Interpersonal Conflict

Interpersonal Conflict

Fifth Edition

William W. Wilmot
University of Montana

Joyce L. Hocker

Boston, Massachusetts Burr Ridge, Illinois Dubuque, Iowa
Madison, Wisconsin New York, New York San Francisco, California St. Louis, Missouri

McGraw-Hill

A Division of The ***McGraw·Hill*** *Companies*

INTERPERSONAL CONFLICT

This book is printed on recycled, acid-free paper containing 10% postconsumer waste.

1 2 3 4 5 6 7 8 9 0 QPF QPF 9 0 9 8 7

ISBN 0-697-32724-8

Sponsoring editor: *Marjorie Byers*
Developmental editor: *Jennie Katsaros*
Marketing manager: *Carl Leonard*
Project manager: *Terry Routley*
Production supervisor: *Sandy Hahn*
Cover designer: *Ellen Pettengell*
Cover image: *Digital Stock Professional; Sunsets, Skies, and Weather*
Compositor: *ElectraGraphics, Inc.*
Typeface: *10/12 Times Roman*
Printer: *Quebecor Printing Book Group/Fairfield*

Library of Congress Cataloging-in-Publication Data

Wilmot, William W.
Interpersonal Conflict / Wilmot/Hocker. — 5th ed.
p. cm.
Hocker's name appears first on the earlier editions.
Includes bibliographical references and indexes.
ISBN 0-697-32724-8
1. Interpersonal conflict. 2. Conflict (Psychology) I. Hocker, Joyce L. II. Title.
HM132.H62 1997
303.6—dc21 97-8560
CIP

http://www.mhhe.com

Contents

Preface

This book is a complete guide to interpersonal conflict. The central principles of effective conflict management are examined in all types of contexts—from romantic relationships to the workplace.

The fifth edition retains all the popular features of earlier editions while incorporating over 200 new reports of the latest research. Many of the chapters are expanded and enlivened with considerably more analysis and examples from the workplace and other public contexts. In addition, throughout the book, increased focus is directed toward the influences of culture and gender.

Chapter 1 reviews conflict assumptions, metaphors about conflict, and the framing effects of culture and gender. The new lens model of conflict demonstrates how partners have different perceptions in all conflicts and how these also differ from outsider views.

Chapter 2 presents the often quoted definition of conflict refined in the previous editions. The spirals of destructive and constructive conflict demonstrate the interactive dynamics that escalate in all disputes.

New illustrations enhance the presentation of content, relational, identity (face-saving), and procedural goals in chapter 3. Here you will find useful new insights forged from intervention into disputes in personal relationships and organizations.

Chapter 4 expands on the major ways people conceptualize power and shows how these views affect struggles as they unfold. This chapter sharpens the treatment of either/or and both/and perspectives found in earlier editions.

New insights appear in chapter 5 regarding avoidance, verbal aggressiveness, and violence. The new information is challenging and worth a close read, for at the heart of all conflict dynamics are the communicative choices made by the parties involved.

The assessment devices that many of you found so useful are still resident in chapter 6. Each of these have been refined in response to your suggestions.

Chapter 7 not only covers the now standard approaches to negotiation but extends the analysis into some of the latest feminist views of negotiation. Many new examples bring negotiation principles into our everyday lives.

Chapter 8 has a dual task—showing how to move out of avoidance and also how to self-regulate destructive moves. You will find very useful information on how to alter both of these patterns and move conflict into a constructive zone.

Chapter 9 has been almost totally revised and expanded. The explosion of interest in mediation is evident in this chapter, with extensive information about types of mediation and the skills needed for successful mediation. A significant component on different cultural methods for handling conflict will pique your interest, for it challenges some widely held assumptions about conflict management and gives us a backdrop for reviewing mainstream cultural practices. Also, new information on how to design dispute systems is useful for preventative conflict management.

If you are interested in becoming a dispute resolver, the appendix is worth a look. Useful resources, many of which can be instantly accessed on the Internet, can be found here. For example, you can locate community dispute centers where you can volunteer, and find graduate programs in conflict management.

Any feedback you have about this edition will be warmly received. Please send correspondence to the following addresses:

Bill Wilmot
Department of Communication Studies
University of Montana
Missoula, MT 59812

Joyce Hocker
210 North Higgins
Suite 309
Missoula, MT 59802

Acknowledgments

From Bill:

In the past few years, numerous people have allowed me to assist them in transforming their work struggles from destructive conflict to collaborative solutions. These leaps of faith have greatly enriched the insights in this book, and I am deeply appreciative of the courageous spirit of these people. Thanks to you all—you have shown that new levels of relationship can emerge from conflicts.

The continuing positive reception to the principles of constructive conflict by participants in classes and workshops serves to energize me. Just when I begin to have an energy dip, someone tells me about the impact this book has had—and I come back to the task with renewed commitment. During my professional career, I have tended to move from topic to topic, seeking new challenges. That I have been teaching conflict for twenty years now is rather amazing, and if it continues to work well for others, I may be dong it twenty years from now. So, "thanks" to you all.

Professionally, Elaine Yarbrough, president of the Yarbrough Group, is a continuing pleasure in our joint work on conflict and mediation. She, Mike Burr, and Lindsay are my Boulder, Colorado, family—a deep and abiding connection over the years. My facilitation, mediation, and training work has been enriched beyond measure by this association.

Effective conflict requires a continuing expansion of one's limits. My spiritual growth has been in response to the kindness of many teachers and fellow practitioners in the Tibetan Buddhist tradition. Special appreciation goes to the Ven. Thubten Chodron, Ven. Kirti Tschensab Rinpoche, Lama Thubten Zopa Rinpoche, and the resident teachers of the Kopan course. The unrelenting emphasis on one's responsibility for one's reactions continues to both challenge and support me. A special debt will always be owed to the fellow members of Osel Shen Phen Ling who warmly welcome me back after each trip and absence.

My sincerest thanks to all the dedicated teachers in my life, from Eva Mae Reub in the primary grades in Upton, Wyoming, to Jerry Davies, my college debate coach. The passing of Dr. Patrick O. Marsh, my first college debate coach, continues to affect me. Finally, in graduate school, Dr. Kenneth Sereno ignited my long-dormant mind, and Dr. Orville Pence wrote AFU on my paper—two crucial turning points.

If you are interested in undergraduate or graduate studies in communication, you might want to check out the superb teachers, mentors, and scholars in the Department of Communication Studies at the University of Montana. We have a fine program, and the faculty actually like one another and treat students well. Our website is http://www.umt.edu/dcs. Thanks to you all for your support over the years—Betsy, Jim, Wes, Sara, Al, George, Debra, and Sally. You are cool.

In my personal life, the reestablishment of a romance with Mada Morgan, my college sweetheart, has brought me full circle and much joy. Who would think that a committed relationship could be so much fun? My grown children, Jason and Carina, continue to be a source of pride. Even if I weren't related to them I would enjoy them. And, Carina, thanks for the professional job on the instructor's manual and for finding some of my typos and other errors. This central cast of three is augmented by many others—my sister Joyce; my friend and "Shabin" co-owner, Roy; Bob, the mayor and chief constable of Southern Cross; and many others. Stan Rose and Greg Patent, both superb chefs, cannot be blamed for my lack of cooking talent in our eight-year-old men's group. Maybe in another decade I can conquer my culinary weaknesses.

Finally, Mom, I really do promise to call you more.

Bill Wilmot
Department of Communication Studies
Missoula, Montana

From Joyce:

From the perspective of five editions and twenty years of authorship of this book, I see clearly that my father, the Reverend Lamar Hocker, along with my mother, Jean Lightfoot Hocker, set in motion all that developed into my lifelong interest in this subject. I am the daughter of a Texas minister who could have kept quiet and let prevailing social norms dictate what happened in the churches he served. But he spoke up, for civil rights, the worldwide ecumenical movement, the integration of our institutions, the movement against war, and later, in partial retirement, against the devastation of our priceless Western land. Our family always knew he was right, but as children we learned that right didn't always prevail. I witnessed almost every form of destructive conflict management, along with some enlightening examples of "a better way," in these struggles among people who were supposed to be able to get along but could not when powerful emotions were engaged. We moved often, hoping the next place would provide a compatible place for the hard truths to be explored in a peaceful environment. I grew up thinking that people ought to be able to resolve conflict while remaining together. This conviction led me to my first career in speech communication and later to my second career as a clinical psychologist. I am deeply grateful to my father for his courage and his clear voice and to my mother for her steady, quiet support along a difficult path. I know of few women my age who still claim their fathers as a hero, but I am one. Thank you to my parents for their love and guidance.

Janice Hocker Rushing, my sister and our best critic, and my brother-in-law, Tom Frentz, have provided humor, perspective, wisdom, and encouragement during this revision. Janice knows this book better than the authors do, having reviewed it many times and taught from it for years, and I value her suggestions and wise eye more than those of any other reviewer. The book was dedicated to Janice several times for this reason. I especially appreciated being able to E-mail Janice at all hours when I ran into various problems. She was always a wonderful help. Thanks again, Tom and Janice.

My women friends and colleagues continued to offer sound advice, personal support, and raucous humor during this revision. I value my longtime colleagues more than they sometimes know. Thank you to Sarah Baxter, Shan Guisinger, Diane Haddon,

Rita Sommers-Flannagan, and Marianne Spitzform, with whom I could let off steam and receive energy to keep going. I especially thank Marianne for one crucial lunchtime conversation when she helped me untangle a mess. Elaine Yarbrough, my dear friend who resolves conflict all over the world for a living, continues to offer wisdom and support. I especially enjoyed coteaching courses on gender diversity with Mike Burr during the time of this edition. Mike and I have developed creative strategies for dealing with conflict in a large corporation with employees who are being challenged to look at gender in a new way.

I am grateful to Bill Wilmot who provided a wonderful array of research resources and personal experience and who took the lead in this revision. Bill's teaching and consultation in conflict management make this book much richer—Bill is known for enlivening situations he enters, and I appreciate his energy, expertise, and timely work on this project. I am glad we are able to continue collaborating on this book, which grew out of many years of dialogue.

Finally, I am deeply grateful, again in edition 5, to my husband, Gary Hawk, who supported me in sticking with this book, working toward excellence, and writing late into the night when the schedule required. Gary often reminded me of stories I had forgotten that belonged in the book and of insights that deserved more attention, and he asked me to trust my own voice, which sometimes recedes under the burden of too much work or insufficient attention. Gary's own fascination with conflict resolution keeps me engaged in this study. I especially appreciate our Wednesdays when we work with couples, talk about the struggles we witness, and try to find ways to help love reawaken.

This is my twentieth year in Montana. I am blessed with human riches in my work and personal life and the blending of a dramatic landscape and a vital community in Missoula. I hope this book helps you appreciate the possibilities that lie hidden in conflict.

Joyce L. Hocker
Missoula, Montana

Both authors would also like to thank the following reviewers for their valuable feedback: Nancy A. Burrell, University of Wisconsin-Milwaukee; David A. Frank, University of Oregon, Honors College; Susan A. Holton, Bridgewater State College; Steven J. Madden, Clemson University; Sara Newell, West Chester University; Shirley A. Van Hoeven, Western Michigan University.

PART ONE

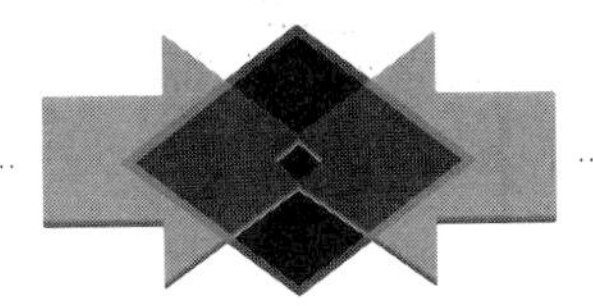

Conflict Components

Chapter 1

Perspectives on Conflict

Conflict Happens

Why Study Conflict?

Conflict happens. It happens on the job, between groups in our society, within families, and right in the middle of our most personal relationships. Conflict is ever present and both fascinating and maddening. The challenges of dealing with differences have rarely been greater.

Conflicts arise naturally in all kinds of settings. On the global scale, nations struggle with one another, both diplomatically and militarily. And with the increased globalization of the world's economy, we are all becoming more interdependent with one another (Brown 1992).

On the job, "conflict is a stubborn fact of organizational life" (Kolb and Putnam 1992, 311). Rather than seeing conflict as abnormal, Pondy (1992) suggests we view organizations as "arenas for staging conflicts, and managers as both fight promoters who organize bouts and as referees who regulate them" (259). Furthermore, Pondy asserts that in the company, agency, or small business, conflict may be the very essence of what the organization is about, and if "conflict isn't happening then the organization has no reason for being." One study surveyed workers and found that almost 85 percent reported conflicts at work (Volkema and Bergmann 1989). And with an increasing awareness of cultural diversity and gender equity issues, it is imperative that we become familiar with issues surrounding promotions and harassment. In fact, one can see training in organizations as a form of preventive conflict management (Hathaway 1995). The recognition of the prevalence of conflict at work has led to books on mediating conflict in the workplace (Yarbrough and Wilmot 1995), showing how managers can learn conflict management skills to intervene in disputes in their organization.

Ongoing, unresolved workplace conflict also has negative impacts that reach far beyond the principal parties. In an electronics plant, for example, if the director of engineering and the director of production are unable to reach agreement about quality controls, the staffs of both engineering and production actively complain about one another, subverting both groups' goals. The continual avoidance of the problem seeps throughout the organization, affecting everyone who has direct contact with the directors. If the executive director of a nonprofit agency and her board cannot get along, employees tend to take sides, fear for their jobs, and, like those above them, wage a campaign discrediting the other group. Ignoring workplace conflict sets destructive forces in motion that decrease productivity, spread the conflict to others, and lead to lessened morale and productivity. In one organization one of us recently entered, the president and CEO was on the verge of reorganizing the structure, affecting 600 people so that two vice presidents would not have to talk to one another!

Some of the advantages to studying organizational conflicts are as follows:

- As an employee, you can learn how to get along with
  - fellow employees
  - your manager
  - the public
- As a supervisor, you can begin to
  - see conflicts coming
  - learn productive responses
  - get more cooperation from employees
  - help employees resolve their disputes with one another
  - keep interpersonal conflicts from spreading to other parts of the organization

In your personal relationships, the study of conflict also can pay big dividends. If you are an adolescent or parent of an adolescent, it will come as no surprise to you that it takes about ten years for parents and children to renegotiate roles closer to equality than their earlier parent-child relationship (Comstock 1994), and at the heart of this renegotiation is the conflict process. The study of conflict can assist in this renegotiation process, letting you see which styles backfire, which ones work best, and how much productive power you have available.

We all know that romantic relationships provide a rigorous test of our skills. Siegert and Stamp (1994) studied the effects of the "First Big Fight" in dating relationships, noting that some couples survive and prosper, whereas others break up. These communication researchers tell us quite clearly that "the big difference between the non-survivors and survivors was the way they perceived and handled conflict" (357). As Wilmot (1995) wrote, "What determines the course of a relationship . . . is in a large measure determined by how successfully the participants move through conflict episodes" (95).

One of the ultimate testing grounds for romantic relationships is marriage. Almost all spouses report "occasional marital disagreement" (Bolger et al. 1989; Metz, Rosser, and Strapko 1994). For many spouses the disagreements may be only once or twice a month, yet for others thay may continue over many days (Bolger et al. 1989). It is common and normal for partners to have conflicts or disagreements, and in fact, managing conflict is one of the central tasks of maintaining a marriage (Gottman 1994). As you might guess, learning to constructively resolve conflict is clearly and directly linked to marital satisfaction. "Findings regarding the link between conflict resolution styles and marital satisfaction have been consistent in indicating that each spouse's marital satisfaction is positively related to the frequency with which each spouse uses constructive strategies to resolve conflict" (Kurdek 1995, 153).

It may well be that the *key skill* in all long-term committed relationships is conflict management—certainly the data on marriages suggest this is true (Gottman 1994). The presence of conflict does not determine the quality of a marriage; rather, how the couple handles conflict situations determines the quality of the relationship (Comstock and Strzyzewski 1990). Even beliefs about conflict are more important to marital happiness than whether or not the two partners actually agree with one another (Crohan 1992).

How you handle conflict spreads to other members of your family. For example, it has been noted that adult children who are taking care of their parents usually have high levels of conflict with siblings (Merrill 1996). Learning effective skills for dealing with your younger brother or sister is far better than engaging in a family dispute that will affect your children and subsequent generations as well.

We need to study conflict management because some of the findings are not intuitively obvious. For example, it isn't just the people who call one another names who have relationship difficulties deriving from conflict. It has been clearly demonstrated that "couples who never engage in conflict are at long-term risk" (McGonagle, Kessler, and Gotlib 1993, 398).

Unresolved conflict has tremendous negative impact. It directly affects the parties themselves—the two vice presidents are so absorbed with their conflict that they cannot carry out their normal job duties. In relationships, unresolved conflict leads to drifting away from one another and sometimes jettisoning the relationship entirely. One study even found that the relapse of compulsive gamblers was related to erupting interpersonal conflicts (Lorenz 1989).

Family research is quite clear about the systemwide effects of destructive marital conflict. First, negative conflict between the parents reduces the family's network of friends and creates more loneliness (Jones 1992). Second, conflict between the parents tends to both change the mood of household interactions and also to shift the parents' attention to the negative behaviors of their children (Jouriles and Farris 1992). For example, interparental conflict leads to fathers issuing confusing and threatening commands to their sons (Jouriles and Farris 1992). Third, parental conflict has direct negative impacts on the children (Comstock and Strzyzewski 1990). Conflict between parents predicts well-being of the children, with more conflict associated with maladaptive behavior on the part of the kids (Dunn and Tucker 1993; Garber 1991; Grych and Fincham 1990; Jouriles, Bourg, and Farris 1991). For example, children of conflicting parents see conflict as aggressive and have behavior problems and lower academic performance (Buehler et al. 1994). Families with delinquent teenagers are found to be more defensive and less supportive than families without delinquents (Prager 1991). Finally, the effects of destructive conflict patterns suggest that "ongoing conflict at home has a greater impact on adolescent distress and symptoms than does parental divorce" (Jaycox and Repetti 1993, 344).

There is evidence that parents who either avoid conflict or engage in negative cycles of mutual damage directly influence the children's subsequent lives. For instance, if your parents avoided conflict, you may be at risk in romantic relationships (Martin 1990). A modest relationship exists between mothers who avoid conflict and their daughters' marital satisfaction (VanLear 1992). On the other end of the continuum, children who are exposed to harsh discipline practices at home (which coincide with a negative and hostile relationship between the parents) are more at risk for aggression, hyperactivity, and internalizing by withdrawing, having somatic complaints, and experiencing depressive symptoms (Jaycox and Repetti 1993). The family effects also reach beyond the immediate environment. One study demonstrated that children from high-conflict homes had much stronger negative reactions while watching a video of angry adults than children from low-conflict homes (El-Sheikh 1994).

Children's own favorableness toward marriage is directly affected by the conflict between their parents. If their parents have frequent conflict, the children have a much less favorable attitude toward marriage (Jennings, Salts, and Smith 1991). A child's general feelings of self-worth are directly affected by interparental conflict (Garber 1991). Finally, it has been fairly well demonstrated that parental conflict has long-term effects on children regardless of family structure (Garber 1991). This means that it isn't primarily the question of whether parents divorce or not that affects the kids but it is the level of conflict present in either the intact family or the restructured family that impacts the children.

Therefore, we need to study conflict in personal relationships for the following reasons:

- How you engage in conflict will directly affect your romantic relationship.
- The long-term satisfaction of your marriage may hinge on how well you manage conflict.
- Your skill at conflict management directly affects your family of origin and your children.

As you will see in chapter 9, "Third-Party Intervention," you might study conflict so you can be of help to others experiencing interpersonal conflict. To be of most help you will need specific intervention skills, but understanding conflict dynamics is an absolute prerequisite for being an effective helper to others—children, friends, family, and work associates.

Finally, learning effective approaches for dealing with interpersonal conflict contributes to overall mental health. The National Institute of Mental Health funded a decade of studies of depression as one of the major public health problems. Depression affects one's personal relationships and results in millions of dollars lost in the workplace due to missed days, medical and counseling costs. Effective conflict management is one aspect of interpersonal therapy, one of the chosen techniques for dealing with depression.

Why study conflict? Because if we don't, we are more likely to repeat the damaging patterns we see on the job and in our homes. Examining the dynamics of conflict will allow us to unpack those dynamics, see what brings on destructive moves, and build more productive options for ourselves both at work and at home. Since the first edition of this book was published in 1978, much more interest in the process of conflict as a natural, inevitable part of communication has been apparent in research and the popular press. Most writers now know that conflict is not different from "regular" communication but is a part of the ongoing flow of the communication between human beings. We might define ourselves as being "in conflict," of varying intensities, many times a day or week. Even people who vastly prefer peace, harmony, and calm interaction find themselves involved in situations that are tense, escalating, and uncomfortable. Truly, we do not have the option of staying out of conflict unless we stay out of relationships, families, work, and community. Conflict happens—so we best be prepared for it.

Your Personal History

Consider your own interpersonal conflicts over the last few months. Take time to recall two or three. How did you respond emotionally to these conflicts? How would you describe your communication, both verbal and nonverbal? Are you generally more comfortable with getting everything out in the open, even if such an effort creates tension, anger, or upset feelings? Or are you more comfortable seeking harmony, peace, and reduction of angry feelings? Keep these recent interactions in mind as you read this chapter, reflecting on your own philosophy and experience of conflict.

In your family of origin you may have learned that to "blow up" was a normal, natural way that people showed they cared about each other. Perhaps your family was quiet, calm, and restrained. Fighting, if it happened at all, went on behind closed doors. Maybe you were punished for raising your voice, physically hurt for talking honestly to an adult, or told to keep your opinions to yourself. Maybe you experienced, as one of us did, hours of sitting around the family dinner table, catching up on the events of the day, talking over what was happening, and being asked how you felt and what you thought about your life's happenings. If so, you might bring a "we can work this out" perspective to conflict. Maybe you learned, as the other author did, that conflict was not talked about and that "actions spoke more loudly than words." You may have been taught not to dwell on problems but just move on.

Think about how your personal history has taught you either to jump right into conflict or to strenuously attempt to reduce or avoid it. None of the ideas and formats in this book are more important than coming to terms with your own life's learnings—which to keep, which to challenge, which to change, and which to discard because they no longer fit your needs. Think also about your role in your family of origin. You may have been raised in several blended families or be raising children in a blended family right now. If so, you may have developed and fill several roles depending on which family you are in at the moment. Do you want to change your usual role? Do you need to learn more about getting along rather than to automatically challenge authority? Maybe you want to learn to speak up in your own clearly heard, authentic voice if you are usually silent or have been silenced by others.

Recently in a class on conflict, the students were asked to choose which of the following would best describe their family of origin: (1) family members avoided most conflict;

(2) family members used collaboration; or (3) family members engaged in a lot of overt yelling, calling of names, and similar aggressive moves. While recognizing the artificial nature of these distinctions (for example, some families will avoid, then be aggressive, then avoid again), what emerged were family "rules" for handling conflict that are quite distinct. Here are some of them:

Avoidant Families

- Conflict doesn't exist, and if it does, don't recognize it.
- If there *is* a conflict, figure out what to do about it on your own.
- Don't tell anyone else if there is a struggle.
- Walk away if something starts to brew.
- Don't ever raise your voice.
- Snide comments are fine.
- Sulking and the silent treatment are good strategies.
- If someone has a concern, don't respond to it.
- Don't express strong feelings.

Collaborative Families

- Have a family meeting or mealtime chat to discuss issues.
- Use good listening skills when someone has a concern.
- Deal with people directly.
- Say openly what you are feeling.
- Parents need to feel resolved about their children's conflicts.
- Regular interaction is important.
- Dirty tricks such as sulking are not allowed.
- Strong feelings are seen as normal and are allowed.

Aggressive Families

- It is survival of the fittest.
- Be brutally honest regardless of the impact.
- Show your emotions strongly even if that hurts someone.
- Establish your position early.
- Have an audience present when you engage someone.
- Don't back down—hold your ground no matter what.
- You have to take it if someone attacks you.
- People who don't engage are weak.

While these lists will vary from family to family, notice how different the three lists are from one another. If you grew up in an avoidant family and your roommate grew up in an aggressive family, it would not be too surprising if a conflict between the two of you was difficult to resolve—*each* of you will break the rules of interaction the other expects you to follow. So our personal history in our families of origin will have a big impact on what we chose to do when conflict starts to rumble below the surface in our relationships.

Our personal history also includes all of our interactions with others up to the present. What we experience as a preschooler, in school, with friends on the playground, and in all of our adult exchanges influences our expectations. Some of us have experiences of working through difficulties with others and find life basically very easy. Others of us expect (and thus receive) constant tension, turbulence, and strife. These people are more likely than others to react with self- and other criticism, blame, negativity, defensiveness, irritability, or selfishness toward daily challenges (Heitler 1990). Of course, these approaches invite a reciprocal response. Think about your current beliefs and expectations about human interaction. Are you primarily hopeful and optimistic, or cynical and pessimistic?

As you might surmise, your particular age group is subjected to unique influences that may shape how you view conflict. If you were raised in the Great Depression you will not likely view the open expression of conflict as positive (Krokoff, Gottman, and Roy 1988), while the younger generation is beginning to learn about constructive conflict in school—a topic not even considered a couple of decades ago.

Your current living situation certainly influences your methods of handling conflict. If you are with people with whom you feel safe and supported, you can experiment with new styles. If not, you will experience less freedom, possibly relying on what you already know how to do. Similarly, some work situations encourage constructive (or destructive) conflict, whereas others reward people for silence and withdrawal. All of these factors of our own personal history feed into our expectations and actions when we are in conflictual situations.

Views of Conflict

Common Assumptions

In a training session held for a large corporation, a revealing dialogue ensued. The agreed-upon topic was "Conflict on the Job: Making It Work Productively." Three days before the training was to take place, a worried manager called. He said the proposed topic "certainly sounded interesting," and he was "sure everyone needed help in the area," but he wondered if the leader would take a more "positive" approach to the subject. He urged a title change to "Better Communication in Business," and explained that his company didn't really have "conflicts," just problems in communicating. He felt conflict was such a negative subject that spending concentrated time on it might make matters worse. The executive's apprehensions about conflict were mirrored by a participant in a recent course called "Managing Conflicts Productively," who said she came to the course because she had never seen a productive conflict—all the conflicts she has witnessed were destructive. Further, her statement suggested that such a thing as a helpful conflict probably did not exist.

Several well-known cultural clichés present a fairly clear picture of how many of us were raised to think about conflict. Parents may tell their children, "If you can't say anything nice, don't say anything at all"; "Pick on somebody your own size"; "Don't hit girls"; "Don't rock the boat"; "Children should be seen and not heard"; "Act your age!" (which means act *my* age, not yours); "Be a man, fight back"; and "Sticks and stones may break my bones, but words will never hurt me!" All of these sayings give a bit of philosophy about conflict: with whom to fight, permissible conflict behavior, injunctions about when to engage in conflict, and the power of words in conflict behavior. All of the sayings make assumptions that are not helpful to persons who want to learn to carry out productive conflict behavior.

If you were asked to list the words that come to mind when you hear the word "conflict," what would you list? People commonly give the following responses:

destruction	anxiety	threat
anger	tension	heartache
disagreement	alienation	pain
hostility	violence	hopelessness
war	competition	

Many people view conflict as an activity that is almost totally negative and has no redeeming qualities. Some take the attitude that "what the world needs now is good communication"; that if people could just understand each other better, they wouldn't have to experience conflicts. While there is an increasing awareness of the potentially positive features of conflict, many widely accepted assumptions continue to work against a positive view of conflict. Some of the most common are presented here.

1. *Harmony is normal and conflict is abnormal.* Years ago Coser (1967) and Simmel (1953) supported the idea that conflict is normal in a relationship that endures over time. They described conflict as cyclical, or rising and falling. No one expects relationships to be in a constant state of upheaval, or they would reach the "critical limit in a degenerative communication spiral and disintegrate" (Wilmot 1995, 70). Observation of people in relationships shows that conflict is not a temporary aberration. It alternates with harmony in an ebb and flow pattern. But common expressions such as "I'm glad things are back to normal around here" or "Let's get back on track" express the assumption that conflict is not the norm.
2. *Conflicts and disagreements are the same phenomenon.* Often people in conflicts assure each other that "this is really just a disagreement." Simons (1972) notes the extensive use of the term *communication breakdown* to describe conflict situations. This term seems to mean that in conflict, one is not communicating. A problem with equating conflicts and disagreements is that people assume that if a discussion is "just a disagreement," it can and should be resolved by reaching a better understanding or by communicating better. As explained in chapter 2, conflicts are more serious than disagreements. They require more than a clarification of terms or more careful listening, although those two communication skills greatly speed the process of conflict management.
3. *Conflict is a result of personal pathology.* Conflict is often described as "sick," and conflict participants may be labeled as "neurotic," "hostile," "whining," "paranoid," "antisocial," "dependent or codependent," or "enabling." Labels offer no substitute for a careful analysis of the elements of the conflict. Conflict results more often from a lack of appropriate personal power and too little self-esteem than from someone with a sick personality. In studying conflict, people's behaviors should be described, not their personalities. Of course, people do get stuck in pathological patterns because of learning or emotional disorders. Sometimes people are so stuck in a destructive pattern that they cannot change and they cannot participate in collaboration. But the process of conflict itself should not be viewed as pathological. If someone is "rigid," they may have too much or too little power. If someone is "defensive," they may be under attack or expect to be threatened.
4. *Conflict should never be escalated.* The term *conflict management* better describes the various options in conflictual interactions than *conflict resolution.* Sometimes, the most productive choice is to temporarily make the conflict larger so it can be seen,

dealt with, and given importance. Sometimes an escalation—not a runaway upward spiral but an emotionally intense expression—is unavoidable and cannot be suppressed without relationship damage (resentment, silent hostility, despair, hopelessness, and private decisions to leave). Conflict management includes learning to make enough noise to be heard and to make conflict big enough to be seen.

5. *Conflict management should be polite and orderly.* Overly nice communication of any kind ensures a lack of authentic, real interchange. Productive conflict management often is disorderly, chaotic, and confusing. Private arguments, especially, seldom conform to public standards of reasonableness, consistency, or relevance in argumentation. Sillars and Weisberg (1987) note that conflicts do not follow rules of polite conversation. Unlike college debaters, conflict participants do not have to respond directly, or in order, or even with relevant expressions. "As conflicts intensify, conversations become increasingly less orderly, clear, relevant, and goal-directed, and increasingly impulsive, emotional and improvisational" (149). With intensity, communication becomes less strategic and rational and more emotionally expressive and relationally focused. A good conflict is not necessarily a nice conflict, although the more people use productive communication, the more likely that the conflict will both solve problems and help the relationship go forward.
6. *Anger is the predominate emotion in conflict interaction.* Another misconception is that the primary emotion associated with conflict is anger or hostility. Instead, many emotions accompany conflict. We are more familiar with the heated, angry, gut-wrenching feelings accompanying conflict than we are with the aching, lonely, sad, and forlorn feelings. Adults are not encouraged in our society to acknowledge fears, loss, feelings of abandonment, and loneliness. When people talk about their conflicts, the experience is most akin to heartbreak. The emotional connection is broken between people. As the relationship changes to one of distance, the natural accommodation and give-and-take that used to come easily is lost. In the experience of brokenheartedness, people turn to avoidance, bitterness, anger, denial, or retaliation. The loss of the emotional bond remains one of the most painful experiences of humankind. The poet Robert Frost has expressed this loss well:

Fire and Ice

Some say the world will end in fire
Some say ice.
From what I've tasted of desire
I hold with those who favor fire.
But if it had to perish twice,
I think I know enough of hate
To say that for destruction ice
Is also great
*And would suffice.**

7. *One should find the right way to resolve differences.* Americans tend to resolve disputes, at least in public, in one of four ways: fight, vote, litigate, or appeal to various authorities (Stulberg 1987). These approaches assume that someone will win or lose and that all will accept the process and abide by its outcome. In trying to employ new forms of decision making in a local church, great disagreement arose over the idea of using collaborative, consensus-based forms of decision making. In one conflict over whether homosexual people should be given full rights and privileges in the church, the debate at the large public meeting centered primarily around whether it was possible to make decisions that were binding without a vote and how to vote without automatically creating "winners and losers." Many appeared more threatened by the change in process than by the possible outcome of the decision. In everyday life, subordinates subvert managers, children disobey parents, and coalitions form after a vote is taken, essentially changing the meaning of the vote. People assent with half a heart then fight against the agreement with all their strength. Sometimes the best method for resolving disputes is not apparent, leading to a struggle over how to struggle. Rather than being viewed as a waste of time, conflict should be viewed as multilayered. Many productive ways to resolve differences can be employed.

Alternative Assumptions

The above set of common assumptions probably reflect the predominate mode of thought in the contemporary West. However, one cannot just say "that is how people see conflict." Many societies, including our own, express contradictory views of conflict—sometimes it is bad, sometimes it is good. Therefore, we may grow up with a confusing perspective on when conflict is helpful or when it should be avoided. We learn few strategies for changing conflictual situations from harmful ones into productive ones. In a study of how children initiate and terminate friendships, Bell and Hadas (1977) found that children had twice as many ideas about how to make friends (e.g., "Ask where they sit so you can sit next to them," or "Just walk up and say that you want to play!") than they did about how to end friendships. The ending strategies relied heavily on ideas such as "Ignore them," "You tell them to go away, or you move," and "Beat them up." The researchers also noticed uneasy silences when children were asked how they ended friendships or what they did when they wanted to make up after an argument. One youngster commented poignantly that friendships were over at the end of the school year anyway, so you did not have to make up.

Children may receive confusing messages about their conduct of conflict. Sports are all right, but violence outside a sports framework is not. Conflicts with peers are all right if you have been stepped on and you are a boy, but talking back to parents when they step on you is not all right. Having a conflict over a promotion is acceptable, but openly vying for recognition is not. Competing over a girl (if you're a boy) is admirable, but having a conflict over a boy (if you're a girl) is catty. And so on. Persons in power send two different messages: (1) fight and stand up for yourself, but (2) only when it is acceptable (Bateson 1972). Thus, people develop mixed feelings about conflict, and many simply learn to avoid it altogether.

Yet, there are some positive views of conflict worthy of our examination. For example, would you list the following words after hearing the word "conflict"?

exciting	intimate
strengthening	courageous
helpful	clarifying
stimulating	opportune
growth-producing	enriching
creative	

One of the assumptions of this book is that conflict can be associated with all of the above words, both the negative and the positive. Conflict does receive some positive endorsement in legal challenges and competition in business. In games, children learn that "hitting hard" and "fighting to win" are positive virtues. Strategizing, scheming, and maximizing your gains are also necessary. To continue the examination of views of conflict, we will present an overview of everyday metaphors people use when describing conflict.

Metaphors Make a Difference

Metaphorical, figurative, and imaginative language pervades everyday speech in informal, formal, spoken, and written contexts. When people spontaneously describe conflict *as* something else, they use a metaphor, which is a way of comparing one thing to another by speaking of it as if it were a different object or process. An army colonel described his office as a windmill, with people going around in circles, not knowing that the pipe connecting the mechanism to the underground well had been disconnected. Through this metaphor, one can picture the pointless confusion and chaos of the office. Karen described her family as a movie scene, in which a train is rushing across a bridge on the point of collapsing. Father, as the engineer, is unaware of the danger since no lookouts are posted to warn of hazards, so he speeds on. The army colonel and Karen used extended metaphors to describe rich scenes.

Our cognitive system itself is fundamentally metaphoric. Imaginative speech makes up much of language (Lakoff and Johnson 1980; Hayakawa 1978; Ortony 1975; Weick 1979). Hayakawa writes that metaphors are not "ornaments of discourse," but are "direct expressions of evaluation and are bound to occur whenever we have strong feelings to express" (109). Conflict brings up such strong feelings that metaphoric analysis, of both the *process of conflict* and *specific conflicts,* aids in analysis, intervention, and lasting change. Using metaphoric analysis of specific conflicts will be explained in chapter 6, "Conflict Assessment." Aristotle understood analogy or metaphor to be the source of truths, a mark of genius. A metaphor or analogy "can take its creator, as well as its hearers, quite by surprise" (Rushing 1983, 2).

In the following section, common metaphors for conflict interaction will be explained. A qualitative study and observations of how people speak and write about conflict itself demonstrate that the way a conflict is characterized metaphorically creates a certain perception of what can happen, what will happen, what should happen, and with what kind of feeling actions might take place (McCorkle and Mills 1992). As you read this book, studying conflict and learning how to manage conflict productively, pay attention to how people express thoughts and feelings about conflict through metaphors.

Metaphors That Limit Conflict

Many images and expressions of conflict cast such a negative tone around the process that creativity is stifled. When metaphors imply that the outcome is predetermined, there is little possibility for productive conflict management.

Conflict Is Warlike and Violent

War and violence is the central metaphor of conflict in the United States and Western Europe. Conflict often is characterized as a battle. The following phrases regarding conflict reflect the metaphor of war and violence:

Your actions are completely *indefensible.*
He *attacked* me where I was most vulnerable—my kids.
That criticism is *right on target.*
Okay, *shoot!*
I feel *beaten down and defeated* after our talk.

When conflict is envisioned as warlike, certain actions seem natural. In a staff meeting, for instance, if accusations are "hurled back and forth" as if by primitives bashing each other with stones, if arguments are felt to be "right on target," then the whole melee is structured as a battle. The *scene* is that of a battlefield; the *actors* are people of warring groups who are committed to wiping each other out since the other is perceived as threatening. The *acts* are those that aim to produce an advantage by killing or reducing the effectiveness of the opponent. The *resolution possibilities* are reduced to offense and defense, and the *purpose* or outcome is inevitably harm, vengeance, a reduction of players, and a repetition of the argument/battle. The war metaphor influences the entire perception of the conflict. Both winning and losing sides feel incomplete; victors desire more power, and losers shore up their defenses for the next attack.

Perhaps you work in an organization whose workers act as if conflicts were large or small wars and fights were battles in the ongoing war. If your organization uses a "chain of command," gives people "orders," "attacks competitors," "wages advertising or public relations campaigns," "fires traitors," "employs a diversionary tactics," or "launches assaults," then the organization may well have evolved a military metaphor for conflict management (Weick 1979). If so, conflict is likely to be solved the way it would be if one were on a battlefield.

"They Are Killing Me"

In a large technological research firm, military metaphors abound. The program directors are under a lot of stress with high-stakes external negotiations, which involve millions of dollars. When they have a meeting with someone who shouts or stomps out of the room, they find it very unpleasant. Between rounds of negotiation, they might tell another program director that "he is killing me." Everyone immediately knows what this metaphor means: (1) this negotiation is very important, (2) I'm concerned that we won't "make a deal" on this contract, and (3) they are acting in ways that make me uncomfortable.

Couples talk in warlike terms, too. They may say:

I just retreat. I fall back and regroup. Then I wait for an opening. . . .
He slaughters me when I cry and get confused.
When I don't want it to come to blows (laughs), I launch a diversionary attack, like telling him the kids are calling me.

"She's Squeezing the Life out of Me"

A divorcing couple, Kent and Jeannie, were at odds over the division of their property. Most of the big items had been decided and they were down to the smaller but more symbolic things such as music, art, family pictures, and gifts to one another. In describing their negotiations, Kent said in the mediator's office, "She's choking me," "These are my lifeblood," and "These things are my life." Because Jeannie saw the items as "just stuff, for heaven's sake," the metaphors the couple used revealed the degree of importance they put on the items.

Chronic use of military or violent metaphors severely limits creative problem solving. People overlook improvisation, alternative actions, and opportunities to contradict the norms instead of following orders. The military image saves us the trouble of inventing new ones. However, "other metaphors are needed to capture different realities that exist right alongside those military realities" (Weick 1979, 51).

Conflict Is Explosive

Perhaps you experience "explosive" conflicts, using phrases like the following to describe the process:

He's about to blow up. Any little thing will set him off.
Larry's got a short fuse.
The pressure's building up so fast that something's gotta give soon!
I just needed to let off steam.
She really pushed my button.
Put a lid on it!

Phrases like these indicate a perception of conflict as being made up of flammable materials (feelings), trigger issues, and an ignition of the explosion that, once started, can't be stopped. Maybe the pressure builds "under the surface," like a volcano, or "in a pressure cooker," such as an overcrowded office. People often say they "blew their stacks" in response to an event.

If people act out explosive conflicts, they often see them as somehow out of their control ("He touched it off, not me"). Explosions blow away familiar structures, often requiring a period of rebuilding and cleanup. The "exploder" may feel better after a release of pressure; the people living in the vicinity may feel blown away.

The explosion metaphor limits creativity in conflict because the only way participants can imagine resolving the issue is to "blow up" or to avoid "touching it off." This image denies personal responsibility for the pressure and mistakenly urges only two avenues for resolution. Additionally, people with "explosive tempers" are often relieved of their own responsibility to do something about the buildup of tension before they have to blow up. Family members are taught to keep from making Dad or Mom mad, thus learning that conflict is avoidable by not provoking someone, thus keeping the peace. Family systems theorists have labeled this pattern as one of the destructive patterns of codependence—of taking too much responsibility for the actions of others.

Conflict Is a Trial

The legal system provides a regulated, commonly accepted system for managing social conflict. The system has evolved over hundreds of years and serves our culture well in many instances. However, Western society has come to rely too much on the legal system, partly as a result of the breakdown of community and personal modes of managing conflict. Thus, legal terms creep into personal or organizational conflict metaphors, since at least the legal system has firm rules and expectations. Phrases like the following indicate that legal metaphors may be shaping conflict behavior:

> He's got the best case.
> The jury's still out on that one.
> You're accusing me.
> She's the guilty party.

Even in conflicts between romantic partners or friends, one person might take on the role of the accusatory prosecuting attorney, one the role of the defender of the accused. Friends might get informally brought in as jury; one might say to friends, "Should I let him off on this one? Do you think he meant to . . . ?" Arguments between interdependent people often go back and forth as if there will be a judgment of guilt or innocence, but often the jury stays out, no judge appears, and the case remains unresolved, to simmer through the system until another suit (interpersonally) arises. Courts maintain clearly delineated processes, basing decisions on law and precedent. Interpersonal situations, however, admit feelings as evidence, do not bind parties to the outcome of a conflict, and maintain no systems of law and order to back up a decision. Few "trials" settle underlying issues in the conflict in personal relationships. Instead, romantic partners or friends keep "going back to court" (keep arguing). The metaphor doesn't fit the usual interpersonal situation, but the participants act as if it does, then remain bitterly disappointed that their understanding of the case doesn't carry the day.

Conflict Is a Struggle

People experience conflict as a hopeless or difficult struggle like "being on a sinking ship with no lifeboat," traveling "a rocky road," working with "a checkbook that won't balance" (McCorkle and Mills 1992), or "arm wrestling." Sometimes conflict is expressed as a power struggle, or a struggle to get "one up." The "conflict as a struggle" metaphor implies that the process takes a lot of emotional and physical energy and may indeed turn out to be fruitless. Sometimes people say, "It was a struggle, but we finally made it," indicating some form of conflict resolution that worked out reasonably well.

Conflict Is an Act of Nature

Conflict is expressed as a negative natural disaster, or at least an uncontrollable act of nature, such as a tornado, a hurricane, an avalanche, being swept away, an earthquake, or a fire raging out of control (McCorkle and Mills 1992). One telling phrase was that experiencing conflict felt like being "a rowboat caught in a hurricane." McCorkle and Mills note, that those who feel powerless may "(a) take little or no responsibility for their own actions that sustain the conflict, (b) feel that the other participant has all the choices, or (c) believe that no one involved has any choices" (64). The best course of action, then, would be to avoid conflict, since no positive outcome can be expected.

Conflict Is Animal Behavior

Human animals often characterize conflict as something done by other members of the animal realm—not ourselves. People may be called "stubborn as a mule" or described as "butting heads," or in a very common phrase, conflict is called "a zoo" (McCorkle and Mills 1992). You may hear phrases like "tearing his throat out," "slinking around," "stalking," or entering into a "feeding frenzy."

Conflict Is a Mess

Another intriguing image is that of conflict as a mess or as garbage. You'll hear "Let's not open up that can of worms," "They got all that garbage out in the open," "Things are falling apart around here," or "Everything's disintegrating." People will ask to "tie up some loose ends." Another clear expression of the "mess" metaphor emerges when people say, "This is a sticky situation," or "Something stinks around here."

Messes are difficult to manage because they spill over into other areas and can't be contained easily without making a bigger mess. A messy conflict usually means one that is full of personal, emotional attachments. This metaphor limits creativity to the extent that feelings are judged to be messy or not amenable to rational treatment. If the opposite of a messy conflict is a clean, or straightforward one, involving only facts and rationality rather than messy feelings, then only part of the conflict can be resolved. The feelings will go underground and "create a stink."

Conflict Is a Communication Breakdown

Calling conflict a "breakdown in communication" is one of the most popular designations. McCorkle and Mills (1992) refer to this breakdown as "one-way communication," in which people "talk to a brick wall" or "argue with someone from another planet." Referring to the process as a breakdown implies a telephone line that is down, a computer that won't communicate, a car that won't run, or a sound system that won't amplify sound. The implication that breakdown can be "fixed," however, often turns out to be inaccurate. Many times people communicate clearly in conflict interactions—only to find out that they are in an intractable conflict. Clarity of communication *usually* improves the process of conflict management greatly, but it is a mistake to assume that clarity removes conflict.

Neutral Conflict Metaphors

A few metaphors indicate that conflict is neither negative nor positive but embodies possibilities for either, depending on how skillfully the conflict is enacted.

Conflict Is a Game

The game, especially ball game, image is popular. People "bat around ideas," "toss the ball into his court," "strike out," go "back and forth," and "make an end run." Some people are judged to be "team players." Images of referees, an audience, or coaches are popular. In the media age you'll hear "Would you do that again on instant replay?" which may mean "I can't believe you said that." The game image assumes the existence of rules defining the game and defining interaction among the players. Rules define fouls, out-of-bounds behavior, winning, losing, and when the game is over. An even more interdependent game is chess, which requires the players to keep in mind at all times the predicted moves of the opponent. Chess is a game that can only be won by a highly developed prediction of the strategy of the other player. If one doesn't take account of the opponent, one loses immediately. This image works well if everyone plays by the same rules.

The game metaphor is limiting when people won't "play fair" or don't see the conflict as having gamelike qualities at all. Many men are raised to feel comfortable with the game image, accepting wins and losses as "all part of the game." Many women are less comfortable with the structure, insisting on talking about what is going on, which men see as not playing by the rules. Game metaphors work poorly in intimate conflicts, since most games provide a winner and a loser.

Conflict Is a Heroic Adventure

The hero image is endemic to conflict images. The superheroes of Western movies, science fiction, myths, and our own childhoods are used even in adult life. This archetypal imagery describes a process in which slightly scared people appoint a leader who is "bigger and better" than they are, then they pledge loyalty to that leader who is bound to protect them. The hero or heroine is one who has found or done something beyond the normal range of experience. "A hero is someone who has given his or her life to something bigger than oneself" (Campbell 1988, 123). The question is whether the hero or heroine is really a match for the task at hand, can really overcome the dangers, and has the requisite courage, knowledge, and capacity to serve.

This desire to follow a heroic leader emerges in all cultures. In social or political movements, leaders such as Martin Luther King organize the energies of many people who overcome many obstacles to reach a common goal. The limit to this heroic metaphor in conflict resolution is that one can become used to passively watching events happen on TV or elsewhere. The spectator feels helpless or unimportant. And if the right leader does not emerge, a wonderful chance for change may be lost. Additionally, people often get stuck in certain roles in the heroic drama, such as damsel in distress, knight in shining armor, lieutenant or helper to the "great one," or victim.

Many of the heroic roles specify men as actors. Roles such as king, dragon slayer, the lone Western gunslinger, the sports hero, or the action hero of adventure movies more often star men than women (Gerzon 1984). However, Rushing and Frentz (1995) indicate that films, especially Westerns and science fiction, are providing more and more heroic roles for women, such as Ripley in the *Aliens* series.

Conflict Is a Balancing Act

Conflict is referred to as a delicate balancing act, like that of a tightrope walker or a rock climber, who must find just the right handholds or fall to sure death. Often negotiations in the formative stages are referred to as "in a very delicate" stage, in which one "false move" will scuttle negotiations. Satir (1972) refers to a family as a mobile, which can be unbalanced by one member having too much weight or getting stirred up, thus making the whole mobile swing and sway.

Metaphors That Expand Conflict Potential

Conflict Is a Bargaining Table

A collaborative approach to conflict is exemplified by the common metaphor of "the table." Diplomacy, labor negotiations, and parliamentary procedure all use this image. The conflict structure and procedure depend on the table as a central feature. Families are urged to sit down to dinner together, labor and management officials "come to the table," and diplomats struggle over actual tables at conferences. These real or imagined tables communicate information about who the conflict participants will be, how they will act, and what their placement will be in relationship to each other. The table is a spatial metaphor defining the relationships.

King Arthur, in historical legend, created a round table to symbolize equal discussion, with each knight having one vote. The idea of "Right makes might" substituted, for a time, for "Might makes right." When the federation disintegrated, the round table, smashed to pieces by dissident knights, became a symbol of the disintegration. Other examples of "table" imagery in conflict management include the following:

In parliamentary procedure, "tabling a motion" stops movement toward a decision, and "bringing a motion off the table" indicates a readiness to decide.

"Under the table" refers to hidden or secretive agreements.

"Turning the tables" comes from a medieval custom of turning from one dinner partner to another to begin conversation. It was done in response to the king or queen's gesture. If the "tables are turned," a person feels an unexpected lack of support from someone important.

Conflict Is a Tide

A second positive metaphor for conflict is the tide. Tides ebb and flow within predictable parameters based on the phases of the moon, the climatic conditions, the shape of the shoreline, and the currents of the ocean. The tides are predictable only through observation and careful record keeping. They must be seriously considered by those on land and sea or they can become life threatening. Every sailor knows the folly of going out on the ocean without knowing the tidal patterns. Tides can be destructive, but they also wash in nourishment and unexpected flotsam, sometimes even treasure. Debris is washed out, exposing new features of the coastline. Tides are repetitive, powerful, and inescapable.*

Thinking of conflict as a tidal rhythm in relationships may help to reduce fear. If the relationship is equal and trusting, conflict will develop its own rhythm that will not wash away the foundation of the relationship. Conflict will ebb, as well as rise. For example, many families experience more conflict than usual when a college student comes home for the summer to work. After being on one's own for several years, possibly in both dorms

*Thanks to Debra Stevens for suggesting this metaphor.

and apartments, many students experience too many restrictions at home, and parents experience what appears to be too little family involvement and accountability on the part of the student. Many times, several "high tide" conflict experiences prompt a family to reset the expectations and boundaries. Then for the rest of the summer, conflict episodes recede to "low tide." Thinking ahead about this possibility helps many family members navigate well through a potentially stormy time.

Conflict Is a Dance

Another positive image is conflict as a dance. People speak of "learning to dance to the same music." In a dance, both or all participants have to learn how close and how far to move, how to regulate distance, when to slow down and speed up, how to maintain contact with partners so you know where they will be, and how to end the dance (Lindbergh 1955). Different flourishes and steps can add to the grace and beauty of the dance. Dancing can be energetic, stimulating, fun, and exhilarating. Sometimes one's partner steps on one's toes, can't dance very well, is awkward, or doesn't know the steps yet. But the whole idea of dancing with partners is to create something beautiful, graceful, and inspiring that depends on each person's skill, training, and individual expression. Dance can give collaborative images of conflict on which to build.

Conflict envisioned as dance is reflected in the following statements:

"I feel hurried. I need more time." (The person is not saying, "I need a different partner.")

"Quit dancing around, and come over here and talk with me, please." (One person may be saying, "I don't know these steps, and I can't reach you. Please let me in.")

"They're just do-si-doing [a square-dancing term] around." (The people look as though they are doing something together but really have their backs to each other and their arms folded—a fairly noninteractive way to dance!)

Conflict Is a Garden

A final expanding image of conflict is that of a carefully cultivated garden. In creative conflict, as in good gardening, seeds are planted for future growth, pests are managed, weeds are pulled, and the garden is watered when needed. Sun and light are needed for the plants to grow, and the most fruitful outcomes occur when the conditions are carefully tended. If constructive conflict can be seen as a garden, many positive outcomes can be experienced. In good gardening, poisons are not put on the ground—thus, rage, fury, and attacks, which are poison in an ongoing relationship, become as unthinkable as putting dry-cleaning fluid on rose bushes. In good gardens, individual plants are given room to grow. Some plants are thinned to make room for mature plants. In human relationships, people learn to leave space for others, to give them room to grow, and to plant compatible varieties together. As a child you may have learned that no amount of watching beans or carrots in a garden would make them grow any faster. Human relationships, especially when conflict has recently been part of the environment, need time to grow slowly, to recover from stress, and to put down roots. The "garden" image thus holds a lot of promise, especially as world understanding shifts to encompass environmental realities, and we begin to understand our Earth as a single garden.

Mixing the Metaphors

Since the images used in conflicts are central to the conflict process, problems occur when people envision conflict in completely different ways. One person may think of conflict as war, with all the attendant warlike images, while the other assumes that conflict is more like a chess game—strategic, careful, thoughtful, and planned. The following box presents two examples of problems arising from different images of conflict.

Is It a Mess or an Explosion?

Lynn and Bart are married to each other. Lynn sees conflict as a mess, something sticky and uncomfortable, even slightly shady or dirty. People in her family believe that husbands and wives who love each other don't have conflict very often. It is distasteful to her. She is likely to say, "I don't want to talk about it now. Let's just leave the whole mess until this weekend. I can't handle it tonight." Bart sees and feels conflict as an explosion—his stomach tightens, his pulse races, and his heart begins to pound. He likes to reduce the pressure of all this emotion. He's a feelings-oriented person, while Lynn is more likely to use a reasoning process if she has to deal with an issue. Bart is likely to say, "I am not going to sit on this until Saturday morning. I'll burst. You can't expect me to hold all this in. It's not fair, you always . . ."

In addition to their specific conflict, Bart and Lynn are fighting over how to fight; indeed, they are fighting over what conflict is and how they experience it. Each assumes that the other thinks about the conflict the way he or she does. They could not be farther from the truth, as they probably will find out.

The following box presents another example of different views of conflict within an organization.

The Trial Begins

Charlotte, the district manager, sees conflict as a trial. She plays various roles when she is in conflict with the assistant managers. Sometimes she asks them to bring in facts to back up their opinion; sometimes she accuses them of not doing their homework. Sue is assistant district manager. She sees conflict as a process of bargaining around an imaginary table. She keeps trying to find areas of compromise, while Charlotte acts as judge or jury, deciding which ideas are best supported. Charlotte later fires Sue for not being able to take a stand, for being indecisive, and for not being aggressive enough in developing her own program. The two managers thought conflict was a different kind of process, and they made no provisions for their differing expectations.

Initiating some process of talking about *what is happening* in a small group, *how decisions are going to be made,* and *how conflicts will be managed* gives potential opponents a chance to understand that their friends or coworkers may have a completely different idea about what is appropriate. One way to generate creative ideas about the management of conflict is to understand what people in conflict think conflict *is*. Their metaphors and your own language and images will help you learn more about the task of conflict management.

Other images of conflict can be detected in ordinary conversation. Listen to the way you and others talk, scrutinize news reports, and pay attention to images in public speeches. See if you can determine the metaphor that shapes a particular conflict in a family, an agency, a social group, the general public, or even the nation. What might it mean, for instance, if conflict is seen as an irritant, as in "She bugs me," or "Get off my back," or "He's just trying to get a rise out of you"? Do you think conflict takes on a life of its own, as when it "snowballs out of control" or is "a runaway train"? Many people experience conflict as an endless circle of repetition, going nowhere, as exemplified by phrases such as "We're just going round and round," "We're on a merry-go-round," or "Here we go again!" The tedium of conflict is reflected in "Same song, second verse." People refer to conflicts as "a drain," "a lot of grief," "a heavy burden," or "poison." Attending to these vivid images can unleash your creativity and help to sort out which images of conflict are limiting and which are helpful.

Framing Effects

Culture Frames Conflict Interaction

> Who knows but one culture, knows no culture.
>
> —Augsburger, *Conflict Mediation Across Cultures: Pathways and Patterns*

The United States encompasses a vast cultural diversity. Think about your own cultural history and roots, whether you and your family have been in the United States for generations or whether you are recent immigrants. To gain a sense of how pervasive cultural differences are, think about the neighborhood in which you spent part of your childhood, your fourth-grade classroom, your experience making a geographical move, or your experience getting to know friends or new family members from a different cultural background from your own.

Every person reading this book experiences cultural diversity at some level. About 150 different languages are spoken in the United States. The southern part of the United States becomes more and more influenced by Hispanic cultures each year. As of this writing, one of every two schoolchildren entering the Los Angeles public schools is Hispanic.* U.S. culture is becoming less of a Western European offshoot in many ways. Changes in the workplace demand that we become sensitive to different ways to process conflict. "Consider the increasing diversity, for instance. The often quoted Hudson Institute Report on *Workforce 2000* predicts that 85 percent of those entering the workforce in this decade will be women, minorities and immigrants" (Yarbrough and Wilmot 1995, 4).

In conflictual interactions, we clearly need to translate, interpret, and become fluent in

*Depending on their descent, some groups prefer the word "Latino" or "Chicano."

several "conflict dialects." We may primarily speak English, but special backgrounds create special expectations. It is not the purpose of this book to provide an overview of cross-cultural communication, but a thorough grounding in diverse cultures precedes excellent conflict management. Otherwise, one remains *ethnocentric,* or biased toward judging all other groups and situations according to the categories and values of one's own culture (Ruhly 1976). Augsburger (1992) states:

> What comprises a conflict in one culture is a daily difference of opinion in another. A serious insult in one setting—crossing one's legs or showing the sole of one's foot, for example—is a matter of comfort in another. An arrogant challenge in one culture—putting one's hands on one's hips—is a sign of openness in another. A normal pathway for de-escalating a conflict in one society—fleeing the scene of an accident—constitutes a serious offense in another. Human boundaries are cultural creations—social boundaries, legal boundaries, and emotional boundaries are all drawn according to each culture's values, myths, and preferences. (23)

Westerners now understand that in many Asian cultures, self-expression is frowned upon if it does not further the needs of the group. In the West, in general, autonomy and self-expression are regarded more highly. Therefore, for Westerners to assume that individual expression is a higher value than harmony in the larger group is to remain in a Western, ethnocentric mode.

Of course, within such an array of different cultural influences, there are many ways in which people process conflict in the United States. In a recent qualitative study in which U.S. students were interviewed about their understanding of kinds of conflict, students identified the following varieties:

- *mock conflict:* conflict that is playful in intent (e.g., "We're just fooling around.")
- *déjà vu conflict:* serious conflict characterized by predictable repetition (e.g., Uh-oh. Here we go again.")
- *indirect conflict:* people know there is conflict even though not a word has been exchanged (e.g., "The tension is so thick around here you could cut it with a knife.")
- *silent-treatment conflict:* silence extends across two or more interactions in which people would usually talk (e.g., "He's freezing me out again.")
- *blowup conflict:* hostility and uncooperativeness lead to heated emotional exchange (e.g., "I've had it! Get out of my face or you'll be sorry!")
- *sarcastic sniping:* indirect hostile sarcasm (e.g., "Oh really? And just how do you propose to do that with no support from anyone? You have a buried treasure, maybe?")
- *civil discussion:* calm and rational discussion (e.g., "Let's sit down and talk this through. We can figure something out.") (Adapted from Baxter et al. 1993)

If this list seems familiar to you, you probably have been raised in mainstream U.S. culture, which exhibits all these variations. However, if you are an exchange student from China, Finland, or Zimbabwe, you might be puzzled by the above descriptions. But you could provide a similar list from your own culture—ways you and your friends understand conflict.

The United States, generally, is a *low-context culture.* A person is supposed to say what he or she means and resolve disagreements through the use of power (as in competition) or by working things out together (collaboration) (Wilson 1992). This approach to resolving differences and communicating relies on assertiveness, relatively equal power, and freedom from fear of reprisal. Since these attributes are seldom present, however, U.S. cul-

Table 1.1 Characteristics of Conflict in Low- and High-Context Cultures

Key Questions	Low-context Cultures	High-context Cultures
Why?	Analytic, linear logic Instrumental-oriented Dichotomy between conflict & conflict parties	Synthetic, spiral logic Expressive-oriented Integration of conflict & conflict parties
When?	Individual-oriented Low-collective normative expectations Violations of individual expectations create conflict potentials	Group-oriented High-collective normative expectations Violations of collective expectations create conflict potentials
What?	Revealment Direct, confrontational attitude	Concealment Indirect, nonconfrontational attitude
How?	Action and solution-oriented Explicit communication codes Line-logic styles Rational, factual rhetoric Open, direct strategies	Face- and relationship-oriented Implicit communication codes Point-logic style Intuitive, affective rhetoric Ambiguous, indirect strategies

Source: Reprinted, by permission of the publishers, from W. Gudykunst and S. Ting-Toomey, *Culture and Interpersonal Communication* (Beverly Hills, Calif.: Sage, 1988). 158.

ture rewards actions that are, for some people in the culture, stressful or even impossible. For example, Barnlund notes, "One of the most frequent shocks experienced by Japanese in coming to America is the resilience of friendships in the face of such strong clashes of opinion: Friends are able to confront each other, to vigorously argue contradictory views and to continue to be close friends in spite of their differences" (1989, 157). In situations in which people enjoy approximately equal power or understand the rules of interaction easily and well, the ideal of clarity and expressiveness works well. But when there is not a common base of assumptions, one's assertiveness can backfire.

Less individualistic, more collective cultures have been termed *high-context cultures* by researchers. In high-context cultures, discrepancies abound between what is meant and what is actually said. Disagreements are resolved through avoidance or accommodation, resulting in considerable face-saving (discussed at length in chapter 3). In high-context cultures, nuances of communication take on major importance, along with expected ways of behaving and working out problems. People are not confronted assertively and directly; to do so is considered rude and ignorant. In high-context cultures, members rely heavily on inferred meaning, whereas in low-context cultures, members strive for an understanding of the literal meaning (Borisoff and Victor 1989, 141).

Communication researchers have provided a clear summary of some of the differences between low- and high-context cultures. Table 1.1 portrays the differences in communicative strategies—direct and open compared to ambiguous and indirect. No wonder cross-cultural communication is now getting more attention; we certainly need all the help we can get!

Similarly, Triandis (1980) notes some of the salient differences between the two orientations. In individualistic, low-context cultures

> many individuals are high in internal control, who emphasize private goals, who pay attention to what the person does rather than who the person is . . . and where one finds more alienated and rootless individuals, where people think that decisions made by individuals are better than decisions made by groups . . . where going one's way and not paying attention to the view of others is acceptable, where personal enjoyment is emphasized, where friendship is a matter of personal choice. (65)

However, in collectivist countries

> there is an assumption that maintaining a strong group is the best guarantee of individual freedom, there is a strong emphasis on doing what the in group specifies . . . shame and loss of face are mechanisms of social control, there is sometimes the tyranny of the group, interpersonal relations are an end in themselves, there are narrow ingroups, there is a concept of limited good, there are more people under external control or motivation, people tend to think that planning is a waste of time, goals tend to be group rather than individual goals, who does something is more important than what she/he does. (66)

Some of the specific differences in styles will be explored in more depth in chapter 5, "Styles and Tactics."

> We live in a cobweb of relationships. When you die you are finally free of this cobweb of relationships—which you leave to your children to carry on.
>
> —Hiroko, former student, on the relationship focus of her Japanese culture

In addition to bridging the gaps between low- and high-context cultures, we need much more exploration of cultural diversity within the United States. For example, many cultural groups share some of the features of mainstream U.S. culture yet are distinct in ways that make conflict management and mediation of their disputes challenging to someone from the dominant culture. Buitrago (1997) outlines some of the key features of Hispanic cultures that require careful consideration, and we need detailed exploration of many other cultural groups as well, ranging from Native American to Black subcultures.

Whatever set of assumptions you choose to use, each framework places boundaries on constructive conflict management. Sometimes effective management requires people to be clear, direct, assertive, and unambiguous. Yet, at other times, deferring until the time is right, focusing primarily on the relationship components, and thinking of indirect ways to manage the dispute is the best approach. To solve the most difficult problems, we cannot rely solely on the teachings of one culture. One major problem encountered in low-context cultures is that we receive little training in the search for *commonly acceptable solutions.* If three people want different things, often the problem is resolved by competing to see who is the strongest ("We'll play it *my* way or not at all!"), or a progressive manager in a business may attempt to come up with a good solution for everyone. Typically, a person has to have enough power to persuade others to go along with a search for a collaborative solution. Therefore, many potentially collaborative ideas generated by low-power people are dismissed as unimportant.

In the United States, even in communication studies departments, students are often taught that directness, ease in public, clarity of expression, assertiveness, and the ability to argue well are prerequisites to participation in conflict management. Indeed, in many contexts these skills are essential. However, for people who hold low-power positions in society, this is a very difficult set of skills to be learned. To correct this imbalance, we need to focus also on communication skills for people in high-power or high-authority positions. Both the high- and low-power people contribute to the tangles that occur in the workplace, and both must participate in better conflict management.

Finally, cultural considerations include nonverbal communication, concepts of time (such as lateness or promptness), place of meetings or talks, whether content, relationship, and process issues can be separated or not, and face-saving (Borisoff and Victor 1989). As you begin to pay attention to the structure of conflict interactions, include these cultural and power issues in your analysis. Conflicts usually are not at all simple. If someone opens a conflict interaction by saying, "It's simple. We just have to do what makes sense . . . ," you can be sure that, if the conflict is ongoing or has raised a lot of emotion, the solution is not simple at all.

Augsburger summarizes this brief treatment of cultural considerations: "Every human conflict is, in some respects, like all others, and like no other. Conflicts are similar, culturally distinct, and individually unique—simultaneously, invariably, and intriguingly" (1992, 17).

Gender Frames Conflict Interaction

Membership in the "gender club" remains exclusive for all of your life, exerting one of the several powerful, pervasive influences on your developing conflict repertoire. Your own gender and the gender of those with whom you engage in conflict may affect your behavior in powerful ways.

One of the primary ways to view the role of gender in conflict interaction comes from the *communication differences tradition,* made popular by scholarly work in communication and linguistics. These traditions have taken a "separate but equal" or descriptive way of viewing communication differences. Rather than presenting women as deficient in "general" (male) communication skills or males as lacking important relational skills that women are assumed to possess, both gender-based preferences are studied openly. Given the scope of that work, only that directly pertaining to conflict interactions will be summarized here. (See Wood 1994 and Pearson, Turner, and Todd-Mancillas 1991 for comprehensive reviews of gender differences and similarities.)

Current research does show that in some circumstances there are female/male differences in enacting conflict. In laboratory exercises, men will often exhibit dominating and competitive behavior and women exhibit avoidant and compromising behavior (Papa and Natalle 1989). In real-life observations of young girls and boys (at age eleven), it has been noted that adolescent girls use indirect means of aggression, whereas the boys use more physical aggression. Interestingly, both sexes used direct verbal aggression equally (Bjorkqvist et al. 1994).

In contrast to these findings, current work on physical aggression and gender is a bit surprising. Women are, in relationships that involve physical aggression, more often aggressive than men in terms of the number of acts initiated. In dating relationships in the United States, women are fourteen more times likely than men to throw something and fifteen more times likely than men to slap (Stets and Henderson 1991). Yet, as you will see in the section on violence, women, because of their smaller size, are usually the ones who sustain the most damage once the aggression escalates.

One other finding shows some consistency across subjects and contexts. When feeling powerless, males tend to "state their position and offer logical reasons to support it" and females' approaches depend on the gender of their opponents (Watson 1994). As another researcher put it, "Men may use a more independent criterion for managing conflict and women a more interdependent one" (Miller 1991, 28), where women will choose responses based on interpersonal obligations and men based on the offended person's rights. As a result of their focus on relationships, females in conflict seem to exhibit fewer self-presentational actions (Haferkamp 1991). In preschool children ages three to five, for example, Sheldon (1992) noted that young girls' expressions of self-interest are often meshed with "an expression of communal interests." Research also indicates that women in lesbian relationships may benefit from both being female in that they have "more optimism about conflict resolution" (Metz, Rosser, and Strapko 1994, 305).

One persistent finding is that in adult marriages, the wife "frequently used conflict management and the husband frequently withdrew" (Kurdek 1995, 161). Gottman's (1994) classic work on predicting divorce reveals that in unhappy marriages "wives are described as conflict engaging, whereas husbands are described as withdrawn" (135). Similarly, in personal relationships, Dutch males reflect a trend that also occurs in other Western countries—That men tend to avoid emotional discussion and soothe over differences (Buunk, Schaap, and Prevoo 1990). In chapter 5, "Styles and Tactics," the more complex issues of engagement and withdrawal will be explored.

Before we decide that "men are like this and women are like that," we need to examine the similarities among men's and women's conflict behaviors. In a comprehensive examination of sex differences, researchers concluded that "no meaningful gender differences in positive affect behavior, influence strategies, autocratic behavior, democratic behavior communication, facilitation and leader emergence" were found. They report "in both survey and observational studies, we discovered more similarities than differences between men's and women's conflict behaviors" (Canary, Cupach, and Messman 1995, 131). Most of the studies that find male-female differences in conflict choices ask college students to answer "in general" rather than for a particular conflict. College students have a stereotyped *belief* that there are gender differences. This leads college students to report gender differences, which then get summarized in research reports about gender differences.

Once people are studied in relational contexts, gender differences tend to diminish. For example, Noller et al.'s (1994) work on marriages showed "no gender effects." Consistent with the early work by Shockley-Zalabak (1981), recent work shows experienced managers manifesting no gender differences in style, but "among participants without managerial experience, women rated themselves as more integrating, obliging, and compromising than did men" (Korabik, Baril, and Watson 1993, 405). Likewise, in a negotiation context, "Women are not necessarily more fair-minded or compassionate" than men (Watson 1994, 124). In the workplace, Gayle (1991) notes that on conflict strategy selection, the effects of gender are "minuscule" compared to a host of other, unidentified factors. It may well be that most of the effects ascribed to gender are due to other relationship factors such as power, gender of the opponent, prior moves of the other, and so on. But, clearly, in a negotiation context, "Women are likely to be just as oriented toward beating their opponents as men are, and just as successful at doing so" (Watson 1994, 123).

One important contribution of gender research is that it has sharpened the focus on key issues in conflict behavior. For example, when we see the self-in-relationship as a theoretical starting point, it allows us to concentrate on the following dimensions of conflict:

- Interdependence rather than power over others
- Mutual empathy as the basis for understanding and communicating
- Relational self-confidence instead of separate self-esteem (autonomy)
- Constructive conflict instead of domination
- Staying engaged with others while in conflict
- Valuing separate knowing and connected knowing
- Utilizing both *report talk* and *rapport talk*
- Continuing dialogue when there is disagreement

New models of constructive conflict are being built on the ideas of partnership and self-in-relationship (Tannen 1990; Young-Eisendrath 1993; Belenky et al. 1986; Jordan et al. 1991; Goodrich 1991; Brown and Gilligan 1992; Jordan 1992; Wilmot 1995). These ideas underlie the development of constructive conflict practices as have been presented in all the editions of this book and will be developed more in depth in subsequent chapters.

Conflict Elements Frame Conflict Interaction

Just as culture and gender frame conflict interaction, the underlying *elements of conflict* set the stage for how a conflict is enacted. The following elements of conflict allow one to unpack conflict dynamics to see what is really operating below the surface.

- How the struggle is *expressed*—the styles and tactics used
- The degree of *interdependence*—how much the parties need from one another
- The perceived *differences in goals* of the parties
- The perception of *scarcity*—that there is "not enough to go around"
- The perception of *interference* by the other

The framing effects of the conflict elements are so important that chapter 2, "The Nature of Conflict," will be dedicated to their exposition.

The Lens Model of Conflict Interaction

Before discussing the conflict elements, the basic components of all conflicts will be overviewed. The building blocks of conflict are represented in figure 1.1, the lens model. For the sake of simplicity, the lens model will be illustrated with just two conflict parties, though many times there will be more than two parties involved.

All conflicts are composed of these minimal features:

Figure 1.1 The lens model of conflict interaction

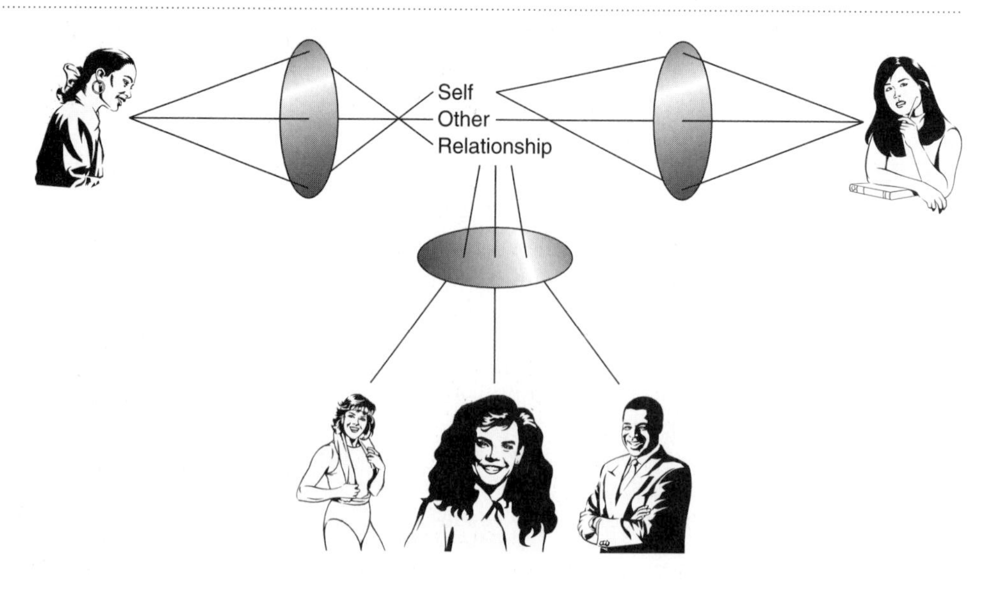

- The communicative acts of each person
- The meanings (attributions) attached to those acts by each person
  - views of self
  - views of other
- The meanings the two people ascribe to their relationship
  - past events
  - current events
  - future projections

The lens model specifies that each person has a view of (1) oneself, (2) the other person, and (3) the relationship they are conjointly creating. Note that each person has a "lens" that gives him or her a particular perspective; they are looking at the conflict from different "sides" of the picture. In the Far East, such as in Nepal and Tibet, a person in conflict might say, "Well from my side, I guess I am getting tired of waiting for him, but from his side I don't know what is going on." The notion of "side" captures just how different two perceptions will be.

It is easy when one is watching someone else's conflict to think that the only important elements are what each person does—the observable behavior or communicative acts. Certainly, that is one big part of conflict management. If, for example, someone who interrupts others and makes snide remarks stops those negative behaviors, the change will have an immediate impact on the interaction. Or, if one of the parties always avoids discussing issues and begins to discuss them, possibilities open up for working through the conflict with the other.

Behaviors do not, however, occur in a vacuum. The *perceptions of and attributions about* the behaviors are at the heart of the conflict process. The work on attribution theory shows quite conclusively that we make different attributions about ourselves than about others. Here are the findings:

- We try to make sense out of behavior by looking for causes.
- We attribute causes of *our* behavior to external factors (e.g., "I failed the test because it was unfair").
- We attribute causes of *others'* behavior to internal dispositions (e.g., "He failed the test because he was lazy and didn't study").

So, when we are exposed to conflict (which has many negative features for most of us), we tend to *attribute the negative effects to the other* rather than to ourselves. This tendency explains the familiar "It's his fault!" Sillars and Parry (1982) found that as the stress of conflict increases, the blame of others also increases. We begin with an attribution of blame, then choose our next conflict move based on our perception that the other is at fault. And, the other party does the same thing. No wonder conflict is so difficult.

The lens model illustrates that people's views of self, other, and relationship are always, to some degree, distorted. We all have "filters" that come into play. As we will see in chapter 3, often in U.S. culture we "save face" for ourselves and "damage face" for the other. The other is probably doing the same thing. If you have ever known both individuals of a broken-up romance you see the two sides very clearly. In fact, their filters are so strong it doesn't even sound like they were in the same relationship!

The following conversation between two people occurred with two listeners present. As you can tell, the people conversing are in conflict with one another. Notice the different internal filters they automatically use that give them their opposing perspectives. The two of them had just hosted a special event and coordinated a series of public meetings for thirteen outside people.

Program coordinator	"The executive director does not listen to me, does not include me in decisions, agrees to include me, then goes her merry way without consulting me. Happened five times this week during the visit of some important people. She is just too controlling. I don't see that this relationship can continue."
Executive director	"The program coordinator is too passive and does not remember when I talked to him. Further, he is being power hungry and wanting to run things himself. I specifically remember inviting him to participate on most of these occasions. What is the beef?"

The two of them then began a round of "did too," "did not." As of this writing, they were beginning to work their way through this dispute. Both remain involved in the organization, with the program coordinator taking more responsibility and the executive director sharing more information.

Outsiders to a dispute, whether they be social scientists or friends, also have their own attributions—adding still other "sides" to the conflict equation. Whereas the parties see the issues, exemplified above, as inclusion, power, control, and assertiveness, an outsider might focus on other issues. For example, during the exchange between the program coordinator and executive director, one of the outsiders was thinking, "Hmmm, if the coordinator doesn't dampen this outburst, it will blow this relationship sky high, and the executive director is looking a bit smug—maybe she excluded him on purpose and is glad she did."

These three "lenses" offer very disparate pictures of the unfolding dispute. Chapter 9, "Third-Party Intervention," will describe the moves mediators make in situations like this. But for now, notice how disparate the starting observations are for *all* the people present in the discussion. The filters are operating at full force. And when the "hardening of the categories" sets in, you can see how people get locked into intense struggles.

In a conflict interaction, you often hear the principal participants say, "Yeah, well that is just *your* perception," as if the other's view isn't relevant. At the heart of *all* conflicts are the perceptions of the parties—they fuel the dispute engine. Research illuminates the importance of perceptions. For example, one consistent finding about married couples is that *believing* they are similar is what produces happiness, not whether they are similar or not (Acitelli, Douvan, and Veroff 1993). On the other side of the coin, when you come to see your work relationship (or personal relationship) as "having no hope," that belief alone predicts dissolution (Wilmot 1995). As a relationship declines, the individuals make fewer dyadic and more individual attributions (Lloyd and Cate 1985). The dissolution of a marriage is speeded up if the two players see it as emanating from individual factors (Siegert and Stamp 1994, 358). If during the "first big fight" the individuals develop a shared view of what happened, their relationship is more likely to survive.

Attributions and meanings about the relationship are central to the struggles we have with others. If your lens for a relationship is "this one won't last long," then it won't (Wilmot 1995). Further, in viewing the relationship, each partner has their own view. Years ago it was called "his marriage/her marriage" to highlight the vastly different filters that develop. Each person develops these three views of the relationship:

- An account of the past of the relationship
- A view of the current state of the relationship
- A projected image of the future of the relationship

These perceptions occur not only in romantic relationships but in families, in business settings, and between nation states—everywhere we have a connection with others. Perceptions of the future are a big part of conflict. Many a romantic relationship has been broken up because someone begins to believe "He/she isn't committed to me" and makes the first strike to kill the relationship when, in fact, the other partner may have wanted it to continue (Wilmot 1995). One study on environmental organizations and the timber industry found that *each side responds to, anticipates, and often copies* the moves they think the other will make (Lange 1993). This same dynamic is present in personal and workplace conflicts as well.

If you are not in touch with the other party, much like the environmentalists and timber industry representatives in Lange's study, then you mull over the conflict in your own mind. Without interaction with the other, the only "information" you have is what is going on in your own mind—your filter doesn't have a chance to get corrected. The result? "Prolonged thinking about disputes in the absence of communication focuses individuals on their own perspective and enhances biases toward seeing disputes as serious and holding partners responsible for conflicts" (Cloven and Roloff 1991, 153). If we run our own stories in our minds, then our view gets even more distorted. Cloven and Roloff found that only 1 percent of the time, individuals reported that they had thought about the conflict from the partner's view (136).

As you can see, the distorted lens can become even more warped in time. Here is an example of such thinking:

Joan

- Why is Jack late?
- He must be tied up.
- He was late last week, too.
- Hmmm, he is moving into the "irresponsible zone."
- I wonder if he is wanting to tell me something about our relationship?
- It has now been twenty-five minutes—he is so inconsiderate.
- I knew he would be like this—Sandy warned me about him.
- Jack is a real jerk.

Jack

- Hi, Joan. Sorry I'm late. I ran out of gas and had to walk. Then when I got to the gas station between your place and mine, their only phone was out of order.

Summary

Your personal history affects your approaches to conflicts. Perceptions about conflict, whether it is an activity to be avoided or sought out and whether it is a negative or positive activity, develop over one's lifetime. In this process, refined images or metaphors develop in one's imagination and language that give shape and meaning to conflict episodes. Cultural perspectives, such as one's access to power and whether the culture is low- or high-context in its structure, also affect perspectives or conflict. Finally, there are conflicting perspectives on the role of gender in conflict, demonstrating that other relationship features may be more important than gender alone. The lens model of conflict is one tool used to clarify the distortions in view that develop in all conflicts.

Chapter 2

The Nature of Conflict

The following dialogue may be familiar to you in tone, if not in content:

Son: My graduation expenses cost a lot more than I thought they would. Would you be willing to pay my car insurance premiums through the summer?

Mother: I thought you were going to pay them out of your work earnings this summer. I haven't budgeted for this at all.

Son: I haven't been able to find a job yet. You know I've been looking. I can't drive if I don't have insurance, and if I don't have a car I can't work.

Mother: This is not what we agreed. The payments are your responsibility after graduation. We've been clear on this all along.

The mother and son are engaged in a pervasive human activity—interpersonal conflict. Their conflict results from their particular communication choices. The son asks for extra help; the mother makes a judgment rather than asking questions. The next few interactions escalate and may damage an important, ongoing relationship. The son may be uncertain how he will look for work if he can't drive. He may want to save money he was given for graduation for other purposes. Yet he also wants his mother's recognition of him as an adult, and he wants to be seen as responsible. The mother wants, presumably, to help her son find work, to teach him to manage money, and to preserve a give-and-take relationship between them. She doesn't want to alienate her son, but she doesn't want to feel taken advantage of or to go against an agreement. Their individual and relational goals can only be met through creative conflict interactions. When conflict is viewed as a problem to be solved instead of a battle to be won or interaction to be avoided, creative solutions can be found.

This book on interpersonal conflict is written to help people manage conflict in productive, creative ways. In the Chinese language the character for conflict is made up of two different symbols: one indicates danger whereas the other indicates opportunity. As you think about these two approaches, decide whether you respond first to conflict as a dangerous, obstructive dilemma or whether you experience conflict as a welcome opportunity for change. The I Ching teaches that the wise person in conflict remains clearheaded, inwardly strong, and ready to meet his or her opponent halfway (Wilhelm 1977). At the beginning of your study of conflict, you might consider the possibilities inherent in conflict and come to experience the activity as an important means of growth rather than a failure or a negative event to be avoided at all costs.

By studying this book and participating in class exercises, you will be able to understand your present conflict behavior, make choices to engage in new behavior during conflicts, and thus act as a change agent in times of crisis and turbulence. People *can* change their conflict behavior. Your approach to conflict is not an inborn set of responses but rather a developed repertoire of communication skills that are learned, refined, and practiced. You don't have to remain the way you have been in the past.

Conflict Defined

All interpersonal conflicts, whether they occur between family members, students and teachers, employees and supervisors, or groups, have certain elements in common. One of the popular definitions of conflict, offered by Coser (1967, 8), asserts that conflict is "a struggle over values and claims to scarce status, power, and resources in which the aims of the opponents are to neutralize, injure, or eliminate the rivals." Notice that this definition grew out of the cold war in which conflict between the United States and the former U.S.S.R. dominated Western approaches to conflict. Conflict was definitely viewed as a win-lose situation. In 1973 Deutsch maintained that "conflict exists whenever incompatible activities occur . . . an action which prevents, obstructs, interferes with, injures, or in some way makes it less likely or less effective" (156). Mack and Snyder (1973) suggested that two parties must be present, along with "position scarcity" or "resource scarcity," in addition to behaviors that "destroy, injure, thwart, or otherwise control another party or parties, . . . one in which the parties can gain (relatively) only at each other's expense" (36). All of these early social science definitions help us distinguish conflict from simple "strain," "disagreement," or "controversy" (Simons 1972; Schmidt and Kochan 1972).

Contemporary definitions focus largely on *interdependence* instead of unalterable opposition. Donohue and Kolt (1992, 3) define conflict as "a situation in which interdependent people express (manifest or latent) differences in satisfying their individual needs and interests, and they experience interference from each other in accomplishing these goals." Jordan (1990, 4) writes that "conflict arises when a difference between two (or more)

Figure 2.1 Continuum of conflict management and resolution approaches

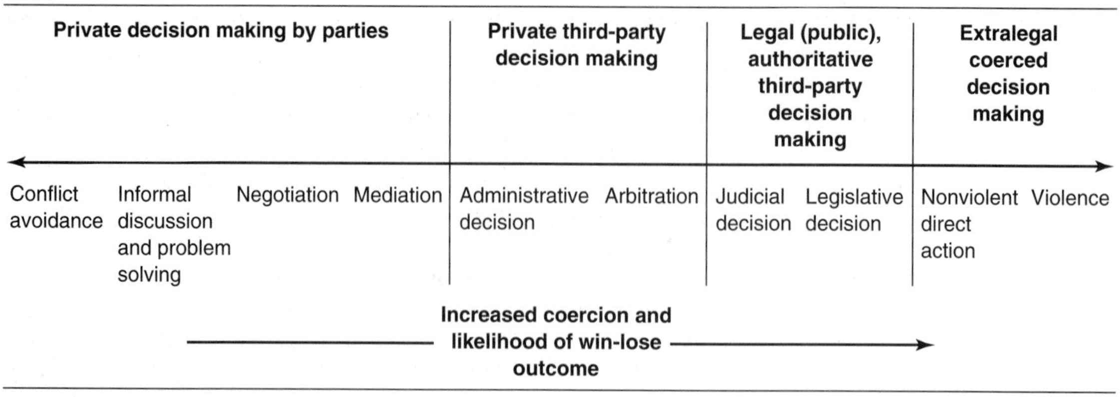

Private decision making by parties				Private third-party decision making		Legal (public), authoritative third-party decision making		Extralegal coerced decision making	
Conflict avoidance	Informal discussion and problem solving	Negotiation	Mediation	Administrative decision	Arbitration	Judicial decision	Legislative decision	Nonviolent direct action	Violence

Increased coercion and likelihood of win-lose outcome →

Source: From Christopher W. Moore, *The Mediation Process: Practical Strategies for Resolving Conflict.* Copyright © 1996 Christopher W. Moore and Jossey-Bass Inc., Publishers, San Francisco, California. Reprinted by permission.

people necessitates change in at least one person in order for their engagement to continue and develop. The differences cannot coexist without some adjustment." Parties are presented as inherently interdependent. Additionally, at least one person may need to change his or her perception of the situation. Conflict is sometimes, but not always, accompanied by anger or strong emotion.

Conflict varies in intensity and range. At least two continua have been advanced to describe the intensity of conflict. It may be seen as a (1) mild difference, (2) disagreement, (3) dispute, (4) campaign, (5) litigation, or (6) fight or war (Keltner 1987). Another continuum (Moore 1996) shows conflict ranging from avoidance to violence (see figure 2.1). Our choices range from low coercion to increased coercion of the other party. Our conflict choices also reflect who is making the decisions, the parties themselves or an external authority.

For purposes of this book, conflict is defined as follows: *Conflict is an expressed struggle between at least two interdependent parties who perceive incompatible goals, scarce resources, and interference from others in achieving their goals.* Transforming a conflict depends on perceptual and/or conceptual change in one or more of the parties. Careful attention to the elements that make up conflict will help you "break apart" an apparently unresolvable conflict. When conflicts remain muddled and unclear, they cannot be resolved. Take the time to analyze an important conflict of your own as you read through the common components of any conflict.

An Expressed Struggle

An interpersonal approach to conflict management focuses on the communicative exchanges that make up the conflict episode. Intrapersonal conflict—internal strain that creates a state of ambivalence, conflicting internal dialogue, or lack of resolution in one's thinking and feeling—accompanies interpersonal conflict. One may endure intrapersonal conflict for a while before such a struggle is expressed communicatively. If you are upset with your father yet do not write him, or phone him less often, and avoid expressing your concern, do you have a "conflict"?

People involved in conflicts have perceptions about ther own thoughts and feelings and perceptions about the other's thoughts and feelings. Conflict is present when there are joint communicative representations of it. The verbal or nonverbal communication may be subtle—a slight shift in body placement by Jill and a hurried greeting by Susan—but it must be present for the activity to be interpersonal conflict. Therefore, although other conditions must also exist before an interaction is labeled "conflict," Jandt (1973, 2) asserts, "Conflict exists when the parties involved agree in some way that the behaviors associated with their relationship are labeled as 'conflict' behavior." Often, the communicative behavior is easily identified with conflict, such as when one party openly disagrees with the other. Other times, however, an interpersonal conflict may be operating at a more tacit level. Two friends, for instance, may both be consciously avoiding the other because both think, "I don't want to see him for a few days because of what he did." The interpersonal struggle is expressed by the avoidance. Intrapersonal perceptions are the bedrock upon which conflicts are built, but only when there are communicative manifestations of these perceptions will an "interpersonal conflict" emerge.

Communication is the central element in all interpersonal conflict. Communication and conflict are related in the following ways:

- Communication behavior often *creates* conflict.
- Communication behavior *reflects* conflict.
- Communication is the *vehicle* for the productive or destructive management of conflict.

Thus, communication and conflict are inextricably tied. For example, the most distinguishing characteristic of happily married couples is their ability to reach consensus on conflictual issues (Mettetal and Gottman 1980). How one communicates in a conflictual situation has profound implications for the residual impact of that conflict. If two work associates are vying for the same position, they can handle the competition in a variety of ways. They may engage in repetitive, damaging rounds with one another, or they may successfully manage the conflict. Communication can be used to exacerbate the conflict or lead to its productive management.

Most expressed struggles become activated by a *triggering event.* A staff member of a counseling agency is fired, setting off a series of meetings culminating in the staff's demand to the board that the director be fired. Or, in a roommate situation, Carl comes home one night and the locks are changed on the door. The triggering event brings the conflict to everyone's attention—it is the lightning rod of recognition.

Interdependence

Conflict parties engage in an expressed struggle and interfere with one another because they are *interdependent.* "A person who is not dependent upon another—that is, who has no special interest in what the other does—has no conflict with that other person" (Braiker and Kelley 1979, 137). Each person's choices affect the other because conflict is a mutual activity. People are seldom totally opposed to each other. Even two people who are having an "intellectual conflict" over whether a community should limit its growth are to some extent cooperating with each other. They have, in effect, said, "Look, we are going to have this verbal argument, and we aren't going to hit each other, and both of us will get certain rewards for participating in this flexing of our intellectual muscles. We'll play by the rules, which we both understand." Schelling (1960) calls strategic conflict (conflict in which parties have choices as opposed to conflict in which the power is so disparate that there are virtually no choices) a "theory of precarious partnership" or "incomplete antagonism." In other words, even these informal debaters concerned with a city's growth cannot formulate their verbal tactics until they know the "moves" made by the other party.

Parties in strategic conflict, therefore, are never totally antagonistic and must have mutual interests, even if the interest is only in keeping the conflict going. Without openly saying so, they often are thinking, "How can we have this conflict in a way that increases the benefit to me?" These decisions are complex, with parties reacting not in a linear, cause-effect manner but with a series of interdependent decisions. Bateson (1972) presents an "ecological" view of patterns in relationships. As in the natural environment, in which a decision to eliminate coyotes because they are a menace to sheep affects the overall balance of animals and plants, no one party in a conflict can make a decision that is totally separate—each decision affects the other conflict participants. In all conflicts, therefore, interdependence carries elements of cooperation and elements of competition.

Even though conflict parties are always interdependent to some extent, how they perceive their mutuality affects their later choices. Parties decide, although they may not be aware of this decision, whether they will act as relatively interdependent agents or relatively independent agents. Both or all may agree that "we are in this together," or they may believe that "just doing my own thing" is possible and desirable. A couple had been divorced for three years and came to a mediator to decide what to do about changing visitation agreements as their three children grew older. In the first session, the former husband seemed to want a higher degree of interdependence than did the former wife. He wanted to communicate frequently by phone, adopting flexible arrangements based on the children's wishes and his travel schedule. She wanted a monthly schedule set up in advance, communicated in writing. After talking through their common interest in their children, their own complicated work and travel lives, the children's school and sports commitments, and their new spouses' discomfort with frequent, flexible contact between the former partners, they worked out a solution that suited them all. Realizing that they were unavoidably interdependent, they agreed to lessen their verbal and in-person communication about arrangements while agreeing to maintain written communication about upcoming scheduling. They worked out an acceptable level of interdependence.

Another example of the struggle over interdependence occurred in a class in which one older student challenged the teacher's choices about the most appropriate way to run the class. This challenge went on for several class periods, with the rest of the large class becoming very restless and annoyed. Finally, a representative of a group of students spoke up to the challenger and said, "Look, you are taking our time to work on this personal conflict, and we are really getting angry. We're not able to do what we came to this class to do. Don't involve us in your personal hassles." The student initiating the challenge said, "But you're involved—you're in the class, and you ought to be concerned about how the sessions are run. You're in this just as much as I am." They engaged in a short-term conflict based not only on the issue of class goals but also on the issue of "How interdependent are we?" The most salient issue at that point was how the parties perceived themselves in relationship to each other. The issue of class goals had to wait until the first-order issue was settled. A basic question, then, in any conflict is, *"How much are we willing to allow each other to influence our choices?"*

Persons who understand themselves as interdependent must determine who they are as a unit after they decide individually how much influence they want the other person to have with them. (Sometimes, these choices are not available.) They must decide, tacitly or overtly, which rules bind them, how they will communicate, where "beltlines" are (Bach and Wyden 1968), and dozens of other relationship issues that define them as a conflict unit proceeding toward mutual and individual goals. People who see themselves as relatively independent are primarily concerned with *acting* issues—where will I go, what will I get, or how can I win? But those who view themselves as highly interdependent must, in addition, decide *being* issues—who are we and how will this relationship be defined? For instance, two persons in competition for a job are more interested in maximizing their own gains than the gains of the ephemeral relationship. They want to win—separately. But the same two individuals one year later, after both have been hired by the company, perceive themselves as highly interdependent when asked to work together to come up with a plan for implementing an environmental impact study. While still in competition with each other for promotions, they must also define for themselves a workable relationship that enhances desired goals for them both.

Sometimes parties are locked into a position of mutual interdependence whether they want to be or not. Not all interdependent units choose to be interdependent but are so for other compelling reasons. Some colleagues in an office, for instance, got into a conflict over when they were to be in their offices to receive calls and speak with customers. One group took the position that "what we do doesn't affect you—it's none of your business." The other group convinced the first group that they could not define themselves as unconnected, since the rest of the group had to be available to fill in for them when they were not available. They were inescapably locked into interdependence. If a working decision is not made, the parties have almost guaranteed an unproductive conflict, with each party making choices as if they were only tenuously connected.

Most relationships move back and forth between degrees of independence and interdependence. At times there will be an emphasis on "me"—what I want—and on separateness, whereas at other times "we"—our nature as a unit—becomes the focus. These are natural rhythmic swings in relationships (Frentz and Rushing 1980; Galvin and Brommel 1982; Olson, Sprenkle, and Russell 1979; Baxter 1982; Bochner 1982; Stewart 1978). Just as we all need both stability and change, conflict parties have to balance their independence and dependence needs.

The previous discussion suggests, for clarity's sake, that relationships and interdependence issues precede other issues in the conflict. Actually, these negotiations over interdependence permeate most conflicts throughout the course of the relationship, never becoming completely settled. A helpful practice is to address the interdependence issue openly in ongoing, highly important relationships. In more transient and less salient relationships, the interdependence may be primarily tacit or understood.

Perceived Incompatible Goals

What do people fight about? (We use the word *fight* to mean verbal conflict, not physical violence.) People usually engage in conflict over goals they deny are important to them. One company had an extreme morale problem. The head cashier said, "All our problems would be solved if we could just get some carpet, since everyone's feet get tired—we're the ones who have to stand up all day. But management won't spend a penny for us." Her statement of incompatible goals was clear—carpet versus no carpet. But as the interviews progressed, another need emerged. She began to talk about how no one noticed when her staff had done good work and how the "higher-ups" only noticed when lines were long and mistakes were made. There was a silence, then she blurted out, "How about some compliments once in a while? No one ever says anything nice. They don't even know we're here." Her stated needs then changed to include not only carpet but self-esteem and increased attention from management—a significant deepening of the goal statement. Both goals were real, carpets and self-esteem, but the first goal may have been incompatible with management's desires, whereas the second might not; the need for recognition may have been important to both the cashiers and management.

We do not support the overly simple notion that if people just worked together, they would see that their goals are the same. Opposing goals are a fact of life. Many times, however, people are absolutely convinced they have opposing goals and cannot agree on anything to pursue together. However, if goals are reframed or put in a different context, the parties can agree. Recently a student teacher's supervisor outlined her goals for the student. Included in the list was the demand that the student turn in a list of the three most and least positive experiences in the classroom each week. The student asked to be transferred to another supervisor. The dean asked why, saying, "Ms Barker is one of our best supervisors." The student said, "That's what I've heard, but I can't be open about my failures with someone who's going to give me my ending evaluation. That will go in my permanent files." In a joint discussion with the teacher and the student, the dean found that both were able to affirm that they valued feedback about positive and negative experiences. Their goals were more similar than they thought; the means for achieving them were different. The teacher agreed to use the list as a starting point for discussion but not to keep copies; the student agreed to list experiences so the teacher would not feel that the student was hiding her negative experiences. Trust was built through a discussion of goals. Perceptions of the incompatibility of the goals changed through clear communication.

Perceived goal incompatibility appears in a couple of forms. First, the conflict parties may want the *same* thing—for example, the promotion in the company, the only A in the class, or the attention of the parents. They struggle and jockey for position in order to attain the desired goal. They perceive the situation as one where there "isn't enough to go around." Thus, they see their goal as "incompatible" with the other person's *because* they both want the same thing. Second, sometimes the goals are *different.* Mark and Tom, for example, decide to eat out. Mark wants to go to Bananas and Tom wants to go to Pearl's. They struggle over the incompatible choices. Similarly, in an organization one person may want to see seniority rewarded, whereas another may want to see work production rewarded. They struggle over which goal should be rewarded. Of course, many times the content goals seem to be different (like which restaurant to go to), but beneath them is a relational struggle over who gets to decide. Regardless of whether the participants see the goals as similar or different, perceived incompatible goals are central to all conflict struggles.

Perceived Scarce Resources

A *resource* can be defined as "any positively perceived physical, economic or social consequence" (Miller and Steinberg 1975, 65). The resources may be objectively real or perceived as real by the person. Likewise, the perception of scarcity, or limitation, may be apparent or actual. For example, close friends often think that if their best friend likes someone else, too, then the supply of affection available to the original friend will diminish. This may or may not be so, but a perception that affection is scarce may well create genuine conflict between the friends. Sometimes, then, the most appropriate behavior is attempting to change the other person's *perception* of the resource instead of trying to reallocate the resource. Ultimately, one person can never force another to change his or her valuing of a resource or perception of how much of the resource is available, but persuasion coupled with supportive responses for the person fearful of losing the reward can help.

Money, natural resources such as oil or land, and jobs may indeed be scarce or limited resources. But intangible commodities such as love, esteem, attention, respect, and caring may also be perceived as scarce. A poignant example concerns dropouts in the school system. By watching videotapes of classroom interactions, researchers could predict by the fourth grade which students would later drop out of school. The future dropouts were those students who received, either by their own doing or the teacher's, very limited eye contact from the teacher. They became, nonverbally, nonpersons. The glances, looks, smiles, and eye contact with the important person in the room became a scarce resource upon which the students were highly dependent. Often children fight with one another over this perceived scarcity—teacher attention. Or they fight with the teacher, resulting in a gain of that resource. A child would rather get negative attention than none. When rewards are perceived as scarce, an expressed struggle may be initiated.

In interpersonal struggles, two resources often perceived as scarce are power and self-esteem. Whether the parties are in conflict over a desired romantic partner or a coveted raise, perceived scarcities of power and self-esteem are involved. People engaged in conflict often say things that may be easily interpreted as power and self-esteem struggles, such as in the following scenarios:

"She always gets her own way." (She has more power than I do, and I feel at a constant disadvantage. I'm always one down.)

"He is so sarcastic! Who does he think he is? I don't have to put up with his mouth!" (I don't have ways to protect myself from biting sarcasm. It feels like an attack. I feel humiliated. The only power I have is to leave.

"I refuse to pay one more penny in child support." (I feel unimportant. I don't get to see the children very often. I've lost my involvement with them. Money is the only way I have to let that be known. I don't want to feel like a loser and a fool.)

"I won't cover for her if she asks me again. She can find someone else to work the night shift when her kids get sick." (I feel taken advantage of. She only pays attention to me when she needs a favor.)

Regardless of the particular content issues involved, people in conflict usually perceive that they have too little power and self-esteem and that the other party has too much. Of course, with each person thinking and feeling this way, something needs to be adjusted. Often, giving the other person some respect, courtesy, and ways to save face removes the need to use power excessively.

Interference

People who are interdependent, have incompatible goals, and want the same scarce resource still may not meet the conditions for conflict. *Interference,* or the perception of interference, is necessary to complete the conditions for conflict. If the presence of another person interferes with desired actions, conflict intensifies. Conflict is associated with blocking (Peterson 1983), and the person doing the blocking is perceived as the problem. For instance, a college sophomore worked in a sandwich shop the summer before her junior year abroad. She worked two jobs, scarcely having time to eat and sleep. She was invited to a party at a cabin in the wilderness, and she really wanted to go. She worked overtime on one day then asked for a day off from the sandwich shop, but the employer was reluctant to say yes, since the student was the only one the employer trusted to open the shop and keep the till. For an angry moment, the employer, who was interfering with what the student wanted to do, seemed like the main problem. Goals appeared incompatible, no one else was available to open (scarce resource), and the two parties were interdependent because the student needed the job and the owner needed her shop opened and the cash monitored. She was about to say, "No. I'm sorry, but I can't cover you." The student volunteered to train someone else, on her own time, to cover for her. The problem was solved, at least for this round, and the conflict was avoided. But if the student had quit in disgust or the employer had said no, both would have sacrificed important goals.

To make matters worse, people in conflict often assume that the other people are willfully interfering with their needs. One person attributes problems to negative, enduring personality traits of the other (Sillars and Scott 1983). In one organization, an administrative assistant was promoted in a way that the others thought was unfair and unjustified. A coalition of employees formed who talked about the assistant and spread the word that she was manipulative, devious, controlling, and overly protective of the manager of the group. She screened calls, refusing to let disgruntled employees talk to the manager. Later, when the team worked on these problems with a consultant, they found that the assistant had been instructed to do this by the manager, who did not want to engage in conflict with the other employees. The interference in the goals of the employees and the manager, to talk with and avoid talking with each other, respectively, was not a product of the assistant at all. But her perceived interference intensified what had been an annoying incident into a full-blown conflict, requiring the services of a mediator.

The Spiral of Conflict

The lens model of conflict, introduced at the end of the last chapter, set forth the basic building blocks for understanding all conflicts—they are composed of self, other, and relationship behaviors and perceptions on the part of both parties. The lens model, though, does not specify the *processes* that unfold during conflict interactions. Conflicts move from episode to episode in a continually unfolding pattern of interaction between the prime parties. The moves and interpretations of each party influence those of the others. Nowhere can we more clearly see the interlocking effects of moves and countermoves than in destructive conflicts.

Destructive Conflict

Conflict interaction can be productive or destructive depending on many factors, including the context in which it occurs (Camara and Resnick 1989) and the kinds of communication used. Conflict is potentially costly to all parties; these costs can exceed the gains if the conflict is drawn out before some kind of settlement is reached (Boulding 1989). If all participants are dissatisfied with the outcomes of a conflict and think they have lost as a result (Deutsch 1973), then the conflict is classified as destructive.

Often the parties cannot predict during a conflict whether it is going to end up as a destructive or constructive conflict. However, several characteristics of spiraling destructive conflict can be identified. Participants can rescue a destructive interaction, making the overall effect more positive, but if the interaction continues to be characterized by the following descriptions, the overall result will be a destructive, win-lose experience for all parties.

Escalatory spirals pervade destructive conflict. Often conflict gets out of hand. What begins as a rational exchange of opposing views deteriorates into an emotion-laden interchange in which strong feelings, usually anger and fear, are aroused, thus causing the primary intentions of the parties to shift from a useful exchange to damaging the other person (Baron 1984). Escalatory conflict spirals have only one direction—upward and onward. They are characterized by a heavy reliance on overt power manipulation, threats, coercion, and deception (Deutsch 1973). In an escalatory conflict spiral, the relationship continues to circle around to more and more damaging ends; the interaction becomes self-perpetuating. Its characteristics are misunderstanding, discord, and destruction (Wilmot 1987). Figure 2.2 illustrates the "runaway" dynamics that occur in a typical destructive conflict spiral.

In this example, two roommates begin with a misunderstanding that accelerates each time they communicate. Brad begins complaining about Steve's messiness. At each

Figure 2.2 Destructive conflict spiral

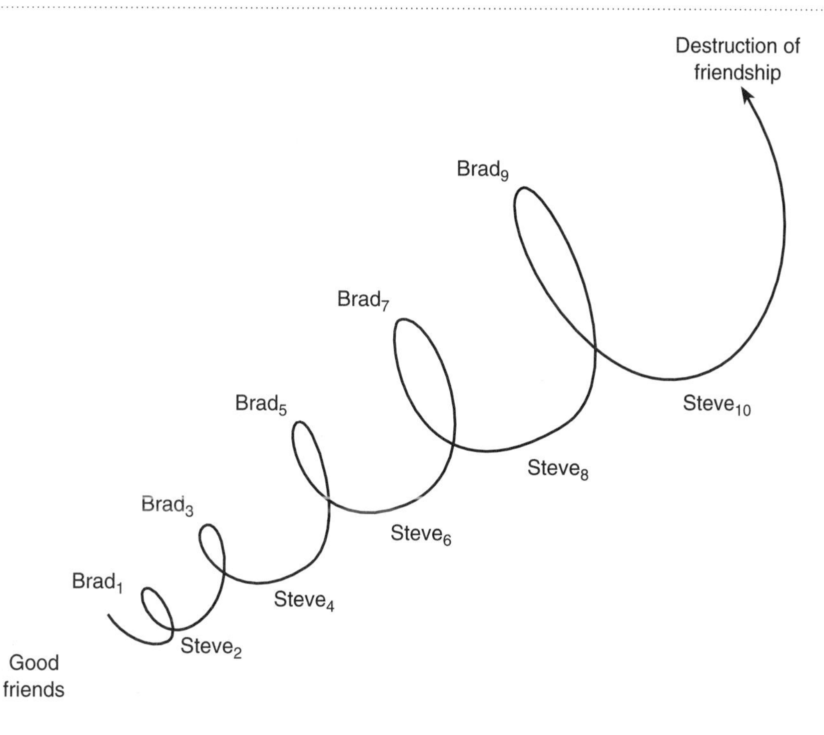

crossover point in the spiral, thoughts and actions might occur as they do in this version of an actual conflict:

1. Brad says to Steve, "Hey, why don't you do your part? This place is a hole."
2. Steve says, "Out of my face, dude!" (He then leaves the apartment.)
3. Brad, still upset about the messy apartment, finds Steve's ex-girlfriend and says, "Has Steve always been such a slob? I can't stand living with him."
4. Steve, hearing from his ex-girlfriend that "even Brad knows that you are a slob," decides that he will get back at Brad for his meanness. So Steve begins deliberately messing up the bathroom, knowing that it will drive Brad crazy.
5. Brad comes home, sees the messy bathroom, and puts an ad in the campus newspaper that says, "If anyone sees Steve K., tell him to clean up his half of the apartment—it's a pigsty."
6. Steve, angered at the public announcement, comes home late one night and, while Brad is sleeping, lets the air out of Brad's tires.
7. Brad runs into a mutual friend the next day and hears that Steve is the one who let the air out of his tires. So Brad goes home, moves all of Steve's belongings into the hall, changes the locks on the door, and puts a sign on Steve's belongings that says, "Help yourself."

The conflict continues to escalate, with more and more destructiveness. A destructive conflict in an intimate relationship between spouses, for example, may be characterized by the above features, in addition to "hitting below the belt" (Bach and Wyden 1968). Each person uses hit-and-run tactics to damage the other person. The injunction "don't fight unless you mean it" is ignored in a destructive conflict, and the interlocking, damaging moves occur repeatedly. In a destructive conflict, one party unilaterally attempts to change the structure, restrict the choices of the other, and gain advantage over the other.

Probably the best index of destructive conflict is when one or both of the parties has a strong desire to "get even" or damage the other party. When you hear a friend say, "Well, she may have gotten me that time, but just wait and see what happens when I tell some things I know about her!" you are overhearing one side of a destructive conflict in action. Wilmot (1995) observed, "if the conflict is responded to in destructive ways . . . it starts sequences of episodes that detract from relational quality" (95). For example, in organizational settings when one's persuasive strategies are not effective, they "become progressively more coercive" (Conrad 1991). The conflict continues unabated, feeds upon itself, and becomes a *spiral of negativity* (see figure 2.3). Each part—the behaviors, the perceptions of others, and the perceptions of the relationship—mutually reinforces the others. Interestingly enough, as behavior becomes more destructive and one's view of the other and the relationship go downhill, each person continues to perceive the self as free from blame (i.e., "It is all his or her fault"). In an organization, for example, one person on the verge of firing an employee said, "Well, I'm a good supervisor. He just won't cooperate. It is all his fault. Besides, he will probably be better off if I fire him."

Escalatory spirals are a cascade of negative effects, self-perpetuating dynamics in which the (1) behaviors, (2) perceptions of the other, and (3) perceptions of the relationship continue to disintegrate (with each party viewing the self as not responsible for any of it). Beck (1988) aptly summarizes the later stages of the process:

Figure 2.3 The spiral of negativity

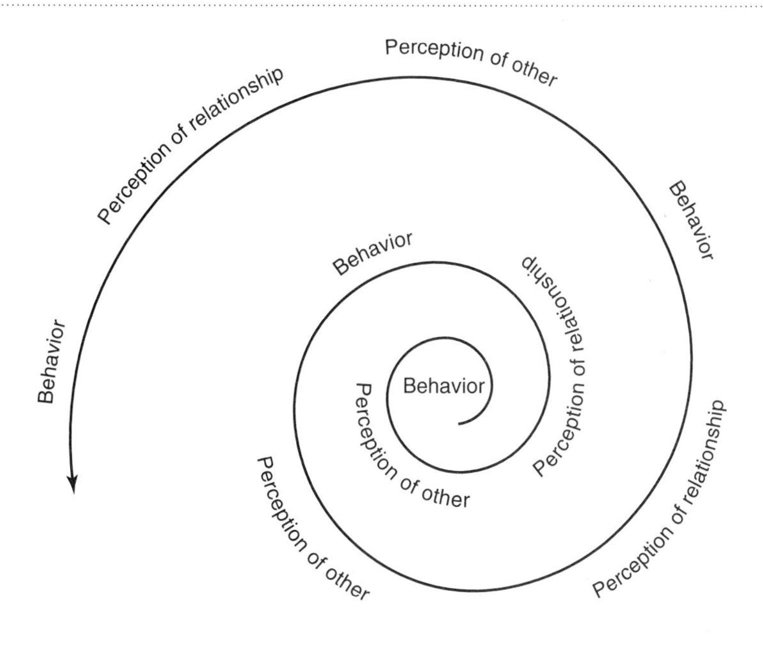

> When a relationship goes downhill, the partners begin to see each other through a negative frame, which consists of a composite of disagreeable traits ("He's mean and manipulative"; "She's irresponsible") that each attributes to the other. These unfavorable attributions color how the offended mate sees the partner; negative actions are exaggerated and neutral actions are seen as negative. Even positive acts may be given a negative coloring (207)

Of course, these declines happen in all kinds of relationships—between social groups (Lange 1993), among marriage partners, between roommates, and within the work setting. Adolescents often experience a transformation in their relationship with their parents. Flannery et al. (1993) wrote that the adolescent and parent relationship is "characterized by increased conflict and declines in positivity," which is exactly what happens in relationships of all types when a negative spiral gains momentum.

Avoidance patterns reduce the chance for productive conflict. Escalatory spirals can be called "fight" patterns. Conflict parties also manifest "flight" patterns of avoidance of the conflict. Avoidance will be discussed extensively in chapter 5. For now, be aware that patterns of avoidance also create and reflect destructive conflict interaction. One form of avoidance is parties lessening their dependence on each other. By doing this, they reduce the influence of the other party on their choices. Both parties then become less invested in the relationship. Many long-term marriages, for example, become devitalized, with the spouses expecting less and less of one another. This is often the natural consequence of lessened interaction. Spouses who are prevented from enriching daily interaction by the pressure of jobs, children, and other stresses become estranged. The barrier between them becomes harder and harder to breach. Avoidance spirals occur in other contexts as well. The child who is not picked for the volleyball team and says, "I didn't want to be on your team anyway," is withdrawing, as is the employee who says, "I don't care if they fire me—who needs them anyway?" The basic dynamics of all avoidance spirals are

- less direct interaction
- active avoidance of the other party
- reduction of dependence
- harboring of resentment or disappointment
- complaining to third persons about the other party

Whereas escalatory spirals are characterized by *overt* expression of the conflict, avoidance spirals demonstrate *covert* expression. At least one of the parties tries to impact the other through lack of cooperation. If you are mad at your supervisor, your late report may serve to get her into difficulty with her boss. Any form of withholding from someone who depends on you can bring negative consequences to the other. For example, when you withdraw, the other party does not know what you want or are thinking. Often the other will say something like, "What is wrong?" Then you say, "Nothing," covering up anger, resentment, or disappointment.

Oddly enough, sometimes people *want* destructive conflict in their relationships (Neimeyer and Neimeyer 1985). Although escalatory and avoidance spirals may appear to be totally negative to outsiders, the conflict party may be getting something valuable from these spirals. For example, if John can stay locked in an overt struggle with Bill, the impasse may give John a sense of power and self-esteem: "I only fight him everyday on the job because the principle is so important." Or, if you are in an avoidance spiral, complaining about your supervisor, employee, spouse, or friend to others builds closeness between you and your listener. For example, a husband and wife may both complain about the other to the children, each thereby building a close bond with the child who is the chosen listener. One can get locked into a position of complaining bitterly about a spouse or coworker but not take any steps to alter the relationship directly. In short, people may be invested in *not* moving past the destructive conflict.

The close-far dance, a destructive pattern usually manifested in intimate relationships, also destroys chances for productive conflict interaction. In the "pursue-flee" pattern, described in detail in Lerner's *Dance of Intimacy* (1989), one partner specializes in initiating conversation, bringing up problems, commenting on the lack of closeness between the partners, escalating feelings and issues to get them resolved, and drawing the other partner out by asking questions like "You seem preoccupied—what's going on?" or "We don't seem close these last few weeks. Is something bothering you?" Then the "dance" of distance is engaged as the other partner minimizes the problems, denies anything is wrong, promises to do better, comments on content problems only, avoids discussion of any relationship issues, or gives excuses such as "I've just been really busy," or "I'm distracted by what's going on at work," or "I'm just premenstrual. Don't take it personally." The conflict remains frustratingly unresolved because each partner specializes in a role that is so prescribed, whether initiating or fleeing, that the issues remain unexplored. These dynamics will be addressed in chapter 5, "Styles and Tactics." For now, as you begin to watch and analyze conflicts around you, pay attention to who initiates and who flees. One way to arrest this pattern is to make a metacommunicative comment about it, such as "I notice that I'm the one who brings up problems, and you feel defensive. We need to do something different." The one who flees can own up to the discomfort caused by the pursuit by saying

Figure 2.4 The four horsemen of the apocalypse

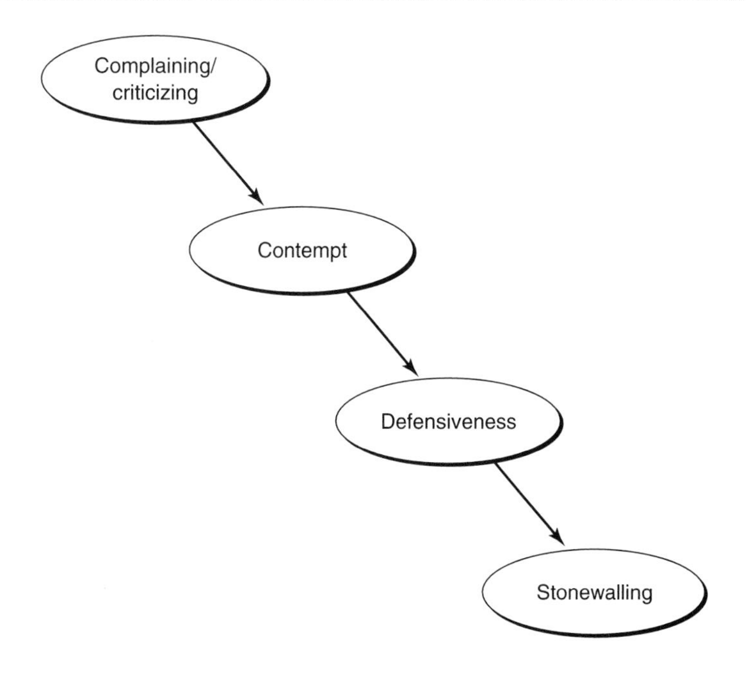

something like "I feel pounced on, especially about my feelings. I need time to sort out what's going on. I will talk to you; I just need to do it at a time when I'm not exhausted or frazzled."

Gottman (1994) discovered that the avoidance sequence illustrated in figure 2.4 leads to unstable marriages and even to divorce. He calls it the "four horsemen of the apocalypse" because of its negative impact. As you can see, avoidance or stonewalling comes after some preliminary episodes. For the marriages Gottman studied, the destructive sequence consisted of complaining, criticizing, contempt, defensiveness, and stonewalling. Thus, avoidance can be viewed within the overall spiral of conflict leading to eventual dissolution of a relationship. Whereas Gottman (1994) used the cascade metaphor to represent the decline from loss of faith in the relationship to divorce, the metaphor also accurately captures the interlocking of behavior and perception that leads to dissolution.

One other feature of Gottman's work is noteworthy: If avoidance is accepted by both partners ("conflict-avoiding couples"), it can stabilize the marriage. It is when avoidance is coupled with dissatisfaction and disagreement, with one person pursuing and the other fleeing, that is damaging.

Retaliation runs rampant in destructive conflicts. Conflict participants destroy chances for change when they pile up grievances, hold grudges, and wait for opportunities to retaliate. "Don't get mad—get even!" is the watchword for this urge to get back at the other person. Retaliation often becomes paired with covert avoidance. One person acts as though everything is just fine while planning a payback move for later. You can probably think of many retaliatory moves that have either been done to you or that you yourself have done. Some examples of retaliatory moves are letters to someone's supervisor complaining about or pointing out some indiscretion that the employee enacted, a snub such as not inviting someone to a function, a blatant move such as emptying out a partner's savings account, running up phone bills and then moving out, and so on. Dirty tricks inevitably ruin the conflict atmosphere.

Inflexibility and rigidity characterize destructive conflict. When parties are unable or unwilling to adapt to changing circumstances, instead following rules "to a T" or "going by the book," conflict often deteriorates. One manager refused to discuss reprimands with employees, instead recording the incidents in letters that could later be used as part of a paper trail in case an employee needed to be fired. As a result, trust plummeted to zero in the office, and employees formed coalitions to protect each other from the inflexible boss. The supervisor, in addition to creating a hostile working environment, received "pretend change" instead of genuine change in employees' behavior. Everyone lost as the cycle of distancing and inflexible communication intensified.

A competitive system of dominance and subordination results in destructive conflict. "Authenticity and subordination are totally incompatible" (Miller 1986, 98). Dominant groups tend to suppress conflict, minimizing and denying its existence. This works reasonably well for those in power since they can make and enforce the rules. In fact, a measure of the dominant group's success and security is often its ability to suppress conflict, to keep it hidden, unobtrusive, and unthreatening to the group's position of power. In a situation of unequal power, in which a myth of harmonious relationships is set forth, the subordinate person is put in charge of maintaining that harmony. Then any recognition of differences is treated as insubordination (Miller 1986; Jordan 1990).

Demeaning verbal and nonverbal communication results in and reflects destructive conflict practices. These tactics will be discussed in detail in chapter 5. Destructive conflict appears in countless examples of verbally abusive, demeaning, shaming, and blaming communication. The tone of destructive conflict often reflects the portrayal of the other party as "unworthy." In a recent example, one city government official said, in an informal caucus, about another elected official, "Let's get this straight. We're dealing with a subhuman species here—this is not a human being we're dealing with."

Humans in various cultures distinguish between the kind of aggression that can be directed against members of their own population and that directed toward other human groups. Stevens (1989) cites a tribe in Brazil, the Mundrucus, who distinguish between themselves, whom they call "people," and the rest of the world population, whom they call "pariwat." These in-group and out-group distinctions allow them to refer to others in the way they would refer to huntable animals (40–41). In North American and Western European cultures, the use of verbally demeaning and abusive communication serves a similar function (Evans 1992). Whole groups of minorities receive demeaning descriptions, and individuals in low-power positions in relationships suffer from pervasive demeaning, shaming, and blaming communication.

Constructive Conflict

As discussed previously, conflict can play an important part in the development of healthy friendships, romantic relationships, and work relationships. This book focuses on how to build constructive conflict interactions from the materials of good communication, careful analysis, and adaptation. At this stage in your analysis of conflict, it will be helpful to recognize healthy conflicts in your own past, those occurring in your present life and in the lives of others around you, and those you can imagine occurring in the future. The building blocks of constructive conflicts include the following:

People change. In the usual course of ongoing relationships at work, at home, and with friends, people adjust, accommodate, and compromise all the time. Flexibility means that most of the time people can work and live together without losing their sense of self-worth or losing track of their own needs. But when interactions begin to escalate into conflict, people must change at some point to stay involved with each other. In constructive conflicts, people try new strategies, communicate differently, and change their goals when necessary. Rigid, insistent communication defeats the purpose of constructive conflict. When something isn't working, try something else!

Inflexibility that locks parties into escalation or avoidance cycles destroys constructive conflict (Folger, Poole, and Stutman 1993, 9). Once tensions have increased to the point of conflict, resisting change means certain escalation of the conflict or even dissolution of the relationship. Good conflict, on the other hand, creates change in the relationship so that all people experience growth (Jordan 1990). Exploring differences offers the possibility of change for both people or what Mary Follett (1940), pioneer of conflict management in the 1920s, called "a creating relationship" (128). At a certain point in the conflict cycle, one no longer has the option of "no change." Following a popular dictum in communication, "one can't not communicate" (Watzlawick, Beavin, and Jackson 1967), "no change" means that some kind of change, whether toward further avoidance or escalation, will surely occur.

People interact with an intent to learn instead of an intent to protect (Paul and Paul 1983). Constructive conflict is viewed as a learning experience, albeit difficult, instead of something to protect yourself against. The basic movement, metaphorically, of constructive conflict is *toward the other* for the purpose of sorting, solving, learning, asking, opening, and changing.

People do not stay stuck in conflict when the conflict is constructive. The conflict episode serves its function of bonding parties together, defining the group or family, clarifying feelings about issues and processes, bringing up the possibility of needed change, or correcting an injustice or ineffective practice. Then the people involved move on to something else—the conflict does not define who they are. It recedes, and other kinds of relating take place. Constructive conflict is a dynamic process that occurs within the bounds of already existing patterns. If the sister says to the brother, "You never pick up your shoes, and I'm getting sick and tired of tripping over them in the dark!" one cannot understand the importance of the event without knowing what has happened before. If this is the first complaint, the episode might proceed quite differently than if she has lodged this complaint unsuccessfully for a month. Complaining unsuccessfully characterizes conflict that stays stuck. Constructive conflict moves and changes.

Constructive conflict enhances self-esteem in the participants. Each person feels a greater sense of zest, feels more productive, has a more accurate picture of oneself and the other person(s) involved, feels more self-worth ("We made it!"), and feels more connected to the other person(s). In addition, one feels motivated to connect with other people even beyond those in the specific conflict interaction (Miller 1986, 3). One becomes more able to bear the tension of conflict because other conflicts have turned out well, so one is more able to trust that growth and healing will take place in the current conflict.

Constructive conflicts are characterized by a relationship focus instead of a purely individualistic focus. When we acknowledge the importance of the relationship *per se,* it allows us to move to constructive conflict. As one set of authors say, "Relational maintenance can be viewed as a function of acknowledging the importance of communicative rules" (Honeycutt, Woods, and Fontenot 1993, 301). One operates from a stance of enlightened self-interest, in which each move is understood as affecting the other; therefore each move must be chosen to enhance the working relationship. If one party is simply out for what he or she can get, at the expense of the other, the win-lose quality of the conflict will result in the classic "winning the battle and losing the war" outcome. The relationship worsens for the future. This singular focus is less of a problem in one-time, transient interactions, such as buying a car or negotiating for a loan.

The focus on the relationship can also be maintained by the practice of *empathy.* Jordan (1984) describes empathy as a cognitive and emotional activity in which one person is able to experience the feelings and thoughts of another and is simultaneously able to know her or his own different feelings and thoughts. Far from being a mysterious, mushy process, empathy requires a high level of maturity. "It is not a question of one person sort of looking into the other person's eyes and feeling what the other person is feeling. It is a question of a process of interacting, engaging and moving along" (Miller 1986, 20). This kind of active empathy provides motivation to take care of the relationship. When each person has been seen and heard, even in the midst of a highly charged situation, a constructive basis for action develops. A focus on the relationship leads to the active maintenance of connections in the midst of conflict, for without these connections, the possibility for creative change is lost.

Finally, *constructive conflict is primarily cooperative.* The rest of the book develops this kind of cooperation in detail. It is enough to remind you now that unrelenting competition and destructive practices result in human losses.

A Short Course on Conflict Management

By the end of your study of conflict management, you will know a great deal about analysis, personal change in conflict, and intervention into others' conflicts. You will know more about planning, using particular tactics for a certain effect, and bargaining. But you might want some ideas right now for managing conflicts. The following simple suggestions will get you started. Keep these practices in mind and use them when you can.

Clarify Communication

Students often say, "I can't remember all that stuff when I'm in the middle of something that has me upset. I just want to strangle him/her." True enough! No one can perform at a virtuoso level of communication all the time. It's often worth stopping to check your technique, or even starting over, to get it right. You might say, "Wait a minute, let me try that another way" or "I don't get it yet. Would you tell me more?" We human beings are notoriously poor mind readers, so it often pays to slow down, practice a skill, check out what you think you heard, or say it a different way. Just like learning to play tennis, care for an infant, play the guitar, operate a new word-processing program, or telemark ski, skills seem awkward at first then become more natural with practice and confidence. Varied skills are needed for different levels of conflict intensity (Sillars and Weisberg 1987; Fisher and Davis 1987) and different kinds of relationships. The skills that serve you well in intimate relationships may be inappropriate with transient, unimportant connections, at work, with casual friends, or with distant family. You will need to adapt these general communication skills to each situation:

1. *Speak your mind and heart.* Someone needs to speak up and say what he or she wants, thinks, or feels. However obvious this point seems, often the expression of conflict is bogged down because someone is afraid to articulate needs clearly. Difficulty in expressing preferences directly may result in indirect, passive, or aggressive communication (Young-Eisendrath 1993; Heitler 1990). Instead of blaming, switching topics, or avoiding, make sure you address the problem as the issue (Fisher and Ury 1981). Speak up!
2. *Listen well.* You are, by this time, aware that listening is a skill that underlies all productive conflict management. Focus on what the other person is saying, not your rebuttal. Search for what *might be right* about what you hear instead of what is wrong (Heitler 1990), and let the other know you are doing this. Give some feedback that indicates that the other has been heard. You might say, "I am intrigued about your idea about taking six months off. I'm worried about how I will cover your job, but let me hear more." Remember that any sentence beginning with "Yes, but . . ." disqualifies anything you are going to say next.
3. *Express strong feelings appropriately.* In conflict you will, at times, feel very strongly. You will be angry, hurt, enraged, sad, joyful, hopeful, and despairing. Careful, respectful expression of these feelings helps, rather than damages, conflicts. Avoid squelching your feelings—just learn to express them clearly in a nondestructive manner. Never attack, for any reason, if you want a long-term relationship!
4. *Remain rational as long as possible.* Remaining rational does not mean staying calm, cool, collected, and distant. Rationality means keeping in mind that you are trying to solve a problem and to stay connected in the interaction. Anything that diverts you from this task hurts conflict management.
5. *Summarize and ask questions.* Review what has been said. Ask about points that need clarification, using open-ended questions. Specialize in asking questions for which you do not know the answer.
6. *Give and take.* Be fair, taking your turn and giving others their turns. No productive resolution comes from one-sided conversation. You may solve a short-term problem; but in the long term, fairness counts.
7. *Avoid all harmful statements.* Attacks create enemies. Biting criticism drives people out of the interaction. Making the other person wrong means reducing the chance that you will ever make anything right. As medical doctors are taught by the Hippocratic oath, "Do no harm."

Check Perceptions

Perceptions of the other and of the situation make more difference than objective reality. People act on perceptions, not on some outsider's view of what is real. When beginning to work through a conflict, make sure the perceptions on which you and the others are operating are as accurate as possible. You can check out the perceptions by going through the *elements of conflict* discussed previously. At first, you may need to do this slowly, reflecting by yourself or talking through conflicts at some length with others. You can practice analyzing conflicts now, using what you know of the conflict elements.

- *Expressed struggle.* Use the seven skills of communication to make sure you and others are communicating as clearly as possible. In addition, you can ask people directly whether your perception of a struggle is indeed accurate, or you can make a cooperative response and then see whether the other person responds cooperatively, thus eliminating the conflict altogether (a successful mini-intervention includes at least two cooperative transactions). You might say or write the following kinds of statements:

  Woman (to new husband, referring to his fifteen-year-old son): I've noticed Brennan is using my towels and other stuff from my bathroom instead of the ones from his bathroom. Do you think he's annoyed because he can't share the upstairs one and has to go downstairs? Or is he being thoughtless? I don't want damp towels all over my bathroom!

  Man: I don't know. He hasn't said anything. Do you want me to check it out, or do you want to?

  Woman: I will.

  This situation could have escalated into a "war of the towels," or notes being left from stepmother to stepson, or the husband defending the son, or many other unproductive scenarios. As it happened, the boy did admit that he was irritated. He and his father had lived together for years without bothering much about whose towel was whose, and he resented being told which bathroom and towels to use. The two worked it out, not perfectly but acceptably.
- *Between at least two interdependent parties.* Perceptions of interdependence vary widely. One person may not know the effects of his or her actions on another. Checking out perceptions of interdependence by letting someone else know how their actions affect you helps clarify the interaction. Kara told her mother about an abusive situation from her childhood—one that was new to her mother. Her mother responded mildly, with little interest. When Kara, a successful doctor, later told her mother how hurt she was, her mother said, "I always saw you as so strong. I didn't think you needed anything from me. I thought you were telling me about something you had already worked out." Kara replied, "Mom, at that moment I was a little girl again. I needed you to be more of a mother to me again, like when I was little. It seemed as though you didn't care what had happened." Both were resetting their levels of interdependence, at least on this issue.
- *Perception of incompatible goals.* Parties in conflict perceive incompatible goals. Again, communicating clearly what these goals are is the only way to check out the perception that they are in conflict. Sometimes they are, and sometimes they aren't. Disclose your goals and ask about others' goals. You might say, "We've been having a lot of money troubles, but I still want to go to Central America this February. I haven't heard you mention the trip in a long time. Do you still want to go?"
- *Perception of scarce resources.* Parties in conflict perceive scarce resources. However, maybe other resources are available, or you can share resources such as computer

time, plan more time together in a busy family instead of assuming that mom's schoolwork and job mean you can't go on any vacations together, or explore sharing a house for a month, as friends recently did, instead of evicting good friends from a rented house because the owners' new house was not yet available. Resources over which people struggle are not always as scarce as they seem.
- *Perception of interference.* Check out your perception that the other person is, or could be in the future, in the way of what you want. Kelly wanted time alone in a lookout tower she goes to every summer as a volunteer—to enjoy the forest, to renew from work, and to just "be." When her college-age kids asked to come along, she hesitated and said she didn't think there was room. They were hurt, since they had spent the year away at school. Mom did not check out whether they would be happy going off hiking during the days, giving her some time alone as well as time spent with them. Everyone ended up with hurt feelings.

In summary, when checking out your perceptions in a conflict, you will find it helpful to look for alternative possibilities:

- ask directly what is going on
- tell others your own reality
- look for flexible "shades-of-gray" solutions
- remember that your history together may not predict your future
- never underestimate the power of initiating a cooperative move

In the following box, a relatively simple interaction illustrates how the elements of a conflict may be transformed from a perception of incompatible conflict to that of a potentially productive conflict.

"Paddle Your Own Canoe"

A man and woman went on a long canoe trip through the Montana wilderness. The couple, still in the "getting to know each other" phase of their relationship, had carefully discussed how they would manage their differing levels of ability to keep paddling in adverse situations. Both were in their fifties and had a lot of outdoor experience, feeling generally competent about their abilities. The general agreement they made was that Greg would either paddle alone or both of them would paddle together, but they would not paddle at different tempos. On the third day of the trip, the following interaction ensued:

Sharon puts down paddle to rest and look at the scenery, then paddles a few strokes, then rests her paddle again. She seems calm and serene.

Grey notices that Sharon is paddling intermittently and waits for her to say she is tired and wants to rest or to begin paddling regularly. He grows more irritated as he waits.

Time passes. Sharon remains unaware of Greg's rising, silent fuming. Greg wants out of there, which is impossible since they are on a river with steep banks, with several days left before they reach the takeout point. Finally Greg explodes.

Greg: Either paddle or don't!

Sharon: I don't have to put up with your controlling. You're not the only adult here!

From here the conflict deteriorated into blame, defense, and ineffective attempts to explain their intentions. They paddled in silence for over an hour, banked, and finally began to talk through the interaction. The story has a happy ending in that the couple was able to complete their trip down the river and at this writing are still together. If one were to coach this couple in a brief form of "Conflict Management for Beginners," they would be reminded to express their own truths clearly and to check out their perceptions. It could have gone like this:

Greg (noticing that Sharon isn't paddling but is looking around, then paddling a few strokes, etc.): Are you tired?

Sharon: No. I'm just enjoying this incredible day. I've never seen the Missouri this clear and the wildflowers so lush.

Greg could pick from the following options:

A. I am loving this day, too. I need to tell you, though, that when you paddle a little bit and then don't, my rhythm is off and I can't just tune out and concentrate on the scenery and talking with you.

B. I've been fuming, I must admit, for a while back here. I didn't know whether you had forgotten our agreement about paddling. Had you? Or did it just not seem very important?

C. I'd appreciate it if you'd stick with our agreement about paddling. I don't mind doing it, although I'll go more slowly if I'm paddling alone. What would be best for you now?

D. I'm really getting tired, Sharon. Could you join in for a while? Or could we stop?

Any of these would have set the couple off on a more constructive conversation—one that didn't use mind reading as the main form of problem solving. You can undoubtedly think of many others.

Toward Productive Conflict

Conflict brings both danger and opportunity, and the dangerous aspects are well-known. Changing our usual behavior, learning to "do what comes unnaturally," requires an examination of one's most deeply held values and spiritual beliefs. At its most effective, conflict resolution can never be simply a set of techniques, put on or cast aside at will. You will want to think and feel through your own principles as you study this subject.

If people are to survive and thrive, working together is not an option but a necessity. Principles learned at the interpersonal level lead to collaborative principles at the global level. In this way, what you learn about collaboration within relationships will affect a much larger plane of well-being. Breggin (1992) reminds us:

> In every aspect of life . . . we need better principles for resolving conflict and promoting harmony within ourselves and others. We need approaches that make personal *and* political sense, that connect us in a rational and caring manner to ourselves as individuals and to the world around us, including people and nature. We need a viewpoint that helps us understand and heal the pain of human conflict. (3)

We are connected human beings who must balance our need for personal autonomy with our need for connection. We can no longer live by the myth that somewhere out there is a place where we can be completely independent and do what we wish. More than thirty years ago, Martin Luther King stated this imperative: "I can never be what I ought to be until you are what you ought to be, and you can never be what you ought to be until I am what I ought to be. This is the interrelated structure of reality" (Martin Luther King Jr., "Strength to Love," 1963).

In conflict, no one set of principles will always work, no one metaphor embraces all the possibilities, and no one set of behaviors avoided can keep you out of conflict altogether. Yet, people do change their orientation to conflict and amaze themselves with their ability to transcend formerly destructive situations. If enough of us are willing to weave webs of connection with others, all our shared hopes for the world can be realized.

Summary

Conflict is a pervasive human activity that can be defined as an expressed struggle between at least two interdependent parties who perceive incompatible goals, scarce resources, and interference from others in achieving their goals. Careful analysis of the elements of this definition will allow one to begin changing conflict. Although conflict serves a valuable function, there are many differences between destructive and constructive conflict. Conflict management involves effective communication, or expression, of the conflict, checking one's perceptions, and transforming the elements of the conflict. Because no one set of conflict behaviors will work in every situation, one must remain open to new visions of constructive conflict interaction.

Chapter 3

Goals: Saving Face and Getting What You Want

An American father and his twelve-year-old son were enjoying a beautiful Saturday in Hyde Park, London, playing catch with a Frisbee. Few in England had seen a Frisbee at that time and a small group of strollers gathered to watch this strange sport. Finally, one Homburg-clad Britisher came over to the father: "Sorry to bother you. Been watching you for a quarter of an hour. Who's winning?" (Fisher and Ury 1981, 154).

Just as in this game of catch watched by an outsider, it is easy to misread goals in conflicts. As the lens model presented in chapter 1 suggests, both insiders and outsiders can misperceive the goals of the conflict participants. In all disputes, the parties are trying to accomplish something, or they would not be struggling with one another. This chapter will overview the types of goals, describe how different types of goals overlap and metamorphose during and after a dispute, and give suggestions for how to clarify goals.

All conflicts are built upon the parties' perceptions of incompatible goals. Whether a sister and her older brother are struggling over limited parental attention, two managers are competing for a coveted promotion in the organization, or a seller and buyer are arguing over the price of a car, the perception of incompatible goals fuels each conflict. In every conflict the interdependence of the parties is built on both common and disparate goals (Rubin 1980), but the parties often only perceive the disparate goals. Conflict builds as people begin to understand that they want different things; often the dawning awareness of conflict's existence comes when people say to each other, "What you want is *not* what I want."

Before a conflict is activated, people often assure each other that "we want the same thing" or "we're headed in the same direction." This assertion may be an attempt to find common ground, or it may be a denial of the genuine differences that are beginning to emerge; conflict is uncomfortable for most people, and at these early stages, denying that different goals exist is a first attempt to resolve conflict. However, as stated in chapter 2, conflict is more than a disagreement. In true conflict, people not only want different things but believe that another interferes with their goal attainment.

Interaction goals often diverge across types of relationships. In a friendship, for example, your main goal might be affinity—wanting the other to like you (Bell and Daly 1984). On the job, you may primarily want to gain information from colleagues or to persuade them about something. Our goals range from obtaining money, goods, services, love, or status to getting information (Foa and Foa 1974). In a conversation, your primary goal might be to express your feelings (Argyle and Furnham 1983).

Many times, especially in emotionally charged conflict situations, we may be unaware of what goals we want to achieve. If you are angry at your roommate you might not know whether (1) you want to punish her for being sloppy; (2) you want to have her like you, but you still want to influence her cleanliness standards; or (3) you want her to get angry and move out, so you can get a new roommate. Most conflict participants initially lack goal clarity; participants only discover their goals through experiencing conflict with the other participants. As we will see later, the goals will probably shift during the course of the conflict. What you want to achieve in the conflict (goals) also affects the tactics you choose during the conflict. For example, if you are "defending yourself" you are likely to use self-oriented tactics—being competitive and looking out only for yourself. On the other hand, if you want to improve a relationship you are more likely to use conflict moves that are integrative—taking account of the others' needs as well as your own (Canary, Cunningham, and Cody 1988). One fact emerges from studying goals in personal and organizational settings—effectively functioning teams have a clear understanding of their objectives. The more clearly individuals or groups understand the nature of the problem and what they want to have occur, the more effective they will be in solving problems. At its best, conflict management is a specialized form of problem solving (Larson and LaFasto 1989).

Types of Goals

Conflict interactants pursue four general types of goals: (1) *content,* (2) *relational,* (3) *identity* (or *facework*), and (4) *process.* The acronym CRIP stands for these major types of goals, which overlap and shift during disputes. These types of goals will be examined one at a time.

The four types of goals pursued during conflict

C Content

R Relationship

I Identity/facework

P Process

Content Goals: *What* Do We Want?

The key question when looking at a conflict is "*What* does each person want?" When parties perceive incompatible content goals, they assume that some course of action, if followed, will lead them more deeply into an incompatible situation—I want A, and you want B. Content goals emerge as different ideas about *what* to do, *what* decisions to make, *where* to go, *how* to allocate resources, or other externally objectifiable issues. Content goals can be listed, debated, argued, supported by evidence, and broken down into pros and cons. For example, Amanda might tell her supervisor, "I have been here six months, and I would like to have a raise." Other examples of content goals are

available student loans	a clean apartment
more free time	meaningful work
a new pair of skis	fashionable clothing
space to work	a different job
a vacation overseas	reliable transportation
a salary raise	an A in the class
to sell a house for $80,000	a VCR

Content goals can be easily seen and talked about; they are external to us—we can point to them and say, "I want that." Yet, although they are objective, people often feel very deeply about them.

Content struggles are of two types: (1) people want *different* things—I want to get the most for my car, and you want to pay the least for it; or (2) people want the *same* thing (same job, same romantic partner, same room in the house). In either case, what happens is a struggle over the goals. And, as mentioned in chapter 2, the perception that there is not enough to go around—a perception of a scarce resource—intensifies the conflict. More examples of struggles over content goals follow:

- A divorcing couple tries to construct a visitation schedule that allows each parent access to their young children but that also fits with each parent's work schedule. The specific visitation schedule is the content goal (at this point, separate goals) of the couple. Mom may state, "I want the kids on Sundays," or "I want to see them one night a week when they are at your house." Dad might say, "I want them on alternate weekends."

- A romantic couple talks about the pros and cons of either being together for the summer and both working in a restaurant, or one going to Glacier Park to be on trail crew and the other to work as a biologist in the River of No Return Wilderness Area. They want to spend the summer together, but both also want to advance their respective careers.
- Three midlevel managers must come to agreement about which benefits would motivate their employees to stay with the company the longest. Jill favors educational benefits, in addition to a basic benefits package, whereas Chuck favors increased insurance options, and Jim wants to increase flextime options. All three managers want to keep employees longer but disagree on how to do that.
- Mary is going to put her house up for sale because she will be moving to a different region. She asks $90,000 for the house, knowing that this price will pay for both her relocation and three months of living while she finds a new job. In addition to this amount of money, she wants to sell the house quickly—also a content goal.

Usually, when you ask someone what they want in a conflict, you will hear a content goal from at least one of the parties—"I just want a different office." For most people, content goals are the easiest to identify and tell others about. Content goals, although important and the beginning point to understanding all disputes, are just one part of the conflict mosaic.

Relational Goals: *Who* Are We to Each Other?

The key question when assessing the relational goals of a conflict is "*Who* are we in relationship to each other during our interaction?" Relationship goals define how each party wants to be treated by the other and the amount of interdependence they desire (how they define themselves as a unit). Additionally, the amount of influence each will have with the other is worked out through relational interaction.

Differing relational goals lead people into conflict just as differing content goals do. People often experience deep disagreement about the question of who they are to each other. The following statements, expressed during actual conflicts, are relational goal statements:

How You Want to Be Treated by the Other

What I need here is some respect.
So, what happened to our collegial relationship?
What I want is for you to support me when we are in public.
I won't put up with that kind of abuse.
Well, you don't have to be nasty about it.

The Amount of Interdependence You Want (Are We a Unit?)

If I want to be best friends I'll tell you.
How can I help if I don't know if you want to stay on the project with me?
We both have our separate lives to live now, so let's get on with it.
What I do is none of your business.
I just don't know who we are to each other any more.

Relational goals will emerge in any ongoing dispute and must be managed. For example, Donohue, Drake, and Roberto (1994) note that "the more mediators ignore disputants' relational concerns, the more difficulty they will experience in reaching agreement" (261). Yet, relational goals seldom become open, spoken messages (Wilmot 1995). Relationship definitions might instead be communicated by who talks first, who talks the most, nonverbal cues such as eye contact, and many other factors. For example, if an employee asks for a raise and is told no, the supervisor might be warning, on the relational level, "Don't push too far. I have the right to tell you what we can afford and what we cannot afford." If the employee says, "Why not? This is the best year we've ever had!" the relational message might be, from the employee's perspective, "I have a right to challenge what you say." Much of the communication regarding relational goals remains tacit and unspoken. Productive conflict interaction sometimes requires that a third party or a participant make overt the tacit relationship definitions. The following are some examples of relational goals:

- A second wife decides not to go to a big family gathering of her husband's relatives. She resents the expectation that since his family gathers at Labor Day every year, she is expected to attend. She prefers to visit with her family at that time of year. If the husband and wife have a conflict over this issue, the content goals may be fairly clear: the husband wants the wife to go to the gathering, whereas the wife wants to visit her family and not attend the big gathering. The wife's relational goals might be varied: to establish equity in the time she spends with her family, to establish her independence from the new family group, or to protect herself from comparison to the first wife. The husband's relational goals might be to please his family, to introduce his second wife to the family in a relaxed setting, or to spend more time together. Each argues about how much influence they will allow the other to have, about what kind of a unit they are, and many other relational issues. If the couple argues about content goals only, they will get stuck on issues about plane fares and what they can afford, or the weather in Georgia around Labor Day, or the accommodations provided. In ongoing relationships such as this one, the goals of *who the participants are to each other* need to be given priority. The content goals take second place. Most people argue content when they ought to be talking about relational goals.
- In a staff meeting, Joan insists that "before we decide on the reorganization, I need to know how committed you all are to staying with the organization." She needs some clarity on how people define their relationship to the larger group before plunging ahead with an extensive reorganization plan.
- Two teenage girls currently are "on the outs" with each other. Jennifer talks about how JoAnn is "high and mighty," then JoAnn complains to another friend that Jennifer has "an abnormal need to be in on everything." The conflict erupted the day after JoAnn canceled her plan to go shopping with Jennifer and went with another friend instead. The content, whether to go shopping together, was not the issue; the relational strain was.

Relational goals are at the heart of all conflict interactions yet are difficult to specify from the outside (and sometimes from the inside as well). That is because each person *translates the same event into their own relational meaning.* A conflict is interpreted differently by each participant. Just as we have no success in translating Ukrainian unless we speak the language, conflict parties must learn the relational language of their conflict partners. For example, a father and daughter fight many evenings when she comes home from school and he arrives home from work. Mother gets pulled into playing peacemaker, trying to urge them to get along better. The following box demonstrates how an event can trigger such a conflict.

> Daughter scatters books, shoes, and lunch box in the living room while she gets a snack. Father comes home an hour later, sees the mess, and explodes. Daughter says, "I forgot," and Father says, "You *always* forget."
>
> Content messages: "I forgot/You always forget."
>
> Daughter's translation: It's not important. I wish he'd pay attention to something that is more important to me.
>
> Father's translation: She doesn't listen. She is getting too independent to care what I think.

The difficulty with relational issues is that we never ultimately know the other person's translations. Just like the daughter and father have different translations for these events, usually the conflict parties cannot accurately guess what the other's translations will be, or if they can, they try to dismiss them. The friend who says "you shouldn't be bothered by not being invited to the picnic" is not accurately keying into what *your* translations are. One technique in conflict management, therefore, is to have conflict parties *share their relational translations* of the content issues.

Other examples of incorrect or incomplete translations of each other's messages are illustrated by the following:

- A couple argues over who should fill the car with gas each week—each feels she or he is doing more work than the other and wants credit for what is already being done. But the man argues that he shouldn't have to do all the work on the car, and the woman argues that he doesn't notice now much work she does for him, such as taking clothes to the cleaners. Not only are they arguing about content, but they are mistranslating the crucial relational goals (which remain unstated).
- Coworkers bicker each day about whose turn it is to lock up the business, which requires staying longer at the end of the day. None of the procedures developed seem to work—people have doctor's appointments, or have to pick up a child, or have a racquetball court reserved, so they have to leave early. This conflict is becoming a big issue. So far, the only way people resolve the issue is to come up with creative excuses for leaving work. But resentments grow daily, factions are created, and pretty soon, the boss will have to step in and make a new rule, which will displease everyone. No new procedure (content solution) will work until leftover resentments are explained and attended to (relational issues). Then new, shared goals can be developed that have a chance of finally working.

Relational goals are often *reactive.* What I want from you is the result of what I think you are doing or what I think you want from me. Once a conflict is triggered each party reacts to what they think the other is doing or wanting. When Sandy says, "I won't take that kind of treatment from Jason," she is reacting to her guess about how Jason will act in the future, too. Once the conflict spiral begins, each person responds to an image of the other that may not be accurate. When Jason replies, "You are just trying to control me," he states his relational reaction to Sandy. In this manner, relational goals escalate into polarized states.

Identity and Face-Saving Goals: Who *Am I* in This Interaction?

The key question in assessing identity goals is "Who *am I* in this particular interaction?" or "How may my self-identity be protected or repaired in this particular conflict?" As conflicts increase in intensity, the parties shift to *face-saving* as a key goal (Rubin 1996).* Of course, face-saving or identity protection are occurring throughout the conflict but will be highlighted more at certain times than others.

In addition to content and relational goals, interaction goals include specific desires to maintain one's sense of *self-identity.* Identity needs have been extensively discussed as *facework* or *saving face* (Folger, Poole, and Stutman 1993; Wilson 1992; Goffman 1967; Brown and Levinson 1978; Lim and Bowers 1991). Often people will say, with frustration, "What are we fighting about?" or "I don't know what is going on!" Many times, a puzzling or maddening interaction can make sense if one analyzes whether one or more of the parties is primarily trying to present a *positive face* by claiming one's need to be approved of, to be included, and to be respected (Lim and Bowers 1991). When face-saving becomes an issue, people are less flexible and engage in destructive moves (Folger, Poole, and Stutman 1993). According to Brown (1977), "In some instances, protecting against loss of face becomes so central an issue that it swamps the importance of the tangible issues at stake and generates intense conflicts that can impede progress toward agreement and increase substantially the costs of conflict resolution" (175).

The importance of identity or saving face can be seen when large corporations or individuals are sued in court. In some circumstances, they can enter an "Alford Plea," which means "we don't admit guilt, but based on the evidence presented we think we would be convicted." Thus, we read news reports of people and organizations saying "we didn't do it, and we paid the plaintiff $75,000." On one hand this seems absurd, but on the other it helps sensitize us to the importance of saving face. The issue is no longer "did I break the law," but "how can I protect how I see myself and others see me."

In each conflict interaction, individuals either save face or lose or damage face. Self-esteem has been discussed as a scarce resource. This is another way of saying that people's sense of self is often tenuous, not fixed. Few people are so full of self-esteem that they do not want to look well in conflicts, be seen as intelligent, honorable, correct, or justified. Likewise, when your opponent begins to perceive that you are damaging his or her sense of self, the stakes get higher. Facework occurs for each party throughout the conflict (see figure 3.1).

In terms of self-interest, what normally happens as a dispute progresses is that people

*Different authors use diverse terms (self, face, identity) for concepts that overlap yet differ in some key assumptions. *Identity* is our preferred term because it suggests that it is constructed socially and highlights the way communication is central to its formation and maintenance. But, the word *face* is used interchangeably with it because of the common usage of the term. However, the assumptions used here are in line with those suggested by Tracy and Naughton (1994).

Figure 3.1 Dimensions of saving and damaging face

	Self	Other
Save face	Save self's face	Save other's face
Damage face	Damage self's face	Damage other's face

protect their own face or identity while damaging the other's face or identity. Productive conflict management demands that we move to the other quadrants. One fascinating study analyzed communication in three cases of hostage negotiations. The cases involved three different people: (1) an armed, suicidal man barricaded inside a TV station, (2) a man suffering extreme emotional instability who was barricaded in a house, and (3) an armed man holding his children hostage. What emerged in the taped FBI transcripts was the necessity to let the men save face while working to get the hostages released. The outside negotiators had to restore the armed men's face, such as by saying, "I think you are an extremely strong person for how you have handled this so far," You've got a whole lot of people who care about you," and "The people you are trying to help, they need you" (Rogan and Hammer 1994). Sometimes face is saved ahead of time and other times it is restored after there has been some loss, like in the hostage situation. Both processes, however, are tied to either keeping identity intact or reestablishing it after it has been lost.

Figure 3.1 also shows the self damaging her or his own face. Though it seems unlikely, people often say negative things about themselves. When you say, "I'm just a terrible parent," or "I'm a lousy student," or "What does someone my age think he/she is doing going back to school?" those statements are damaging to one's own face or identity. In the hostage situation, the armed men were, in effect, saying "I'm just crazy," and the job of the outside negotiators was to get the men to start to see their own behavior as not quite so damaging to their view of themselves. Paradoxically, once face is restored one is more free to give up extreme defensive tactics, such as holding hostages.

People try to avoid loss of face by defending their self-images against humiliation, embarrassment, exclusion, demeaning communication, or general treatment as unimportant or low-power individuals. Attempts to solve a problem or stop a conflict by causing another person to lose a sense of dignity and worth never work in the long run. Extensive overuse of power may temporarily solve a problem. Any time losers are created, however, the losing group or individual waits for a time and place to "make it right," either by getting back at the winners, subverting the ongoing process, or leaving the relationship, work setting, or group. Demeaning communication creates ongoing pain and dissatisfaction, and the conflict remains unresolved at a deep level.

Face-saving and giving others face are extremely important in all cultures but take precedence over content issues in Asian cultures. It is now well-known in the business community that entirely different kinds of negotiations are required in Asian cultures. Attempt to give others face support and avoid at all costs the loss of face of the other are part of the requirements of polite interaction among many Pacific Rim cultures. One would never pin an opponent down or attempt to prove him or her wrong.

The box labeled "Going Public," from a biweekly newspaper column about mediation in different types of disputes, briefly treats the necessity of saving face, even in this culture.

Going Public: Like Dirty Laundry, Gripes Are Best Aired in Private

Ask a Mediator
by William Wilmot, Ph.D. & Roy Andes, M.A., J.D.

Reader: I'm an employee of a business that's falling apart. We have a high profile in the community and could easily pressure the management by going public with our complaints. Should we?

Mediators: We are a society addicted to two values at odds with one another: Privacy & public disclosure. Nowhere more than in conflicts do those values collide. Although the public likes to know what's going on, and the press likes the pizzazz of conflict, people whose relational dirty laundry gets hung out in public suddenly become more positional, more intransigent and more likely to use lawsuits and other formal or hostile procedures.

Why? The answer is privacy and face-saving. We all want people to feel good about us, to like us and to give us strokes. We feel that if we are completely open about our dilemmas and conflicts people are less likely to give us the things we want. How many of us tone down, postpone or even entirely avoid family arguments in public? How many of us in conflicts with friends or co-workers prefer to talk "privately" rather than in the presence of strangers? ALL of us, of course, do so. It's only natural. It's just as true for public officials and corporate executives as for the rest of us. People want privacy when they have to confront strong feelings and disagreements.

Destroying that privacy is as much an escalation of a conflict as throwing a bomb into the room. In response to such a "bomb," most people respond aggressively. They are certainly less likely to be cooperative, and less willing to try to work collaboratively to help you get what you want and need.

If you want to solve problems rather than preach about them, do it in private. If you want sincerity and openness, privacy is the best way to go. This is why mediators provide absolute confidentiality of mediation discussions. It's also why good negotiations take place out of the glare of press attention. Collaboration and problem-solving take mutual commitment, safety, patience, and thoughtfulness. None of those virtues emerge in a 30-second sound bite.

You can tell that attempts to save face are being employed when you or others engage in the following kinds of communication (adapted from Folger, Poole, and Stutman 1993):

1. *Resisting unjust intimidation.* Content goals take second place to this specific kind of relational goal—to stand up to another's attempt to take over. People accuse others of taking advantage, declare their resistance to unjust treatment, and often seek support from outside parties when they are being treated unjustly.
2. *Refusing to step back from a position.* A person who no longer feels comfortable with an earlier position may choose to stay with it, even in light of new information, because looking foolish or inconsistent results in losing face. Thus, content and larger relational goals are set aside to avoid looking weak, ill-informed, or

incompetent. In a community in a Western mountain state, water rights became a major conflict for a group of summer home owners in the mountains. A larger community was trying to claim water rights to a small creek that flowed through the home owners' property. One man resisted the efforts of a majority to build a legal defense fund because he had said at a meeting, "I'm not going to pay some lawyer to fritter away my money on something we can't stop anyway!" As several summers wore on, this embattled individual refused to step back from his position of "no money to lawyers," and "we can't make any difference anyway." He wrote letters to others in the home owners' group, bitterly protesting the intimidation of the majority group in assessing a fee for each home owner to build the legal fund. Clearly, as new information came in strongly supporting the efforts to fight the large community's water claim, as when the district court judge supported the summer-home group, the man who was fighting to avoid losing face found himself in a dilemma—to fight further might be to lose face even more. Eventually, he pretended he had supported the legal efforts all along but just thought the fees were too high. This was a face-regaining effort, and the home owners' group wisely dropped the issue so the man could be part of the community again. For him, the content and relational goals had become temporarily unimportant.

3. *Suppressing conflict issues.* People also try to save face by refusing to admit that a conflict exists, since to acknowledge the conflict might mean that events are out of control, making people feel uncomfortable and incompetent. In the water rights conflict discussed previously, several longtime friends of the dissident home owner said things like, "Well, Kent is just cantankerous. He'll get over it," or "Well, these things bring up strong feelings." Since the association had few effective means of conflict resolution, some people felt that to acknowledge conflict at all would mean that their group was in danger of losing a sense of camaraderie and community spirit. One board member tried to schedule a meeting that the dissident individual could not attend because of his travel schedule—an attempt to suppress or avoid the issue of face or identity needs.

In productive, ongoing relationships, several kinds of communication will help people restore their lost face or prevent further loss of face. You can increase flexibility and problem solving by

1. *Helping others increase their sense of self-esteem.* Treat others with good will, giving them the benefit of the doubt even when they have been belligerent or unproductive. You might say things like, "Everyone gets upset sometimes. We can get past this," or "You must not have had all the information I had. You couldn't have known about the Grandview project yet, as I did." Even saying something like, "I know you were doing what you thought was best" gives the other person the benefit of the doubt and is usually true. People do tend to do what they think is best at the time.
2. *Avoiding giving directives.* Parents can tell their teenage children, "I want you to honor the house rules we've discussed. I want to be able to trust you and not worry about monitoring you—you're almost grown and can make decisions for yourself." This approach is much better than "If you don't follow the rules we've set up you can find somewhere else to live!" As will be discussed later, it's better to avoid direct threats and to use persuasion and face-saving communication instead. No one wants

to be pushed around. Even if you have "right on your side," it may not always be wise to be "right," as this creates winners and losers.

3. *Listening carefully to others and taking their concerns into account.* Even when you don't have to listen because you have the power to make a decision independently, listening and taking care of others' concerns as best you can helps them feel included, approved of, and respected.
4. *Asking questions so the other person can examine his or her goals.* By asking questions instead of attacking, the other person has a chance to change in the interaction instead of entrenching and digging in (note the warlike metaphor).

In conclusion, helping others protect their self-identity as a good, worthy, competent, and intelligent human being goes far toward helping resolve conflict by allowing people to focus on goals other than self-protection.

Process Goals: What *Communication Process* Will Be Used?

The key question when assessing process goals is "What communication process would work best for this conflict?" Many times people disagree about how to formally or informally conduct a conflict. A group might argue over the merits of consensus or voting. Intimates often disagree about whether strong emotions hurt the process of conflict or not, or whether the partners should stay up and talk when one is sleepy or wait until morning. Work groups go back and forth about whether to send out opinion questionnaires, talk informally in a series of meetings, delegate certain decisions, or put off deciding certain issues. All these relate to the *process* of conflict interaction and will impact content, identity, and relational goals.

Different processes of communication may change the relationships involved. For instance, minorities may be given more power with a free flow of communication, whereas higher-power people might maintain their power with a more tightly organized form of interaction, such as one that relies heavily on written communication. One of the current trends in the workplace is that people want more processes that enhance equality and open participation. People struggle in organizations and small groups over the pros and cons of consensus, informal discussion, information gathering, delegated decisions, written summaries, voting, and parliamentary procedure. Women, more so than men, are more comfortable soliciting everyone's opinion (Brown and Gilligan 1992). Process goals also vary in different cultures, with some being quite authority oriented and others relying on equal participation. In Native American tribal politics, a long process of consensus building is often required before a decision is considered valid by the tribe. The tribal members delegate less to their elected officials than do Western European cultures.

In addition to changing the levels of influence, different processes encourage or discourage creative solutions. Quick, well-defined processes may decrease creative, innovative solutions. Longer, sometimes confusing processes that build in time for reflection and evaluation improve the chances for creativity. Thus, different processes affect the outcome of a conflict interaction, as well. For instance, one couple began to struggle over when to buy a house. The wife wanted to buy a house in the next few months, whereas the husband wanted to save more money before they looked seriously. The husband suggested that they first discuss with each other their financial goals and then talk about the house. This discussion resulted in the wife's decision that she, too, wanted to wait at least a year so that they could better their financial situation. By changing from content issues, such as the interest rate, the availability of houses in the desired neighborhood, or the likely tax consequences, to a different process, such as talking about other goals, the couple change the relational conflict ("I've got to get her/him to listen to me") to a mutually acceptable process.

Large public meetings are arenas for process conflict. In one conservation organization, the planning group struggled over whether to have a symposium of speakers presenting their ideas on biodiversity or whether to break the participants up into small groups to discuss different ideas then bring questions back to the resource people. The executive group, anxious to present their organization's views on the importance of biological diversity, decided on a process they could control, the symposium of carefully chosen speakers. This led to a clear but noninvolving presentation.

Conflicts over process involve face-saving or face-giving goals, as well. People who know they are in the minority often argue over correct parliamentary procedure, which provides more options for hearing from the minority than does, for instance, informal large-group discussion followed by voting. Often, process conflicts change as individuals are heard. People drop their obstruction to a certain process if they are assured of being heard and counted (face/identity issues) and when they see that their content and relational goals are being protected. As in struggles over differing content, relational, and identity goals, process conflicts blend into the other conflicting goals. Shifting from one level to another often helps parties avoid becoming stuck in an unproductive conflict.

The Overlapping Nature of CRIP Goals

Now that each type of goal has been explained and illustrated, it is appropriate to deepen our analysis of goals in conflict. A number of features about conflict goals need to be highlighted.

Feature 1: Not all types of goals emerge in all disputes. Raging disputes go on in which no process or procedural issues emerge. In the workplace, for example, there may be a heated disagreement between two supervisors, yet neither wants to change any of the processes used, how frequently they meet, or who is included. Similarly, many examples of conflicts can be cited in which there are no content issues. Two friends may be locked in a struggle over how responsive they are to one another, a relational issue that doesn't involve "content." It is often puzzling to parents how their children can fight for hours over "nothing"—no identifiable content issues. But rest assured, if there is a struggle and no content issues are apparent, the struggle *is* about something. The dispute rests on identity, process, and/or relational grounds.

Feature 2: Interests overlap with one another and differ in primacy. When you begin a dispute over your grade (the content goal), you also want to be treated well by the professor (the relational goal) and want to think that you tried hard (the identity or face-saving goal). Figure 3.2 demonstrates how this might look from your side. As you can see, you begin a discussion with the professor with the content issue paramount in your mind; the relational and identity issues are there but not as important to you. Note therefore that even though they differ in prominence, *different goal types emerge.* The professor, on the other hand, may be most concerned that she be seen as a fair and kind person, so a diagram of her goals at the beginning of the conversation might look like figure 3.3. She may be most concerned about relational issues, such as others seeing her as a fair person who treats

Figure 3.2 Content goals paramount

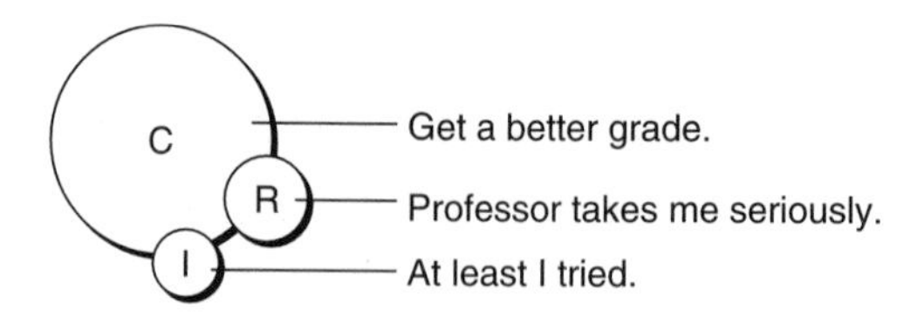

students equally, and identity issues ("I'm doing this job the way it should be done; I like how I respond to student concerns"). Her primary goals, then, are relational and identity goals. The content goal of the student's grade is much less significant, unless the student feels he or she is being treated unfairly.

A second example illustrates how a procedural goal might be utmost in one party's mind. You are a member of a departmental student group and would like to run for president. You were out of town last weekend, and this Tuesday in class someone said, ""Hey, what do you think about Stan being president of the student club? We had an election last night." For you, the procedural issue of not being notified of a meeting when others knew you wanted to run for president is your paramount issue, as shown in figure 3.4. Note that in this case, the procedural issue looms largest followed by identity and relational issues of equal weight.

The examples illustrate that *for each party,* the paramount interests probably differ from those of another person in the same situation. Notice that all of these examples included relational and identity goals because it is rare to have a conflict that does not involve identity and relational issues.

Feature 3: Identity and relational issues are the "drivers" of disputes; they underlie content and process issues. As you listen to people describe conflicts, you begin to notice a pattern—at the core of the disputes are their concepts of *who they are* and *how they want to be treated* in relationships. In most business disputes, for example, regardless of the content issue, someone is concerned about trust, treatment, or communication—relational issues. Further, the face-saving discussed earlier is a key element in *all* disputes. Because we are human beings, our inherent subjectivity drives disputes. Think back to when you were not chosen to play as a kid or were excluded from some high school activity, and you may remember just how important relational and identity issues are. As discussed under Feature 1, relational and identity concerns will almost always overlap—who you are with others is intricately tied into how you are in that relationship. Figure 3.5 illustrates which goals are almost always present and, in fact, "drive" almost all disputes.

Figure 3.3 Relational and identity goals paramount

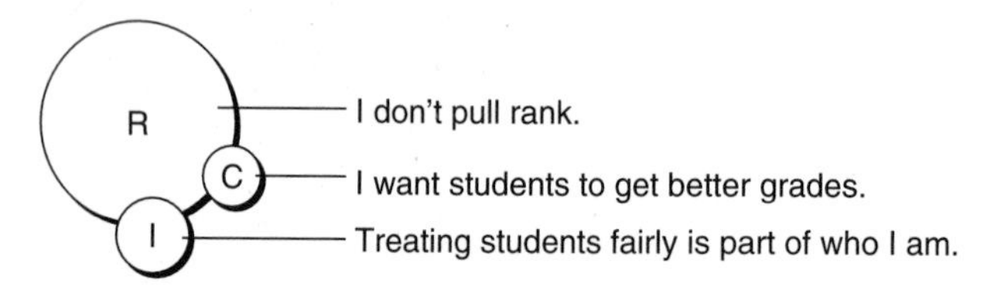

Figure 3.4 Process goals paramount

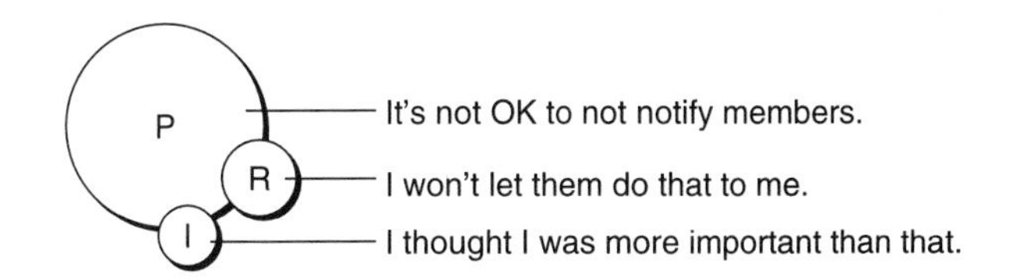

Note that the relational and identity issues are the more subjective forces that propel the content and process issues into focus. It is paradoxical that even though the identity and relational issues are the most difficult to talk about, they are the most potent issues in conflicts. One interesting feature of how people operate, given that relational and identity issues are the foundations of all conflicts, is that sometimes *identity and relational interests may be met indirectly.* For example, it may not be common in your family to say "I feel excluded," but rather, family members may watch others at the family picnic, see who is left alone, and seek them out for a talk. In an organization, it may not be within the cultural norms to say "I don't feel very valued here," but the president may give you access to the boardroom for meetings if he or she guesses that you are feeling pushed aside. Similarly, watch little kids at play. One of the kids may be left out, and another may turn to that child and say, "Want to play dolls with me?" Such content moves reverberate on the relational and identity level, without anyone ever talking about it. When Bill, one of the coauthors of this book, was twelve and not getting any time with his dad, he was rather hyperactive and on the verge of delinquency. Francis Cowger from Upton noticed him, offered him a summer job driving his tractor, and served all kinds of relational and identity needs for Bill via a John Deere tractor. If Francis had approached Bill's dad and said, "I think your kid needs some attention, but I know you are working fourteen hours a day, so how about I give him a job on my ranch this summer?" Bill's dad would have been insulted. But the indirect offer to help circumvented a conflict with the father and allowed Francis to help out. By being alert to the "relational translations" someone else might make, you can serve both relational and face-saving needs indirectly through content.

Indirect, content-only solutions do not work in intense conflict situations, however. The more severe and strained the conflict, the less satisfying the content approaches will be. This leads to the fourth feature of conflict goals:

Feature 4: In a serious dispute, content-only solutions are rarely satisfying to conflict parties. If you know someone who has ever won a lawsuit, ask them, "How do you feel

Figure 3.5 Relational and identity goals propelling a dispute

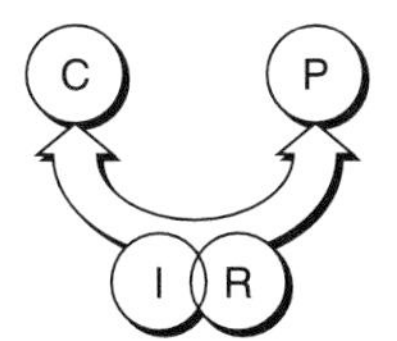

about the other party and the process you went through?" Guess what? You will hear anger, frustration, and exasperation, with the person usually launching into a tirade about both the other party and the other party's attorney. That is because (unless it is a very unusual case) only content issues have been addressed, and the needs to save face, to be listened to, and to be told that you weren't crazy have not been attended to. During the dispute there is often so much threat to each person's identity that content solutions alone are not satisfying. In this type of situation, if an outsider says, "You got $150,000, what more do you want?" the plaintiff will usually answer, "An apology."

Feature 5: Conflict parties often specialize in one kind of goal. Conflict parties in ongoing struggles often highlight one type of goal and limit themselves to it, as in the following dialogues:

In the Family

Grandfather:	"My daughter is just not a good mother to her kids—she needs to learn how to be a better mother. The kids need to be cleaner, and they are always late to school. Those kids need a better Mom." (content specialization)
His daughter, the mother of two small boys:	"I am just not willing to have the kids spend time at their grandparents' house until Dad learns how to treat people better. He only criticizes me and the kids and never says anything positive." (relational and identity specialization)

In the Organization

Faculty member:	"This is a ridiculous place to work. I put in a lot of hours and no one notices. I'd just once like to get some credit for what I do here." (relational specialization)
Chair of department:	"Dr. Samuels just doesn't do a very good job in the classroom. I can't support him for promotion until he begins to get higher marks from the students. I'll have to have some hard-hitting sessions with him outlining how a professional person does a job like his." (content specialization, then a shift to relational specialization)

In these conflicts, the participants separate and specialize—one party on content goals and the other on relational goals. This split tends to keep the conflict going—as the content specialist continues to expect better "performance" from the other, the relational specialist becomes more and more critical of the treatment he or she receives.

Specialization in either content or relational goals often reflects the parties' relative power. All too often, high-power parties are the ones who focus exclusively on content. Failure to acknowledge relational goals may be due to a lack of skill or can show hostility, lack of caring, or even a desire to compete. Focusing only on content devalues the other person and his or her concerns. The most powerful group member usually wins by structuring the conflict and ignoring troubling relational issues from lower-power people. Content discussion is simpler and requires less investment in the other person. Similarly, lower-power members may wish to bring in goals other than content as a power-balancing mechanism. If a lower-power person can get the higher-power person to agree that rela-

Figure 3.6 Relational goals emerging in content form

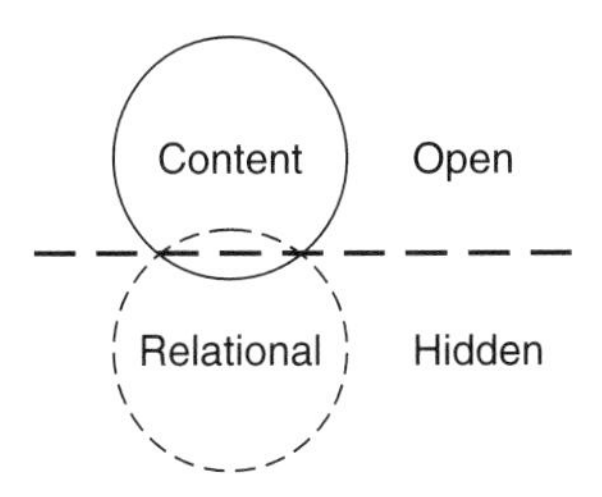

tional goals, including process and identity goals, are important, the lower-power person is "empowered" and becomes a legitimate party in the conflict.

Feature 6: Goals may emerge in a different form. Sensitivity to the different types of goals allows you to recognize when one type of goal is being acted out in terms of another. Any one of the four can come to the surface in a different form. Content goals emerge as relational, identity, or procedural goals. Relational goals can emerge as content, identity, or procedural goals, and so on—there are twelve possible substitutions. One of the most common is illustrated in figure 3.6: a relational goal carried by content.

Many times conflict parties are simply unable to identify their relational goals. Instead, they act them out at the content level. For example, you may feel devalued by your boss, so you wage an ongoing persuasive campaign to change the performance evaluation system used by the organization. Or, you think your brother does not respect you, so you argue that he doesn't have the training to handle your aging mom's finances. In "Stay for Dinner," notice the shift in goals.

"Stay for Dinner"

Connie, Sharon, and Janene, seniors at a university, share an old house near campus. They have known each other for years; they grew up in the same town. Their roommate relationship has, thus far, been fairly smooth, although recently an issue has emerged. Janene eats two meals a day on campus at the food service. Connie and Sharon like to cook, so they prepare their meals at home. They have invited Janene to share their evening meal several times, and Janene has occasionally accepted. It's Thursday night, Janene is rushing to get to the food service before it closes, and the following dialogue ensues:

Connie: Hey, Janene, you might as well stay and eat with us. It's late—you'll never make it.

Janene: No big deal. If I miss it, I'll get a hamburger or something. (She rushes out the door.)

Connie (to Sharon): That's the last time I'm going to ask her to eat with us. She thinks she is too good to be bothered with staying around here with us.

A few weeks later, Connie and Sharon find someone who is willing to room with them, share cooking, and pay a higher rate. So they approach Janene and say, "We are struggling with finances, and we have someone who will eat here, share expenses, and save us all money on food. Would you rather pay a higher rate or move out?

Figure 3.7 Identity goals emerging in content form

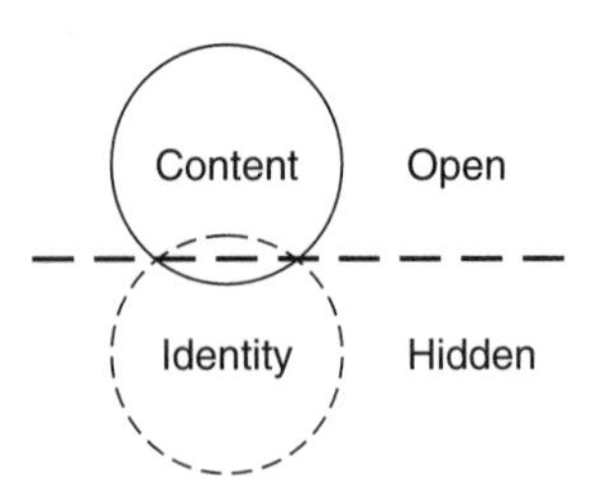

As you can see, this dispute began with two people feeling excluded and quickly degenerated into a content-only conflict. By ignoring relational issues, a longtime friendship was lost.

Identity conflicts, as well, often erupt on the content level, as shown in figure 3.7. "I'm Right/Are Not/Am Too" is an example of an identity-driven dispute that gets played out on the content level. Each person starts by wanting to feel right (identity or face-saving). Watch what quickly happens.

"I'm Right/Are Not/Am Too!"

Duane and Kathy are going to a movie. Duane is driving, and they both notice a red car passing them.

Duane: That's a Datsun, like the kind I was telling you about.
Kathy: No, I think it was a Toyota. But it's pretty.
Duane: No, it was a *Datsun!*

They argue back and forth about the rightness of their claims. Neither is a car expert, but both are adamant, using sarcasm and biting humor.

Kathy: Well, you may be right, but I still think it was a Toyota.
Duane: Look, I know I'm right!
Kathy: You never think I know anything!
Duane: You don't know anything about cars. Blow if off. It's not important.

Kathy sits silently for ten minutes.

The couple will continue to argue about identifying cars, but both have stated relationship concerns. Kathy feels she is not given credit as a knowledgeable person. Duane states that he needs to be right on things he knows more about. The couple appears to be negotiating about who has preeminence in certain areas of expertise. They haven't worked out how to "call off the conflict" or how to ask for more respect from each other. They are likely to find other content issues to fight over until the relationship is addressed directly. The following box presents two openings that might start them off more productively.

Duane: I get bothered when you challenge me about something I know a lot about. I start thinking you don't think I'm very smart.

or

Kathy: Duane, I'm not that interested in Toyotas, or Datsuns either. But I've been thinking that you get the last word on most topics we discuss. It makes me want to never give in—even if I know I'm wrong.

Here, in shortened form, are some more examples of how conflicts emerge in different forms:

Relational/identity ⟶ Procedural

A person feels devalued as the new accountant and, as a result, argues for getting signature authority over all disbursements.

Content ⟶ Relational

Two men have a land dispute. The issue gets passed down through the generations, and eventually, the grandchildren of both families are told not to speak to each other.

Identity ⟶ Content

A faculty member is not given tenure. So begins writing a newspaper column arguing that "the University is not serving its mission."

Content ⟶ Relational/procedural

The Forest Service makes a decision about logging. An interest group argues that "there was not enough public input" and that the process needs to be redone.

Shape Shifting of Goals

Goals, once identified, don't stay static but undergo transformation before, during, and after disputes. They will emerge as one type and, during the course of the dispute, flower into another type. Even after the struggle is over, goals will shift and change retrospectively. Additionally, multiple goals for interactions usually exist. People may hold different content, relational, and identity goals, may hold different short- and long-term goals, and may disagree about which shared goals are most important and deserve the most energy, as shown in the following box.

How Much Is Too Much?

Mr. Quentin, the program director at a hospital, is conducting the biannual review of employees. Ms. West, who has been public relations director at Metro Hospital for one year, is reading her review letter prior to the conversation.

Ms. West (to herself): He wants me to show more initiative! I'd like to know how I can do that when he's made it clear that I need to check everything out with him first. I'll ask him about that.

In Mr. Quentin's office:

Mr. Quentin: Ms. West, the one area I'd like you to give some attention to is showing more initiative. You see I've checked you the lowest in that regard.

Ms. West: I'm glad you are giving me the opportunity to change in that area. I have some ideas I'd like to try.

Mr. Quentin: That's great. Your job is to come up with some new ideas for keeping us first in the community.

At the next biannual review, Mr. Quentin placed Ms. West on probation for acting without the authority of the program director and the hospital administrator. Ms. West was appalled, thinking she was supposed to act with less "checking." Mr. Quentin, however, wanted her to initiate more new ideas so that he could take them to his boss, the administrator, and the administrator could decide which way to go in the public relations effort. No one clarified goals, and now the conflict is structured overwhelmingly against Ms. West. The hospital may lose a talented employee if the parties cannot untangle the conflict over multiple unshared, unclear goals.

Prospective Goals

The word *goals* most commonly connotes intentions people hold before they engage in conflict. For instance, Sally might say to Dorothy, "What do you hope to accomplish at the board meeting? The last one was awful—so much confusion and disorganization." Dorothy might reply, "I want to sort out who's in charge of the budget decisions and how we're supposed to come up with $5,000 more next year than we took in this year. I don't want to take responsibility for more fund-raising." Dorothy has stated her *prospective goals*—those she can identify before the board meeting begins. Simply stated, she hopes that the board will decide who makes budget decisions and delegate fund-raising to some responsible party. Most of the other board members will come to the meeting with their own prospective goals. An effectively managed meeting will take account of all the prospective goals members bring, whether they are readily stated or not.

Prospective goals can be shared in families, intimate relationships, organizations, and staff groups. Taking the time to clarify what it is that people want from a particular interaction lays the groundwork for more effective conflict. Each person's concerns are heard, listed (if appropriate), and attentively clarified. When this step precedes a later conflict episode, parties can back up, restate what each person wants, and suggest ways to accomplish those goals. The expectation of collaboration establishes a positive tone for the discussion.

Transactive Goals

In many conflicts "goals are quite complex and ephemeral" (Sillars and Weisberg 1987), and they only become clear as the conflict unfolds. For example, during a struggle with your housemate over financial misunderstandings, you discover that what you really want is to move—which you did not know you felt until the argument began. You have just stumbled onto a *transactive goal,* or one discoverd during the conflict itself.

Transactive goal development takes place *during* expressed conflict episodes rather than before or after. You may have been absolutely certain that you wanted an assistant to carry out the new project your boss assigned to you, but during a staff meeting in which the goals of the whole team are expressed, you may change your demand for an assistant. You may now say that you can do the work without an assistant for at least six months. What happened? Did you back down? Did the boss win? Did you have "no guts"? More likely, you became aware of the interdependent nature of your work team and decided to change your demand, given the needs of the entire group. You may have been given recognition for the difficulty of your job. Maybe your boss said in front of the group, "I'd like to give you an assistant, but I don't have the money in the budget and don't know where I can get it" (a face-saving message). Your conflict goals changed because of the communication transaction. Adaptability makes continuing interdependence possible:

> Adaptability is probably the most distinctive characteristic of life. In maintaining the independence and individuality of natural units, none of the great forces . . . are as successful as that alertness and adaptability to change which we designate as life—and the loss of which is death. . . . There are two roads to survival: fight and adaptation. And most often—adaptation is the more successful (Selye 1974, 57).

A school board member was trying to decide how to handle her strong opposition to the closed, or "executive," sessions of the board that her colleagues on the board supported. She discussed the incipient conflict with friends ahead of time, rehearsing what she was going to do (prospective goal). When the next board meeting arrived, she did not give her prearranged speech. She compromised and agreed with her colleagues that some closed meetings, in limited circumstances, were acceptable. This change is an example of transactive goal development.

The concept of transactive goals developed from the conviction that communication, itself, is transactional. To describe communication accurately, we must look at what happens when people are together instead of looking at each person's separate experiences (Wilmot 1987; Laing, Philipson, and Lee 1966). Relationships are interpenetrative, with each person influencing and being influenced by the other (Wilmot 1995). To say that the board member in the example was persuaded by the other board members is simplistic. Neither did she persuade them to adopt her point of view. They all influenced each other, creating new, transactive goals through the process of a democratic board meeting.

You may have noticed that your goals change in conflicts as you get a chance to express your feelings, be heard, and talk through your opinions and wishes (while the other party does the same). If you are a person who says, "I don't know what I want until we get a chance to discuss it," you understand transactive goals. The following box exemplifies the way new goals develop as a conflict progresses. Note that the two friends see themselves as interdependent and that they value their relationship as well as solving the immediate problem (finding the lost object).

Verbal Communication		Goal Analysis
First phone call:		
Amy:	You know that silver star pendant I loaned you? I guess you didn't return it with the rest of the jewelry, because I can't find it.	Amy's #1 prospective goal is to *get the pendant back from Janice.*
Janice:	I don't have it. I remember that I didn't borrow it because I knew it was valuable to you. You must have misplaced it somewhere. But I'll look.	Janice's #1 prospective goal is to *convince Amy that she is not responsible for the disappearance of the necklace,* a goal that is incompatible with Amy's prospective goal.
Second phone call:		
Amy:	I still can't find it—I'm getting panicky. I'll hold while you go look. Please check everywhere it might be.	Amy maintains prospective goal #1 by escalating her previous goal statement. Amy and Janice still have incompatible goals.
Janice:	You're upset about the necklace, and I don't know what I can do since I honestly don't think I have it. But what really concerns me is that you are upset at me. You mean a lot to me, and this hurts.	Transactive goal #2: *Affirm the relationship in spite of the loss of the necklace.*
Amy:	I know. I really don't want to put it all on you. I'm glad you understand, though. You know, John gave me that necklace.	Amy reaffirms transactive goal #2, making it mutual. She agrees to discuss, affirming the relationship as a new, additional goal.
Janice:	Well, what can we do to get this solved? I feel awful.	Janice restates transactive goal #2 and offers transactive goal #3: *Find the necklace together without damaging the relationship.*
Amy:	I'll hang up and we'll both go look everywhere and then report back.	Amy advances transactive goal #4: *Share the responsibility with a new plan of action.*
Janice:	OK. And then we'll come up with something if we don't find it right away. Cross your fingers.	Janice accepts transactive goal #4 and advances transactive goal #5: *We will keep working until we solve this problem.*

Changes in your transactive goals reflect your success at managing a conflict. When you are not able to move toward a productive conflict, you shift toward wanting to belittle, injure, cut down, or lessen the other's power. In fact, it is precisely this shift from content to negative relationship or identity goals that characterizes the destructive conflict described in chapter 2. In diagram form, the goal change occurs as follows:

1. You want a promotion:
   You ————————→ Promotion
2. When you ask her for a promotion, your supervisor says, "No way. You aren't going to get a promotion as long as I'm the boss here. Your work has been substandard, not

worthy of promotion." Your boss interferes with your original goal, and you begin to focus most of your attention on her interference and your attempts to gain power.
You ————————→ Supervisor

3. You then begin to lose sight of your original goal and spend energy trying to get even with the boss. You talk to people at home and at work about her, tell others how biased she is, spread rumors at work, and do other things to undercut her authority.

This example describes a typical pattern of *goal shifting* in a conflict. What began as a content goal, getting a promotion, turns into a relational contest between the two of you—you shift from a positive content goal to a negative relational goal. Such shifts occur often and can be either automatic and spontaneous, or strategic (Infante and Wigley 1986). Two business partners, for example, who begin by wanting to help each other earn sizable amounts of money, experience a misunderstanding over a contract and then spend the next two years trying to one-up each other during board meetings and to get others in the organization to side with them. The partnership begins to flounder as each one thinks the other is more trouble than he is worth.

One other type of goal shifting occurs in conflicts. Often, a person who is frustrated over the content of a conflict (the vote doesn't go your way; you can tell the outcome of the discussion will be unfavorable) will shift from content to process. Concerns about fair process, equal treatment, and other process issues often surface when one has not been successful at attaining a desired content goal. The teenager who launches an appeal to use the family car and is turned down may resort to arguing that "you listened to Steve, but you didn't let me tell you why I needed the car. You treated me unfairly." She is switching from the unsuccessful content attempt to a discussion of process. Similar process concerns arise in many conflicts after the participants realize their content goals have been thwarted. A change in any type of conflict goal spills over to the other types of conflict goals. Often, as in previous examples, identity issues become intertwined with relational goals. When you feel powerless in relationship to another person, your sense of effectiveness or worthiness is challenged. Thus, identity goals rise in importance.

Conflict parties also *sacrifice* content for relationship goals or relationship goals for content. When the spouse never argues, avoids expressing any disagreement, and always says "whatever you want dear," he or she is sacrificing content goals in order to maintain the relationship. Acquiescing to others and never telling them what you really feel are types of content goal sacrifice. Alternatively, if you are intently set on your content goal (making money, negotiating the best possible contract, or always winning), you may be sacrificing the relationship in order to win the content. If you never consider the wishes of the other and always try to win, you are probably destroying valuable relationships in order to accomplish your goals. If you own a business and treat employees unfairly (in their eyes), you are sacrificing your relationship with them in order to maximize profit. The other party may pressure you to balance the varied types of goals.

In conclusion, conflict goals change over time. As one goal is frustrated, others a
more importance. You may not know which goals, whether content, relation
process, hold the most value for others unless you ask. Some people prima
process to be just right, others specialize in relational goals, and others see
content goals.

Retrospective Goals

Goals continue to change and grow long after conflicts are over. Toulmin (1958) and Weick (1979) suggest that most people spend a large part of their time and energy justifying decisions they have made in the past. Understanding assumes a retrospective quality, with people needing to explain to themselves and others why they made the choices they did. This process often happens with intimates who, for example, have an intense conflict over discipline of the children. After the first triggering comment or episode, they may say, "Let's decide what's best for the children, not just what fits our own upbringing" (prospective goal). During subsequent conflicts over specific instances of discipline, they discuss everything from how the individual children react to whether Mom and Dad should support each other's choices, even if they don't agree. If they decide that discipline is to be handled differently from the way it was in past episodes, Mom might say retrospectively, "I mainly wanted to see whether you would begin to share the discipline with me." Dad might say, "All along I was really trying to get you to see that you need to loosen up on the kids." Assuming that the couple came up with a wise agreement they can follow in future episodes, the retrospective sense making helps them to define who they are and to make meaningful statements about the place of the conflict in their lives. Monday morning quarterbacking is important in ongoing relationships as well as in sports.

Since we do not know the implications of a conflict until we look back on it, retrospective goals serve an *explanatory* as well as a predictive function. Weick (1979) explains this sense-making process as the reverse from the usual way of looking at goals. He explains organizational behavior as "goal interpreted." People act in an orderly fashion, coordinating their behavior with each other, but with little notion of how this is accomplished until after the fact. Then they engage in retrospective meetings, conversations, paper writing, and speeches to explain why they did what they did. "The organism or group enacts equivocal raw talk, the talk is viewed equivocally, sense is made of it, and this sense is then stored as knowledge. . . . The aim of each process has been to reduce equivocality and to get some idea of what has occurred" (134). Talking about what happened after an involving conflict is as important as talking about what will happen before a conflict episode. In these retrospective accounts, prospective goals for the next episode are formulated. Thus, we learn from experience.

Retrospective sense making also serves the function of *face-saving.* Visitors to the United States often comment on our lack of face-saving social rituals compared to those in Japan, China, and other countries. Brown and Levinson (1978) argue, on the basis of cross-cultural data, that helping one's fellow communicator to validate a positive social identity in interaction is recognized universally as socially necessary. Even if you have been involved in a competitive conflict and have won, rubbing it in or gloating over the loser will only serve to alienate and enrage the person, perhaps driving him or her to devious actions in retaliation. If you can provide accurate and empathic ways to give respect to the *person,* even if you did not agree with the *position,* the person's "face" will be saved, and you will lay the groundwork for collaboration in the future. Following are some face-saving comments:

> Employer to job applicant: We looked very highly on you and your application. Our offer to Ms. Shepherd was based on her experience in our particular kind of operation. Even though you and I have been at odds for some time over organization of the new program, I want you to know that your new ideas are always sound and well organized. I just have different priorities.

> Mother to teenage daughter: I know you didn't want to cause us worry. You couldn't have known how upset we'd be that you were four hours late. But since you did not follow our agreement, we are grounding you for a week, as we said we would if the rule was not followed.

Improving Conflict Goals

As noted above, how conflict parties formulate, alter, and explain their goals in a conflict determines to a large degree the success of the conflict experience. This section gives suggestions for better articulating and working with goals to improve one's conflicts.

Clarify Goals

Goals that are unclear, ambiguous, or hard to specify usually produce more conflict. One study demonstrated that in organizations, unclear and ambiguous goals produced more conflict between employees (Schnake and Cochran 1985). A careful specification of everyone's goals lets you decide which ones to abandon, which ones to trade, and which ones to maintain (Hermone 1974). Further, as Papa and Pood (1988a) demonstrated, clarity about goals before the conflict interaction results in increased satisfaction with the discussion with the other party.

Sometimes, however, a discussion of goals in interpersonal conflict elicits the same avoidance reaction mentioned in earlier chapters: "I don't want to be manipulative. If I figure out what I want ahead of time, I'm being pushy and presumptuous—I'll let the chips fall where they may." However, all effective communication is *rhetorical,* or goal directed (Phillips and Metzger 1976). This means that communication is purposive, not that it is manipulative, and that people communicate for reasons and to reach goals. Since no one can avoid being goal directed, especially in conflict communication, productive conflict management depends on parties taking open responsibility for their goals. In other words, know what your goals are, state them clearly to yourself, and communicate them in a flexible manner with your conflict partners. Advantages of clarifying your goals follow:

1. *Solutions go unrecognized if you do not know what you want.* If parents are not clear about whether they want their eighteen-year-old to live at home or to board in the dorm at a local college, they will not know how to manage the conflict with the son who wants to live in the dorm but does not have a job. If saving money is the primary goal, the parents might allow the son to live in the dorm and get a job. If the parents have decided that they do not want him to live in the dorm under any circumstances, the son's offer to get a job may trigger a covert conflict that is unclear and unproductive for all parties.
2. *Only clear goals can be shared.* Since people cannot read your mind, you must clearly communicate your goals. An example of this kind of goal sharing occurred in an academic department. The chairperson complained that the faculty was not paying enough attention to university politics. He made several statements over a period of a week or so, urging more attendance at meetings, more discussion of long-term budget and curriculum plans, and voluntary participation in activities around campus. Since all this happened at the beginning of a quarter, when the rest of the faculty

were feeling busy, hassled by bureaucratic demands, and underappreciated, the response from the faculty was negative. A genuine conflict began to brew. Finally, the chairperson said, "Since keeping us involved in the university is my job, I feel really down when nobody supports what I'm doing. I need some feedback on what you think so I'm not just floundering around." Because he changed his goal statement from "Why don't you people work more?" to "I need support for what I'm doing," the conflict was reduced and productively managed.

3. *Clear goals can be altered more easily than vague goals.* One agency was embroiled in conflict over whether to fund and provide staff support for a new program to aid recently unemployed families. The three staff members who had been charged with setting up the new program did not know whether the agency director wanted to support that particular new program or whether he wanted to demonstrate to the funding sources that the agency was committed to being responsive to families in general. When the director clarified that the specific program should serve an undeserved population, the staff members altered their previous goals so that the new program would assist with community problems of child abuse. The change in staff goals was possible because the larger goals were clarified for the staff members, along with their important role in reaching the goals.
4. *Clear goals are reached more often than unclear goals.* Having a map helps travelers reach a destination. Similarly, Raush et al. (1974) found that 66 percent of the conflicts in which the issue was clearly stated were successfully resolved, whereas only 18 percent of the conflicts in which the issue remained vague and nonspecific were resolved. For example, a couple is considering where to move after college. If they choose the first option, "We will stay in the same city no matter what," they will have made a significantly different choice than if they choose the second option, "We will both get the best jobs we can." Those with shared individual and relational destinations are more likely to arrive at some desired point together. Clarifying goals has one risky outcome: it may make seriously incompatible goals apparent. However, they will become apparent sooner or later. Additionally, when goals are "stated explicitly and directly there is control of escalation" (99). When one's goals are unclear, they often promote overreaction from the other person, who misjudges the nature of the conflict. We are remarkably poor at second-guessing the goals of our conflict partners.

Often people create difficulty by assuming that their goals cannot be attained—that the other party will stand in their way. How many times have you planned and schemed for days, only to find that others were perfectly willing to give you what you wanted? A friend was miserable because her children would not give her any free time on the weekends. She began to believe they did not respect her needs. Finally one night she said in tears, "If I don't have some time alone, I'll go crazy." The teenagers were glad to make plans to give her time with no responsibilities. She simply never had asked. Even if the goal is a difficult one, allotting time to accomplish a clear goal allows for its attainment (Neale and Bazerman 1985).

In conclusion, clarifying goals is a key step in conflict management. People assess the conflicts in which they participate by making decisions about which goals are worth pursuing. In common language, they get a "grip" on the situation before deciding how to proceed.

Collaborative Goals

The best goals are clear, as explained previously, and help conflict interactants collaborate on resolving the conflict while protecting their ability to work, live, or interact with each other in important ways. The following statements characterize *collaborative goals* and may be used as a checklist for "good goals":

1. *Short, medium, and long-range issues are addressed.* Many times people engage too forcefully with others at the beginning of a conflict because they are afraid their ideas will not be heard. Collaborative goals build in ways for people to be involved in the process as it unfolds. To form collaborative goals, plan for evaluations along the way. Give as much attention to a few weeks or months from now as to "right now." Looking at longer-range goals helps de-escalate the importance of initial, prospective goals. One city council, meeting in a retreat, specified which goals, over a time line, were important to them. They set up a plan to specify *who* would do *what* by *when* and with what *evaluation process.* A year later, only those goals that had been broken down into a specific time line were achieved. Goals that are set up on a time line are less overwhelming than global goals such as "Let's change the way we get along as a family," or "I want more say about the financial structure of our family."
2. *Goals are behaviorally specific.* Doable goals (Phillips and Metzer 1976) can be checked. "I'll try to do better" might become a doable goal with specification; at present, it is a positive statement but not a collaborative goal. Terms used in intimate relations are often more vague than statements in business relationships. A corporate vice president could not get away with telling the president, "I will try the best I can to remember to turn the monthly reports in on time," but intimates make such vague promises frequently. Specificity helps the parties know when a goal has been accomplished. The following examples illustrate how to make vague statements more specific:
   - Instead of saying, "Please respect my things more," say, "I want you to ask me before you borrow any of my possessions. I'm usually glad to oblige, but I want you to ask me, all right?"
   - Instead of saying, "Let's get this show on the road" (and then showing nonverbal impatience during a meeting), say, "I need to leave this meeting at 5:00 sharp. I'm anxious to discuss the vacation replacement plans. Could we start?"
   - Instead of saying, "This time, young lady, you're going to listen to what I say!" a parent might say, "Last time we talked about your messy room I wasn't pleased with where we got. This time, I want you to listen to me, and I will listen to you, and then I want us to decide on what is reasonable. OK?"
3. *Statements orient toward the present and future.* The language of change uses what can be done now instead of what should have been done in the past. Hopeful statements instead of blaming statements set the expectation that agreements can indeed come about. A department head might say, "I want our program group to increase services to clients without increasing hours worked by our counselors," instead of, "We have got to be more efficient than we were last year."
4. *Goals recognize interdependence.* In all conflicts, tension arises between serving self-interest and the interests of the other party. In Western cultures we have overemphasized self relative to community interest, whereas Eastern cultures tend to

focus on the interests of the group or community (Dien 1982). Research consistently indicates, however, that when conflict parties operate with *both* concern for self and concern for others, the agreements that emerge serve the parties best (Tutzauer and Roloff 1988; Holloway and Brager 1985). This does *not* mean that you give in to the other; you can remain firm in achieving solutions that work for you while simultaneously seeking to please the other (Tutzauer and Roloff 1988). When one has low concern for the other coupled with a high demand for one's own goals, however, coercion and manipulation result (Kimmel et al. 1980). High concern for self and the other coupled with high demand that one's own goals remain important gives the parties an opportunity to develop creative, integrative solutions to the conflict.

5. *Collaborative goals recognize an ongoing process.* An overriding goal of constructive conflict is to remain committed to the *process* of constructive conflict. The particular content can be transcended by adhering to a collaborative process. Fisher and Ury (1981) remind conflict managers that goal setting begins with the participation of all conflict parties. "Give them a stake in the outcome by making sure they participate in the process" (27). For collaborators, "the process *is* the product" (29).

We discussed earlier that the goal of any conflict is to reach agreement and enhance future conflict management. The outcome of constructive conflict should be wise agreements, if such agreements are possible. Wise agreements are fair and durable and take the interests of all parties into account (Fisher and Ury 1981, 4). The struggle for wise agreements is exemplified by a couple with children that goes to court for a divorce. The agreement should be representative of both sides, should be fair to all parties, including the children, should keep the couple out of court in the future, and should set up care for the children if they are too young to care for themselves. The process should be efficient, involve all parties' interests, and improve or at least not damage the relationship between the parties.

When conflict parties work together to clarify goals and specify what the conflict is and is not about, destructive conflicts subside. Collaboration is a high-energy alternative to avoidance, violence, coercion, frustration, despair, and other forms of destructiveness. You may feel that the view of collaboration presented thus far is overly altruistic. Selye (1974), however, sees altruism as a kind of collective selfishness that helps the community: "By making another person wish that we prosper because of what we have done—and hence, are likely to do for (him) again—then we elicit goodwill" (53). Collaboration is not always possible, but when it is, destructive conflict is transformed into constructive problem solving.

The participants should come to see themselves as working side by side on a problem, attacking the problem instead of each other. The overarching process goal is *"We, working together, can solve this problem that is confronting us."* Part of the self-interest of conflict parties is preserving a workable relationship; focusing on the problem instead of the other people assists in relational maintenance. The problem is faced as one would face an enemy, working cooperatively *with one's conflict partner* to solve the problem.

Relational preservation becomes a superordinate goal, as in the classic Sherif and Sherif (1956) study where groups of boys were placed in situations that aroused conflicts of interest between the two groups. The researchers then introduced a common enemy, thus stimulating the two groups to work together, which reduce their intergroup hostility. In interpersonal conflicts, *long-term* relational, process, identity, or content goals can become superordinate goals that reduce conflict over *short-term* goals, but only if the conflict parties can separate the people involved from the problems.

Summary

People in conflict initially perceive their goals as incompatible with those of the other party. As a conflict unfolds, we see content, relational, identity, and process goals emerge. Content goals are the "objective," verifiable issues that people talk about. Relationship goals are those pertaining to the parties' influence on each other. Who gets to decide, how they treat one another, and other aspects of their communication characterize relationship goals. Identity or face-saving goals have to do with the needs of people to present themselves positively in interactions and to be treated with approval and respect. Process goals refer to parties' interests in how the interaction is conducted. Although most conflict parties center their discussions on content goals, the relationship, identity, and process components often fuel the feeling in a given conflict.

Goals change in the course of a conflict. *Prospective goals* are those identified before interacting with the other parties. Specifying them ahead of time helps with productive conflict. *Transactive goals* are those that emerge during the communication exchanges. Transactive goals often shift; a destructive conflict is characterized by a shift from original goals to a desire to harm the other party. *Retrospective goals* are those explained after the conflict episodes have occurred. Unregulated, unplanned, fast-paced conflicts keep many people from understanding their goals until they later have time to reflect on the transactions.

Productive conflict management is enhanced by clarifying goals and working to build collaborative goals with the other party. Working against or without consulting the other party often sets destructive forces in motion that preclude integrative management of the conflict.

Chapter 4

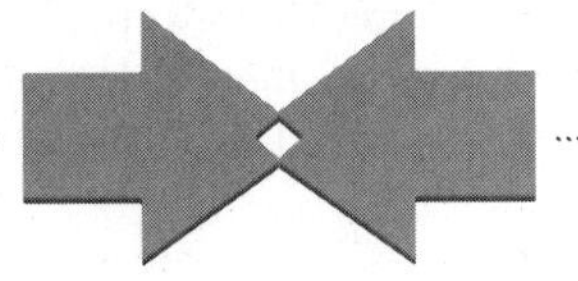

Power

> The stick, the carrot and the hug may all be necessary, but the greatest of these is the hug.
> —Kenneth Boulding, *Three Faces of Power*

What is Power?

Just as energy is a fundamental concept in physics, power is a fundamental concept in conflict theory. In interpersonal and all other conflicts, perceptions of power are at the heart of any analysis. There are literally hundreds of definitions of power, but they tend to fall into two camps. Power is seen as (1) *distributive (either/or)* or (2) *integrative (both/and).* Distributive definitions of power stress that "with force, control, pressure or aggression, one individual is able to carry his or her objective over the resistance of another and thus gain power" (Dahl 1957, 3). Distributive approaches focus on *power over* or *power against* the other party.

Integrative definitions of power highlight *power with* the other. Integrative views stress "joining forces with someone else to achieve mutually acceptable goals" (Lilly 1989, 281). Integrative definitions focus on "both/and"—both parties have to achieve something in the relationship. As we shall see, it is not what outsiders say about power but rather the *views of the conflict parties themselves* that determine the outcomes of their conflicts.

This chapter examines the role of power in conflict by examining common assumptions people have about power. Power currencies are then analyzed, a relational view of power is explored, and finally, ways to assess and rebalance power so constructive conflict can take place are presented. Sometimes all we can do in conflicts is keep the destruction from spiraling out of control, or negotiate an uneasy "balance of terror." But, as you will see, there are alternatives for the top-down exercise of power. Integrative use of power solves problems, enhances relationships, and balances power so the best qualities of each party can flower. When that happens, the hard work that goes into learning about conflict management seems worth it!

Views of Power

In chapter 1, the lens model of conflict was outlined (see figure 1.1). You learned that your particular view of self, other, and relationship are the key ingredients in a conflict (along with the other's perceptions). When a dispute occurs between two people, they often talk about power, and their perspectives on how it operates will predispose them to certain communicative moves. For example, if you are a student intern in a real estate firm and you feel that brokers have all the power, you are likely to keep silent even when you disagree—giving the impression that you agree when you don't. If, on the other hand, you feel that both you and the brokers have sources of power, you will be more likely to engage in discussion to work through issues. As an intern, you may have sources of power such as a different set of acquaintances and new ideas about zoning regulations.

You probably have a gut level response when you hear the word "power." As Kipnis notes, "Like love, we know that power exists, but we cannot agree on a description of it" (1976, 8). Respond quickly to the word "power," as you did with the word "conflict" in chapter 1. What comes to mind? The following are common associations:

power play	power source	power corrupts
high powered	power behind the throne	devious
bullheaded	run over	authority
power politics	powerhouse	overpower
low powered	sneaky	strong-arm
bulldozed	powerful	influence

As reflected in this list, people have differing views of power, some positive and some negative. One group of researchers (Cavanaugh et al. 1981a, 1981b; Goldberg, Cavanaugh, and Larson 1983) classified differing views of power. Using samples of salespeople, government employees, corporate executives, and law enforcement personnel, they concluded that the prime orientations toward power were varied. Some people viewed power as good—that the responsibility and challenge of power are exciting and that they would like to be powerful. Others saw power as instinctive—something we all possess innately. Still others saw power as consisting of valued resources, such as political skill; as a charismatic thing that people "have" within themselves, or as reflected in control over others and autonomy of the self.

Either/Or Power

Take a look at the list of words associated with power—most show an either/or association. You have power in order to move others against their will; it becomes a contest of the wills when you are in a "power struggle." When you examine typical newspaper stories about power, you read about the either/or (distributive) notions of power. In fact, it is difficult to even find examples of any other orientation toward power in the popular press. Many people think that power is only "force"—pushing others around against their will. When you examine nations using military might against other nations, you see either/or power in operation.

Once a relationship begins to go downhill, *concerns with power increase.* As any relationship deteriorates, the parties shift to a more overt focus on power—and this shift is reflected in their discourse (Beck 1988). When partners are abusive to each other, their communicative interactions show a lot of "one up" responses, attempts to demonstrate conversational power over each other (Sabourin and Stamp 1995). Partners might say, "She is just trying to control me," or "I'm not going to let him push me around." People, whether married couples or work colleagues, try to "keep score"—watching the "points" they have vis-à-vis the other party (Ross and Holmberg 1992). When partners develop an overt concern with power, their struggles over power are directly related to relationship satisfaction (Kurdek 1994). Figure 4.1 demonstrates how concerns rank in a distressed relationship.

As Ury, Brett, and Goldberg (1988) so aptly note, the focus for a dispute becomes power—who has the right to move the other. The teenager who says, "You can't boss me around," the spouse who shouts, "Just who do you think you are?" and the coworker who states, "Well, we'll see who the boss is around here!" are all highlighting power and giving it center stage in the dispute. These struggles often escalate. Dissatisfied couples are more than three times as likely to escalate episodes and focus on power than satisfied couples (Alberts and Driscoll 1992). We are not suggesting that power shouldn't be an issue. In fact, the parent-child relationship (at least when the child is young) is inevitably "one of domination by the parent" (Boulding 1989, p. 38). And in many organizations, like the military, people have the power to dictate what others do, but that doesn't work too well in the family back at home.

Notice in figure 4.1 that disputes also involve "rights" and "interests." Rights include not being discriminated against, being free from physical harm, and other constitutional

Figure 4.1 Power emphasized in a distressed system

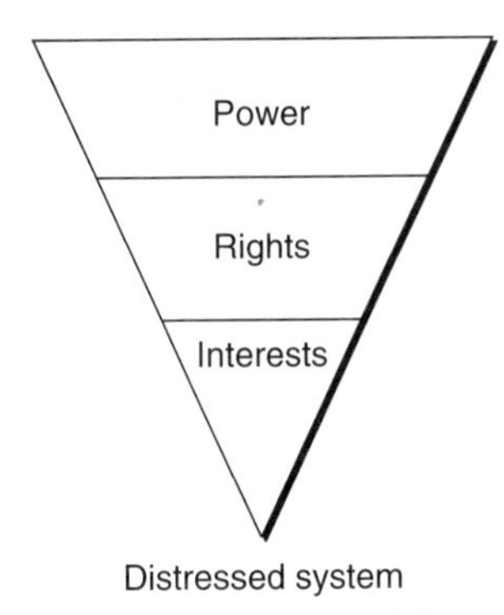

Source: From William Ury, Jeanne M. Brett, and Stephen B. Goldberg, *Getting Disputes Resolved: Designing Systems to Cut the Costs of Conflict.* Copyright © 1988 Jossey-Bass Inc., Publishers, San Francisco, California. Reprinted by permission.

and legal guarantees we have as citizens. Sometimes it is more appropriate that disputes get settled on the basis of rights rather than power or interests. For example, if the famous *Brown v. Board of Education* case in 1954 outlawing segregation in public schools had been settled on the basis of power, it would have resulted in a struggle in the streets. If, on the other hand, it had been settled on the basis of interest, Brown might have negotiated his way into school, but the country's social policy would not have changed. When we solve a dispute based on interests, the goals and desires of the parties are the key elements. For instance, if you don't want your teenage son to use the car, you can (1) tell him it is not OK as long as you are the "head honcho" in the house (power); (2) let him know that you own the car and have all the rights to its use (rights); or (3) let him know that you are dissatisfied with how he drives, and until you are convinced he will be safe, you will not lend the car (interests). Thus, disputes can occur on any one of the three levels.

Figure 4.2 illustrates an effective system where the emphasis is on interest, with rights and power playing smaller but still important roles. As you can see by comparing figure 4.1 with figure 4.2, an overemphasis on power is symptomatic of a distressed system.

Both/And Power

There is, however, at least one alternative to viewing disputes as power struggles. Boulding notes that "the great fallacy, especially of political thinking in regard to power, is to elevate threat power to the position of dominance" (1989, 10). Interpersonal relationships reflect the same fallacy—many people just can't envision power in terms other than "either/or" or "win/lose." Yet a study of the dynamics of successful disputes and ongoing relationships reveals that power functions on a broader basis than either/or thinking. *Disputes are power struggles if the parties allow them to be defined as such.* If we think of power "merely in terms of threat, we will get nowhere" (250). Conceptually, the alternative to framing disputes as power struggles is to place power in a subordinate position to rights and needs.

Figure 4.2 Power de-emphasized in an effective system

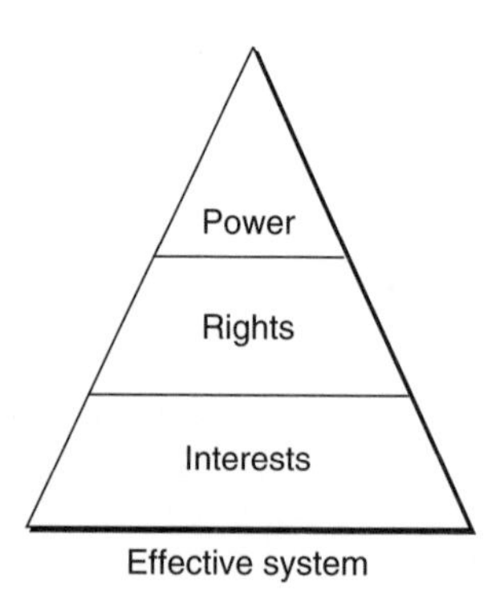

Source: From William Ury, Jeanne M. Brett, and Stephen B. Goldberg, *Getting Disputes Resolved: Designing Systems to Cut the Costs of Conflict.* Copyright © 1988 Jossey-Bass Inc., Publishers, San Francisco, California. Reprinted by permission.

To help us understand the cultural basis of our assumptions, Augsburger (1992) details the lack of verbal fighting in some other cultures. In these cultures, power is activated as "both/and."

> There are cultures, the Japanese and Javanese, to name two obvious examples . . . where harmony and cooperation are basic values, verbal contradiction is not the automatic first choice in conflict. A more accepted process is to affirm the strengths of each other's position, let them stand without attack, and then join in exploring other options. Both parties search for superior options (59)

"Power sharing" and how it works in disputes will be discussed later as an alternative to the "power over" thinking that is so prevalent in our culture.

Power Denial

Some people are so "antagonized by any discussion of power" (Madanes 1981, 217) that they may deny that power and influence are appropriate topics for discussion. We often try to convince ourselves and others that control is not part of our interpersonal patterns. One student wrote that in her relationship with her boyfriend, "No one has to have power—we just listen to each other, try to respond with love, and always put the relationship and each other first." She seemed to think that acknowledging the use of power would destroy her perfect relationship with her boyfriend.

Many people view power as negative and find "explicit references to power . . . in bad taste" (Kipnis 1976, 2). Cahill, conducting research on married couples, encountered this view when he interviewed them about their relationships. When he asked them about decision making, persuasive techniques, and disagreements, the discussion flowed smoothly. But when he asked about their relative amounts of power, he encountered long silences, halting answers, obvious embarrassment, and reluctance to speak of the topic (Cahill 1982). Similarly, McClelland (1969) noted that people who were told they had high drives to achieve or affiliate derived great satisfaction from the feedback, but people who were told they had a high drive for power experienced guilt.

In its extreme form, reluctance to talk about power emerges as power denial. Haley (1959) listed four common attempts people use to deny that they exercise power. These four forms of denial are presented in the following box.

Denying Power Use

1. Deny that *you* communicated something.
2. Deny that something *was* communicated.
3. Deny that you communicated something *to the other person.*
4. Deny the *situation* in which it was communicated.

The speaker can deny that *he or she* is doing the communicating by using a number of common ploys, such as saying, "I'm not myself when I drink," or, "It's just the pressure I'm under that's making me act like such a grouch." You may hear the claim, "I can't help it. I *told* you I was jealous. I'm not responsible for what I said." To say that you are not responsible for your communication lets you exercise control (if others accept your claim) while denying that you are doing so.

Denying that *a message was communicated* is another way to ignore the existence of power. The simplest way to deny communication is to say, "I did not say that." Since this kind of denial usually gets you in trouble after a while, another form develops, such as, "I forgot I said that. Did I really say that? I didn't mean to." For example, one supervisor might consistently forget to include the new members of a staff in the lines of communication in an agency. As a result, the newer, less powerful members are often late for meetings or miss them totally, having to reschedule other meetings at the last minute. When confronted by the workers left out of the message flow, the supervisor might say, "I thought that was taken care of. I'm sorry."

Denying that *a message was communicated to a particular person* is another way of expressing discomfort with the exercise of power. For example, a salesperson rings the doorbell of an apartment complex, and the following dialogue ensues:

Salesperson: Hello, I'd like to take this opportunity . . .

Apartment dweller: People are bothering me too much! Oh, I'm not talking about you. It's just that everyone bugs me day in and day out. I get no peace of mind. I wish the world would calm down and leave me alone.

Salesperson: Maybe I can see you another time. I'm sorry I bothered you. . . .

The person who was bothered is exercising considerable control in the communicative transaction and at the same time is denying that control by pretending that the remarks are not meant for that particular salesperson. Another common way of denying that your comments were addressed to the other person is to claim that you were "just thinking out loud" and did not mean to imply anything toward the other person. For instance, a boss might say, muttering under his or her breath, "If I could count on people . . ." Then when a subordinate asks what is wrong, the boss might say, "What? Oh, nothing—just a hard day."

The last way to deny communicative power attempts is to deny that what has been said applies to *this situation.* Saying, "I'm used to being treated unfairly by others; I probably always will be," denies the clear implication that the person now present is acting in a demeaning manner.

All of the preceding examples are ways that people can deny exercising power in a relationship when, in fact, they really are exercising power. Whenever you communicate with another, what you say and do exercises some communicative control—you either go along with someone else's definition of the conflict, struggle over the definition, or supply it yourself. Even if you would rather be seen as a person who does not exert power, *you exercise influence on how the conflict interaction is going to be defined.*

Working with Power

Power does not have to be viewed as finite (either/or), as a limited commodity that can be used up. Whereas competitive, power-over conflict management is part of life, constructive conflict management almost always depends on the *search for power with others.* Constructive power use, and ways to think about power integratively, will now be presented.

Power is Ubiquitous

We all try to exert some form of communicative influence—to influence others in order to accomplish our goals. This influence can focus on either independent, individual goals or goals that are interdependent and relationally oriented. Attempting to gain more power and influence in a conflict does not have to be seen as negative; power is necessary to move a conflict along to some kind of resolution. If people have no influence over each other, they cannot participate in conflict together, since their communication will have no impact. With no influence, people are not in a conflict but are simply in a mutual monologue. In addition to the constructive use of influence, the use of power that directly harms relationships or hinders individual goals will be discussed. Power is central to the study of conflict and can be used for collaborative or destructive ends—it is always present.

The centrality of power in conflict can be seen in the following example.

Power Play

In a medical clinic in a rural town, a conflict over flextime had been brewing for several months. The doctor in charge of the clinic traveled frequently since she had a split appointment, with responsibilities elsewhere. The administrative assistant in the office had been formally warned twice about her less-than-satisfactory performance. Her supervisor warned her against excessive use of sick days, coming in late, and overall negligent work. The administrative assistant used typical low-power tactics such as forgetting, making mistakes, calling in sick, apologizing, and losing files. She was unhappy with the way the office policies, especially policies related to flexible time and travel, were set up, believing them to be unfairly weighted toward professional staff and against hourly employees. When the assistant had trouble with child care or needed to go to appointments, she had to work out these plans with the administrative office. The physician was also a mother with two young children, like the administrative assistant. However, because the physician was classified as professional staff, she did not have to clear her plans with anyone in the office but worked her schedule out with a supervisor in another state.

The conflict about flexible time finally erupted. When the doctor was at a professional meeting in another state, she discovered that no hotel reservations had been made, the conference fee had not been paid, and the slides that were supposed to have been mailed to the conference had not arrived, making it difficult to give the presentation she had planned. When the doctor arrived back at the office, ready to fire the assistant, she found that the assistant had resigned without notice.

In "Power Play," a seemingly unequal power situation was suddenly balanced by the resignation of the assistant—a classic "got you now" move on the part of the low-power person. Each of the participants in this conflict attempted to exercise communicative influence (Millar and Rogers 1987). In fact, exercising influence or control is one of the basic human needs. Schutz (1966) postulates that all people need a sense of inclusion, affection, and control to be satisfied and to grow in their relationships. Even the youngest infant exercises influence. Bell's (1968, 1971) research demonstrated that infants and their caretakers mutually influenced one another. In fact, the behavior of the caretakers was more dependent on the infants than vice versa (Huston 1983). The ability to meaningfully influence important events around you is necessary for a sense of well-being and personal effectiveness.

That power is central to the study of conflict does not mean that people are always sneaky and try to get power illegitimately. Rather, the productive exercise of personal power is crucial to your self-concept. Without some exercise of power in your interpersonal relationships, you would soon feel worthless as a person. As you read this chapter, use your sources of feedback (friends, memories, personal writing, family members) to gain understanding about your own uses of power. Try to gain a "power profile" of your own behavior—the way you really communicate, not just the way you might want to be seen. Sometimes there is a difference! Remember that just as one cannot not communicate (Watzlawick, Beavin, and Jackson 1967), *one does not have the option of not using power.* We only have options about whether to use power destructively or productively for ourselves and relationships.

A Relational Theory of Power

A common perception is that power is an attribute of a person. If you say, "Lynn is a powerful person," you may, if she is your friend, be referring to such attributes as verbal facility, intelligence, compassion, warmth, and understanding. Or you may refer to a politician as powerful, alluding to her ability to make deals, call in her debts, remember names and faces, and understand complex economic issues. In interpersonal relationships, however, excluding situations of unequal physical power and use of violence, *power is a property of the social relationship rather than a quality of the individual.* Lynn, for instance, has power with her friends because she has qualities they value. When she suggests something to do, like going on an annual women's backpacking trip, her friends try to clear their calendars because they like her, have fun with her, and feel understood by her. Lynn has a way of making a group feel cohesive and at ease. But if an acquaintance hated backpacking, did not like some of the other people going on the trip, and was irritated at Lynn because of a misunderstanding that had not yet been cleared up, Lynn's power with the irritated acquaintance would lessen considerably. Similarly, if a politician did not show any interest in a bill that a human rights group was trying to get on the table in their state legislature and, furthermore, if the politician were a congresswoman representing another state, the congresswoman would have little power with the human rights group. Would she still be "a powerful person"? She would be to her constituents but not to the interest group in question.

Power is not owned by an individual but is a product of the social relationship in which certain qualities become important and valuable to others (King 1987; Rogers 1974; Harsanyi 1962a; Deutsch 1958; Dahl 1957; Soloman 1960). Deutsch (1973) states the case well: "Power is a relational concept; it does not reside in the individual but rather in the relationship of the person to his environment. Thus, the power of an agent in a given situation is determined by the characteristics of the situation" (15). Rather than residing in people, "power is always interpersonal" (May 1972, 23). In the strictest sense, except when violence and physical coercion are used, power is *given* from one party to another in a conflict. Each person in a conflict has some degree of power, though one party may have more *compared to* the other, and the power can shift during a conflict.

One way to analyze one's degree of power has been explored by Emerson (1962), who specified that a person's power is directly tied to the nature of the relationship. In terms of two people, A and B, person A has power over person B to the extent that B is dependent on A for goal attainment. Likewise, person B has power over person A to the extent that A is dependent on B. The following box expresses this simple formula.

$P_{AB} = D_{BA}$
(the power of A over B is equal to the dependence that B has on A), and
$P_{BA} = D_{AB}$
(the power of B over A is equal to the dependence that A has on B).

Your dependence on another person is a function of (1) *the importance of the goals the other can influence* and (2) *the availability of other avenues* for you to accomplish what you want. As Emerson states, "The dependence of Actor B upon Actor A is directly proportional to B's motivational investment in goals mediated by A, and inversely proportional to the availability of those goals to B outside of the A-B relation" (1962, 31). When trying to expand your power, it becomes important to increase the other person's dependency on you. This process builds a relationship and takes time to accomplish (Donohue and Kolt 1992). Increasing another's dependencies on you can be constructive or destructive. In the example cited earlier, when the administrative assistant assured the physician that she would take care of the arrangements for the conference and then did not, she destructively increased (temporarily) the doctor's dependence on her. If the supervisor and physician had rethought the flexible-time needs of the office staff and then given desired resources (flexible time off) if the staff followed the new guidelines, this change would be an example of constructively increasing dependencies.

One way to reduce power others have over you is to change your goals. If after a few years in a new job a person is not valued by an organization, a change of goals will likely occur. The disenchanted employee might remark, "It is not important to me what they pay me for this job. I'll just do the minimal amount of work and expend all my creative energy on my hobbies." By altering the importance of the goal, you reduce the power the other has over you. And the often heard remark, "There are other fish in the sea," when a person has been dropped in a love affair is just another way of saying that you have alternative sources for accomplishing your goals. (Or at least you hope you do, and you want other people to think you do!)

Power Currencies

You may have had the experience of traveling in a foreign country and trying to adapt to the use of different currencies. Drachmas, used in Greece, are worthless in Italy, where lira are used to buy items of value. A pocketful of pounds is worthless in France unless you exchange it for the local currency. Just as money depends on the context in which it is to be spent (the country), your power currencies depend on how much your particular resources are valued by the other persons in your relationships (Rodman 1967, 1972). You may have a vast amount of expertise in the rules of basketball, but if your fraternity needs an intramural football coach, you will not be valued. *Power depends on having currencies that other people need.* In the same manner, if other people possess currencies you value, such as the ability to edit a term paper or the possession of a car, they potentially maintain some degree of power over you in your relationships with them. Conflict is often confusing because people try to spend currency that is not valued in a particular relationship.

Power currencies are classified many different ways by researchers. Raven and French (1956) label the bases of power as reward, coercive, legitimate, referent, and expert. Kipnis (1976) maintains that influential tactics are best classified as threats and promises, persuasion, reinforcement control, and information control. May (1972) notes five types of power: exploitative, manipulative, competitive, nutrient, and integrative. Folger, Poole, and Stutman (1993) supply this list: special skills and abilities, expertise about the task, personal attractiveness and likability, control over rewards and/or punishments, formal position in a group, loyal allies, persuasive skills, and control over critical group possessions. Despite the various labels, the consensus is that everyone has potential currencies that may be used to balance or gain power in a relationship. Even when you are used to devaluing your own currency, a careful analysis can show you areas of wealth. The following box presents a list of general power currencies.

R

Resource control: Often comes with one's formal position in an organization or group. An example is the controlling of rewards or punishments such as salary, number of hours worked, or firing. Parents control resources such as money, freedom, cars, and privacy for teenagers.

I

Interpersonal linkages: Your position in the larger system, such as being central to communication exchange. If you are a liaison person between two factions, serve as a bridge between two groups that would otherwise not have information about each other, or have a network of friends who like each other, you have linkage currencies.

C

Communication skills: Conversational skills, persuasive ability, listening skills, group leadership skills, the ability to communicate caring and warmth, and the ability to form close bonds with others all contribute to interpersonal power. All people need to be related to others, to matter to others, and to be understood by others. Those who communicate well gain value and thus interpersonal power.

E

Expertise: Special knowledge, skills, and talents that are useful for the task at hand. Being an expert in a content area such as budget analysis, a process area such as decision-making methods, or a relational area such as decoding nonverbal cues may give you power when others need your expertise.

Resource control often results from attaining a formal position that brings resources to you. The president of the United States, regardless of personal qualities, will always have some resources that go along with the job. Leadership and position, by their very nature, place a person in a situation in which others are dependent upon him or her, thus bringing ready-made power. Whatever your position—secretary, boss, chairperson, teacher, manager, or volunteer—you will be in a position to control resources that others desire. Many resources are economic in nature, such as money, gifts, and material possessions (Warner, Lee, and Lee 1986). Many people try to be close and supportive to those around them by buying gifts. They trade on economic currencies in order to obtain intimacy currencies from others. Their gifts are not always valued enough to bring them what they want, however. Not surprisingly, people who give gifts to each other often try to work out an agreement, probably implicitly, about the amount of money that can be spent to keep the dependence (and power) equal. If an inordinate amount of money is spent by one person, then typically the other person feels overly indebted. As Blau (1964, 108) writes, "A person who gives others valuable gifts or renders them important services makes a claim for superior status by obligating them to himself." People with little money usually have limited access to these forms of power. College graduates who cannot find jobs must remain financially dependent on parents, thus limiting independence on both sides. Elderly people whose savings shrink due to inflation lose power; mothers with children and no means of support lose most of their choices about independence, thus losing most of their potential power. Economic currencies are not the only important type of power currency, but they operate in small, personal conflicts as well as in larger social conflicts.

Another cluster of power currencies comes from one's *interpersonal linkages,* a set of currencies that depend on your interpersonal contacts and network of friends and supporters. People often obtain power based on whom they know and with whom they associate. For instance, if you have a good friend who has a mountain cabin you can share with others, then you have attained some power (if your family or friends want to go to the cabin) because of your ability to obtain things through other people. Young children try to trade on their linkage currencies when they say such things as, "My Uncle Ben is a park ranger, and he will give us a tour of the park."

Interpersonal linkages help one attain power through coalition formation. Whenever you band together with another (such as a good friend) to gain some sense of strength, this coalition can be a form of power (Van de Vliert 1981). The small boy who says, "You better not hit me, because if you do, my big sister will beat you up," understands the potential value of coalitions. Similarly, Jason, a four-year-old boy, invented a friendly ghost, Karsha, who would come and help him in times of difficulty. After one particularly trying day with his younger sister (who was two years old), Jason recited to his father the virtues of Karsha. Karsha was "bigger than a mountain, a giant, who comes in the mornings and kills spiders with his hands. Karsha also makes electricity and has long hair. And Karsha is mean to babies that bite little boys."

One's *communication skills* also serve as potential power currencies. The person who can lead a group through effective decision making or galvanize political action with skills of persuasion may be granted considerable power by others. Conversationally, your skills make a considerable difference, too. As Millar and Rogers (1988) demonstrated, when others allow us to dominate the conversation we have attained a source of power. Likewise, if you can facilitate the social process of a group, serve as the fun-loving joker in the family, or get conversations started at work, others typically will value you. It is not only the qualities, per se, that bring power but that these currencies are valued by others.

Communication skills also include the ability to form bonds with others through love, sex, caring, nurturing, understanding, empathic listening, warmth, attention, and other characteristics of intimate relationships. If a father provides genuine warmth and understanding to his teenage daughter who is going through a tough time at school, his support is a currency for him in their father-daughter relationship. Some people draw others to them because they listen attentively, remember what is important to others, and ask questions that show the importance of the others. These qualities should not be viewed as manipulative because if one's words and actions are not sincere, the phony quality of the communication becomes evident and power is not enhanced. Conflict management skills depend on a thorough grounding in communication skills. One cannot become an effective conflict manager without excellent interpersonal communication skills. These skills provide a positive base for the exercise of *power with others,* or relational power.

Expertise currencies are involved when a person has some special skill or knowledge that someone else values. The worker who is the only one who can operate the boiler at a large lumber mill has power because the expertise is badly needed. The medical doctor who specializes in a particular area has expertise power because the information and skills are needed by others. Almost all professions develop specialized expertise valued by others, which serves as a basis of power for people in the profession. Family members develop expertise in certain areas that others within the family come to depend on, such as cooking, repairing the car, or babysitting.

We limit our own power by developing some currencies at the expense of others. For example, women have traditionally been most comfortable using power to bond with others (Miller 1991), providing more warmth and affection that men do (Johnson 1976). If this particular communication skill is developed at the expense of the ability to clarify a group discussion, a woman unnecessarily limits her power potential. The person who trades on currencies of interpersonal linkages, such as access to the boss, may neglect the development of expertise. The person who gains power by controlling resources, such as money or sex, may neglect the development of communication skills, resulting in a relationship based on coercive instead of shared power; withdrawing warmth in intimate relationships too often substitutes for good communication skills. A coworker who focuses on the development of expertise in computer programming and systems analysis may ignore the power that can be developed through interpersonal linkages, thus furthering a tendency toward isolation in the organization. The most effective conflict participant develops several forms of power currencies and knows when to activate the different forms of power. A repertoire of currencies is a better base for sharing power than exclusive reliance on one form of power, which too often leads to misuse of that power.

Clarifying the currencies available to you and the other parties in a conflict helps in the conflict analysis. People are often unaware of their own sources of productive power, just as they do not understand their own dependence on others. Desperation and low-power tactics often arise from the feeling that one has no choice, that no power is available. Analyze your power currencies when you find yourself saying, "I have no choice." Usually, you are overlooking potential sources of power.

Assessing Power Accurately

Since power is a dynamic product of shifting relationships, the amount of power parties have at any one time cannot be measured precisely. One maxim to remember when you are in the middle of a conflict is this: "Each person firmly believes that the other person has more power." Many of the pathologies or misuses of power arise because the image people have of their power (and others') is unrealistic (Boulding 1989, 65). Because each person in the conflict so often believes that he or she is in the low-power position, the conflict escalates. People use devious, sneaky, and manipulative tactics, since they truly think they have no choice. This perception is almost always inaccurate. In this section, ways of assessing power more accurately than by using one's emotional state are presented. Of course, you won't get out a conflict assessment instrument to have everyone fill out right in the middle of an interaction. But familiarizing yourself with these instruments and concepts will help you think through what is happening, what has happened in the past, and what you would like to have happen in future interactions. Several assessment approaches are useful (Huston 1983; Millar and Rogers 1988; Witteman and Fitzpatrick 1986; Millar and Rogers 1987). The most common way to measure power is to compare the relative resources of the parties in a conflict (Berger 1980; Galvin and Brommel 1982; McCall 1979). For instance, in organizational work, it is generally agreed that power accrues to "those departments that are most instrumental in bringing in or providing resources which are highly valued by the total organization" (McCall 1979). People have power in the organization when they

- are in a position to deal with important problems;
- have control over significant resources valued by others;
- are lucky or skilled enough to bring problems and resources together at the same time;
- are centrally connected in the work flow of the organization;
- are not easily replaced; and
- have successfully used their power in the past (McCall 1979).

This method of assessing power places high reliance on the resources controlled by a person or group on whom the organization is dependent. Although it provides a useful starting point, this method has two limitations:

1. It defines resources too narrowly (Berger 1980).

2. It puts too much emphasis on the *source* of the influence. Overemphasis on the source is characteristic of most studies of power, such as the "bases of power" work of Raven and French (1956) and the research of Kipnis (1976). Most assessments of power view the relationship as one-way. Person A is seen as exerting influence on person B. In diagram form, the relationship looks like this:

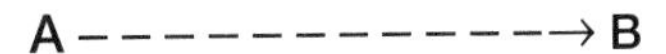

The relational perspective presented thus far characterizes the communication as two-way: each participant has power with the other. The relationship looks like this:

A ←-----------→ B

Most research presents power as a static property and disregards the dynamic elements of power (Bochner 1976). Resources are treated as possessions rather than as a changing part of the relationship process. One would assess power, using this perspective, by examing the resources that one party possesses. Many popular books on power take this individualistic approach.

Research on power has also focused on *decision making* or *conversational control* within the family unit. Decision-making approaches began with the classic Blood and Wolfe (1960) study of Detroit housewives. They asked wives questions such as "Who decides where the family will take a vacation?" and "Who decides what job to take?" Researchers in subsequent years tried to analyze power similarly by asking "Who has the last say about spending money?" (Safilios-Rothschild 1970), "Who is the real boss in the family?" (Heer 1963), and "Who would decide how you would spend $300?" (Kenkel 1957). It seemed reasonable that the most powerful member of a family would be the one who decided most of the important decisions; unfortunately, there were difficulties with this popular method of measuring power. First, the researchers did not ask both spouses the questions. They might have received different answers if they had asked each partner separately. Second, the questions asked for "perceived authority"—who the participants thought made most of the decisions rather than who actually did (Bochner 1976; McDonald 1980). As a result, the participants may well have answered according to who they thought *should* have been making decisions. Given the sex-role stereotypes of that time period, a woman may have not wanted to tell a researcher that she was "the real boss." Whether accurate or not, women usually reported that their husbands made most of the decisions (Turk and Bell 1972).

In other cases researchers have studied decision making in the laboratory by presenting decision-making tasks such as responding to conflict stories or trying to match subtly different colors (Olson and Straus 1972; Olson and Rabunsky 1972). The problem with this approach was that many times the people completing the decision-making tasks together were strangers to each other. Obviously, people act differently with strangers than they do with intimates. In an extensive review of the decision-making assessments of power, McDonald says, "After twenty years of studying marital decision making, we actually may know little more than the authority expectations of couples" (1980, 850). He then argues that more research should focus on the "powering processes" or the interaction between the parties (Sprey 1972; Scanzoni 1979).

Conversational control is the other main way researchers have attempted to study power (Millar and Rogers 1987, 1988). At one time or another, you have probably judged someone as powerful because he or she controlled the conversation. Many researchers have studied conversational control in couples (Mishler and Waxler 1968; Rogers and Farace 1975; Rogers-Millar and Millar 1977; Ellis 1979). Assuming that conversational control and power were the same thing, these researchers studied who talked the most, who interrupted the most, who changed topics the most, and who engaged in more "one up" moves.

These two measures of power, decision making and conversational control, do not measure the same concept. If you look at different measures of power, you will probably reach different conclusions about who is most powerful (Olson and Rabunsky 1972; Turk and Bell 1972; Bochner 1976; Berger 1980; McDonald 1980). With a group of people serving as the audience, try this experiment: watch a movie, role play, or video presentation of two people in conflict, with the audience making notes on who appears to be more powerful. You will probably find that almost everyone in the audience has a different way of deciding who *really* is more powerful. For some it may be nonverbal dominance, for others, vocal quality, for still others, amount of time spent in overt argument, and so on. In essence, no single validating criterion for assessing power has been discovered by researchers; such a surefire technique may not exist (Gray-Little 1982; Berger 1980).

Power is especially difficult to assess when influence is exercised covertly or in hidden ways. Most of us have trouble deciphering covert power, or choices made based on another person's potential influence. For example, Will is an outdoors man who would like to take a weeklong hunting trip, but he knows that his wife will not like being left alone for such an extended period of time since she works and would have to assume all the care of the children. Will proposes a two-day trip and, in the process, talks more and controls the discussion. An observer might guess that Will was in control of both process and outcome, since he and his wife agree that he will go on the two-day trip. Yet Will's conversation was structured around his estimate of his wife's reaction. Her power was important to his decision, yet an outside observer could not have known that without asking.

People who look the most powerful to outsiders often are less powerful than they appear. In fact, without knowing the structure of a relationship, you cannot guess who has the most power, since people balance their power currencies in complex ways. For instance, if one person "lets" the other do the talking for the group, the person who gives tacit permission for the other to talk is actually controlling the situation. Gender issues come into play, since women in our culture cannot usually become the powerful aggressor without facing social disapproval or physical danger. Many women learn to seek safety and power by hiding, becoming invisible, or becoming relationally oriented. Whereas a woman's safety and power needs are often met *by becoming smaller and less visible,* the traditional masculine style of seeking safety is by becoming the feared individual, *by becoming bigger and more visible* (Kaschak, 1992, 126). A woman's use of power often exposes her to denigration and attack, whereas a man's use of power may be viewed as evidence that men are insensitive to the feelings of others.

Power is exercised in supposedly weak ways, also. Sometimes the most powerful behavior is to submit, go weak, or act in a nonresistant way. An example of this form of power was Martin Luther King Jr.'s civil rights tactics, based on Gandhian principles, in which civil rights workers were trained to sit down when confronted by powerful persons, to protect their bodies if attacked but not to attack in response, and to use nonaggressive verbal responses. As happened in India, weakness in the face of strength made stronger persons question their use of force and coercion. A less productive "weak" way of exercising power is that of the apocryphal army private who, when ordered to do KP duty, does as sloppy a job as possible while asking constantly, "Is this the way?" "Am I doing it right?" This "reluctant soldier" example can be seen in offices, in families, and on work crews where one person is "trying" (but failing) to get it right. The supervisor, parent, or crew boss then gets disgusted and does the job himself or herself.

Another supposedly weak way to gain power is to refuse to cooperate when other people are depending on you. When this tactic is used in conjunction with unexpressed anger, it is labeled *passive aggressive behavior.* In passive aggression, a person acts aggressively (in one's own self-interest, without much regard for the other) by being passive or unconcerned when the other person needs a response. Passive aggression is displayed when people feel they have low power, whether they do or not, since it appears to be a safer way of expressing anger, resentment, or hostility than stating such feelings directly. Additionally, "nice" people (Bach and Goldberg 1974) may use passive aggression instead of direct conflict statements because they have been taught that it is not nice to engage in conflict. Bach and Goldberg's (1974) list of common passive aggressive behaviors has been expanded to include the following:

- Forgetting appointments, promises, and agreements
- Slipping and saying unkind things, then apologizing
- Acting out nonverbally, such as slamming doors and banging objects, but denying that anything is wrong
- Getting confused, tearful, sarcastic, or helpless when certain topics come up
- Getting sick when you've promised to do something
- Scheduling two things at once
- Evading situations so that others are inconvenienced

The following box presents a case of passive-aggressive communication.

> Two college roommates have a practice of borrowing each other's possessions. When Jan and Cheryl first moved in together, they decided it would be inconvenient to ask each time they wanted to use a CD or borrow an article of clothing. Cheryl has been keeping Jan's things longer than Jan wants her to, however, often causing Jan to have to look for her CDs, textbooks, car keys, sweaters, skis, and gloves. Recently, Jan lost several of Cheryl's possessions, including a CD she took to a party. She feels justified since Cheryl has been misusing the privilege, too. They are avoiding the issue and spending time away from each other.

The "cure" for passive aggression is to confront angry feelings directly instead of indirectly. The college professor who double-schedules may feel overloaded and underappreciated and may be communicating that fact by mixing up schedules. A better practice would be to tell people directly that too many appointments are interfering with the rest of his or her work so that people know why the professor is less available.

Power, in summary, is a complex and elusive concept. Conflict parties inevitably have different views of the power dynamics in their relationships; these discrepant perceptions keep the conflicts going. Power, as we have seen, is a difficult concept to assess accurately. One kernel of wisdom to remember is this: assume that you and your conflict partner measure each other's power differently, disagree on who has the most, and disagree on who should have the most.

Power Imbalances

In most relationships, there are times when the participants become aware of discrepancies in their relative power with one another. Conflict behaviors highlight different levels of power and allow participants to see the discrepancy (Rummel 1976; Dahl 1963; Rollins and Bahr 1976). If one party has more power than the other, the conflict is unbalanced; many of the choices the parties then make are attempts to alter these imbalances. Keep in mind that power is always a relative judgment—each party has sources of power even during times of imbalance. Such power asymmetries have predictable effects on both the higher- and lower-power parties, and the imbalance produces system-wide effects on the relationship.

High Power

The exercise of social power for most people in Western culture is satisfying and even produces joy (Bowers and Ochs 1971; May 1972). High power is often a goal that people strive for; those with less power often feel, "If I were just the boss, things would be a lot better around here." The major difficulty with having higher power than someone else is that it may corrupt. *Corruption* is more than a word that describes a crooked politician. Corruption means moral decay, rottenness, and inability to maintain the integrity of the self. Constant high power may "eat into" one's view of self and other, forming a perceptual distortion that may take on monstrous proportions. Higher-power persons, organizations, or nations may develop altered views of themselves and other parties. Constant feelings of power can result in these consequences:

1. A "taste for power" and the restless pursuit for more power as an end in itself
2. The temptation to illegally use institutional resources as a means of self-enrichment
3. False feedback concerning self-worth and the development of new values designed to protect power
4. The devaluing of the less powerful and the avoidance of close social contact with them (Kipnis 1976, 178)

The undesirable consequences of a power imbalance can take many forms. For instance, studies show that if a teacher uses strong power over a student, the relationship disintegrates into the exclusive use of coercive strategies (Jamieson and Thomas 1974; Raven and Kruglanski 1970). Or the person highest in power may claim benevolence, that harmful actions are actually "for the good of the other person," thereby dismissing the negative consequences to the lower-power person. When someone is fired from an organization, it is common to hear, "It was for her/his own good—he/she will be better off spending time doing X." According to Guggenbuhl-Craig (1971), persons in helping professions, such as ministers, teachers, health workers, and others, can lose touch with their need to exercise power in order to feel valued and needed. Although helpers undoubtedly are in their professions in order to help, they also must have "helpees," or they have no function. How can a physician be a physician without people who need healing? How can teachers teach if no one values learning? If helpers do not understand that helping also contributes to their own sense of self-worth and personal fulfillment, the act of helping can become a high-power move. Just as during the Inquisition, when the learned scholars were sure that they were helping the persons accused of heresy, unrestrained high power may make the powerful party blind to the havoc wreaked on the less powerful party. You may have had times in your personal relationships when power became unbalanced; if so, you know the harm that unrestrained power can bring, whether you were the one with too much power or the one without enough power.

Striving for higher power can destroy even the best of relationships. For example, in intimate relationships, the person who is least invested in the relationship has the most power (the "Principle of Least Interest," Waller 1938). Paradoxically, decreasing the investment for the purpose of gaining higher power is ultimately self-defeating, since you have to continue your decreasingly fragile investment in order to remain more powerful. And the lessened dependence can lead to the demise of the relationship. If you convince yourself that "I don't have to put up with this," then you don't usually stay in the relationship.

Finally, persons or nations with higher power can deny that power is exercised; they may deny that there is a conflict (it is a "minor disagreement") or use any of the other forms of denial mentioned earlier. Unrestrained higher power can corrupt the power holder's view of the self and view of the other, and it can set the stage for continued unproductive interaction.

Low Power

Just as power can corrupt, powerlessness can also corrupt (May 1972). If lower-power people are continually subjected to harsh treatment or lack of goal attainment, they will likely produce some organized resistance to the higher-power people. When one reaches the stage where "nothing matters" (one cannot attain his or her goals through accepted means), violence or despair is spawned. It is the person who feels powerless who turns to the last resort—giving up, aggression, or violence (Richmond et al. 1984; Kipnis, Schmidt, and Wilkerson 1980; Falbo and Peplau 1980). Too much losing does not build character; it builds frustration, aggression, or apathy. A typical example of how perceived unequal power results in aggression is the relationship between students and teachers. In one study, when students were asked what they considered doing to resolve conflicts they had with more powerful teachers, they replied on paper, "Use a .357 magnum," "Blow up his mailbox," "Sabotage him," and "Beat him up" (Wilmot 1976). At the very least, asymmetry in perceived power can lead to coercion in an attempt to "get even" (Jamieson and Thomas 1974; Raven and Kruglanski 1970).

In severe, repetitive conflicts, *both* parties feel low power, and they continually make moves to increase their power at the other's expense. Since, as noted, the assessment of power is problematic, it is very difficult to determine the exact levels of power in a conflict. However, if each party *believes* she or he has less power than the other, a destructive, escalatory spiral of conflict usually results. Each party attempts to increase power at the other's expense, with the next round bringing yet more destructive moves. Each person feels "behind" and justified in engaging in dirty moves because of what the other did.

A Power Spiral

Tom and Paula were a married couple with two small children. Tom felt the financial pressure of providing for the young family since he and Paula had decided that Paula would work at home, caring full-time for the children until they were at school. Tom, a dentist, scheduled more patients during each day and arrived home later than he used to. To release the increased stress, he set up golf games with friends on the weekends, something he and Paula used to do together. Paula felt lonely and upset that Tom was spending more time at work and with his friends. She let Tom know that she needed more help at home and asked him to pitch in with some of the chores around the house and with getting the children bathed and put to bed. Tom resented being asked to do more at home, since he felt his financial contributions to the family were unappreciated. Paula felt taken for granted and tired of being alone with the two children. Both *felt* low power but acted in ways that communicated to each other that they were really *higher* in power than the other. Both felt justified in their escalating anger at each other. Both felt lonely, unappreciated, misunderstood, and scared. They were only a few weeks away from "dirty tricks" when they sought professional help.

Often, as with Tom and Paula, even if the lower-power person wants to act aggressively, there are restraints against doing so. The powerless will try to restore equity, and if that fails, they have few options; one option is to use passive-aggressive behavior, as discussed previously. In addition, Madanes (1981) notes that developing severely dysfunctional behavior is an exercise of power that affects all close associates. Lower-power parties will sometimes destroy a relationship as the ultimate move to bring about a balance of power.

The combination of denigration from the higher-power person and destructive power-balancing moves from the lower-power person contributes to a system of interactions that is not productive for either party. A cyclical, degenerative, destructive conflict spiral characterizes the ongoing interactions. The power disparity promotes struggles over power (Brown 1983), increases the underlying bases of the conflict (Raven and Kruglanski 1970), and leads to lessened involvement in the relationship for both parties. The following box presents an example of power disparity.

Nobody Wins

Craig is a supervisor in a community agency, and Marilyn is a staff member who works part-time. Craig coerces Marilyn to take on a community volunteer program—a job she neither wanted nor had time to develop at a competent level. Marilyn resists working on the program, and deadlines are looming. Craig, noticing her subversion, forces her in a public meeting to agree to work hard on the program. Marilyn accedes (on the surface) but talks to her friends about how poorly she is treated. After two months of Craig's disapproval with her progress and of her seeking social support elsewhere, she resigns.

In the example presented in the preceding box, Craig did not accomplish his original goal of starting the community program, and Marilyn lost her job. They achieved a power balance in an unproductive manner, much like a game of leapfrog. When one person is behind, he or she then jumps into the lead, and the other person, sensing that he or she is "losing," does the same. Pretty soon the relationship is suffering, and neither person has achieved any of the original goals.

In cases of power disparity, agreements are "basically unstable since they are grounded on unilateral threats rather than on mutually established norms" (Apfelbaum 1974, 151). The ever accelerating unproductive moves are the result of attempts at power balancing through counterproductive means. The alternative is to balance the power through productive avenues and recognize that with extreme power asymmetry, effective long-term management is not likely.

Sharing Power and Collaboration

Integrative power depends very much on the power of language and communication, especially on the powers of persuasion.

—Boulding, *Three Faces of Power*

To this point, four sets of words have been used interchangeably—integrative power, both/and power, collaboration, and sharing power. What is the rationale for viewing power in such terms? This section will highlight how power can actually be shared in ongoing relationships.

Since destructive conflicts are often set off by struggles over power, and given that power is relational, it is impossible to not share power—the only question is how one goes about doing it. If you struggle with someone because "you won't give in," you are trying to block their exercise of power—and they are probably doing the same thing. The paradox is that *the more you struggle against someone the less power you will have with them.* From a both/and perspective, the more powerful we feel, the more we are setting ourselves up for resistance from the other party. Put bluntly, power-against is usually eventually blocked and diminished. Boulding says it well: "Power over human beings is very complex. Other human beings can answer back, fight back, obey or disobey, argue and try to exercise power over us, which a tree never does" (1989, 53). We must recognize that while we need to exercise appropriate power and influence, the other person needs to exercise influence as well, so we might as well cooperate with each other so we can both be effective. The both/and perspective assumes that you both want to accomplish your goals and that you need each other to do that. Since it is the other who is blocking you (and you blocking him or her), integrative power moves beyond the tug of war and to a new plane of relationship.

Whereas destructive struggling for power leads to a downward spiral of more thwarting and interference and to a lessened ability to accomplish your goals, shared power leads to a *synergy of power creation through productive communication.* As you work with each other, each of you stops directly interfering with the other and actively assists the other in getting what he or she wants (when you can), and the communication between the two of you serves a transcendent function (Wilmot 1995). Via cooperation you actually create more power than either of you could have created separately.

As Gray says, "Collaboration operates on a model of shared power" (1989, 119). Rarely will you be in a life situation where all the power resides with the other, which means that collaboration is almost always possible. Research on a number of fronts makes this clear. Alberts and Driscoll (1992) demonstrated that satisfied couples will "pass, refocus, mitigate or respond" to the other rather than struggle over power. The sense of "we-ness," working *together,* pulls romantic couples through their first big fight (Siegert and Stamp 1994).

"It's *Their* Fault"

Bruce is the production manager of a large electronics manufacturing facility, and Lenny is the engineering manager. They each supervise a five-person team of managers. Lenny's engineers are responsible for (1) designing systems for production and (2) quality control. Bruce's production employees are responsible for minimum output—they have to get the product out the door and shipped to customers. Over a two-year period, the two teams were really at loggerheads. Engineering staff were, both in their staff meetings and to the plant manager, saying, "Those production people—we design good systems for them to follow, they don't follow them, and then quality slips. What is their hang-up?" Meanwhile, production employees were openly criticizing the engineers on the manufacturing floor by saying, "They think they are so hot—yet their elaborate designs don't work, they treat us like slaves, and they don't know how we are being held to a minimum number of units produced."

Finally, the plant manager had to ask for outside help. The production and engineering managers met, as did the work teams. They agreed (1) to shift quality control to the production side, (2) to have the engineers provide training to the production employees so they could enforce quality control, (3) to not make any more negative public comments about the other team, and (4) to require the production and engineering managers to attend each other's staff meetings. What was a "power-against" situation became, over a period of a month, a "power-with" situation. The plant manager was very pleased that his two key players in engineering and production were now *helping* each other accomplish their goals rather than interfering with one another. Production output and quality both improved.

Conflict participants are more likely to make a long-range relationship work if they move toward equality in power. Models for productive power balancing, although scarce, do exist. In everyday life individuals *can* learn to cooperate and to reach agreements if power is distributed equitably or fairly (Apfelbaum 1974, 138). For relationships to work over time, people must continually realign the power balance as the situation warrants (Rummel 1976).

What can friends, coworkers, family members, or intimates do when they discover power asymmetry in their relationships? They can (1) work to make the relationships more equal, (2) try to convince themselves and their partners that the relationships are more equal than they might seem (by restoring psychological equality), or (3) eventually abandon the unbalanced relationships (Hatfield, Utne, and Traupmann 1979). For instance, family members negotiating household tasks may say, "I should get more credit for taking out the garbage than you do for cleaning the counters because I *hate* to take out the garbage and you don't mind doing the counters." The person who hates taking out garbage is trying to balance power by restoring psychological fairness. We are all too familiar with friendships that fail because of inadequate power balancing.

An interpersonal relationship with a power disparity between participants can achieve a more productive focus by moving toward balance. Just as the destructive attempts by lower-power parties to balance power are a move toward reciprocity, a move toward some balanced arrangement of power can lead the way to effective management (Wehr 1979). Power must be realigned in order for sharing to exist. The following techniques are ways for both high- and low-power parties to realign power balances.

Realigning Power Balances

When power is greatly unbalanced, people can take steps to realign power so work can proceed creatively and the relationship issues do not supercede the content issues.

Restraint

As unlikely as it might seem, higher-power parties can *limit their power* by refusing to use the currencies they have at their disposal. A militarily powerful nation that refuses to invade a neighboring country and a physically powerful spouse who refuses to inflict damage on the other spouse are examples of a higher-power party limiting power usage. If the high-power person refuses to engage in "natural" responses, this restraint can alter the automatic nature of a destructive cycle. Art, a college teacher, refuses to use punitive power when students present last-minute pleadings for more time to write final papers. Instead, Art simply says, "Why don't you set a deadline for the final paper that you can meet, and it will be fine with me. What day and time do you want to hand it in?" A married couple found a way to lower one member's economic power, thereby providing more balance in their relationship. They valued monetary equality and were used to having separate accounts and almost the same spendable income. The husband got an unexpected raise, however, and suddenly had more money to spend. They started arguing frequently because he would propose expensive weekends for recreation and his wife had difficulty paying for her half. In response to increasingly destructive arguments, he had more withheld from his monthly paycheck, to be put in a joint long-term savings plan. Then they would use this money occasionally for a "lost weekend." Even though he still had more money than his partner, the effect on them as a couple was lessened, while he gained the long-term advantages of saving more money. He limited his immediate use of his higher monetary power, with positive effects on the couple's balance of power.

Focus on Interdependence

One way to balance the power in a relationship is for lower-power individuals to focus on ways the people involved in the conflict are dependent on each other instead of demanding attention to their own individual needs (Donohue and Kolt 1992). Higher-power individuals usually try to minimize interdependence; therefore, lower-power individuals need to point out how the conflict parties are more related than it might appear. (The strategy of searching for overlapping interests will be discussed in detail in the next chapter.) When individuals are scared and feeling powerless, they often angrily demand that their own needs be met or begin to use threats. These are ineffective approaches, since the higher-power person has the ability to move away or lessen the interdependence.

A thorough understanding of interdependence clarifies power relationships. If John and Sarah are dating and decide to live together, they both increase their dependence on the other. Following Emerson's formula, as John becomes more dependent on Sarah, Sarah's power increases. Likewise, Sarah becomes more dependent on John, thereby increasing his power. When two people elevate their dependence on each other, *both* increase their sources of power. Each one expands his or her currencies that are valued by the other. Therefore, power in enduring relationships is *not* finite—it is an expandable commodity. The focus shouldn't be the singular amount of power each one has but the balance of power between them. John and Sarah may have little power with each other at the beginning of their relationship. Later, as each develops more power, the other's power rises approximately equally. The absolute amount of power may change, but the crucial issue is the comparative dependence that John and Sarah have on each other.

"Quick! It's an Emergency!"

Conflict Parties: Tom, a midlevel manager in an office; Helen, the secretary for four people in the office

Repetitive Conflict: Often when Helen is too busy to get all her work done immediately, she will set priorities and plan her schedule based on known deadlines. Tom's work makes up the largest share of Helen's work. Tom and the other three supervisors ranked equally on the organizational scale. However, when Tom is busy and pressed, he rushes to Helen's desk with work that needs to be done immediately.

Tom: Helen, I have just this one little thing that has to go out today.
Helen (sighing noticeably): Yes, Tom, I know—just one little thing. But I have to get this out for Joe today, and it must be done first.

Tom puts more pressure on Helen to do his job first by saying that it won't take long and that just this once she needs to respond to the emergency pressures. Helen gets angry and tries to persuade him that it can wait one more day. Then she pouts a bit.

Helen: I am only one person, you know. Just put it there and I'll *try* to get it done.
Tom: Helen, you're a sweetheart. When this madhouse calms down, I'll take you out to lunch. I knew I could count on you.

Helen then stays late to finish the work, but she asks her office manager to speak to Tom again about interfering with her ability to manage her work. Tom apologizes a few days later.

Tom: I didn't mean to make you mad. I didn't think that one report was going to tick you off so much.
Helen: It's OK; it's just that I can't please everybody.

In the scenario presented in the preceding box, the power may appear to be organized such that Tom has more because he is the boss and Helen has less because she occupies a lower position in the organization. A closer look reveals that the parties are fairly well-balanced in power. The balancing act is, however, taking a toll on their relationship, and the work could be managed more creatively. Tom is dependent on Helen for getting his work out error free, quickly, and with the benefit of Helen's experience. He depends on Helen to respond to his needs before those of the others in the office, since he is carrying more of the work in the office than the other three at his level. He sees himself as a pleasant and noncontrolling person whose employees work because they want to. He depends on Helen to view him as a reasonable and professional person because this is how he views himself. Helen, meanwhile, depends on Tom for some of her self-esteem. She prizes her ability to skillfully organize her work so that it gets done on time. She wants to be treated as a valuable, decision-making employee. She knows, too, that if Tom becomes dissatisfied with her work, he will complain to her immediate supervisor in the office, and she might be overlooked for promotions or might even lose her job. So Helen depends on Tom for positive ratings, a good work climate, and self-esteem. Restructuring their interactions could allow them to achieve more of their independent and interdependent goals. Helen could ask Tom to help her respond to disparate pressures; Tom could ask Helen how to set up a way to take care of emergencies. A problem-solving approach to conflict management would allow both to balance their power more collaboratively.

The Power of Calm Persistence

Lower-power people in a conflict often can gain more equal power by persisting in their requests. Substantive change, when power is unequal, seldom come about through intense, angry confrontation. Rather, change results from careful thinking and from planning for small, manageable moves based on a solid understanding of the problem (Lerner 1989, 15). When intensity is high, people react rather than observe and think. We overfocus on the other instead of the self and an analysis of the problem, and we move toward polarization. Lower-power parties cannot afford to blow up. One source of power the lower-power person has, however, is careful, calm analysis that directs attention to the problem. If lower-power people have patience and avoid giving up out of frustration, they have "nuisance value," and the higher-power person or group often listens and collaborates just to get them to go away.

Several examples of calm, clear, thoughtful persistence illustrate this strategy for increasing one's power. Ellen is the head of a large, successful consulting organization. She travels a lot and has a tightly organized schedule. A few years ago her daughter, Linda, whined and pouted about not being able to go horseback riding alone with her mother. This was ineffective since Ellen hates whining tactics. Finally, Linda, at age 8, hit upon a solution. She asked her mother for a "management meeting," in which she pointed out her complaints and asked for what she wanted. This approach so impressed her mother that with affection and humor, they broke through an avoid-pursue spiral. Linda gained power, and Ellen felt much better about how the two of them were spending time.

Individuals in conflict with institutions often experience frustrating, demeaning powerlessness as they are shunted from voice mail to clerk to yet another voice mailbox. Phone calls may not be returned, each succeeding contact passes the complaint along to someone else, and frustration rises dramatically. Sometimes only calm, clear persistence increases an individual's power enough for him or her to be heard and dealt with. Some suggestions for dealing with large, impersonal institutions are as follows:

- Identify the individuals on the phone by name and ask for them when you call back.
- Stay pleasant and calm. State clearly what you want, and ask for help in solving the problem.
- Follow the rules even if you think they are ridiculous. If they want five copies of a form, typed and folded a certain way, do it. Then point out that you have followed the rules and expect results.
- Write simple, clear memos summarizing what you want, what you have done, when you expect a response.
- Avoid taking out your frustration on low-power individuals in the organization. They may respond with, "I'm just following the rules," avoiding personal responsibility—and who could blame them? Instead, be courteous, and ask for help. Humor always helps if it is not at someone else's expense.

Stay Actively Engaged

Remaining in a low-power position, assuming that one's weakness is a permanent instead of a temporary condition, and adopting low-power tactics sets up a dangerously unbalanced situation that benefits no one, not even the high-power person. The higher-power person, who has the power to define the terms of the conflict in his or her own favor, often understands only one side of the conflict. Therefore, the higher-power person may not be able to find a constructive solution. People who perceive themselves as powerless usually do not talk effectively about their own needs and, after a while, may adopt a self-defeating, accommodating style that becomes fixed. When one person believes that the other person can go elsewhere for whatever is needed, the lower-power person tends to avoid conflict (Folger, Poole and Stutman 1993). If the fixed power position becomes intolerable, the lower-power person may act out of desperation, such as resigning, leaving a romantic relationship, blowing up and antagonizing the high-power person so that he or she ends the relationship, or threatening self-destructive behavior, such as, "Just do what you want. Just tell me what to do. I'm tired of fighting. You win." This unstable situation invites escalation on the other person's part and may lead to the end of the relationship.

Rather than remaining in self-defeating spirals, (Lerner 1989, 35) suggests that people in low-power positions adopt the following moves:

- *Speak up and present a balanced picture of strengths as well as weaknesses.* One might say, "It's true that I am afraid to ask my boss for a raise, even though you want me to. But I earn a steady paycheck and budget and plan well for our family. I want some credit for what I do already contribute."
- *Make clear what one's beliefs, values, and priorities are, and then keep one's behavior congruent with these.* An entry-level accountant in a large firm was asked by the comptroller to falsify taxable deductions, hiding some of the benefits given to employees. The accountant, just out of school and a single parent, said, "When you hired me I said I was committed to doing good work and being an honest accountant.

What you are asking me to do is against the code of ethics and could result in my losing my license. I can't afford to take that risk. I'm sure you'll understand my position."

- *Stay emotionally connected to significant others even when things get intense.* It takes courage for a low-power person to let another person affect him or her. One teenage son was furious and hurt when his father decided to remarry, since the son did not like the wife-to-be at all and felt disloyal to his mother. After some tough thinking, he decided to tell his father honestly how he felt, what he did not like, and what he feared about the new marriage instead of taking another way out, such as angrily leaving his father's house to live with his mother in another state. This conversation balanced the power between father and son in an entirely new way.
- *State differences, and allow others to do the same.* The easiest, but often not the best, way for a low-power person to manage conflict is to avoid engagement. Again, courage is required to bring up differences when a power imbalance is in place. Brad, a college freshman, worked at a fast-food place during school. He was unhappy because the manager kept hiring unqualified people (without checking their references) and then expected Brad to train them and provide supervision, even though Brad was barely making more than minimum wage. Finally Brad told the manager, "I have a different way of looking at who you should hire. I try to do a good job for you, but I have to try to work with people who have no experience and maybe don't have the personality to pitch in and work hard as part of the team. Would you consider letting me sit in on interviews and look over applications?" The manager was pleased with Brad's initiative and said yes.

Empowerment of Low-Power People by High-Power People

Sometimes it is clearly to the advantage of higher-power groups or individuals to purposely enhance the power of lower-power groups or individuals. Without this restructuring of power, working or intimate relationships may end or rigidify into bitter, silent, passive-aggressive, and unsatisfactory entanglements. Currencies valued by higher-power people can be developed by lower-power people if they are allowed more training, more decision-making power, or more freedom. For instance, in one social service agency, Sharon was not doing well at directing a grant-funded program on finding housing for homeless people. Jan, the director of the agency, realized that Sharon was a good fund-raiser but not a good program director. By switching Sharon's job description, the agency gained a good employee instead of continuing a series of negative job evaluations that would have resulted in Sharon's eventual termination.

Empowerment also occurs when third parties are invested with the power to intervene on the behalf of less powerful persons. For instance, children who have been abused by their parents or caretakers can be empowered if their plight is reported to the proper agency. The legal system will provide attorneys, caseworkers to monitor the situation, counselors to work with the parents, judges to arbitrate decisions involving the children, and free services to help the children recover from the effects of the abuse. Our society has decided, by passing certain laws, that extreme forms of power imbalance, such as abuse, will not be allowed to continue when they are discovered. Children are empowered by laws that give them rights and give responsibilities to others.

Metacommunication

Another way to balance power is to transcend the win-lose structure by jointly working to preserve the relationship during conflict. By *metacommunicating* during or before conflicts (talking about the relationship or about how the parties will handle their conflicts), the parties can agree about behaviors that will not be allowed (such as leaving during a fight). True, they are not forced to keep their agreements, but the moral force behind such agreements propels many people into more productive struggles. They can agree to bring in outside mediators or counselors if either person begins to feel like leaving. They can agree that whenever a serious imbalance occurs, the high-power party will work actively with the low-power party to alter the balance in a meaningful way. Usually romantic partners, friends, family members, and work partners can accomplish such joint moves if they agree that the maximization of individual power, left unrestrained, will destroy the relationship. They see that individual power is based relationally, that dependence begets power, and that successful relationships necessitate a balancing of dependencies and therefore of power. The lack of a balanced arrangement is a signal to *reinvest* in the relationship rather than a clue that the relationship is over. The person temporarily weaker in the relationship can draw on the relationship currencies, almost as if the relationship were a bank and the currencies were savings. The weaker party can claim extra time, space, money, training, empathy, or other special considerations until the power is brought back into an approximation of balance. The following box presents an example of an interpersonal peacemaking agreement.

"I'm Not Your Slave!"

Cheryl and Melissa are two teenage girls who share a room in a foster home. Cheryl is more outgoing and friendly than Melissa, who is shy in groups but demanding of Cheryl's time and attention. Recently, Melissa escalated small demands for Cheryl to shut the door, turn down the radio, bring her a drink of water, include her in phone gossip, and lend her clothes, records, and other items. Cheryl, after discussing the situation with several helpers, decided she did not want to continue to respond to Melissa in anger and disdain (e.g., "Get your own water—I'm not your slave!"). She then took the following steps to restore the balance of power:

1. She reminded Melissa that they had agreements about chores in the room, made at a family meeting, that Cheryl wanted to follow.
2. She voluntarily began to fill Melissa in on happenings at school that involved people whom Melissa admired.
3. She complied with Melissa's requests the first time they were made, such as getting her a drink of water, but then said, "I'm glad to get it this once, but remember we agreed to be equal in who does what in the room. So you're on your own now."
4. She asked Melissa to go to basketball games with her and her friends. Melissa became sociable, made new friends of her own, and needed Cheryl's assistance less.

Granted, Cheryl was a remarkably compassionate teenager. But she reported that her life was better, too, since she got along so much better with her roommate.

Most of us are caught in a paradox of power. To be effective people, we need to maximize our abilities, take advantage of opportunities, and use resources at our disposal so we can lead the kinds of lives we desire. Yet within the confines of an ongoing relationship, maximization of individual power is counterproductive for both the higher-power and lower-power parties. The unrestrained maximization of individual power leads to damaged relations, destructive moves, more destructive countermoves, and the eventual ending of the relationship. Since people are going to take steps to balance power—destructively if no other means are available—we can better manage conflict by working to balance power in productive and creative ways. Equity in power reduces violence and enables all participants to continue working for the good of all parties, even in conflict.

Summary

Power is a central concept in conflict management theory. Even though most people dislike discussions of their own power, one cannot avoid using power. Power is a necessary part of conflict management, since interdependence presupposes mutual influence. Power currencies of expertise, resource control, interpersonal linkages, and communication skills provide ways to enact this mutual influence.

Power is a product of the social relationship, not an attribute of the individual, and it grows from mutual dependencies. Although researchers have tried to measure decision making and conversational control as indicators of power, accurate assessment of power remains difficult. The difficulty is compounded by the common use of covert or supposedly weak power moves such as passive aggression. Power imbalances over time harm relationships, since negative results occur from both too much and too little power. Power balancing can restore productive conflict management; limiting the power of the high-power party, focusing on interdependence, persisting in a calm manner, staying actively engaged, empowering the low-power party, and metacommunicating are power-balancing techniques.

Chapter 5

Styles and Tactics

I guess my boss is mad at me. I have left three messages for her to return my phone calls, and she hasn't. I wonder why she is avoiding me.

My boyfriend is really something. Every time I ask him to change something, even small things like what time we'll go out, he explodes at me.

John is a good manager. He can sit and listen to our problems without being defensive or jumping in to argue. He somehow gets us all to work out our problems.

I handle conflicts with my wife by not talking to her. If I tell her that she is doing something I don't like, she pouts for two days. It's just better to avoid the whole thing.

Kevin and Sharon are quite a pair! They fight all the time and don't seem to get anywhere, except ready for the next round of fighting.

Style preferences develop over a person's lifetime based on a complicated blend of genetic predispositions and life experiences, such as level of activity, introversion/extroversion, education, family background, and personal philosophy. By the time you are an adult, your basic orientation to conflict is in place. Your preferences for either harmony and calm or high-energy engagement are apparent. Constructive conflict management depends on the ability to choose from a wide repertoire of styles and tactics to support a specific desired outcome. For instance, if you traditionally go on a final, end-of-summer backpack trip involving ten or twelve friends, and the main goal is a wonderful time of fun and friendship, it would make no sense for you to stubbornly insist on going where you want to go. Instead, cooperating to find a place to go fits the goals of the group. Developing diverse styles and tactics may require some stretching of your comfort zone. This chapter will introduce you to a variety of styles and tactics used in conflict situations and will show you the impact each style or tactic typically has on these situations.

Styles and Tactics Defined

Most people do not carefully plan their approach or individual moves in conflict situations, except when they are very stressed or threatened. Usually, people communicate in generally consistent ways in the same context, changing when they perceive a need to do so. *Conflict styles* are patterned responses or clusters of behavior that people use in conflict. *Tactics* are individual moves people make to carry out their general approach. Styles describe the big picture, whereas tactics describe the specific communicative pieces of the big picture.

Because conflict styles have been researched more than any other topic in interpersonal conflict management, a variety of ways to classify styles have been developed. The classifications range from the two-style approach to the five-style approach:

- Two styles: Cooperation and competition (Deutsch 1949; Tjosvold 1990)
- Three Styles: Nonconfrontation, solution orientation, and control (Putnam and Wilson 1982)
- Four Styles: Yielding, problem solving, inaction, and contending (Pruitt 1983b); accommodating/harmonizing, analyzing/preserving, achieving/directing, and affiliating/perfecting (Gilmore and Fraleigh 1992); aggressive/confrontive, assertive/persuasive, observant/introspective, and avoiding/reactive (Robert 1982)
- Five styles: Integrating, obliging, dominating, avoiding, and compromising (Rahim 1983; Rahim and Magner 1995); collaboration, accommodation, competition, avoidance, and compromise (Thomas 1976; Kilmann and Thomas 1975)

Most trainers and researchers are currently using a five-style approach; therefore, this approach will be used for the remainder of the chapter. Kilmann and Thomas (1975) most clearly defined the five styles when they graphically located them according to two dimensions: (1) concern for the self and (2) concern for the other. The five styles are presented in figure 5.1.* Notice that avoidance represents low concern for yourself and low concern for the other. Accommodation represents low concern for yourself but high concern for the other (you give them what they want). The opposite of accommodation is competition—

* Because of the differences between various writers in labeling styles, one set of labels is being used throughout this chapter. The original Kilmann and Thomas graph has been slightly modified, and Rahim's style questions and labeling have been modified for consistency in this presentation.

Figure 5.1 Conflict styles

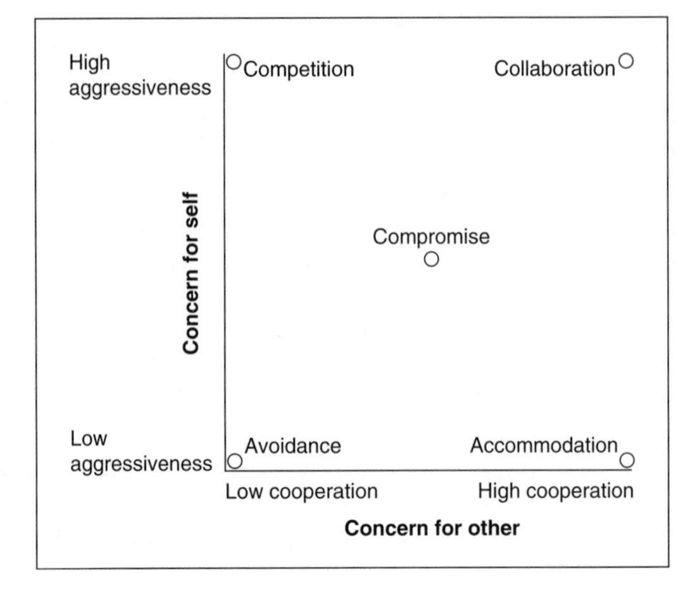

you are highly concerned for yourself but have only low concern for the other—you "go for it" regardless of the desires of the other. Collaboration factors in both your concerns and the other's concerns. And compromise is a middle ground, where there are moderate degrees of concern for self and concern for other.

These five styles and the way that they operate will be discussed one at a time. But before examining the specific styles, we will discuss the basic choice that people in conflict tend to make—whether to engage or to avoid. This basic "branch" leads to the five different styles of conflict.

The Basic Choice: Avoid or Engage

Recall a conflict in which you felt intense emotion. In such situations you may not be aware of making a specific choice about whether to engage or not, yet that choice defines all future interactions. Earlier it was noted that destructive spirals occur when one person pursues and the other distances. This preference for engaging or avoiding the other can develop into a rigid style, and when this happens, constructive conflict becomes difficult. One needs to choose when to protect and disengage and when to engage and extend. Neither style is always the right choice. As Kaplan (1975) writes, one chooses "maintenance-by-*suppression*" or "maintenance-by-*expression*." For example, the following couple is struggling over how much engagement they will have:

He: There is something bothering me.
She: I'm busy.

He: I'm upset about what you said about me at the party.
She: All you do is pick on me. Leave me alone!
He: Well, you do things that bug me!
She: I'm going for a walk. See you later.

This couple will probably replay these exchanges at other times, too. He wants to engage the conflict and she wants to protect herself by avoiding it. Each time an issue surfaces, they will have to reach agreement on avoidance/engagement, or this metaconflict will subsume and exacerbate any other emerging issues. Until they manage their metaconflict on avoidance/engagement, they will be unable to manage their other conflicts. Their fundamental issue is "How much conflict am I willing to risk to get what I want?" (Stuart 1980, 295). Of course, during the next conflict on a different topic, she may push for engagement and he may avoid.

If whether to avoid or to engage is the fundamental issue, which is the best style for use in conflict? Read the four statements below and put a check mark by the one that you feel is the most accurate:

1. Avoidance of conflicts leads to unhappy marriages and work relationships—it just keeps important issues buried.
2. Avoidance of unnecessary conflict helps promote harmony and keeps people from getting involved in unnecessary upsets.
3. The only way to really manage conflict is to work through it by engaging the other person.
4. Engagement of conflict leads to escalatory spirals and hurt for all parties.

If you agree with one of these statements more than with any other, you have a clear preference for engaging or avoiding conflicts. Although we may want to argue for our own personal preferences, neither style is necessarily better than the other. The presence of conflict per se does not signal relationship distress, nor does the absence of conflict indicate a lack of stress (Stuart 1980). Similarly, avoidance can represent unexpressed discord or can be part of a functional relationship (Raush et al. 1974).

Both avoidance and engagement are workable options in different circumstances (Canary and Spitzberg 1987; Canary and Cupach 1988). Recall the example of the couple struggling over their level of engagement. The woman's avoidance may have prompted the man to examine his reaction, decide that he was too sensitive, and back off to reduce the conflict. Or her avoidance may have signaled to him that she did not care for his feelings and that he should start exiting the relationship. Avoidance and lack of overt conflict may indicate that the participants are unable to reach accommodation, that they cannot work through problem areas, and that they will gradually drift apart.

Avoidance of conflict often leads to a cycle that is self-perpetuating. Here is a typical pattern that occurs when one avoids conflict:

1. We think of conflict as bad.
2. We get nervous about a conflict we are experiencing.
3. We avoid the conflict as long as possible.
4. The conflict gets out of control and must be confronted.
5. We handle it badly (Lulofs 1994, 42).

Such avoidance patterns tend to recycle, preventing us from constructively dealing with the conflict. You are more likely to avoid conflict in personal relationships if you are concerned that your partner might respond aggressively to a conflict issue. Predictions about a partner's potential aggression "chills" your expression of your feelings about the issue. Cloven and Roloff (1993) call this the "chilling effect"—anticipating aggressive reactions leads to withholding grievances in personal relationships.

Avoidance can lead to a stressful relationship with considerable unexpressed discord; it can preclude needed change in a relationship (Raush et al. 1974), leading to less understanding and agreement (Knudson, Sommers, and Golding 1980). Avoidance is paradoxical. It is designed to protect the self and other from discord, yet the avoidance may lead to lack of clarity and set the stage for later uncontrollable conflict (Bullis 1983).

Avoidance can also be productive for a relationship. Avoidance serves as a defense against engagement or confrontation with the partner (Raush et al. 1974, 65). Spouses who practice avoidance within a bond of mutual affection often describe their marriage as happy. On the other hand, if the relationship is not important to you, avoidance can conserve energy that would be expended needlessly. We cannot invest equally in all relationships. Similarly, when someone attempts to engage you in conflict over an *issue* that is of trivial importance to you, your best choice is avoidance (Thomas 1976).

The tension between avoiding and engaging can be seen in the following dialogue:

Marjorie: Hi, Terry, what's going on?

Terry: Oh, not much. (He is thinking, "If I say how upset I am, we'll get into it, and I just want to cool out.")

Marjorie: You don't look very happy. (She's thinking, "I know you're upset about last night. We might as well talk about it.")

Terry: No big deal. ("I hope she just lets it go.")

Marjorie: Are you mad at me? ("He must be more angry than I thought. This doesn't look good. Uh-oh.")

Terry: Why do you always have to blow everything out of proportion?

The conflict then escalates as they struggle tacitly over whether to engage or avoid. In the following section, *avoidance as a style with specific tactics* will be presented.

Avoidance

Avoidance is a style characterized by denial of the conflict, equivocation, changing and avoiding topics, being noncommittal, and joking rather than dealing with the conflict at hand. There are many types of avoidance tactics. Generally speaking, however, you practice the style of avoidance if you agree to the following statements (Rahim 1983; Rahim and Magner 1995). Although this instrument was designed for use in organizations to provide a rough index of degree of avoidance with supervisors, employees, or peers, you can fill in the blanks with a specific person from any context (like your parents, friends, etc.) to see if you are practicing avoidance. You might also fill in a context such as work, a friendship group, your family, or your current living situation. Because there are some differences in versions of the instrument, only the most recent version (Rahim and Manger

1995) is used throughout this section. You might wish to use this scale to mark each item: 1 = never, 2 = seldom, 3 = sometimes, 4 = often, and 5 = always.

____I attempt to avoid being "out on the spot" and try to keep my conflict with ______ to myself.

____I usually avoid open discussion of my differences with ______.

____I try to stay away from disagreement with ______.

____I avoid an encounter with ______.

____I try to keep my disagreement with ______ to myself in order to avoid hard feelings.

____I try to avoid unpleasant exchanges with ______.

____I generally avoid an argument with ______.

The avoider may sidestep an issue by changing the topic or simply withdrawing from dealing with the issue. Just as use of the competitive style does not mean that one will get what one wants (because of interdependence with the other party), the use of avoidance as a style does not mean that the avoider will be ineffective. For instance, if a person is having a conflict with a large organization that overcharged for some goods, the organization can enhance its position by not responding to correspondence on the matter. By pretending that the conflict does not exist, the high-power party is freed from dealing with the low-power party.

Avoidance can serve similar functions in interpersonal conflicts as well. If two roommates are both dating the same women, they may refuse to discuss the subject openly, even if both of them are aware of the problem. Furthermore, in intimate relationships the style of avoidance is often invoked during conflict over sensitive matters. If a couple is having some difficulty in dealing with each other's families, they may not feel free to discuss the problem. Avoiding a conflict, however, does not prevent it. Conflict occurs when parties have the perception of incompatible goals, regardless of the style they choose to use in responding to this perception. Avoidance is simply an alternative mode of conflict expression.

Some of the advantages and disadvantages of avoidance are presented in the following box.

Avoidance

Advantages

Avoidance can supply time to think of some other response to the conflict, as some people cannot "think on their feet." It is useful if the issue is trivial or if other important issues demand one's attention. If the relationship itself is unimportant to one person or if others can manage the conflict without his or her involvement, avoidance is a wise choice. Avoidance can also keep one from harm if he or she is in a relationship in which anything other than avoidance will bring a negative response from the other party. If one's goal is to keep the other party from influencing him or her, then avoidance helps to accomplish that goal.

Example:

Shirley is a twenty-three-year-old graduate who has recently broken off a long relationship with a man her parents like very much. They ask her to tell them "what went wrong" and offer to pay for a trip to visit him. Shirley decides not to take them up on the trip offer and says, "Many things happened to make us want to break up. Thanks for caring about me." She avoided a discussion that she felt would end in conflict.

Disadvantages

Avoidance tends to demonstrate to other people that one does not "care enough to confront" them and gives the impression that one cannot change. It allows conflict to simmer and heat up unnecessarily rather than providing an avenue for improving it. It keeps one from working through a conflict and reinforces the notion that conflict is terrible and best avoided. It allows partners to each follow their own course and pretend there is no mutual influence when, in fact, each influences the other. It usually preserves the conflict and sets the stage for a later explosion or backlash.

Example:

Professor Lane has recently made several sarcastic comments about low class attendance. Chuck has missed three classes. Upon receiving a midterm grade of C, Chuck decides to wait for a while before asking for the reasons for the low grade. Later he decides to forget trying to get a B in political science and instead to concentrate on geology, in which he has a higher average.

In marriages, avoidance of conflict relates to lower satisfaction in general. In one study, partners who believed in their first year of marriage that conflicts should be avoided also reported lower happiness in the first three years of marriage than those who believed that conflicts should not be avoided (Crohan 1992). In some traditional marriages, however, stability and predictability are emphasized and continual renegotiation of what the spouses expect of one another is not useful. As Pike and Sillars (1985) found, "Satisfied couples used conflict avoidance to a greater extent than dissatisfied couples" (319). Similarly, for couples who are not traditional and who lead somewhat independent lives, "Avoidance may be a satisfying style of communication" (321). Finally, older couples in our culture can often be characterized as happy, although inexpressive—they often avoid conflict (Zietlow and Sillars 1988). Based on intervention experiences in conflicts in organizations and families, avoidance can be useful and appropriate when (1) open communication is not an integral part of the system (family or organization); (2) one does not want to invest the energy to "work through" the conflict to reach accommodation with the other—he or she wants to stay at arm's length and not get close; (3) the costs of confrontation are too high (Van de Vliert 1985); or (4) one simply hasn't learned how to engage in collaborative conflict management.

Whether avoidance is productive or destructive generally depends on the *culture* and the *relationship.* Cultures differ in their valuing of avoidance. The Japanese avoid conflict in order to preserve congeniality and consensus and out of sensitivity to others' feelings. In one study, Japanese students avoided a potentially conflictual relationship 80 percent of the time (Barnlund 1989). The impact of avoidance varies in different cultural settings. For example, in a high-context culture, if you avoid a conflict, others will talk to you about how to heal wounds, make amends, and solve the conflict in indirect ways. In individualistic cultures, on the other hand, if you avoid someone as the result of a conflict, your friends might cheer you on, suggesting that you "don't have to take that junk" and making other escalatory suggestions. Depending on the culture, those around you either push you to reconciliation or into continual fighting. In high-context cultures, one is "more concerned with the group's needs, goals and interests than with individualistic-oriented interest" (Trubisky, Ting-Toomey, and Lin 1991, 67). Thus, avoidance serves *different functions* in collectivist cultures than in individualistic ones. In collectivist cultures, avoidance represents "indirect working through," but in individualistic cultures, avoidance represents "indirect escalation."

Within Western cultures, the *type of relationship* determines the effects of avoidance. Although avoidance can serve constructive purposes in long-term relationships, it should not be used exclusively as a style. For example, people in distressed marriages use more avoidance than people in nondistressed or satisfied marriages (Noller et al, 1994; Alberts and Driscoll 1992; Gottman 1994; Martin 1990; Courtright et al. 1990). As Noller et al. (1994) say, "On the whole, then, conflict avoidance tends to be counterproductive" (245). Siegert and Stamp (1994) capsulize it well: "If the conflict is not negotiated to the satisfaction of both individuals, it could become an unmanageable burden and contribute to the eventual demise of the relationship."

Two types of avoidance were noted by Raush et al. (1974): (1) both parties tacitly approve of avoiding the topic with a sort of "joint contract," and (2) one person avoids engagement in disagreement. Older couples who are happy often practice the first type of avoidance, as do many individuals in workplaces. The second type of avoidance is often represented by the husband who is defensive and withdrawn and the wife who wants him to engage. This kind of avoidance, *nonconsensual avoidance,* is the one that is highly destructive and leads to dissatisfaction. A high-power person can avoid a conflict as a way of ignoring the other person's legitimate stake in the conflict. Or a romantic partner may avoid dealing directly with issues while the relationship is crumbling around him or her. Sometimes a person gets "stuck" avoiding a conflict, while others attempt ineffectually to work through the conflict. Especially when the avoider is in a position that greatly affects others—a supervisor, minister, manager, or parent—avoidance damages relationships. In these cases, the effects of avoidance are passed on to others. The parishioners, kids, or employees are greatly affected by the lack of responsiveness in the system and become disenchanted, angry, frustrated, and blocked from productive influence.

The lists of tactics presented in table 5.1 are from the work of Sillars et al. (1982), Sillars (1986), and Zietlow and Sillars (1988). This coding scheme is revised from earlier

Table 5.1 Avoidance Tactics

Conflict Codes	Illustrations
A. Denial and equivocation	
1. *Direct denial.* Statements that deny that a conflict is present.	"That's not a problem."
2. *Implicit denial.* Statements that imply denial by providing a rationale for a denial statement, although the denial is not explicit.	"We've never had enough money to disagree over" (in response to a question about disagreements over money).
3. *Evasive remarks.* Failure to acknowledge or deny the presence of a conflict following a statement or inquiry about the conflict by the partner.	"That could be something that a person might resent but I don't know."
B. Topic management	
4. *Topic shifts.* Statements that terminate discussion of a conflict issue before each person has fully expressed an opinion or before the discussion has reached a sense of completion.	"Okay, the next issue is . . ." (the preceding statement occurs before each person has disclosed his or her opinion on the topic).
5. *Topic avoidance.* Statements that explicitly terminate discussion of a conflict issue before it has been fully discussed.	"I don't want to talk about that."
C. Noncommittal remarks	
6. *Noncommittal statements.* Statements that neither affirm nor deny the presence of conflict and are not evasive replies or topic shifts.	"The kids are growing up so fast I can't believe it."
7. *Noncommittal questions.* Unfocused and conflict-irrelevant questions.	"What do you think?"
8. *Abstract remarks.* Abstract principles, generalizations, or hypothetical statements that are not also evasive remarks.	"All people are irritable sometimes."
9. *Procedural remarks.* Procedural statements that supplant discussion of conflict.	"You aren't speaking loudly enough."
D. Irreverent remarks	
10. *Friendly joking.* Friendly joking or laughter.	"We need to either clean the house or torch it" (stated with friendly intonation).

Source: Reprinted, by permission of the publisher, from A. L. Sillars, "Procedures for Coding Interpersonal Conflict," rev. (Department of Communication Studies, University of Montana, 1986), 7–16.

work and has been applied in various forms to conflict between college roommates and between marital couples. The codes have been rearranged for this presentation. Readers wishing to pursue the scheme in greater detail should consult Zietlow and Sillars (1988) and Sillars (1986).

Many times multiple forms of avoidance are used in combination. For example, a person in a low-power position may refuse to engage the other by using both topic management and noncommittal remarks. Often avoidance takes the form of what Brockriede (1972) termed "seduction," which Sillars would classify as a combination of joking, evasive remarks, and topic avoidance. The low-power person using seduction tries to charm or trick the other conflict party into going along with what he or she desires. Argument tactics vary from classical reasoning, such as "ignoring the question, begging the question, the red-herring appeal, and appeals to ignorance or to prejudice" (Brockriede 1972, 4), support this avoidance strategy. The clash between issues is not direct; the issues are circumvented in a sometimes deceptive, charming, or even "cutesy" way. It is not important to the seducer to appeal to the other party's sense of free choice. She or he wants what is wanted, no matter what, but is not willing (or perhaps able) to ask for it directly.

For instance, Liz asked friends of hers to help her find a job for the summer. She appeared weak, took little initiative, and became stuck in a low-energy period in her life. She frequently dropped in on her friends, politely asking for "any suggestions" they might have in finding a job, but was evasive and confused when friends suggested that she needed help from an employment service. It appeared that she was trying to "seduce" her friends into taking responsibility for her but that she needed to preserve own self-concept to avoid any direct clash with her friends. Finally, her choice of the avoidance strategy became a great disservice because her friends got tired of trying to help her and started avoiding her in return. All of the avoidance tactics in table 5.1 involve refusing to engage in the conflict. Note, however, that *postponement* of a conflict may not be avoidance per se but rather temporary avoidance with a promise to engage in the future. Bach and Wyden (1968) suggest that setting a time for a later conflict is a productive tactic. They suggest "fighting by appointment." Here are two examples of a conflict—the first using avoidance and the second using postponement:

Gloria is upset. She wants to talk to her husband Sam late at night. Sam, however, has an appointment at eight o'clock in the morning.

Gloria: I am so upset that I can't sleep. Whatever possessed you to talk about our summer plans to the Carters at the party? You know we've been trying to get free of doing things with them. You said last week . . .

Sam: Can't we talk about this in the morning?

Gloria: It's fine for you to say that. You don't have to deal with Sandra when she calls tomorrow to decide where we'll take our families for a joint vacation. *I* have to talk to her and tell her we changed our minds.

Sam: I'm sorry I brought it up. But I'm sleepy, and I don't want to talk about it.

At this point, the avoidance tactic Sam is using—"Maybe if I close my eyes all this hassle will go away"—is certainly not productive. His twin goals—to get some sleep and to avoid further antagonizing his wife—are not likely to be met. By this time Gloria is probably angry not only about his lack of discretion at the party but also about his refusal to talk to her about it. An example of a productive postponement tactic follows:

Sam: Gloria, I know you're upset. I also feel foolish. But I am exhausted, and I really don't want to deal with all the issues now. When Sandra calls tomorrow, tell her we haven't had a chance to talk yet and you'll call her back. Then when I come home from work tomorrow, we'll discuss the whole thing.

Gloria: You always say that, and it never gets talked about.

Sam: This time it will. We'll sit down before dinner, banish the kids, and the two of us will talk. I know you're upset.

Gloria: OK, if we really will. I know it's hard to know what to say in public like that. They presume so much. . . .

Postponement as a tactic works best when several conditions are present. First of all, emotional content of the conflict needs to be acknowledged while referring other issues to a later time. Sam said, "I know you're upset," acknowledging the depth of Gloria's feelings. She would not have been likely to go along with the postponement if he had said, "It's stupid for you to be upset. We'll work it out later." After the emotional content is acknowledged, all parties have to agree on a time that is soon and realistic. If Sam had said, "We'll talk about it sometime soon," that would not have been precise enough. The other party has to believe that the postponer really means to bring up the issue later. Postponement does not work well as a tactic if the other people involved think they are being put off, never to return to the issue. Vague statements such as "We'll have to work on that sometime" or "Let's all try harder to get along" are often giveaways that the person wants avoidance rather than genuine postponement.

As you study avoidance tactics in table 5.1, note that although avoidance comes in many costumes, its function is always to deflect, avoid, or not engage in the conflict. Whether a professor who is confronted about a grade says, "That's an interesting point. It brings up an interesting question" (abstract remark), or a supervisor says, "That's enough complaining. Let's get back to the job" (topic shift), the basic dynamic is the same—to avoid the conflict.

Competition

A *competitive* or "power over" style is characterized by aggressive and uncooperative behavior—pursuing your own concerns at the expense of another. People with competitive styles attempt to gain power by direct confrontation, by trying to "win" the argument without adjusting to the other's goals and desires. A person with a competitive style is one who usually thinks it necessary to engage the other participant in overt disagreement. The conflict is seen as a "battleground," where winning is the goal and concern for the other is of little or no importance. Someone who adopts a competitive style in conflicts would probably agree with statements such as, "Once I get wound up in a heated discussion, I find it difficult to stop," and "I like the excitement of engaging in verbal fights." The following items, adapted from Rahim (1983) and Rahim and Magner (1995), fit into the competitive frame:

____I use my influence with ______ to get my ideas accepted.

____I use my authority with ______ to make a decision in my favor.

____I use my expertise with ______ to make a decision in my favor.

____I am generally firm in pursuing my side of an issue with ______.

____I sometimes use my power with ______ to win a competitive situation.

Some sample items from Putnam and Wilson (1982) further clarify the nature of competitive responses:

____I insist that my position be accepted during conflict.

____I raise my voice when trying to get other persons to accept my position.

____I dominate arguments until other people understand my position.

____I argue insistently for my stance.

Competitive tactics can be employed in an assertive rather than an aggressive manner. Usually, however, aggression creeps into a competitive style. Whereas nonassertive people deny themselves and inhibit their expression of feelings and open striving for goals, assertive people enhance the self, work toward achieving desired goals, and are expressive. The aggressive person, however, carries the desire for self-expression to the extreme. Goals are accomplished at the expense of others. The aggressive style results in a put-down of others while actively working against their goals. The assertive person can be competitive without berating, ridiculing, or damaging the other. The aggressive person is competitive primarily by trying to destroy the opponent's options.

The competitive style of managing conflict is productive if one competes to accomplish individual goals without destroying the other person. Competition can be productively used in conflict, especially if the participants agree about the amount of aggressiveness that can legitimately be used in their conflict. The following box summarizes the advantages, as well as the disadvantages, of competition.

Competing

Advantages

Competition can be appropriate and useful when one has to make a quick, decisive action, such as in an emergency. Competition can generate creative ideas when others respond well to it or when one is in a situation in which the best performance or ideas are rewarded. It is useful if the external goal is more important than the relationship with the other person, such as in a short-term, nonrepeating relationship.

Competition also informs the other of one's degree of commitment to the issue and can be used to demonstrate to the other party the importance of the issue. Competition can be useful in situations in which everyone agrees that competitive behavior is a sign of strength and in which such behavior is treated as a natural response, such as in games and sports or in a court battle. In these cases, other styles may confuse the resolution of the conflict.

Example:

A human service agency competes with others for grant money from United Way. A limited amount is available, so the best proposal for solving a human service problem will be funded. The director of the agency competes with other directors for funding. The larger good of the community is served by the best program gaining support.

Disadvantages

Competition can harm the relationship between the parties because of the focus on external goals. Rands, Levinger, and Mellinger (1981), for example, show that continued escalation in marriages is related to unhappiness with the marriage. Competition can be harmful if one party is unable or unwilling to deal with conflict in a head-on manner. Conflict waged competitively can encourage one party to go underground and use covert means to make the other pay. Competition tends to reduce all conflicts to two options—"either you are against me or with me," which limits one's roles to "winning" or "losing."

Example:

Greg and Marcie, both young, competitive salespeople for the same company, live together. High sales, naturally, are rewarded by their manager. The couple keeps track of who's ahead of the other by placing a chart on the refrigerator. The week's loser has to do the laundry for the week. However, when Marcie's sales are low because she has been ill and has missed a lot of work, she angrily proclaims to Greg, "I'm not your slave! Do your own damn laundry!"

A competitive style is useful in showing the other party how important an issue is to you. Especially when both parties agree that competitive styles are the norm, the style can be useful. Competitiveness can be a sign of strength or commitment. For example, two attorneys who one-up each other during negotiation are each attempting to persuade the other to alter his or her position.

On the other hand, as mentioned previously, competitive tactics can damage a relationship, lock the participants into round-robin sequences of attack on each other, and deprive the participants of collaborative, cooperative solutions to their problems. In severe cases a competitive style can become self-encapsulating—the participants can't give up or stop because they get too caught up in winning at any cost. When people launch never-ending court challenges against one another or continue to verbally abuse their ex-spouses for many decades, such approaches indicate a frozen position of competitiveness. The ever competitive combatants lose all perspective on the original goal, and they dedicate their energies to triumphing over the other.

Table 5.2 Competitive Tactics

Communication category	Illustrations
1. *Personal criticism.* Remarks that directly criticize the personal characteristics or behaviors of the partner.	"Sometimes you leave, and you don't say goodbye or anything. You just walk right out."
2. *Rejection.* Statements in response to the partner's previous statements that imply personal antagonism toward the partner as well as disagreement.	"Oh, come on." "You're exaggerating."
3. *Hostile imperatives.* Requests, demands, arguments, threats, or other prescriptive statements that implicitly blame the partner and seek change in the partner's behavior.	"If you're not willing to look for a new job, then don't complain to me about it."
4. *Hostile jokes.* Joking, teasing, or sarcasm that is at the expense of the partner and that is accompanied by hostile intonation.	"It's very easy to say, 'Gee, I *really* appreciate you' [said mockingly], but that doesn't mean anything." "Every time you send me flowers, two days later I get the bill."
5. *Hostile questions.* Directive or leading questions that fault the partner.	"Who does most of the cleaning around here?"
6. *Presumptive remarks.* Statements that attribute thoughts, feelings, motivations, or behaviors to the partner that the partner does not acknowledge.	"You're purposely making yourself miserable."
7. *Denial of responsibility.* Statements that minimize or deny personal responsibility for conflict.	"That's not my fault."

Source: Adapted, by permission of publisher, from A. L. Silars, "Procedures for Coding Interpersonal Conflict," rev. (Department of Communication Studies, University of Montana, 1986), 7–16.

Competitive tactics involve "verbally competitive or individualistic behavior" (Sillars et al. 1982, 83). These tactics focus on a win-lose orientation and often reflect a belief that what one person gets, the other loses (Thomas 1976). As a result, the party using competitive tactics will try to one-up the other party to gain an advantage (Rogers and Farace 1975). Table 5.2 displays various competitive tactics (Sillars et al. 1982; Sillars 1986; Zietlow and Sillars 1988).

With these tactics the conflict participant pushes for self-interest, often at the expense of the other. These competitive tactics are so commonplace that many people see them as synonymous with conflict. If you saw two business partners calling each other names, finding fault with each other, and acting in forceful or controlling ways, you would conclude that a conflict is present. At their core, all competitive tactics involve pressuring the *other* person to change.

Confrontational remarks, as summarized in table 5.2, are the essence of competitive tactics. If someone personally criticizes you, rejects your statements, or acts in a verbally hostile manner (with threats, jokes, or questions), you become vividly aware of the competitive nature of the exchange. Confrontational remarks are at the heart of "I win–you lose" perspectives on conflict. Just as with avoidance tactics, competitive tactics are often used in combination. Denial of responsibility for the conflict ("I didn't cause it!") is usually linked with presumptive remarks ("It's your fault"). Whatever the specific tactical move, a competitive approach demands that the other give in, take responsibility for the conflict, and solve it.

When competitive tactics are extreme they are characterized by the "rapist" style. In the rapist style (this metaphor is not mean to imply only sexual behavior but all kinds of dominating communicative behavior), participants "function through power, through an ability to apply psychic and physical sanctions, through rewards and especially punishments, and through commands and threats" (Brockriede, 1972, 2). The conflict or argument is often escalated, since participants are interested in coercion instead of gaining assent through carefully reasoned argument. The intent of those using the rapist style is to manipulate and violate the personhood of the "victims" or other parties in the conflict. In some situations, such as the courtroom, legislative hearings, political debates, and forensic tournaments, the structure of the conflict encourages the coercion, or rapist, strategy.

When one person has chosen, however tacitly, the rapist strategy, the other person functions as the victim, even though most people certainly do not want to be victimized. Often, the person who feels powerless and victimized escalates to a point, then gives up, thinking, "There's nothing I can do to win anyway." In effect, the participants cooperate in the escalation. A very angry person was once observed trying to take over the microphone and the floor at a convention. He shouted loudly, disrupted the proceedings, and was finally given five minutes to state his case. He did so, supporting with vehemence the pullout of his church group from a large national group, which he perceived as being too liberal. He chose the rapist style to escalate the direction of the conflict—soon he and the chairman were yelling back and forth at each other, and tensions were rising.

Threats

The most commonly used competitive tactic is the threat. We rush to use threats because we believe they are effective (Rubin, Pruitt, and Kim, 1994). Many parents are quick to say, "If you don't eat your spinach, I'll spank you," or supervisors to say, "If you employees don't do what I say, someone will be gone tomorrow, and it won't be me." Sillars (1986) categorizes threats as a subtype of "hostile imperatives." For most of us, any hostile comment directed to another is classified as a threat. But when the exasperated father shopping in the grocery store says to the child, "If you don't stop taking candy off the shelf, Santa Claus will not visit you this year," he is not issuing a credible threat.

It is important to clearly understand what is and is not a threat, then to know the conditions under which they can be effective. Table 5.3 shows that a threat has to meet two criteria—the source of the threat must control the outcome and the threat must be seen as negative by the recipient. If you (the source) control the outcome ("If you don't go to bed, I'll spank you") and the sanction is seen as negative, then it is a threat. Similarly, if the professor says, "If you don't get your paper in on time, I will dock your grade," it is a threat. However, if the source does not control the outcome (a friend says, "If you don't get your paper in on time, it will hurt your grade"), it is not a threat—it is a warning. Many parents get confused between warning and threats. For example, "If you drink too much, you'll never graduate" seems like a threat, but it is not because the parent does not control the

Table 5.3 The Nature of Threats

	Source controls the outcome	**Source does not control the outcome**
Negative sanction	Threat	Warning
Positive sanction	Promise	Recommendation

outcome. Or, if you say to a friend, "If you step out on your boyfriend, he will leave you," it is not a threat, it is a warning.

Small children understand the difference between a positive and a negative sanction. If the parent says, "If you don't do the dishes, you'll have to spend the evening in your room," and the child has a Nintendo game, computer, or TV so that going to the room is not negative, the child may likely retort, "Is that a threat or a promise?" As you can see, if the source controls the outcome and the recipient sees the outcome as positive, the threat is, instead, a promise.

A threat is credible only if (1) *the source is in a position to administer the punishment,* (2) *the source appears willing to invoke the punishment,* and (3) *the punishment is something to be avoided.* If your friends say, "You had better quit trying to get your dad to buy you expensive gifts, or he will get mad and not give you anything," this is not a credible threat but rather a warning. Similarly, if your romantic partner says, "You better study harder or you will flunk out of school," it is not a threat. The threat is credible only if the person making the threat is capable of invoking the negative sanction.

Often the other party is *able* to administer a threat but not *willing* to follow through on the threat. A coworker who threatens to tell the boss that someone's work is not up to par may not carry out the threat if the boss dislikes "whistle-blowers." Similarly, in an intimate relationship, one intimate might say, "If you want to make your summer plans alone, go ahead. But if you do, then don't expect to find me here when you come back." Such a threat (relational suicide) is effective only if the person who makes the threat is willing to lose the other person over this one issue. It is the *perception* that the other party is willing to carry out the threat that makes it effective. As a result, intimates and others often avoid testing the willingness of the other party to invoke the threat and instead live under the control of the other person for years. In poker, a "bluff" is the ability to convince the other party that you are willing to bet all your winnings on a single draw of cards. The only successful bluff is one that the other party believes is true.

Finally, threats are effective only if the sanction is something the threatened party wants to avoid. If you threaten to leave a relationship and your partner says, "So you think I'm going to cry over you?" your threat was not credible. So before you issue your next threat to a close friend or family member, keep in mind that your threat is effective only if he or she does not want the "undesirable" end result. Similar scenarios happen in all levels of relationships. One faculty member was offered a job at a competing university; when he went to the department chair and threatened to leave unless his salary was raised, the chair replied, "I hope you enjoy the climate down south."

As you have seen, threats can be either constructive or destructive. They can be used constructively to highlight the importance of the conflict topic to you, to get the attention of the other party, and to clarify one's perceptions of the power balance. On the other hand, threats tend to elicit the same behavior from the other, starting escalatory conflict spirals. They also block collaborative agreements and undermine trust in the relationship. Worse, we can become enamored with them (Kellermann and Shea 1996). If two dormitory roommates have been getting along well except for the issue of sweeping the floor, then a threat of "If you don't sweep more often, I'll process a room change!" might damage the trust in an otherwise good relationship. The recipient of the threat will likely respond with a feeling of "OK, then go ahead. Who needs you anyway?" Unless trust can be regained, forging agreements will be extremely difficult. Once a threat has damaged the trust in the relationship, it often leads to further destructive tactics.

In the case of nations that threaten one another with military intervention, "Threats are not bad merely because they do not work. They are also bad because they are dangerous" (Fisher 1986, 151). Threats are overused, used too quickly, destroy trust, and tend to promote retaliation.

Verbal Aggressiveness

Verbal aggressiveness is a broader category of communication than threats. Verbal aggressiveness is a form of communicative violence. Rather than just telling someone what might happen to them, when you use verbal aggression you "attack the self-concepts" of other people (Infante and Wigley 1986). Character attacks ("You are just a rotten wife"), insults ("Well, I suppose someone with your intelligence would see it that way"), rough teasing, ridicule, and profanity all are forms of verbal aggressiveness. Many conflict parties, when engaged in struggle, immediately begin attacking each other. Once one focuses on the other as the sole cause of the difficulties, it is easy to slip into disparaging personal remarks. Therefore, whether you label it as "personal criticism" or "verbal aggressiveness," this competitive tactic involves attacking the other person. The following are examples of verbal aggressiveness:

You're so stupid.
You're a cretin.
You're an imbecile.
You're ugly.
You're low class.
I wish you would die/get hit by a car/fall off the face of the earth.

In individualistic cultures, verbal aggression is typically against a *person,* as in the previous examples. These remarks attack the other's character, background, abilities, competence, physical appearance, and the like (Carey and Mongeau 1996). The more important your relationship with someone, the more verbal aggression within the relationship hurts

(Martin, Anderson, and Horvath 1996). In a collectivist culture, on the other hand, the most damaging verbal abuse is directed toward a person's *group,* clan, tribe, village, or family, such as when you say, "He's a drunken Irishman" (Vissing and Baily 1996), or, "You people are all animals."

One study examined the use of verbal aggression in college-aged couples and found that based on five thousand American couples, men and women engage in equal amounts of verbal aggression (Sabourin 1995). Yelsma (1995) found that 70 percent of partners in dating relationships reported some form of verbal abuse. If an occasional lapse into verbal aggression occurred, partners seemed able to absorb it, but in distressed relationships, verbal aggression was associated with ineffective skills and was much more frequent than in satisfactory relationships.

The impact of verbal aggression is felt by most of us. When we hear someone in public "going after" another, we cringe. The person engaging most often in verbal aggression doesn't see it as all that bad. People who are "high verbal aggressives" claim that 46 percent of their verbally aggressive messages are humorous (Infante, Riddle, et al. 1992). But others view verbally aggressive people as less credible and as having fewer valid arguments than those who don't aggress (Infante, Hartley, et al. 1992). If a couple is verbally aggressive, they tend to aggravate each other and lack the skill to undo the relationship damage (Sabourin 1995). As shown in the following diagram, verbally abusive couples differ from nonabusive couples by how they talk:

Abuse Talk		**Nonabusive Talk**
vague language	vs.	precise language
opposition	vs.	collaboration
relational talk	vs.	content talk
despair	vs.	optimism
interfering with interdependence	vs.	facilitating interdependence
complaints	vs.	compliments
ineffective change	vs.	effective change

The "relational talk" listed in the diagram is of the destructive type, such as "You are always trying to control me." While the context of one's talk will determine whether the talk is abusive, this list portrays forms of language that are commonly associated with verbal abuse. Clearly, the impact of verbal aggression on a relationship is not positive.

In fact, verbal aggression is closely associated with physical aggression. Verbal aggression is a precursor to and predictor of physical aggression in adolescents (White and Humphrey 1994). Similarly, verbal aggression in marriage is correlated with marital violence (Sabourin and Stamp 1995). Adding injury to insult, verbally aggressive couples do not see their aggression as a problem (Vivian and Langhinrichsen-Rohling 1994)!*

Sometimes, researchers label verbally aggressive tactics as "harassment." A direct verbal attack on another can have serious consequences. In Sweden, for example, an estimated one to three hundred people each year commit suicide as a result of harassment by work colleagues (Bjorkqvist Osterman, and Lagerspetz 1994). One study found that in a

* For a comprehensive treatment of sexual harassment, which is beyond the scope of our discussion here, see Albrecht and Bach (1997, chap. 10).

Finnish University, women were more often harassed than men, and women holding administrative and service jobs were harassed more than female professors (Bjorkqvist, Osterman, and Hjelt-Back 1994). Making negative comments about appearance or clothing is considered harassment if the speaker is in a high-power relationship with the "target" person. Additionally, if a high-power person ridicules a low-power person's mode of speech or makes sexually explicit suggestions or observations, harassment is occurring. Finally, when a high-power person negatively labels a low-power person's personality, such as "brain-dead," "loser," "whiner," "bitch," or "wimp," the target person is being harassed. Such comments, whether labeled "harassment" or "verbal aggression," can occur at home, on the job, in public, or in any type of relationship. And sometimes, these destructive verbal tactics escalate to the next level—physical violence.

Violence

Incidence

The ultimate competitive tactic is physical violence—when conflict interactions move beyond threats and verbal aggressiveness. We are faced with an epidemic of violence in the United States, with much of it occurring in the home and the workplace. Violence can occur in many forms. One scale measuring such physical aggression (Straus et al. 1996) lists these items:

Threw something at my partner that could hurt
Twisted my partner's arm or hair
Pushed or shoved my partner
Grabbed my partner
Used a knife or gun on my partner
Punched or hit my partner with something that could hurt
Choked my partner
Slammed my partner against a wall
Beat up my partner
Burned or scalded my partner on purpose
Kicked my partner

The more severe forms of violence occur less frequently (Deal and Wampler 1986). However, although we will never know the precise rates of violence, it is more common than we usually assume. Ponder for a moment these rates of incidence found in various surveys:

- Almost four out of every ten women and one-third of all men report having been violent at some point in dating relationships (Gyrl, Stith, and Bird 1991).
- Almost 20 percent of people experienced a violent episode in the past year of their romantic relationship (Marshall 1994).
- Premarital violence is a serious social problem that affects more than 30 percent of the young people in the United States who date (Sugarman and Hotaling 1989).
- In unhappy marriages, 71 percent of the couples reported physical aggression in the prior year (Vivian and Langhinrichsen-Rohling 1994).

As you might expect, during times of crisis or transition (such as the breakup of a marriage), the incidence of physical assault increases. In Minneapolis and Portland, for example, in cases of custody and visitation disputes that went to court, 80 percent of the women and 72 percent of the men report experiencing abuse. "Although intimidation was the most frequent and enduring form of abuse reported, over half of the men and two-thirds of the women reported being physically abused. Severe abuse (beating or choking) was reported by over 38% of the women and 20% of the men" (Newmark, Harrell, and Salem 1995).

In another study of dating relationships, 23 percent of students reported being pushed, grabbed, or shoved by their dating partner (Deal and Wampler 1986). Studies of college students have indicated that rates of physical aggression against a current mate are between 20 and 35 percent, with all forms of physical assault decreasing dramatically with age. Women reportedly engaged in more frequent physical aggression, regardless of whether the aggression was measured by partner or self report. The most common forms of physical aggression practiced by both men and women were pushing, shoving, and slapping (O'Leary, Barling, Arias, and Rosenbaum 1989). Additionally 16.3 out of 1,000 children were reported to be abused and/or neglected, and in 16 percent of homes, some kind of violence between spouses had occurred in the year prior to the survey (Gelles and Cornell 1990).

In summary, most researchers conclude that "violence is indeed common in American families" (Gelles 1987). Further, "These incidents of violence are not isolated attacks nor are they just pushes and shoves. In many families, violence is patterned and regular and often results in broken bones and sutured cuts" (192). Violence spans all social and economic boundaries, though it is more prevalent in families with low income, low educational achievement, and low-status employment.

A working definition of violence is "an act carried out with the intention or perceived intention of causing physical pain or injury to another person" (Gelles and Cornell 1990, 22). In conflict terms, violent behavior is an attempt to force one's will on the other—to get him or her to stop doing something or to start doing something. Clearly, it is a one-sided tactic designed to force the other to do one's bidding.

Patterns

The following are some tenets of violence, based on the current research (adapted from Lloyd and Emery 1994):

Tenet 1: Physical aggression is almost always preceded by verbal aggression. Small, insignificant acts lead to verbal sparring, which then escalates into physical aggression or abuse. For instance, you burn the toast, your spouse screams at you, "Why can't you even do simple things right?" you shout back, "So what makes you think you are so high and mighty?" and the cycle continues unabated with the two of you shoving each other around the kitchen. The spiral of destruction continues until the physically stronger one, usually the man, gets an upper hand. The important feature here is that the physical abuse does not just arise out of nowhere—it follows other hostile, competitive verbal acts (Evans 1992; Lloyd and Emery 1994). The partners engage in an "aggression ritual" that ends in violence (Harris, Gergen, and Lannamann 1986).

Tenet 2: Intimate violence is usually reciprocal—both participate. Aggression and violence are reciprocal—once one partner engages in violence, the other is likely to respond in kind. In intimate male-female relationships, the woman is more likely than the man to engage in violent low-power tactics: the woman is fourteen times more likely than the man to throw something and fifteen times more likely than the man to slap (Stets and Henderson 1991). Both participants are likely to report being both victims and perpetrators of physical aggression; 85 percent of couples report that the aggression is bidirectional (Vivian and Langhinrichsen-Rohling 1994). These statistics suggest that there is an attack-counterattack sequence to the majority of violent episodes (Deal and Wampler 1986). Once violence begins, both people tend to participate—it is a dyadic, interactive event.

The cycle of violence goes something like this. Stage 1: tension builds; stage 2: violence occurs; stage 3: emotional or physical distancing occurs; and stage 4: loving calm returns (Gyrl, Stith, and Bird 1991). More precise specification of the tactics each person employs would allow us to see the different patterns in place and to begin generating ways to alter these destructive patterns.

Tenet 3: Women and children suffer more injuries. Violence, regardless of the cycle of interaction leading up to it, damages women and children more than men. Advocates for battered women point to a "cohesive pattern of coercive controls that include verbal abuse, threats, psychological manipulation, sexual coercion, and control of economic resources" (Dobash and Dobash 1979; Schechter 1982). The greater the strength and size of the men, the greater the injury (Stets and Henderson 1991). Additionally, many women learn not to confront, and remain unskilled in effective verbal defense. Many women try to placate rather than leave the scene. Socialization of women that teaches them to be forgiving also leads to women staying in abusive relationships. All you have to do is volunteer at a battered women's shelter or read in the newspaper about child abuse to see who loses. As Gelles says, "When men hit women and women hit men, the real victims are almost certainly going to be the women" (1991, 128). Throughout history, women have been the victims of overwhelming amounts of violence.

Tenet 4: Victims of abuse are in a no-win situation. Once the cycle of abuse begins, the victim of the abuse has few good options (Lloyd and Emery 1994). For example, it is fruitless to try to use aggression against a stronger and more violent person. Yet, on the other hand, it is extraordinarily difficult to leave because the perpetrator is trying to control all your actions. The complexity of abusive relationships is evidenced by the fact that nearly 40 percent of victims of dating violence continue their relationships and that most women who seek help from a battered women's shelter return to their spouses (Sugarman and Hotaling 1989). Many women go back to abusive situations because with children and only welfare to support them, they cannot make a living. Many women feel guilty about the failure of the relationship and go back believing the abuser's promises to change. One study documented that 70 percent of fathers who sought custody of their children were successful, so many women, especially poor women, are afraid of losing their children if they stay away (Marano 1996). Tragically, abusers escalate their control tactics when victims try to leave. More domestic abuse victims are killed when they try to leave than at any other time. It is even more difficult for women with children to flee when they are totally dependent on the very persons who are violent with them.

Tenet 5: Perpetrators and victims have discrepant narratives about violence. One of the reasons that it is so difficult to decrease violence is that perpetrators of the most violent acts see their behavior as something "that could not be helped or as due to external, mitigating circumstances. Thus, they may cast themselves as unjustly persecuted for a minor, unavoidable, or nonexistent offense" (Baumeister, Stillwell, and Wotman 1990, 1003). One fascinating study asked the participants to recall situations where they were perpetrators of violence and then write about the events. They also were asked to recall situations where they were victims and reflect on those events. What emerged was that "perpetrators apparently see the incident as a brief, uncharacteristic episode that has little or no relation to present circumstances whereas victims apparently continue to see harmful consequences and to feel lasting grievances" (1001).

The discrepancies in accounts of violence extend to the underreporting of violence. Husbands are more likely than wives to minimize and deny their violence (Browning and Dotton 1986). Furthermore, husbands are more likely than wives to count choking, punching, and beating someone up as self-defense rather than violence (Brygger and Edleson 1984), but what abusers often report as "self-defense" is in reality violent retaliation.

Explanations

Why does violence occur in personal relationships? One explanation is that violent responses to conflict are learned—those who experience violence have experienced it before, witnessed it in their family of origin or in previous relationships. Studies find that perpetrators of violence were often *victims* of violence in their childhood and in their earlier relationships (Straus, Gelles, and Steinmetz 1980; Deal and Wampler 1986; Bernard and Bernard 1983). Yet, saying that "violence is passed on" is not a totally satisfying answer. We need to know much more about people who *do not continue* the patterns. Why do some people who are exposed to violence and aggression in childhood not continue these patterns into adulthood (Lenton 1995)? Patricia, for example, suffered both verbal and physical abuse at the hand of her father. He said and did terrible things to her when she was a child, and she ran away from home at age seventeen. Yet, in raising her children, she did not once verbally or physically abuse them. We need much more research on people like this who break the intergenerational transmission of aggression. Similarly, what about people in families and romantic relationships who *stop escalating sequences* of verbal aggression that might lead to violence? And, finally, why do some people who were not previously exposed to violence and aggression develop violent and aggressive behaviors?

A second explanation for violence centers on the elements of a patriarchal culture that insists the man is always right. It has been found that the more discrepant the power between the husband and the wife, the greater the violence. In "asymmetric power structures" (husband-dominant or wife-dominant marriages) there is "a much greater risk of violence than when conflict occurs among the equalitarian couples" (Coleman and Straus 1986, 152). When the power is "asymmetric," conflict episodes more often trigger violence. Similarly, one study demonstrated that the more dependent a wife is, the more tolerant she is of violence against her (Kalmuss and Straus 1982). Yet, as appealing as the patriarchal explanation is, it does not account for the incidence of physical abuse in lesbian relationships (Lenton 1995) nor for aggression that occurs in less-than-patriarchal heterosexual relationships.

A third explanation for violent tactics is that violence is the result of lack of communication skills in a situation of powerlessness. It has been found that physically aggressive wives and husbands display rigid communication patterns, automatically responding in kind to their partner rather than with an alternative response (Rosen 1996). If you can effectively argue (without being verbally aggressive), then you have a sense of power and impact. If you feel that you can have an impact on your spouse, there is no need to resort to physical aggression, even in the heat of conflict (the section on argumentation in chapter 7 expands on this perspective). Yet, there are also people who are both verbally skillful and physically violent.

Clearly, no one explanation can account for the complexity of violence. For example, why does a strong belief in pacifism correlate to fewer violent behaviors for Quaker women but not for Quaker men (Brutz and Allen 1986)? Why do surveys indicate that men are more often the recipients of violence than women? Is it because males are more likely to see any violence as a violation and report it? And why do people in marriages with a lot of physical aggression often not see it as a problem (Vivian and Langhinrichsen-Rohling 1994)?

Regardless of one's perspective on the incidence, patterns, and explanations of violence, it is time for us as a culture to take a firm stand on it. We desperately need to approach violence from a variety of platforms—in the home, in the schools, in the churches, synagogues, and gompas, and in the workplace. We are in need of pilot programs to teach us how to stop violence in all contexts. We need to give assistance to both perpetrators and victims so the cycles of destruction can be stopped.

If you or someone you know suffers from physical or sexual violence, help is available both locally and nationally. Contact local programs that help victims of violence and/or contact the National Domestic Violence Hotline at 1-800-799-7233 (1-800-799-SAFE).

Compromise

Compromise is an intermediate style resulting in some gains and some losses for each party. It is moderately assertive and cooperative. A compromising style is characterized by beliefs such as "You have to be satisfied with part of the pie," and "Give a little and get a little." When compromising, parties give up some important goals to gain others. Compromise is dependent on shared power because if the other party is perceived as powerless, no compelling reason to compromise exists. The following items, adapted from Rahim and Manger (1995), reflect compromise:

____I try to find a middle course to resolve an impasse.

____I usually propose a middle ground for breaking deadlocks.

____I negotiate with ______ so that a compromise can be reached.

____I use "give and take" so that a compromise can be made.

Compromise is frequently confused with problem-solving or collaboration because often a greater degree of energy is spent, creative solutions are generated, and flexibility is crucial. Compromise differs, however, in that it requires trade-offs and exchanges (Folger, Poole, and Stutman 1993). Many times people avoid using compromise because something valuable has to be given up. While North American norms, especially in public life, encourage compromising, the style is not often the first choice in personal relationships. When power is unequal, compromising more accurately reflects giving in or giving up. The following box summarizes the advantages and disadvantages of compromising.

Compromising

Advantages

Compromise sometimes lets conflict parties accomplish important goals with less time expenditure than collaboration requires. It also reinforces a power balance that can be used to achieve temporary or expedient settlements in time-pressured situations. It can be used as a backup method for decision-making when other styles fail. Further, it has the advantage of having external moral force; therefore, it appears reasonable to most parties. Compromise works best when other styles have failed or are clearly unsuitable.

Example:

Mark and Sheila, ages ten and eight, both want to play with the new video game they received for Christmas. After a noisy argument, their parents tell them to work something out that is fair. They decide that if no one else is using the game they can play without asking, but if they both want to play at the same time, they have to either play a game together or take turns by hours (every other hour). The compromise of taking turns works well as a conflict reduction device. The parents can intervene simply by asking, "Whose turn is it?"

Disadvantages

Compromise can become an easy way out—a "formula" solution not based on the demands of a particular situation. For some people, compromise always seems to be a form of "loss" rather than a form of "win." It prevents creative new options because it is easy and handy to use. Flipping a coin or "splitting the difference" can be a sophisticated form of avoidance of issues that need to be discussed. These chance measures, such as drawing straws or picking a number, are not really compromise. They are arbitration, with the "arbiter" being chance. True compromise requires creative, personal involvement in the proposed solutions.

Example:

Two friends from home decide to room together at college. Sarah wants to live in Jesse dorm with some other friends she has met. Kate wants to live in Brantley, an all-female dorm, so she can have more privacy. They decide that it wouldn't be fair for either one to get her first choice, so they compromise on Craig, where neither knows anyone. At midyear, they want to change roommates since neither is happy with the choice. Sarah and Kate might have been able to come up with a better solution if they had worked at it.

Research has not clarified compromise tactics to the extent of the two styles previously discussed, but the tactics shown in table 5.4 have been compiled to exemplify compromise.

One's view of compromise is a good litmus test about how you view conflict in general. Think about the famous "the cup is half empty" versus "the cup is half full" aphorism that applies to compromise. Some see compromise as "both of us lose something" and others see it as "both of us win something." Clearly, compromise means a middle ground between you and the other but involves a moderate and balanced amount of concern for self and concern for other.

Table 5.4 Compromise Tactics

Communication category	Illustrations
1. Appeal to fairness	"You got what you wanted last time." "It's not fair to ask me to do all the writing. We both are getting the grant support. Why don't you do your part and I'll do mine." "I don't make as much money as you do. It's not fair to make me pay half of all the expenses."
2. Suggest a trade-off	"How are we going to pay for all that summer help? Are you willing to wait to start the staff development program for half a year or so?" "I won't give on my expectations that you pay me back for the car accident, but I will consider your working off some of the money by doing jobs for me."
3. Maximize wins/minimize losses	"I'll give up the idea of going to my folks for Christmas if you'll take a real vacation so we can spend some time together.
4. Offer a quick, short-term solution	"Since we don't have time to gather all the data, how about if we do it my way for a month and then reassess when the data comes in and you get a chance to see how you like it."

Source: Adapted, by permission of publisher, from A. L. Sillars, ""Procedures for Coding Interpersonal Conflict," rev. (Department of Communication Studies, University of Montana, 1986), 7–16.

Accommodation

One who practices *accommodation* does not assert individual needs and prefers a cooperative and harmonizing approach. The individual sets aside his or her concerns in favor of pleasing the other people involved (this relational goal may be the most important goal for the accommodating person). The following items, adapted from Rahim and Manger (1995), represent the accommodating style. As you read these items, mentally fill in the blanks with a particular person (my mother, my employee, my friend, etc.).

____I generally try to satisfy the needs of ______.

____I usually accommodate the wishes of ______.

____I give in to the wishes of ______.

____I usually allow concessions to ______.

____I often go along with the suggestions of ______.

____I try to satisfy the expectations of ______.

One may gladly yield to someone else or may do so grudgingly and bitterly. The accompanying emotion can be highly divergent for those using accommodation, from gentle pleasure at smoothing ruffled feelings to angry, hostile compliance because one has too little power to protest what is being done. The accommodating person may think that he or she is serving the good of the group, family, or team by giving in, sacrificing, or stepping aside. Sometimes this is true; often, however, the accommodator could better serve the needs of the larger group by staying engaged longer and using a more assertive style. Sometimes people who habitually use this style play the role of the martyr, bitter complainer, whiner, or saboteur. They may *yield* in a passive way or *concede* when they have to (Folger, Poole, and Stutman 1993).

The following box summarizes the advantages and disadvantages of accommodation.

Accommodating

Advantages

When one finds that he or she is wrong, it can be best to accommodate the other to demonstrate reasonableness. If an issue is important to one person and not important to the other, the latter can give a little to gain a lot. In addition, accommodation can prevent one party from harming the other—one can minimize losses when he or she will probably lose anyway. If harmony or maintenance of the relationship is currently the most crucial goal, accommodation allows the relationship to continue without overt conflict. Accommodation to a senior or seasoned person can be a way of managing conflict by betting on the most experienced person's judgment.

Example:

A Forest Service manager asks the newest staff member if he is interested in learning about land trades with other federal agencies. The new employee knows that the manager must assign someone from his office to help the person in charge of land trades. The employee says, "It's not something I know much about, but I wouldn't mind learning." The manager, who could have assigned the new employee anyway, thanks him for his positive attitude about new responsibilities. The new employee's goals would not have been well served by saying, "I have no interest in getting into that area. There is too much red tape, and it moves too slowly."

Disadvantages

Accommodation can foster an undertone of competitiveness if people develop a pattern of showing each other how nice they can be. People can one-up others by showing how eminently reasonable they are. Accommodation of this type tends to reduce creative options. Further, if partners overuse accommodation, their commitment to the relationship is never tested, since one or the other always gives in. This pattern can result in a pseudosolution, especially if one or both parties resent the accommodation; it will almost surely boomerang later. Accommodation can further one person's lack of power. It may signal to that person that the other is not invested enough in the conflict to struggle through, thus encouraging the low-power party to withhold energy and caring. A female student wrote the following example of a learned pattern of avoidance and its resulting accommodation.

Example:

"In our home, conflict was avoided or denied at all costs, so I grew up without seeing conflicts managed in a satisfactory way, and I felt that conflict was somehow "bad" and would never be resolved. This experience fit well with the rewards of being a 'good' girl (accommodating to others), combining to make a pattern for me in which I was not even sensitive to wishes and desires that might lead to conflict."

Table 5.5 Accommodation Tactics

Communication category	Illustrations
1. Giving up/giving in	"Have it your way." "I don't want to fight about this."
2. Disengagement	"I couldn't care less." "I won't be here anyway. It doesn't matter." "I don't need to be involved in this." "I don't have time to be working on this issue."
3. Denial of needs	"I'll be fine here. You go ahead." "It's OK. I can stay late and do it."
4. Expression of desire for harmony	"It's forgotten. Don't worry about it" (referring to a previous discount or hurt). "It's more important to me that we work together on this than that I do what I want." "I am miserable when we fight. Let's put all this behind us and start over. I don't even remember what we are hassling each other about."

Source: Adapted, by permission of publisher, from A. L. Sillars, "Procedures for Coding Interpersonal Conflict," rev. (Department of Communication Studies, University of Montana, 1986), 7–16.

Table 5.5 presents tactics that accompany an accommodating style.

Collaboration

> Collaborative processes unleash this catalytic power and mobilize joint action among the stakeholders.
>
> —Barbara Gray, *Collaborating: Finding Common Ground for Multiparty Problems*

Collaboration demands the most constructive engagement of any of the conflict styles. *Collaboration* shows a high concern for one's own goals, the goals of others, the successful solution of the problem, and the enhancement of the relationship. Note that collaboration, unlike compromise, involves not a moderate concern for goals but a high concern for them. Refer back to figure 5.1 to clarify the differences between these two styles. Collaboration is an "invitational rhetoric" that invites the other's perspective so the two of you can reach a resolution that honors you both (Foss and Griffin 1995). The following items, adapted from Rahim and Manger (1995), reflect collaboration:

____I try to investigate an issue with ______ to find a solution acceptable to us.

____I try to integrate my ideas with those of ______ to come up with a decision jointly.

____I try to work with ______ to find solutions to a problem that satisfy our expectations.

____I exchange accurate information with ______ to solve a problem together.

____I try to bring all of our concerns out in the open so that the issues can be resolved in the best possible way.

____I collaborate with ______ to come up with decisions acceptable to us.

A collaborative conflict does not conclude until both parties are reasonably satisfied and can support the solution that has been found. Relationships are better, not worse, than when the conflict began. No one person ends up feeling justified or right. The style is cooperative, effective, and focused on team effort, partnership, or shared personal goals. It is also sometimes called mutual problem solving. It is the style that calls on all your best communication skills.

Collaboration involves making descriptive and disclosing statements and soliciting disclosure and criticism from the other party. One makes concessions when necessary and accepts responsibility for one's own part in the conflict. Collaboration does *not* mean taking total responsibility, such as saying, "It's all my fault. I shouldn't have gotten angry." Rather, collaboration is a struggle with the other to find mutually agreeable solutions. Parties engage at an exploratory, problem-solving level rather than avoiding or destroying each other.

Collaboration is characterized by statements such as "When I get in conflict with someone, I try to work creatively with them to find new options," or "I like to assert myself, and I also like to cooperate with others." Collaboration differs from compromise because in compromise, the parties look for an easy intermediate position that partially satisfies them both, whereas in collaboration, the parties work creatively to find new solutions that will *maximize* goals for them both. Consider the use of collaboration in the following example: A married couple are experiencing conflict over their priorities. The wife thinks the husband works too much and does not spend enough time with her. The husband believes the wife is not interested enough in his work. One way to manage the conflict would be for him to shorten his work hours to spend more time with his wife and for her to increase her interest in his work. But if the two parties collaborated, they could work together to identify the concerns underlying the conflict. It may be, for example, that both of them want more warmth and affection in the relationship, and the conflict arose because neither one's way of seeking affection was working. Through collaborative effort, they explore the disagreement and learn from each other's insights. They may discover, for instance, that *when* they spend time together makes a big difference. They may be able to meet for lunch occasionally, or the husband may be able to work at home during the evening.

Research on the effect of integrative styles is quite consistent—when one learns how to use them they are successful tools for conflict management. Collaboration results in "high joint benefit for the bargainers" (Tutzauer and Roloff 1988) and provides a constructive response to the conflict (Rusbult, Johnson, and Morrow 1984). Collaborative styles in a variety of contexts result in better decisions and greater satisfaction with partners (Sillars 1980; Wall and Galanes 1986; Tutzauer and Roloff 1988; Pruitt 1981; Gayle-Hackett 1989a). Cooperative styles allow conflict parties to find mutually agreeable solutions, whether the conflict occurs in an intimate or work situation. Dating couples who survived the "First Big Fight" believe that a successful relationship requires joint problem-solving (Siegert and Stamp 1994). When college students in collaborative, or win-win, relationships were asked to predict if the relationship would last, 85 percent said yes (Knox, Schacht, Turner, and Norris 1995).

One of the downsides to collaboration is that one party sometimes uses it exclusively and denigrates the other conflict party for not using it. For example, if one party is trying to collaborate and the other party is avoiding or competing, the first party might say, "I tried to solve the conflict, but he wouldn't." Negative views of the other's chosen style can become a sophisticated form of "one-up"—in other words, if what "I" did was fine, the other person must be the cause of the continued conflict.

The following box summarizes the advantages and disadvantages of collaboration.

Collaborating

Advantages

Collaboration works well when one wants to find an integrative solution that will satisfy both parties. It generates new ideas, shows respect for the other party, and gains commitment to the solution from both parties. Because collaboration incorporates the feelings of the concerned parties, they both feel that the solutions are reality based. Collaboration is a high-energy style that fits people in long-term, committed relationships, whether personal or professional. Collaboration actively affirms the importance of relationship and content goals and thus builds a team or partnership approach to conflict management. When collaboration works, it prevents one from using destructive means such as violence. It demonstrates to the parties that conflict can be productive.

Example:

Anne, an intern at a hospital, has been given a "mission impossible" that requires that she diagnose and chart patients under the supervision of four different doctors. Her fellow interns work collaboratively to relieve her of some of the work. They want to demonstrate the need for more reasonable assignments, support Anne as a friend, and avoid being assigned Anne's work if she gets sick or resigns.

Disadvantages

Like any style, if collaboration is the only style used, one can become imprisoned in it. If investment in the relationship or issue is low, collaboration is not worth the time and energy consumed. Further, people who are more verbally skilled than others can use collaboration in very manipulative ways, resulting in a continued power discrepancy between the parties. It can be used as a one-up move. For example, if one party uses collaboration, he or she may accuse the other of being "unreasonable" because of choosing a different style. Often, high-power persons use pseudocollaboration to maintain the power imbalance. These latter cases are not really collaboration because at least two people are required to collaborate. However, one avoider can frustrate the intentions of four collaborators.

Example:

Members of a small group in a communication class are under time pressure to finish their project, due in one week. They overuse collaborative techniques such as consensus building, brainstorming, paraphrasing, and bringing out silent members. Quickly breaking up into subgroups would better serve the individual and relational goals of the group, but the group clings to a time-consuming method of making decisions long after they should adapt their style to meet the deadline.

The collaborative tactics presented in table 5.6 induce or persuade the other party to cooperate in finding a mutually favorable resolution to the conflict. They reflect a "mutual versus individual" orientation (Canary and Cupach 1988). Collaboration involves both parties working together for solutions that not only end the conflict but also maximize the

Table 5.6 Collaborative Tactics

Conflict codes	Illustrations
A. Analytic remarks	
1. *Descriptive statements.* Nonevaluative statements about observable events related to conflict.	"I criticized you yesterday for getting angry with the kids."
2. *Disclosing statements.* Nonevaluative statements about events related to conflict that the partner cannot observe, such as thoughts, feelings, intentions, motivations, and past history.	"I swear I never had such a bad week as that week."
3. *Qualifying statements.* Statements that explicitly qualify the nature and extent of conflict.	"Communication is mainly a problem when we're tired."
4. *Solicitation of disclosure.* Nonhostile questions about events related to conflict that cannot be observed (thoughts, feelings, intentions, motives, or past history).	"What were you thinking when you said . . . ?"
5. *Solicitation of criticism.* Nonhostile questions soliciting criticism of oneself.	"Does it bother you when I stay up late?"
B. Conciliatory remarks	
1. *Supportive remarks.* Statements that refer to understanding, support, acceptance, positive regard for the partner, shared interests, and goals.	"I can see why you would be upset."
2. *Concessions.* Statements that express a willingness to change, show flexibility, make concessions, or consider mutually acceptable solutions to conflicts.	"I think I could work on that more."
3. *Acceptance of responsibility.* Statements that attribute responsibility for conflict to self or to both parties.	"I think we've both contributed to the problem."

Source: Adapted, by permission of publisher, from A. L. Sillars, "Procedures for Coding Interpersonal Conflict," rev. (Department of Communication Studies, University of Montana, 1986), 7–16.

gains for both parties. The term *integrative* can be used to describe collaborative tactics, since the tactics help people recognize their interdependence (Walton and McKersie 1965). Collaborative tactics have also been labeled *prosocial* (Roloff 1976; Sillars 1986). The goals of the individuals and the relationship as a whole are paramount.

Collaborative tactics involve a stance toward conflict management that is very different from competitive tactics. A competitive tactic assumes that the size of the pie is finite; therefore, one's tactics are designed to maximize gains for oneself and losses for the other.

Collaborative tactics, however, assume that the size of the pie can be increased by working with the other party. Both can leave the conflict with something they value.

Some people experience only avoidant or competitive attitudes toward conflict and have a difficult time visualizing a collaborative approach. If each time you have conflict you immediately say to your conflict partner, "You are wrong," you will likely receive a competitive response in return. Collaboration calls for a willingness to move *with* rather than against the other—a willingness to explore and struggle precisely when you may not feel like it. You do not give up your self-interest, you *integrate* it with the other's self-interest to reach agreement. Usually, a collaborative approach to conflict management involves the use of multiple tactics listed in table 5.6.

You need not like your co collaborators. Collaboration, however, does require "we" language rather than "I" language. Because parties work together for mutually desirable outcomes and protect their own as well as each other's interests, many times respect, caring, and admiration develop as by-products of the collaborative effort.

In table 5.6, the first major classification of collaborative tactics is "analytic remarks," which allow one to collaborate by making descriptive, disclosing, or other types of statements. The following examples reflect *descriptive statements,* which are the first category of analytic remarks (Yarbrough 1977):

- *Describe without interpretation.* Describe what you sense, feel, see, hear, touch, and smell instead of your guesses about the behavior.
  Example: "You're so quiet. Ever since I said I didn't want to go out tonight and would rather stay home and read, you haven't spoken to me," *not* "You never understand when I want to spend some time alone!"
- *Focus on what is instead of what should be.*
  Example: "You look angry. Are you?" *not* "You shouldn't be angry just because I want to stay home."
- *Describe your own experience instead of attributing it to the other person.*
  Example: "I'm finding myself not wanting to bring up any ideas because I'm afraid you will ignore than," *not* "You are getting more critical all the time."

One makes *disclosing statements* by saying such things as "I am having trouble tracking this issue" or other reports of your feelings while in the conflict. The flip side of the coin is to *solicit disclosure* from the other party, such as saying, "What makes you so upset when I bring up the summer plans?" As table 5.6 illustrates, one can also make *qualifying statements* and *solicit criticism* as ways to move the conflict toward collaboration.

The final three categories of collaborative tactics, classified as *conciliatory remarks,* are (1) *supportive remarks* ("I can see why that is difficult—we have all been ganging up on you"); (2) *concessions* ("OK, I agree I need to find new ways to deal with this problem") and; (3) *acceptance of responsibility* ("Yes, I have been acting aggressively lately"). All conciliatory remarks acknowledge one's own role in the conflict and offer an "olive branch" of hope and reconciliation to the other, paving the way to successful management of the conflict. All of the collaborative tactics move the conflict into a third dimension where partners neither avoid nor blame but grapple with the conflict as a joint problem to be solved.

Collaborative tactics are associated with successful conflict management. Although conflict participants use collaboration infrequently (Barnlund 1989), participants who do use collaboration report "relational intimacy" (Cupach 1980); "perceived communicator appropriateness, effectiveness and attractiveness" (Canary and Spitzberg 1987); "satisfaction with the partner and relationship (Gottman 1982; Sillars 1980); and "satisfaction with the conflict outcomes" (Canary and Cupach 1988, 306; Wall and Galanes 1986). Similarly, popular prescriptions for conflict management specify that one should work with the partner to establish mutual gain and to preserve the relationship and should engage in neither avoidance nor verbal aggressiveness but try to find mutual solutions to the problems (Fisher and Ury 1981; Fisher and Brown 1988).

Cautions About Styles

Although considerable research has been done on individual conflict styles, there are some serious limitations to the research. Especially when one decides to pursue partnership, collaborative, and mutual-influence approaches, purely individual styles do not exist. One is always influenced by others, and should be, when striving for cooperative goals. For instance, if you want to practice constructive, partnership approaches, you will not automatically respond to a sarcastic threat (competition) with a counterthreat or by backing down (accommodation or avoidance). You will, instead, look for ways to reframe what has happened and for more constructive options, even if you feel justified in blasting back at what feels like a threatening opponent (we will present self-regulation techniques in the next chapter). You will find it useful to thoroughly understand the styles and their supporting tactics so you can make educated choices about moves and approaches that are available to you during conflict. One limitation of the research on conflict styles is that *most studies are based on participants' "perceptions" of their conflict styles.* One's vantage point can significantly alter the given response. Various instruments measuring conflict style have been administered to hundreds of people experiencing conflict in the workplace. When participants fill out the conflict style scales on themselves and on others, two predominant findings emerge:

- People most often see *themselves* as trying to solve the problem (using integrative styles).
- People most often see *others* as using controlling or aggressive styles.

These results indicate that one's perception of conflict style depends on whether one is rating the self or others. People tend to see themselves as trying to solve the conflict and the other as blocking the resolution of the conflict. Although no large-scale studies have been completed on the differences between self and other perceptions of conflict styles, Thomas and Pondy (1977) asked sixty-six managers to recall a recent conflict and state which style was used by each party. Overwhelmingly, the managers saw themselves as cooperative or collaborative and the other party as primarily competitive, demanding, and refusing. Gayle (1991) found a similar social desirability bias (giving answers that "look good"). Unfortunately, your perception of what you did will probably not be corroborated by the other person. In conflict, we tend to see ourselves in a positive light and others in a negative light. Human beings tend to value their own individual approaches to life. All too often we assume that our choices about behavior, values, and goals are the *right* ones. Therefore, we are right if we are "aggressive," "cooperative," "polite," "fair-minded," or "realistic." Since we evaluate styles depending on whether they are ours or someone else's, our vantage point determines our perceptions.

Reporting problems also extend to issues about gender. People often want to know if men and women enact conflict differently. Research demonstrates mixed results—some studies show differences between the genders and some show no differences (Gayle-Hackett 1989b). When style studies are done on high school and college students, women report themselves as more collaborative than do men, who report themselves as more competitive. However, when studies are done in the workplace with older adults, male-female differences disappear (Gayle-Hackett 1989a; Rahim 1986; Bell, Chafetz, and Horn 1982; Renwick 1977; Rossi and Todd-Mancillas 1987; Schockley-Zalabak 1981; Portello and Long 1994; Korabik, Baril, and Watson 1993; Gayle 1991). In real-life settings, conflict styles are more closely related to location in the structure (as supervisor, employee, or owner) than to gender.

Another reporting bias is the underreporting of the amount of avoidance people actually use (Gayle-Hackett 1989a; Gayle 1991). When a questionnaire asks you about an ongoing conflict, you answer about conflicts that are important to you. Those you have avoided and have no interest or investment in are likely not even remembered, thus we underreport the amount of avoidance we actually use.

A second limitation of conflict style research is that *measures are not process oriented.* Some individuals develop preferred *sequences of styles;* for example, one may begin a conflict by avoiding, then move to competing, then finally collaborate with the other party. Most measuring instruments or quizzes, however, treat personal styles as if they are traits belonging to one person—something one always does or something that describes the *person* instead of the *behavior.* The accurate assessment of one's conflict style should presuppose some change over time to reflect the variability that most people enact in their lives. Baxter (1982), for example, demonstrated that conflict expressions of small-group participants differ depending on the phase of group decision making in which the group is engaged. The following chart illustrates predominate styles with fluctuations across time. Note the variability within the styles used by the two people, both of whom predominately avoid conflict.

	Time 1	Time 2	Time 3	Time 4	Time 5	Time 6	Time 7	Time 8	Time 9
Person A:	avoid	avoid	compete	avoid	avoid	avoid	compete	avoid	avoid
Person B.	avoid	avoid	accommodate	avoid	avoid	avoid	accommodate	avoid	avoid

Both would score as "avoiders" on a general style measure, yet over time, each one demonstrates a distinctly different pattern. Measuring general styles does not reflect over-time differences between people.

Not only do our styles change with the progress of the conflict, they also change as a result of our life experiences. A young man who is always competitive learns from his romantic partner how to collaborate—thus changing his style. Alternately, someone who avoids conflict learns through trial and error to engage the conflict earlier, thus changing her predominant mode. One *can* change preferred conflict style, especially if the old style ceases to work well.

A third limitation of conflict style research is that *measures give the impression of consistency across settings and relationships.* Most of the instruments, in fact, ask you to respond "in general." Of course, for many people "in general" doesn't capture the changes they experience from relationship to relationship. When people respond to style measures "for a particular relationship" or conflict, about 50 percent of the people report disparate styles in different contexts. For example, many people compete at work but avoid conflict at home. Similarly, many avoid conflict at work but collaborate at home. Yet most instruments don't account for these differences. Recent work is finally beginning to assess conflict styles across contexts and is confirming that many people have disparate styles in different contexts (Marin, Sherblom, and Shipps 1994).

Even within one setting, such as work, we use different styles with different partners. Putnam and Wilson (1982) demonstrated that employees prefer nonconfrontation when in a peer-related conflict in an organization, but they choose forceful communication to manage conflict with subordinates. For example, Eric, a college debater who uses an analytic approach to conflict, competes every chance he gets within public situations. He loves to match wits with others, push hard for what he wants, and win arguments. He is a good-humored and driven young man in public situations. Yet in private with his wife, he avoids conflict as though it were a dreaded disease. When Joan brings up conflictual issues, Eric either avoids or completely accommodates—he cannot stand conflict within an intimate relationship for fear of losing the relationship. Yet if Eric were to fill out a widely used style instrument, he would be asked to report how he acts in conflicts, without a specific context designated. It is easy to watch someone in conflict and assume that the chosen style reflects some underlying personality dimension. But since most people adapt to different situations, with a preferred choice in one context and another choice in a different context, to give them a single label, such as a "compromiser," is a gross oversimplification.

A fourth limitation of conflict style research is that *one's style of conflict is assumed to be a clear reflection of an underlying motivation—a stable personality trait.* Competers, however, may not want to "run over you," and avoiders may actually care about their relationships. For example, in Ellen's first marriage, she developed the pattern of occasionally throwing dishes when she was intensely angry. Her first husband would then leave the house. A few years later, after she had married Mick, they got into a screaming argument. Ellen threw a dish at Mick, who promptly went to the kitchen and threw some dishes back at her, smashing them on the wall and shouting that she wasn't going to throw dishes at him! In response to this competitive, or at least aggressive, interaction, Ellen realized that what she wanted was someone who would stay and fight out the problem instead of leaving the scene. Neither has thrown a dish since. At first glance, one could say that Ellen's aggressive style was an attempt to get her own way, stifle all opposition, and dominate Mick. The "true" motivation emerged in the interaction—which was a desire for intimacy.

A final limitation of current research is that *attempts to measure individual conflict styles ignore the interactive dynamics in a conflict situation.* As noted previously, our choices are not just the results of some personality quirk—they are responses to many elements of a conflict. This issue is of such fundamental importance that the next section will examine it in detail.

Interaction Dynamics

Whether we are looking at an isolated tactical move or the overall conflict style of an individual, *we cannot understand conflict dynamics by examining the individual in isolation.* The *interaction* of two or more people determines the outcome of the conflict. No matter how hard one person tries to resolve a conflict, the outcome will not be constructive unless the other person is involved in working things out, too. Figure 5.2 shows two very different

Figure 5.2 Tactics in an interaction context

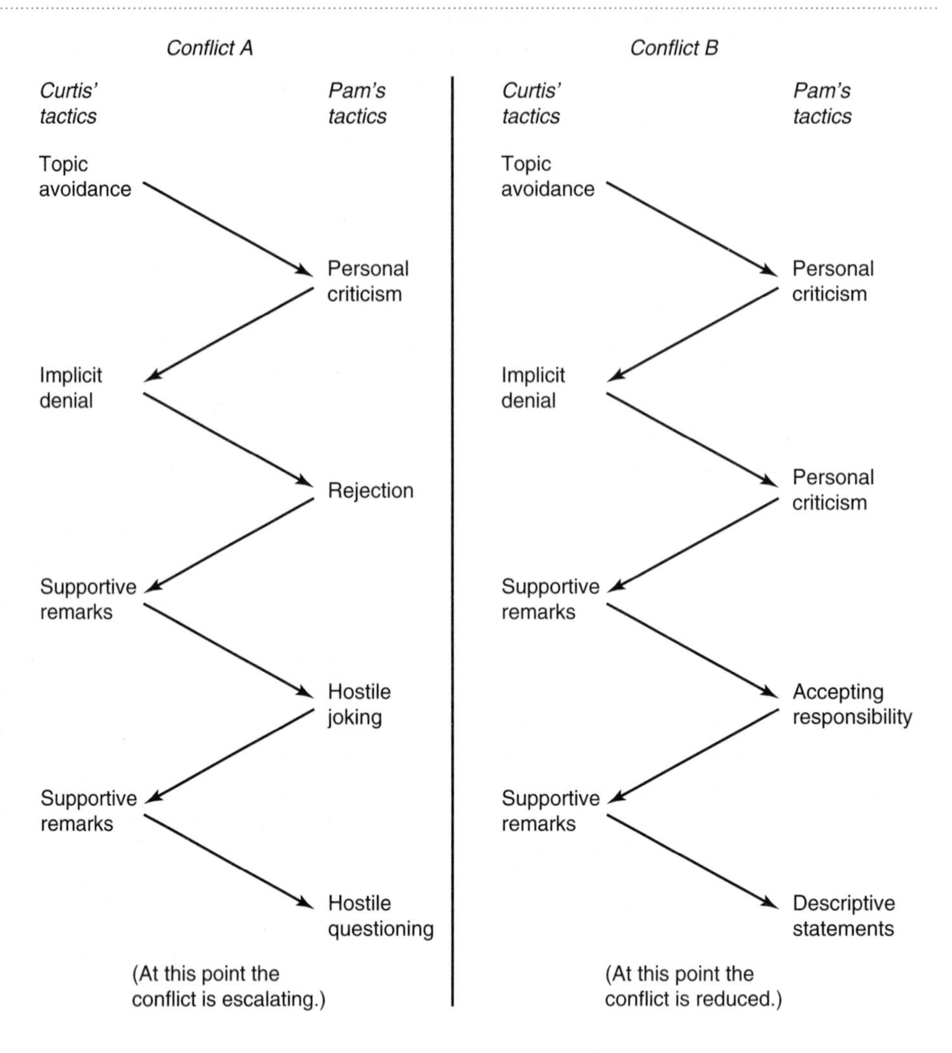

outcomes of conflict even though Curtis uses exactly the same tactics throughout. In one case the conflict escalates between the two participants. In the other, Pam's alternative tactics reduce the conflict. The outcome is the *joint product of both choices,* not some inherent personality trait on the part of either participant.

One chooses his or her conflict tactics and styles based on "attributions about the partner's intent to cooperate, the focus of responsibility for the conflict, and the stability of the conflict" (Sillars 1980, 182). Analysis must shift from the individual to the relationship level, viewing conflict preferences as a system of interlocking behaviors rather than as a function of personality (Knapp, Putnam, and Davis 1988). Relational variables (whom you interact with, how congruent your perceptions are with those of the other party, what intent you think the other party has, and the mirroring of each other's responses) explain conflict style choices better than does personality (Putnam and Poole 1987; Knapp, Putnam, and Davis 1988). When you are a party to a conflict it is your perception of the other's choices that accounts for the choices you make (Rogers, Castleton, and Lloyd 1996).

Even though each conflict interaction is unique, two patterns of interlocking behaviors are worthy of note. They are (1) *complementary patterns* and (2) *symmetrical patterns.*

Complementary patterns are tactics or styles that are different from one another but mutually reinforcing. For example, if one person tries to engage and talk about the conflict and the other avoids, each one's moves reinforce those of the other. The engager begins to think, "If I don't force the issue, he will never talk to me," while the avoider thinks, "If she would just leave me alone, it would be all right." The more she engages, the more he avoids; the more he avoids, the more she engages; and they produce a "communication spiral" with each one magnifying his or her chosen response (Wilmot 1995).

Such complementary patterns occur in many contexts. In business settings, for example, supervisors and subordinates use different styles (Richmond et al. 1984), and in personal relationships, one person is often conciliatory and the other coercive. Raush et al. (1974) found that there was a "Jekyll-Hyde" quality to spouses in unsatisfactory marriages (Pike and Sillars 1985). In the first interaction one person would be coercive and the other conciliatory, then they would reverse roles. The individuals changed styles, but the overall interaction pattern was the same! Subsequent research has demonstrated a consistent pattern of tactics and styles in unsatisfactory marriages. In unhappy marriages wives are conflict engaging and husbands are withdrawn (Gottman and Krokoff 1989). The interlocking communication of *both* parties determines the state of the relationship (Gottman and Krokoff 1989; Canary, Cunningham, and Cody 1988; Pike and Sillars 1985; Raush et al 1974). Over the long term, if the husband stays withdrawn, whining, defensive, and stubborn, the marriage suffers (Gottman and Krokoff 1989). This pattern has also been expressed as the "fight-fight" pattern composed of complementary, interlocking tactics on the parts of husbands and wives (Pike and Sillars 1985).

Two people can engage in complementary interactions that are not causing serious relationship difficulties. For example, nine-year-old Carina, when confronted by her father about being responsible, says, "Who cares?" (with a giggle). But, if the patterns persist for years they can keep the two parties in recurring conflict.

Symmetrical sequences occur in conflicts when the participants' tactics mirror one another—both parties escalating, for example. One type of symmetrical pattern is when the parties both avoid a conflict, refuse to engage the conflict overtly, and create a *devitalized spiral.* As a result, the relationship loses vitality and the partners become so independent of each other that the relationship withers away. Various labels for symmetrical patterns exist. For example, repetitive attempts to coerce and retaliate keep destructive sequences going (Oliver 1984). Gottman (1982) noted that there is a "chaining" of identical tactics in distressed marriages. Distressed spouses get stuck in cycles of competitive tactics. For example, a sequence might occur as follows:

Husband: threat
Wife: counterthreat
Husband: intensified threat
Wife: intensified counterthreat

People match their spouse's competitive tactics with an increase in their own. Such *escalatory* spirals lead the couple into irresolvable conflicts. In organizations, what starts as an "attack-defend" pattern evolves into symmetrical "attack-attack" patterns, with each party trying to one-up the other (Putnam and Jones 1982b). These patterns have been characterized in the following ways:

- attack-attack
- retaliatory chaining
- negative reciprocity
- cross-complaining
- threat-counterthreat
- round-robin attacks
- escalatory spirals

Other conflict tactics and styles, then, are best seen in the context of the relationship. Based on available research, the following conclusions are warranted:

1. If the conflict parties both want to avoid the conflict and, as a norm, do not generally work through conflicts, joint avoidance can be functional (Pike and Sillars 1985; Raush et al. 1974).
2. Once a conflict is engaged, dissatisfaction can be caused by either fight-flight or threat-threat patterns. Either the complementary pattern or the symmetrical pattern can be dysfunctional for the parties, especially when they get rigidly locked into habitual tactics and styles.
3. Once engagement has occurred, the conflict is best managed by moving to collaborative, integrative tactics (Pike and Sillars 1985; Raush et al. 1974). One useful sequence is (a) the agenda-building phase, (b) the arguing phase, and (c) the final, integrative negotiation phase (Gottman et al. 1976).

In summary, to preserve a good relationship while pursuing a goal that appears incompatible with that of the other person, collaborative tactics are needed. You may begin the conflict by avoiding, accommodating, compromising, or escalating, but at some point collaborative engagement is usually necessary. Competent communicators are those who use constructive, prosocial, collaborative tactics at some stage of the conflict (Cupach 1982). As Schuetz (1978) says, "In situations of conflict, as in other communicative events, the competent communicator engages in cooperative interaction that permits both persons (factions) involved to achieve their goals" (10). Sillars's work (1980) demonstrates that roommates who engaged in conflicts characterized by collaboration, rather than by avoidance or competition, were more satisfied with each other and more likely to successfully resolve conflict. Furthermore, various family researchers have clearly demonstrated the link between collaboration and relationship satisfaction (Gottman 1994; Noller et al. 1994). Collaborative tactical and stylistic choices depend on a certain level of cognitive complexity (Applegate 1982; Delia and Clark 1977). Collaborative tactics involve supporting a positive, autonomous identity for the other while working toward your own goals. Such multiple demands, although difficult to master, lead to productive results for both parties, for in the end you are working with rather than against the other for mutual collaborative gains.

Whatever tactical or stylistic moves you make, the basic question is whether those choices lead to the effective management of the conflict over time. No one set of moves at any point will guarantee productive conflict, but collaborative tactics at least set the stage for the containment and management of the conflict if both parties move toward a problem-solving perspective. When in doubt, collaborate.

System Styles

Just as individuals develop characteristic styles, so do entire systems. Papp, Silberstein, and Carter (1973) note that in systems theory analyses, "attention is focused on connections and relationships rather than on individual characteristics. The central ideas of this theory are that the whole is considered to be greater than the sum of its parts; each part can only be understood in the context of the whole; a change in any one part will affect every other part" (197). Each communication system has an identity that is more than the sum of the individual players. If Sally is aggressive, Tom is accommodating, and Linda avoids, simply combining their individual preferences for conflict does not tell us how they will manage conflict as a system. The following comments reflect systemwide observation:

> The research and development department runs like a scared rabbit whenever the bottom line is mentioned.
> They fight like cats and dogs, but they always make up.
> That whole group is plastic. They look so sweet, but I wouldn't trust them farther than I could throw them.

Unlike individual styles, systemwide styles have not been widely researched. Some of the most useful system descriptions will be presented, and hopefully, more research on the impact of various system styles will be forthcoming.

Many system descriptions have emerged from researchers of family interaction (Fisher 1982). Lederer and Jackson's seminal book on the *Mirages of Marriage* (1968) focused attention on how marital partners act as a unit rather than as individuals. In that book, such phrases as the "gruesome twosome" and the "heavenly twins" were used to describe marriages rather than individuals. Cuber and Haroff (1955), often cited, described marriages as

1. *conflict-habituated* relationships, in which conflict recurs constantly but has little productive effect. The fighters "don't get anywhere."
2. *devitalized* marriages, in which the relationship is a hollow shell of what originally was vibrant and living.
3. *passive-congenial* relationships, in which both partners accept a conventional, calm, ordered marriage that maintains little conflict.
4. *vital* relationships, which involve intense mutual sharing of important life events.
5. *total* marriages, characterized by the sharing of virtually every aspect of life, fulfilling each other almost completely.

The impact of conflict itself, as well as the way it is enacted, differs depending on the relational type. In a conflict-habituated couple, for example, conflict is so common that it may go almost unnoticed, but if slowly drains the energy that the couple needs for important growth or conflict. Devitalized partners might experience conflict as so devastating that it tears apart the fragile fabric of their shared life. Conflict, after all, is energy producing *and* energy draining, which may destroy a devitalized couple. Likewise, avoidance in a total relationship would be a distress signal, whereas anything but avoidance in a passive-congenial relationship might break its implicit rules.

Another system-level description comes from Rands, Levinger, and Mellinger (1981), who provided an alternate view of conflict resolution types. They found that couples could be seen as belonging to one of four types:

Type I: *Nonintimate-aggressive* relationships foster escalation without corresponding intimacy. Couples are aggressive toward each other without enjoying the benefit of growing emotional closeness. Conflict for couples who maintain this pattern is usually not satisfying, since more energy is drained than is gained.

Type II: *Nonintimate-nonaggressive* couples lack vitality, intimacy, and escalation. Thus they are more satisfied than Type I people, since they do not have to contend with escalating conflict.

Type III: *Intimate-aggressive* couples combine intimate behavior with aggressive acts. Their conflict usually results in intimacy, even though they use aggressive or attacking conflict modes. Their satisfaction depends on whether their conflicts lead to intimacy or someone derails the predictable outcome by aggression that is too vicious or comments that are "below the belt."

Type IV: *Intimate-nonaggressive* partners use small amounts of attacking or blaming behavior, retaining their intimacy in other ways. These couples are satisfied, whether they are "congenial" (i.e., they avoid full discussion of issues) or "expressive" (i.e., they confront important issues).

Rands et al. (1981) demonstrate that multiple paths may be taken toward the goal of satisfied relationships. In an intimate relationship, for example, conflict avoidance reduces feelings of satisfaction for the couple, but in a nonintimate relationship, avoidance tends to increase satisfaction. The nature of the relationship, its definition, and its underlying patterns determine the existence and impact of conflict.

David Mace (1982), one of the originators of marital enrichment programs, has set forth a workable scheme for conflict patterns in marital systems. He finds that couples react to conflict in one of four ways. They may avoid it, tolerate it, attempt to fight fairly, or process it, which involves active listening and telling the emotional as well as factual truth.

How systems process conflict can also be put on a continuum, such as least processing to most processing. Guerin et al. (1987) have provided a four-stage model of marital conflict. Conflict within other systems, such as families or organizations, can also be classified according to the following stages:

Stage I: Members experience a *minimal amount of conflict,* openly communicate, and share power. The level of conflict causes no distress for the system.

Stage II: Members experience *significant conflict that they see as causing a problem.* Criticism increases, but still there is little power polarization or overt struggle for control. Usually, one person is pursuing and the other is distancing, and as a system, they have some difficulty agreeing on how much separateness they should have.

Stage III: Members are in *turbulence,* experience *high intensity,* and are moving toward *polarization.* They are unable to exchange information accurately and frequently criticize each other. Their power struggle is now serious and there is a life-or-death quality to much of their communication.

Stage IV: Members have *lost the ability to work through their conflicts* and have engaged the *services of a third party.* They see the relationship as adversarial and work to enhance their own individual bargaining positions. At this stage, a couple is headed toward disengagement and divorce (Guerin et al. 1987).

Just as with individual approaches to styles, a systemwide view has some limitations. First, conflict can be occurring in the system because the participants disagree about the type of system they want. One partner may want to be enmeshed, involving the other in all decisions, whereas the other may want more disengagement. In such cases, individual behaviors indicate a struggle with the definition of the system as a whole. Rather than categorizing a system as "nonintimate-aggressive," the system may reflect a struggle in process. When people work toward defining who they will be together, the rules that shape their interaction may be in flux. Some of the typologies discussed in the previous section may have given the impression that conflict patterns are fixed. However, they actually may change rapidly. Sharon and Don, for example, are the parents of three children who are entering their teens. In the past, the family could be described as "nonintimate-nonaggressive." Now that the children are growing up, the parents are rediscovering their intimacy with each other, which results in confusion in the family interactions, since the children are used to being the center of attention. No system description adequately reflects the complexity the family experiences during transition.

Second, just as with individual styles, various systems styles can be functional or not, depending on the needs of the situation. Not all groups are automatically better off with a highly processed or "intimate-nonaggressive" style all the time. Relationships go through cycles of change on various dimensions. Mutual avoidance of conflict may be appropriate, for instance, if a remarried couple is determined to avoid the tense escalatory behavior of their first marriages. Avoidance may not continue to work for this couple for ten years, but it may serve their goals well at first.

Third, descriptions of system styles have emerged relatively recently in communication and the other social sciences. The precise role of conflict in each system is yet to be charted, and other systemwide conceptualizations will undoubtedly be created.

Flexibility Creates Constructive Conflict

As has been demonstrated, the willingness, skill, and courage needed to adopt a flexible style determine how constructive conflict interaction will be.

Individual Adaptability

On the individual level, people often get "frozen" into a conflict style. Each time they are in a conflict, they make the same choices. The work associate who always avoids any conflict, smooths over everyone's feelings, and habitually refuses to talk about the difficulties between herself and others is frozen in a particular style. Individual lack of adaptation can occur in many forms. For example, a person might always avoid conflict until it heats up, at which he or she engages in violent behavior. The pattern is self-sealing and difficult to alter. The person who competes on the job and is unable to relax off the job is just as stuck as the person who is unable to openly admit that conflict exists. People who are inflexible in their style selection are often unaware that their choice of style is an important contributor to the conflict.

People often get stuck in behaviors from their "golden age." The golden age is that period in which you felt best about yourself and from which you possibly still draw many positive feelings. The forty-five-year-old history teacher who fondly recalls participating in high school athletics might operate from the rule that "the way to handle conflict is to get out there and give it everything you've got, fight to win, and never let anything keep you from your goal." This rule probably worked beautifully in a football game, but it may cause real havoc if the principal does not want to work with aggressive teachers and recommends a teacher's transfer to another school.

Often people are stuck in a personal style because of their gender identity. Young girls may have been taught to smooth others' feelings and not "make waves." If you were raised with such prescriptions and bring them to a conflict situation, you will accommodate the other and fail to assert your own desires. In the following excerpt, a woman details some of the disadvantages of this particular lack of flexibility:

> As a child, I was forbidden to "talk back." As a result, I stifled all my replies until I was of sufficient age to walk out and did so. That was fifteen years ago—I have never been back. . . . Thus, my strategy has been one of avoidance of a conflict to which I can see no resolution. Because I was raised by my father and stepmother, I scarcely knew my mother. When I was seventeen, I went to live with her. She wanted a mother-daughter relationship to which I could not respond. Legally bound to her, my attempts at confrontation ended in failure. Once again I walked out—this time into marriage. After seven years of marriage and abortive attempts at communication, I again walked out—this time with two children.

Likewise, many men are taught to compete regardless of the situation, learning that accommodation, compromise, or collaboration are all signs of weakness. Although the competitive style might be appropriate for certain business situations, in which everyone understands the tacit rules making competition functional, carrying competition as one's only response into an intimate relationship can often result in its destruction. Gender conditioning, whatever its particular form, is just one kind of learning that helps keep people stuck in conflict styles that may not work in other situations.

How can you tell if you are stuck in a conflict style? Use the following diagnostic aid to determine if you are stuck in patterns that do not work well for you:

1. *Does your current conflict response feel like the only natural one?* For example, if you friends or family suggest that you "might try talking it through" rather than repetitively escalating conflict, do such new options seem alien and almost impossible for you to enact?
2. *Does your conflict style remain constant across a number of conflicts that have similar characteristics?* For example, in every public conflict, do you accommodate others regardless of the issues at hand or your relationship with the others involved?
3. *Do you have a set of responses that follow a preset pattern?* For instance, do you "go for the jugular" then back off and accommodate the other because you fear you have made a "scene"? If you follow regular cycles of behavior, whatever the particulars, you may be in a process that could be altered.

4. *Do others seem to do the same thing with you?* If different people engage in similar behavior with you, you may be doing something that triggers their response. For instance, has it been your experience that in public conflicts, others are *always* competitive? If so, their behavior may be a reaction to a competitive posture that you take toward public conflict. If you were more conciliatory, others might not feel the need to respond competitively to you.
5. *Do you carry a label that is affectionately or not so affectionately used to describe you?* If you grew up as "our little fireball," you may not have learned how to collaborate. If you are referred to as a "powerhouse," a "mover and shaker," or "a bulldog," your conflict style might be overly inflexible. If you're known as "the judge" or "the dictator," you may need to take notice of an overly rigid style. Labels, although they often hurt and overgeneralize, may carry embedded grains of truth.

Individuals who can change and adapt are more likely to be effective conflict participants, accomplishing private and group goals better than people who avoid change. Hart and Burks (1972) discuss the concept of *rhetorical sensitivity,* the idea that people change their communication style based on the demands of different situations. The following five communication characteristics describe people who are rhetorically sensitive:

1. They are comfortable altering their roles in response to the behaviors of others.
2. They avoid stylizing their communication behavior, so they are able to adapt.
3. They develop skills to deal with different audiences and are able to withstand the pressure and ambiguity of constant adaptation.
4. They are able to monitor talk with others to make it purposive rather than expressive. They speak not so much to "spill their guts" as to solve problems.
5. They adapt and alter behaviors in a rational and orderly way.

In other words, effective interpersonal communicators expect change and adapt to change in their communication with others. They avoid getting "stuck" in certain conflict styles.

One reward for developing a repertoire of conflict styles is that we are then able to see the behavior of others in a different, more objective light. When we have a wide repertoire of conflict behaviors, we assume that other people do, too. We are far less likely to judge the behavior of others automatically as having evil intent, being childish, or being improper. After all, if *we* are reasonable and justified in our choices, we will probably be able to judge others as reasonable when they choose different styles.

Another reason for actively working to widen one's repertoire of conflict styles is that many styles were developed from rules of etiquette that may be outdated. These rules often help us make sense out of social situations—without some expectations of what constitutes appropriate behavior, we would be confused much of the time. However, although it may be appropriate to "respect your elders" when you are eight years old, overgeneralizing that rule to include avoiding conflict with respected elders when you are an adult is much less appropriate. Learning to seek permission to speak might be fine behavior in the third grade, but waiting for permission to speak in a bargaining session, whether formal or informal, will assure that you will never be heard. Using polite forms of conversation may foster accommodation; overusing parliamentary procedure sometimes stifles debate. Rules of etiquette must be tempered with the exigencies of conflict behavior. Raising one's voice may not be as great a sin as stifling it.

Your choices of individual conflict styles are vitally important. By unfreezing your style options, you can adapt to conflict situations depending on the goals you have for yourself and the relationship with the other person. Most of us learn retrospectively that our styles are dysfunctional. We examine our past conflicts and see that we have been stuck in a particular style or style sequence. Developing a repertoire of style choices opens the way to productive management of our conflicts within personal relationships and work, group, or public relationships.

Flexible Systems

Systems can develop repetitive patterns of conflict management that need to be challenged. On the system level, repetitive patterns become *rituals.* For instance, a father and his daughter have a ritual that goes like this: She comes home and is upset with his limitations on her freedom (she is fifteen, going on twenty). He tends to be inflexible about the hours he has set for her to be home from social occasions. About every three weeks, the girl comes home, starts talking about not having any friends, and starts crying. The father, each time this occurs, responds by saying, "Oh, let her cry. It will blow over the way it always does." He characterizes the conflict as the emotional outbursts of a teenager, and she characterizes the conflict as the inflexible position of her father. This conflict, in fact, can be viewed from many perspectives (such as by analyzing the power moves that each participant makes), but the ritual is acted out in a similar fashion each time. And the father and daughter continue to build up hostility.

Rituals for conflict develop most frequently in ongoing relationships in which the participants want some sense of order, even if they experience frequent conflict. If the parties perceive themselves as very interdependent—two coworkers who share in the profits or two intimates, each of whom invests emotionally in the other person—then rituals will develop as guides for their ongoing interaction. As a result of the typical relationship styles that develop over time, people tend to develop beliefs about who they are. For instance, new couples like to focus on the lack of overt hostility as a sign of relational health. The "Heavenly Twins" (Lederer and Jackson 1968), when asked, "How is the relationship going?" respond with, "Great! We haven't even had a fight yet." The Heavenly Twins settle on the ritual of avoidance and convince themselves that since there are no open disagreements, everything is fine. They undoubtedly have other ways of managing their conflicts, but they cling to the "no conflict" ritual.

Another common ritual, especially for intimates, is the game of "Uproar." In Uproar, the parties get into frequent battles. The fighting may serve the function of avoiding intimate situations (Berne 1964) so that every time intimacy is appropriate, like before bed, someone picks a fight over a trivial matter. Because participants characterize the nature of their relationship based on how they, as a unit, conduct conflict, fighters are often heard to say such things as, "We fight a lot, and we really love each other," or "It may seem that we are unkind to each other, but we both understand that underneath all this acrimony is a real commitment to work things out. We find that by sharing our disagreements openly, we are then free to love openly, too."

> Dan and Betsy are two college seniors who have been dating for several years. Betsy has taken the role of "encourager" of Dan and is supportive of his future plans. Dan appreciates Betsy's help but sometimes wants to be left to figure things out for himself. The following conversation ensues:
>
> Dan: "I worked five hours at the recreation program booth at the fair today."
>
> Betsy: "With all that homework? How do you expect to get any schoolwork done? Don't you care if you get anywhere? You have got to take more responsibility!"
>
> Dan: "I don't know."

Dan and Betsy's ritual developed as a way for them to work as a team—Betsy felt positively about Dan's future career goals, whereas Dan was not so sure about his desires and abilities. Through time, however, the problem-solving focus, "I'll push a bit so you'll feel more confident" (Betsy), and "I'll let you know this is hard for me, but I want to move ahead so I'll use your help with thanks" (Dan), became an overused communication structure, ineffectively applied to too many events in the couple's lives.

Summary

Conflict participants face the basic choice of avoiding or engaging a conflict. This choice leads to the five individual styles of conflict management: avoidance, competition, compromise, accommodation, and collaboration. Competitive tactics take many forms, such as threats, verbal aggressiveness, and violence. There are advantages and disadvantages to using each style of conflict management. One must be cautious about overinterpreting individual styles, however, for the measures of style often do not reflect process, situational constraints, and the desire to appear socially acceptable, and styles are not measures of one's personality. Systemwide styles of conflict can also be charted. Many times individuals and systems become stuck in particular styles and rituals that keep people from engaging in flexible communication.

PART TWO

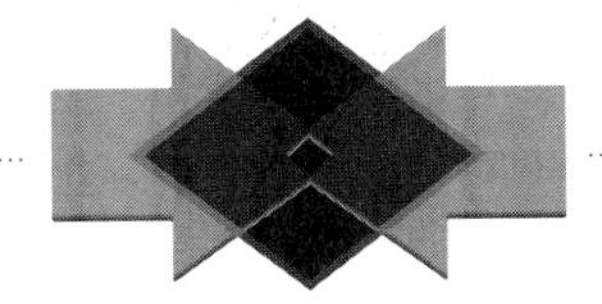

Conflict Intervention

Chapter 6

Conflict Assessment

Have you ever been in a conflict in which you were so perplexed you asked, either silently or out loud, "What is going on here?" Or have you talked with a friend or work associate whose conflicts appear to be totally confusing and impossible to understand? If so, this chapter will help you "get a handle" on the *structure* of conflicts. The assessment guides are useful for describing conflicts whether you are a party to the conflict, a concerned third party such as a parent or friend, or a professional third-party intervener. Some of the techniques presented in this, as well as the following, chapter can be practiced as class or workshop activities. Later you might want to use the techniques for assessment and intervention as a manager, trainer, teacher, parent, or organizational consultant. If you are asked to perform an in-depth analysis of a conflict, either for a conflict of your own or as a service to a group, you can choose several of the assessment devices in this chapter to help you describe the conflict with minimum bias.

Conflict assessment guides can help you understand your own conflicts as most of us are notoriously inaccurate at describing our own behavior in a conflict. We develop blind spots about our own behavior and fail to see certain aspects of the conflict. People repeatedly impose on others that which they later claim was imposed on them. The person who believes the world is a competitive, win-lose place often doesn't see that this view sets competitive processes in motion (Weick 1979). Self-fulfilling prophecies are enacted over and over as we provoke the very behavior we accuse the other in the conflict of perpetuating. Then we each make ourselves out to be the other's victim (Warner and Olson 1981).

Conflicts often appear confusing and unpredictable. As we have learned while working as consultants to families and organizations, each conflict at first appears new, different, and beyond comprehension. One city council is not like another, one family is different from the next, and the mental health agency down the street seems totally distinct from the one across town. As we become immersed in each conflict, taking notes and interviewing the conflict parties, we often feel like Taylor (1979): "My ability to accumulate data often exceeds my capacity to integrate it. . . . I struggle to take in a mass of information that overloads me in some ways and leaves me in the dark in others" (479). The assessment approaches presented in this chapter can help with this kind of overload; they are "confusion-organizing tools" (480). As an assessor of conflicts, it is important that you identify some organizing scheme for reducing confusion before you begin the assessment. One such framework is *systems theory,* which offers a broadly based perspective on all social systems and is particularly useful when assessing an interpersonal conflict. The specific assessment tools used are only part of the overall orientation.

Systems Theory: An Organizing Framework

Full assessment of a conflict can best be accomplished by (1) *assessing the workings* of the overall system, (2) *determining recurring patterns* inside the system that are associated with conflict, and (3) *identifying individual contributions* to the overall system. A combination of these methods, drawn from the different approaches discussed in this chapter, will provide you with data that can serve as background for constructing helpful interventions. When multimodal and multilevel assessment is not used, one runs the risk of an undue focus on one's own area of concern or expertise, whether that be power structures, reduction tactics, improving the atmosphere, problem solving, negotiation, or any other facet of conflict.

General systems theory has provided the framework for a rich body of literature about the workings of entire systems and subsystems in organizations, small groups, and families. Many effective intervention techniques for productive conflict management derive from systems theorists who experiment with change. In this section, systems concepts will be presented that have been the most helpful to us, our students, and our clients. The myriad approaches to assessment can be put in perspective by referring back to these principles as you devise change attempts. The genius of systems theory as a framework for assessment and intervention is that it provides a way to understand conflicts by giving information about patterns, interlocking sequences, functions of the parties, and methods of processing information. Conflicts are seldom managed productively by attention to blame or causality, seeking the truth, finding the initiator and responder, or detecting the persecutor and victim. If you do succeed in tagging someone with the "perpetrator" label, you have not managed the conflict; you have only created an enemy.

Extensive discussions of systems theory applied to various contexts can be found in Gregory Bateson's two major works, *Steps to an Ecology of Mind* (1972) and *Mind and Nature* (1980), cornerstones of systems theory writing and research. The systems approach to describing normal family processes is discussed thoroughly by Galvin and Brommel

(1986) and Walsh (1984). Overviews of systems theory and the change process helpful to counselors and therapists are provided by Minuchin (1974), Neill and Kniskern (1982), Hoffman (1981), and Napier and Whitaker (1978). Systems theory applied to organizations and organizational change, helpful to consultants, workshop leaders, and organizational development professionals, are provided by Weick (1979) and Johnson (1977).

Selected principles derived from systems theory will help you understand the wholistic or systemic nature of any conflict. The following suggestions are adapted from a practical and helpful article by Papp, Silberstein, and Carter (1973):

1. *Conflict in systems occurs in chain reactions. People cannot be identified as villains, heroes, good and bad people, or healthy and unhealthy members.* Rather than pinpointing one person as the cause of the conflict, look instead for predictable chain reactions because what every person does affects every other person. *Study the chain reactions*—see who picks up what cues and identify the part each plays in the runaway spiral. Satir (1972) uses an image of a family as a mobile in which members respond to changes in each other. If one member responds to a situation, the other members must consciously or unconsciously respond to the movement in the system. The same kind of interdependence exists in organizations and small groups. One cannot *not* affect other members of a system.

   Systems operate with *circular causality,* a concept that suggests that assigning a beginning is less important than looking at the sequence of patterns in the conflict process. Punctuation, interrupting a sequence of behavior at intervals, is important for giving meaning to the behavior but not for assigning the "cause" of the behavior. Most of the time, conflict participants identify the other as the cause while portraying the self as innocent. The boy who runs home screaming, "Sasha hit me!" is clearly ignoring his part in the system (he threw dirt at her). All systems are characterized by circular causality—each one affects the other.

   Descriptive language is the basic tool for assessing the system from a "no blame" perspective. Note the difference in the following vignettes:

   Wife: He's too needy. I don't know how he expects me to come home from a pressured day at work, wade through the three kids, all of whom want my attention, and ask him calmly, "How was your day?" while kissing him sweetly on the cheek. He should grow up.

   The same vignette using descriptive language:

   Wife: Scott wants to be greeted by me when I first get home. What happens, though, is that by the time I hit the front door, all three children clamor for my attention. Scott's usually in the back of the house, so by the time I physically get back to him, I'm involved with one of the children. Then he doesn't get my full attention.

   In the second scenario, ideas for change already present themselves, whereas in the first scenario, Scott's wife labels Scott as the problem. The couple will not likely find solutions to the conflict while the wife views Scott as the villain who is causing the problem.

2. *Each member gets labeled, or programmed, into a specific role in the system.* Labeling serves a function for the entire group. Most labels keep people from

changing; however, the labeling process itself can be changed. For instance, the "watchdog" in an organization may be carrying too much of the quality control. Conflicts arise because if the watchdog stops performing the function reinforced by the group, others will try to pull her back into the role.

When certain individuals in the system specialize in specific functions, others may not develop those capabilities. For instance, in one sorority house, Jan was known as the "peacemaker" of the group. She could be counted on to help people solve their problems. In one ongoing conflict, however, Theresa and Pat disagreed vehemently with each other over how literally to enforce some house rules. They blew up at each other, knowing they could count on Jan to help patch things up. Theresa and Pat were not forced to make their own peace because Jan always rushed in.

3. *Cooperation is necessary among system members to keep conflicts going.* One person cannot sustain an interaction. Therefore, the cycle can be changed by any one person changing his or her behavior. Healthy systems are characterized by morphogenesis, or "constructive system-enhancing behaviors that enable the system to grow, innovate and change" (Olson et al. 1979). Conflict can be managed by one person initiating change or by members deciding together to initiate a change in their structure. A system that maintains conflicts by avoiding genuine change is called a *morphostatic system,* one characterized by moves designed to sustain the status quo, or no change.

   If you are stuck in a system that does not change, one choice you always have is to change your own behavior, even if you cannot get others to change. In the Shepherd family, for instance, one of the five members usually felt left out. The family expectation was that four people together were enough but five people together were trouble, since each parent wanted to "take care of" one child. The family was able to change and make more room on the merry-go-round when Dad began sharing his time with all three children instead of paying attention to one child at a time.
4. *Triangles tend to form in systems when relationships are close and intense.* When one person feels lower power, the tendency is to bring in another person to bolster the low-power position. This maneuver forms an *alliance* if the resulting relationship is an open one or a *coalition* if the relationship is hidden. Since the person brought in to build up the position of the low-power person maintains multiple relationships in the system, interlocking triangles begin functioning over and over in predictable ways. If these triangles lead to destructive behavior, they are termed *toxic triangles* (Satir 1972; Hoffman 1981; Minuchin 1974).
5. *Systems develop rules for conflict that, no matter how dysfunctional, are followed as long as the basic structure of the system does not change.* What may develop is a prescriptive rule about conflict that states, "If we are a happy family, we do not have conflict," or "We have polite conflict." At work there may be a rule that "if you have conflict with the boss, you will be fired." Some departments only enact conflict in writing. Others require conflicts to happen only in meetings, whereas some postpone or "table" most potential conflicts. System rules often block collaborative conflict. At one time they may have served the system well. Parents may have decided, for instance, never to fight in front of the children. When the children were infants, the rule protected them from angry faces and loud voices. But with children twelve and sixteen years old, the rule makes little sense, as the children can always tell when Mom and Dad are in a conflict and are thus being brought up to avoid overt conflict.

6. *The conflict serves a function for the system.* The conflict may be substituting for other forms of intimacy and connection, for problem solving, or for expression of dissatisfaction. Never assume that members of a system want the conflict to be resolved. They may fear a vacuum in their interaction if the conflict is no longer serving its particular function. Although almost everyone in a conflict will say, "Of course we want this over and done with," the fact that people keep conflicts going, sometimes for years at a time, indicates that some system function is served by the conflict. One church congregation carried on a repetitive conflict at board meetings about the propriety of using the church buildings for partisan and special interest group meetings. A third party helped them discover that the debate was a substitute for a subgroup's dissatisfaction with the minister's involvement in social action projects. The board had been reluctant to confront the minister with their disapproval, so they always centered the discussion on "use of the building." The conflict allowed them to express their disapproval in an indirect way.

The following section presents techniques for identifying exactly how the conflicts occur inside the system.

Identifying Conflict Patterns

One focus for assessing conflicts is the pattern of the conflict relationship between the parties. The conflict is composed of system regularities such as patterns of communication, rules for behavior, characteristic dynamics of the system. Often the structure of the conflict is only expressed indirectly or implicitly so that assessment approaches cannot be constructed by asking the parties, "What is the structure of your conflict?" Rather, the structure has to be derived from inductive approaches, a few of which will be overviewed. These include (1) metaphoric/dramatic analysis, (2) conflict triangles, (3) sculpting or choreography, (4) system rules, (5) microevents, (6) observation, and (7) interviews.

Metaphoric/Dramatic Analysis

Metaphors, discussed previously, can be elicited by the third party or by conflict participants to present an accurate description of a conflict. Haley (1976) notes that metaphors can be reflective of relational themes. Conflict parties can be asked to compare their conflict to a novel, film, or television program. One group of nurses said they were like characters in a detective novel, looking for "whodunit." A family saw themselves as a pioneer family in a Western movie, circling their wagons against possible attack, pulling together on the trail but scattering once they were not in danger. Some people can write poems or draw pictures about their conflict. Others can visualize disconnected images then talk about what the images mean. One group generated the following images for the divorce process: "drowning," "having the road map taken away," "playing cards with no rules," and "being in surgery and waking up to find that you're on an artificial heart." One foster child, when asking her counselor for placement in a different family, said, "They speak, I don't know, Spanglish or something, and they won't teach me the language." Children can look through magazines to find pictures that represent how they feel in a conflict. Children also respond well to puppet shows in which they act out several conflict roles at once. Let your imagination be your guide in helping conflicting parties express the feel and structure of their conflicts.

During interviews and observation, people spontaneously speak of their conflicts in metaphoric ways. These expressions should be carefully noted and used in your overall analysis. You can ask people to explain how the metaphor works. For instance, a counseling center has a plaque reading "The Little Mental Health Center on the Prairie" hanging in the staff room. Values of neighborliness, assistance in times of trouble, and "pulling together" are evident in staff relationships. The following structured technique allows people to use metaphors to manage their conflicts:

1. Parties *generate a metaphor* for an important conflict, using one of the previous suggestions. Each party writes out their own metaphoric image.
2. One person *shares the image* with the group of conflicting parties or the discussion group. The group then asks clarifying questions of the person sharing the metaphor, using the images developed in the original metaphor.
3. The group then *brainstorms,* still using the imaginary mode, about ways to resolve the conflict.
4. The facilitator or leader then asks the group to *translate* these imaginary resolutions into *practical steps* for conflict management.
5. The primary party, or the group, then *chooses the options* that will most likely lead to *collaborative conflict management.*
6. After all the conflict parties have repeated this procedure, a *contract* is made for selected change.

The following boxes present examples of this exercise.

Beth and Ted

Beth and Ted are a couple who have been intimate for one year. Beth has considered leaving through the National Student Exchange program for one year at a school in Philadelphia, two thousand miles away. She wants to continue the relationship with Ted while at school but also wants freedom to date others. Ted wants a more intimate relationship and feels that can be achieved only if he and Beth can see each other often.

Beth and Ted agree that the following image describes their current attempts to solve their conflict:

We open a messy, heaping cupboard and upon seeing the disorganization and mess, we hurry to slam it shut before all the cans and bottles fall out, injuring one of us.

After following the discussion steps listed above, Beth and Ted agree that a new image will guide them to more productive conflict management:

We open a messy, heaping cupboard. We roll up our sleeves, take all the items off the shelves, clean up, throw out the spoiled goods, and put everything that is left back into a larger cupboard without doors—for easy reorganization.

The Dangerous Minefield

Margaret, a college student, writes:

My father and I are in a minefield. The sky is blue, the sun is shining, there is green grass and sudden death underneath. Each of us is responsible for some of the mines underfoot, and we have to avoid our own mines as well as those planted by the other person. There are scattered trees and bushes around the field, which is quite large. They provide limited cover. We are each trying to get in close enough to the other to get a good look without being seen.

My father throws rocks at me to try to flush me out into the open. I back around a bush and meet him.

Boom! There's a big explosion—we both flee, wounded, only to begin the standoff over again.

Here are some metaphoric solutions translated into practical steps for conflict management:

Metaphoric Solutions	*Communication Possibilities*
1. Dig up my mines, or tell him where they are	Disclose myself
2. Get a metal detector, locate his mines, and	Psych him out and
a. dig them up;	a. confront him;
b. throw heavy objects from a distance to set them off;	b. back stab him;
c. avoid them	c. avoid him or "be nice"
3. Wear explosion-proof armor	Decrease my dependence
4. Throw rocks at him	Attack or goad him
5. Abandon the field; leave	Don't communicate at all
6. Hold on to him when explosion goes off so we can't run from each other	Increase closeness and interdependence
7. Cut down the foliage	Describe our behaviors and feelings to each other
8. Use binoculars to see each other	Get information on him from other sources; focus carefully
9. Whistle as I go around the field	Let him know "where I'm coming from"
10. Stand in the open so he can see me	Give him the opportunity to get information about me; write him a letter

Options 1 and 7 through 10 seem to be moves that would help productively manage the conflict. Many more exist, but these are a good start.

A Shady Deal

We're playing poker at a card table covered with green baize cloth, which is hanging down so no one can see under the table. Kevin is the dealer, and he also plays against me. He has the right to change the rules; sometimes I don't even know the game we're playing. The stakes are high; my tension mounts as the game progresses. Kevin smiles mysteriously; I hide my feelings, trying to bluff. An audience gathers, encouraging me to get out of such a lopsided game. I always stay for another hand, thinking that *this time* I'll understand the rules and have a fair chance. My tension continues to mount.

The shady deal mentioned in the previous box is an elaboration of a comment made by a student in a conflict class. Frustrated with a romantic relationship, she said that sometimes it seemed to her that Kevin "dealt all the cards." In class, her discussion group expanded this description of the "shady deal" and provided imaginary ways the game could be changed. People often use metaphoric language to communicate about the pattern of interaction they experience in a conflict. Many times, the person generating the metaphor is amazed at the precise insights strangers gain about the elements of the interpersonal conflict, based on the metaphor alone.

Conflict Triangles

Conflicts can be structurally analyzed using diagrams. Several researchers note that the triangle is the basic unit of analysis for conflict communication (Satir 1972; Hoffman 1981; Minuchin 1974; Wilmot 1987). Why triangles? When people perceive that they are the low-power party in a two-person conflict, their typical response is to try to form a coalition (hidden) or an alliance (open) with another person who can bolster their power. If another party joins the low-power party, that person then becomes part of the conflict, as you may have discovered if you have taken sides with a friend or coworker who was in conflict with someone else. "Three's a crowd" is a cultural cliche based on sound reasoning. Three people find it difficult to maintain balance in a conflictual relationship. Usually they are structured as a "dyad plus one" (Wilmot 1987). However, three people may be able to interact with ease over a long period of time if they are not engaged in conflict. Triadic analysis can be used to study the relationships that make up an ongoing conflict of more than three people. The method is especially useful in conflicts involving five or more people. After interviewing and/or observing the conflict parties, follow these steps:

1. Ask about recurring experiences in the conflict system. Which are puzzling, painful, frustrating, or triggering of conflicts? Note these by drawing and labeling them.
2. Draw triangles demonstrating the different relationship combinations among the conflict parties. Mark conflicting dyads with ←┼┼┼┼┼┼┼┼┼┼→. In a conflict consisting of many people, choose the most problematic triangles to work with first.

   The following toxic triangles refer to Tom and Mary, a married couple who have both been married before. The word *toxic* (Satir 1972) was first applied to these kinds of relationships to describe the poisonous, dangerous, and potentially devastating nature of the relationships.

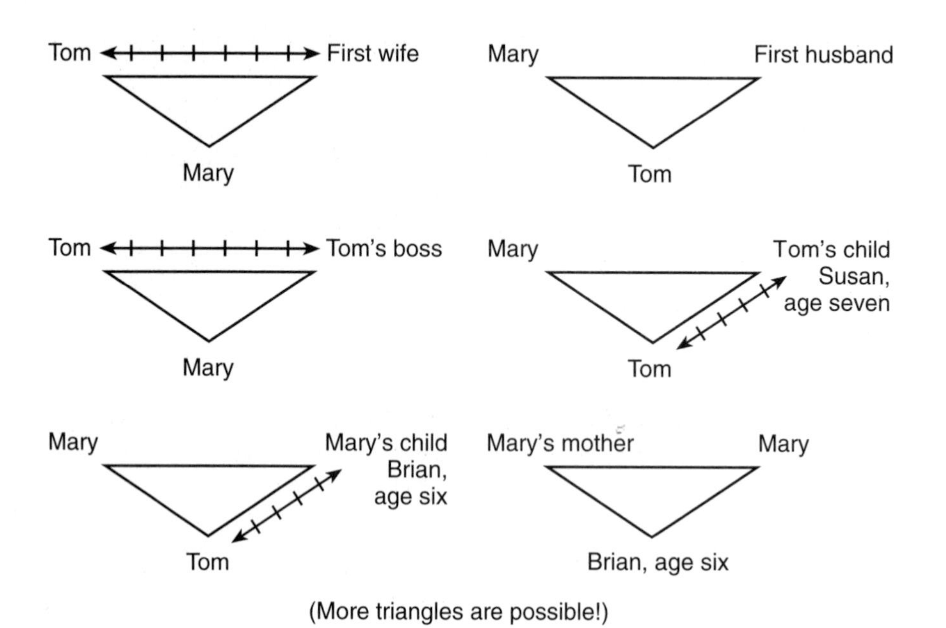

3. Code high-power persons with a + and low-power persons with a –. Whether a person is high-power or low-power may vary depending on the triangle he or she is in.

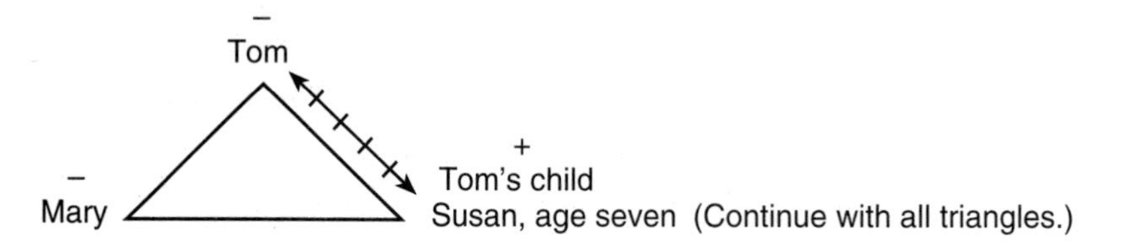

4. Identify alliances with a double arrow: <–> Identify coalitions with an arrow in parentheses:(<–>)

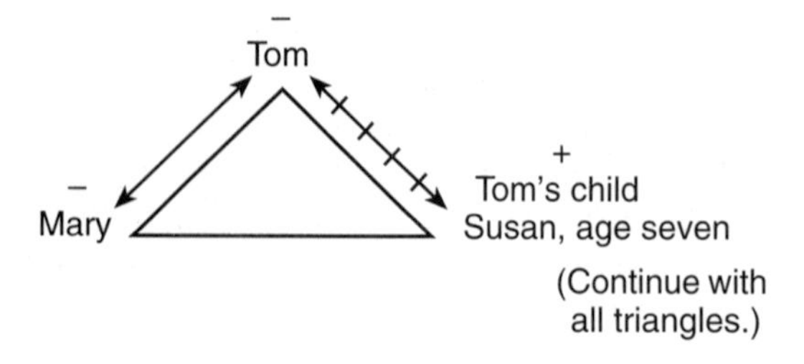

5. Identify isolates, or persons who are in few or no triangles. Can they be drawn in to productively restructure the conflict?

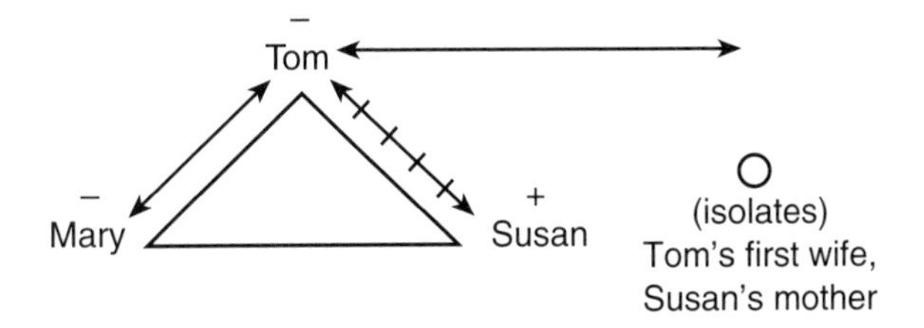

6. Identify persons involved in many or all the triangles. Can they withdraw from some toxic triangles?

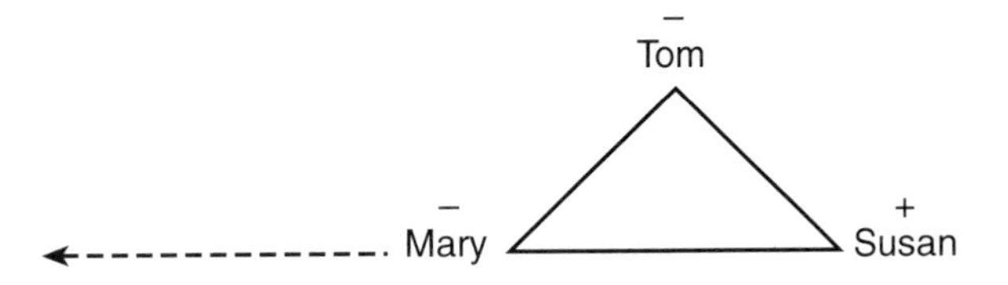

In this example, Mary could withdraw from active participation in Tom's and Susan's conflict, giving them the opportunity to communicate directly with each other.

This might result in two collaborative dyadic interactions:

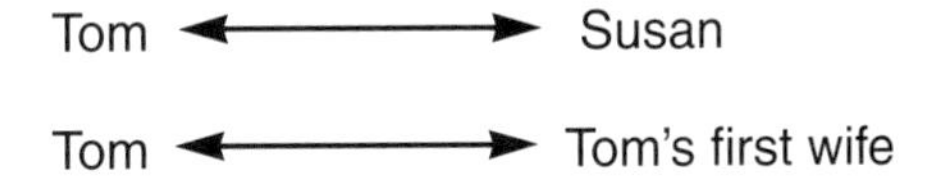

7. Discuss all toxic triangles (the ones that produce the most conflict), deciding how they might be productively restructured. (See chapter 4 for ideas on power balancing.)
8. Choose several options to begin management of the conflict.
9. Have each person keep a list of agreements for change made during the session. These agreements are negotiated by the parties involved and the trainer, and involve self-centered rather than other-centered action.

Diagrammatic techniques are not limited to personal relationships; they can also be applied to conflict in small groups, work groups, or subunits of an organization. Although conflicts do change rapidly, the most confusing, recurring, and damaging conflicts in systems present stable underlying dynamics. They occur over and over in different *content guises,* as discussed in chapter 3. Using a method such as identification of triangles makes the process understandable to members in a way that helps depersonalize the problems. In organizations, staff groups can participate in such an analysis, putting the triangles on a board and working cooperatively to understand what goes wrong and why. When members of a system understand that low-power people act in predictable ways, the members can more readily change the power balance in a productive way.

Sculpting or Choreography

Sculpting, or choreography, is a nonverbal method of demonstrating the structure of a conflict by having each member of the conflict "arrange the other members in a tableau that physically symbolizes their emotional relationships with each other" (Papp, Silberstein, and Carter 1973). Each party creates a live portrait, placing other parties together in postures and spatial relationships that show the essence of one's experience of the conflict. This "picture is literally worth a thousand words." Confused feelings are given form.

Before detailing the technique, however, a word of caution is in order. Sculpting should only be conducted if you as a teacher or facilitator are comfortable with emotional expression and feel that it is appropriate for the classroom. The beauty of the approach is that it "pulls" hidden dynamics to the surface—but of course, that is the downside too. It can also be used to represent dynamics that occur on the job, and for many people this application might be more comfortable than applying it to a close family situation.

This art of representing family roles spatially comes from Papp (Papp, Silberstein, and Carter 1973) and her colleagues Duhl, Kantor, and Duhl (1973) and Satir (1967) as demonstrated in her many training workshops. The sculptor acts in a scene while at the same time explaining his or her actions. Miniature figures can be used to facilitate sculpting (Howard and Hocker 1981; Hocker and Bach 1981). Such sculpting techniques can also be used with less intimate conflict parties, such as staff members. Triangles, alliances, and coalitions, as well as rules about who may talk with whom, often emerge with startling clarity.

After each party to the conflict gets a chance to place members in relationship to each other, the parties are directed to slowly move in their usual directions. The incompatible goals, scarce resources, and other structural elements of the conflict usually become quite evident. Sculpting is a technique that can potentially clarify conflict because the changing, interactive nature of the system dynamics becomes vividly apparent. A variation on this technique is to use people *not* in the actual conflict system as role-players. The verbal dynamics and nonverbal movement provide an imaginative way to observe a conflict, to sit back, watch, and listen. The teacher or facilitator directs the drama, pointing out system dynamics as they unfold. Another variation is to draw the figures in position on a board, allowing observers to analyze the revealed dynamics.

One example of how sculpting can illuminate conflict patterns was provided by Fred in a workshop. His parents, Joe and Patricia, were having recurring conflicts that were drawing in Fred and the other family members. Joe and Patricia were retired; Patricia's mother was elderly and living in the same town in her own apartment. Although Joe and Patricia paid for a part-time caretaker for her mother, Patricia visited her mother every day and assisted her with small tasks. Each time Fred visited his parents, Joe complained bitterly that "Patricia is spending all her time with her mother." Patricia was avoidant; she did not openly discuss the issue with Joe and tried to deflect such discussion. Over time, Joe became more isolated from Patricia, and Patricia's alliance with her mother became stronger. When Fred sculpted this conflict, he represented Patricia and her mother as standing close together and Joe as a long distance from them and slowly moving farther away. Joe was also far from the other family members—his complaining drove them away. The emotional gap between Joe and Patricia was represented by spatial distance from each other in the sculpture.

Patricia, recognizing that she did not want Joe to be so far away, began the following dialogue:

Patricia: "But I don't want him so far away!"
Facilitator: "See if you can get closer to him."

(Patricia walks closer to Joe, and the woman playing Patricia's mother pulls her back. Patricia is stuck in the middle.) After discussion, Patricia decided she could set aside time when she and Joe could be together so that she did not feel pulled between Joe and her mother. Joe helped her decide when would be the best time for her to visit her mother each day. Joe reported that he had begun to think that Patricia did not care about him and that he had not realized that she felt so strongly pulled from both sides.

Choreographing conflicts works best when the parties are present together, each has a chance to choreograph the movements of the system, and they work together to solve their joint problem.

System Rules

You have undoubtedly experienced conflicts in which you wanted to say, "Here we go again. Same song, fourteenth verse." Sometimes, no matter what content is being discussed, the outcome is the same. The same people collude together, the same people are left out, and the same indirect strategies are used (like "forgetting," avoiding the issue, and putting off a decision until something must be done). As we have seen, repetitive, unsatisfactory conflicts often operate on a set of unstated but very powerful rules that limit genuine change.

Rules used in this context means the underlying communication structure of the interaction. Usually, no one person dictates the rules. Instead, the rules guide behavior in more subtle ways. They are "the way things are done" in a family, a business, a department, or a group of friends. A more precise definition of a rule is that it is *"a followable prescription that indicates what behavior is obligated, preferred, or prohibited in certain contexts"* (Shimanoff 1980, 57). Usually the rules of communication remain implicit. However, analysis of conflict benefits from an explicit listing of the rules, so they can be understood and changed. The following are some examples of rules that conform to this definition:

1. *Rules are prescriptions for behavior* stated in the following form:
   "When in context X, Y must/must not occur."
   "When Father shows sadness or anger, Mother must soothe him."
   "When the program director decides to assign a case to a counselor, the counselor must accept the case or convince the program director to reassign it."

2. *Rules are stated in prescriptive, not evaluative, language.*
   "When brother and sister fight, Dad must intervene to stop it," not "Dad feels responsible for stopping brother and sister's fights even though they can handle them without interference" (this is interpretive and evaluative).

One of the characteristics of important rules in a system is that some implicit message *against knowing or stating the rule directly* is usually present. It's as if people must follow the rules but can't say what they are. For that reason, listing rules for the way a certain system of people engages in conflict may not be easy. Rules may be elicited from conflict parties by following these steps:

1. List explicit and implicit rules that prescribe your own and others' behavior in conflicts.
2. If you have trouble thinking of rules for your system, think of times when the rule was broken. How did you know the rule was broken? How was the violation communicated? Write about the prescription that *became* obvious upon breaking the rule.
3. Make sure you generate rules both for behavior that must and must not be performed.
4. Go back over your list. Make each rule simple and prescriptive. Write rules even for "obvious" communication patterns. They may prove to be important possibilities for change.
   Example: When new staff members attend the staff meeting they must not express opinions unless they have a sponsor who is an older staff member.
5. Code each rule as to the following:
   a. Whose rule is it?
   b. What keeps the rule going?
   c. Who enforces the rule?
   d. Who breaks the rule?
   e. What function does the rule serve?
6. Discuss how the rules help or harm the productive management of conflict. Make decisions for change.
   Example:
   Old rule—When Dad is angry at younger brother, older brother must protect younger brother from Dad's disapproval.
   Result—Older brother and Dad engage in conflict often, reducing effect of the protection (a toxic triangle).
   New rule—When Dad and younger brother get into a conflict, they must talk about their conflicts without older brother (a new affiliation).

Many groups are amazed at the complexity of their conflict rules. A first step in collaboration can be to generate the list of rules together, brainstorming to add to the suggestions made by each member, then refining the rules for accuracy. Often groups and families can decide together which rules obstruct collaborative conflict management.

Microevents

Microevents are repetitive patterns that carry information about the underlying conflict structure. The identification of such recurring episodes can lead to morphogenesis or system change. Microevents are "repetitive loops of observable interpersonal behaviors . . .

with a redundant outcome" (Metcoff and Whitaker 1982, 253). The microevent reinforces the structural patterns of relating to one another by supplying a repeatedly experienced interaction. As such, microevents are similar to rules, but microevents are descriptive, not prescriptive, of behavior. They are clusters of behaviors organized into structurally repetitive episodes.

Perhaps the clearest keys to the nature of an underlying structure are the "substitutable communication events that reveal the structure" (Metcoff and Whitaker 1982, 258). Metcoff and Whitaker provide the following example of such repeatability:

> Every time the husband { scratched his ear / rubbed his nose / tapped his right foot } during
>
> an argument with his wife, one of the children
>
> would { ask to go to the bathroom / slap a sibling / begin to cry } so that the
>
> husband-wife dispute was never resolved. (258–259)

The implicit, unstated structure underlying these repetitive conflicts can be summarized as follows: "When the husband and wife begin to initiate a conflict, one of the children makes a move to gain their attention, and the husband-wife conflict is not resolved" (259). Each system will, of course, have a different structure underlying the observable conflict. The microevent serves to define the conflict because it "embodies themes of stability and change within the family system" (263).

Once the underlying structure is decoded, one can begin to predict where, when, or how conflict will erupt. Emily and Gordon are a married couple in their sixties whose children are all grown and living elsewhere. Before each vacation, Gordon decides where they should go then tries to persuade Emily of the wisdom of his choice. Emily won't agree to go, but neither will she say no. Then, the night before the trip, Gordon stays up most of the night packing, and Emily reluctantly goes with him. Their repetitive conflicts are structured in the following manner:

1. He always initiates.
2. She is always convinced (reluctantly) to go.
3. No discussion of their relationship is engaged; all issues are handled through content.
4. Neither receives positive results from their respective stances.
5. Neither one can solve nor escape the conflict.

Their next conflict, over whether, when, and where to go for Christmas, will be based on a similar structure.

One can begin decoding the structure underlying a microevent by focusing on these questions:

1. Who initiates and in what way?
2. Who responds and in what way?
3. Who else is present but is not identified as a party to the conflict?

4. Does anyone "speak for" someone else? If so, does this keep the participants embroiled in the conflict?
5. If there were no conflict, what would be missing?
   a. Who would not be connecting to whom?
   b. How would the parties structure their time?
   c. Would conflicts continue with new parties entering into the fray?
6. Is the conflict serving to fill emotional space so other parties cannot fight?

The communication patterns created in a conflict often cycle back and imprison the players. For example, Beverly went through a divorce two months ago, and her son Randy is having difficulty at school. At least twice a week, Beverly and Randy struggle over his poor work in the fifth grade. He has been labeled as a "troublemaker" at school and has been sent home from school three times in the last month. This is embarrassing for Beverly; she also gets very angry at Randy for his "stupid behavior." The repetitive microevent that Beverly and Randy enact has the following features:

1. Beverly initiates each conflict by being distressed about Randy's school performance or disruptive behavior at school.
2. Randy responds by being sullen, pretending he is deaf and can't hear requests, and withdrawing.
3. The unemployed older brother is present in the house but serves as a bystander.
4. Randy and Beverly are both isolated parties—neither has anyone to come to his or her aid during the conflict.
5. Aside from the conflict, mother and son have few common interests. Beverly can't think of things that might be interesting for the two of them to do together. This recurring conflict both illustrates and crystallizes the family structure.

The following are some ways you can discover and describe microevents:

1. Act as a qualitative researcher who performs observation and interviewing to determine patterns.
2. Obtain a professional third-party (consultant, mediator, or therapist) description of common conflicts.
3. Keep a journal of conflict episodes that seem repetitive—those that have a "here we go again" theme.
4. Ask newcomers to a system, such as new employees, new family members, or new committee members, to describe what they have experienced so far.

Microevents can suggest ways to change the conflict structure just as rules can. In the following case, Melissa decided to give her schedule to her grandparents as soon as she arrived for a visit so her grandmother would not be left wondering about Melissa's schedule and Melissa could be open about her plans.

The Broken Plans

Every time there is a break from school and work, I go down to Medford to visit my relatives. I usually begin by staying at my grandparents' house, then spend a night or two at my brother's house, then visit my cousin or aunt. The following communication patterns are repeated the first morning of every visit with my grandparents:

When I get up, Grandma has already fixed my breakfast and has it set out on the kitchen table—cereal, toast, juice, fresh fruit, et cetera. Grandma always goes to great lengths to have everything perfect. "Would you like an egg, dear?" she asks.

"No thank you, Grandma; this is fine. You really don't have to fix me breakfast. I could do it fine."

"Well, we don't get to see our girl very often; you don't mind being spoiled a bit, do you?" She and Grandpa then bring their coffee into the kitchen and sit down and drink it while I eat my breakfast.

"What are your plans for this time?" asks Grandma. I have already told her that I only have three days, but I haven't mentioned what I am doing.

"Well, I'm not really sure. I hadn't really decided," I answer. At this point I am stalling a bit because I have actually already decided that I am going to leave later this evening and visit my brother. However, I don't want to hurt my grandparents' feelings. "I hope you will be able to spend a little more time with us," says Grandma. Her hopeful look melts my strong will about sticking to my plans.

"Let her do what she wants," says Grandpa. "Must be pretty boring for a young girl like her hanging around with a pair of old fogies like us." He winks or pats me on the knee. "You know we love having you, dear, but there are other people who want to see you, too."

"She has plenty of time to see everyone else!" argues Grandma. "For once, I would like her and I to have a nice visit without worrying about her running off to visit someone else." "We will have a nice visit, Grandma," I say. By this time I am even more reluctant to mention my plans because I don't want to hurt her feelings. "Remember over Christmas I spent nearly a week with you, and the rest of the family only got a few days." I attempt to rationalize.

"Oh, that was months ago," she answers. "Can I get you something else for breakfast?"

"Grandma, I'm fine," I answer.

"I just want to make sure you're not hungry or anything. Whenever you are at our house, you just get whatever you need. You don't have to ask; you just get what you want," Grandma says. "Grandpa and I really enjoy having you, even though we don't get to see you that much."

I can sense her watching me while I concentrate on my dish of shredded wheat, which has gone soggy during our conversation. Breakfast usually ends with me deciding that it is better to spend an extra day with my grandparents instead of feeling guilty during the rest of my visit. The repetitive patterns of "We love you and will do nice things for you if you please stay with us" win out over my initial plans for the break.

(Courtesy of Melissa Price)

Observation and Interviews

Looking, listening, and asking structured questions when possible can give the analyst of conflict a wealth of rich information. Observation and interviewing are essential tools for a third-party facilitator, such as a mediator, manager, or supervisor, or sometimes parents and teachers. One recent graduate of a communication program was asked by the program director in the hospital in which she worked to provide a workshop on team building. Since Carol, the new program assistant, had worked in a similar program in the same hospital, she was aware that some conflicts had gone on for several months, primarily over what kind of advertising should be done for community service programs sponsored by the hospital on alcoholism, self-esteem for children, and caring for older parents. Carol realized that the director who asked her to provide a two-hour workshop on team building had one perspective, and two other program assistants seemed to share a different perspective on how to advertise. Carol chose to interview several of the people involved, so she could specify how to build teamwork in this particular situation. Interviews help participants think through their current conflict, enable the interviewer to coach people on how to present their ideas and search for common interests, build rapport with an outsider who might be able to help, and begin the process of helping people change (Yarbrough and Wilmot 1995). Questions can be drawn from the Wilmot-Hocker assessment guide presented later in this chapter.

As you try to understand complicated conflicts, remember to *observe* what happens—who says what, in what order, about what topics, and with what kind of nonverbal communication. Acting like a good anthropologist helps one become a good conflict analyst. And sometimes other people's conflicts seem as strange as a different culture. Understanding motivation is less important than clearly describing communication behavior.

In the case mentioned earlier, Carol observed, through interviewing and gathering written materials, that more advertising was done for certain courses. She noticed what people said about budget, teaching, personnel, and successful versus unsuccessful courses. Gradually she realized that the program director's agenda was for some courses to fill more quickly than others—the courses the program director thought were most important. Carol realized that clarifying goals had to be part of the team-building workshop.

Quantitative Assessment

This section differs from the preceding ones in that the focus here is on providing sources for available instruments rather than detailing each individual instrument. If you want to use any of these instruments you will need to go to the original sources and secure copies of the scales. Consult the reference list at the end of the book for full source citations.

A variety of instruments are available for the quantitative assessment of conflict. Some are used for workshops and discussion groups and are not intended for research, whereas other instruments have been specifically formulated for research purposes. Many research instruments, however, are also useful in workshops and training sessions because of their specificity and validity. In this review, when a scale has not been researched extensively, it will be labeled as a "discussion starter." Citations to instruments will specify the articles that detail the instrument and its uses. Some of the instruments can only be obtained by writing to a specific address listed in the appendix. Other instruments are only available from the first author of the article, and in almost all the published articles, the author's institutional affiliations are listed.

For purposes of research or teaching, one can tap conflicts retrospectively or create a conflict in a laboratory or classroom for observation and coding. Two of the most useful techniques for highlighting past conflicts are the Revealed Differences Technique (Strodtbeck 1951) and the List of Problem Areas for Spouses (Weiss, Hops, and Patterson 1972). In addition, the Structured Family Interview (Watzlawick 1966) has some useful subparts. Although used primarily for spouses, these basic techniques can be adapted to a variety of contexts such as the work setting. If one wants to observe a conflict rather than rely on retrospective self-reports, the conflict parties can be asked to replay a conflict they have had (Knudson, Sommers, and Golding 1980), or they can be given a conflict scene and asked to improvise a conflict (Raush et al. 1974). Structured game approaches to conflict have been used for both research and teaching purposes. In these games, the rules produce conflict situations of the win-lose variety, which may be useful for observation purposes. The most widely used and known is the Prisoner's Dilemma, described in many sources (Rubin and Brown 1975) and the first edition of this book (1978). In addition, the Parcheesi Coalition Game (Vinacke and Arkoff 1957), Acme-Bolt Trucking Game (Deutsch and Krauss 1960), and Bilateral Monopoly Game (Siegel and Fouraker 1960) are available. Rubin and Brown (1975) provide an overview of these structured approaches. The Color Matching Test (CMT) requires a dyad to reach a joint decision about matching a color presented to them. Unknown to the participants, the charts they are using are coded differently, which sets the stage for a conflict (Goodrich and Boomer 1963). A similar technique of presenting slightly different information to the conflict parties and asking them to reach agreement is the Olson-Ryder scenario method. In this simulation, two disparate descriptions of a "conflict" between spouses are given to the players, and they decide which person described in the scenario is "primarily responsible" for the conflict (Olson and Ryder 1970). The real-world nature of the scenarios makes them particularly useful. However, many of these scenarios are dated and gender-biased, and should be rewritten for use today.

If one wishes to create more lengthy conflict interactions, longer simulation may be useful. Any approach, whether relying on retrospective self-reports, asking for a replay of a conflict, creating a script for improvisation, or putting participants in a highly structured simulation, has advantages and limitations. One needs to have experienced leaders available for debriefing any intensive conflict experience created by structured games or simulations. For an overview of the validity and representativeness of games and simulations to real life, see Knudson, Sommers, and Golding (1980), Glick and Gross (1975), Ryder and Goodrich (1966), Barry (1970), and Raush et al. (1974).

Conflict parties' overall reactions to conflict can be solicited by a variety of means. The following Conflict Attitudes Questionnaire was constructed by the authors. It is a helpful discussion starter used to sensitize people to their own and other's attitudes toward conflict. It can be used in class and workshops to explore the advantages and disadvantages of a variety of orientations to conflict.

Conflict Attitudes Questionnaire

Read each statement then indicate the extent to which you agree or disagree by placing the appropriate number in the margin.

(1)	(2)	(3)	(4)	(5)
Strongly agree	*Agree*	*Don't know*	*Disagree*	*Strongly disagree*

_____ **1.** Once I get wound up in a heated discussion I find it difficult to stop.
_____ **2.** If people communicated more there would be a lot less conflict.
_____ **3.** I am productive under pressure, and enjoy the challenge of a deadline.
_____ **4.** When they are upset, people shouldn't discuss important issues.
_____ **5.** I try not to show overt anger when working with everyday acquaintances.
_____ **6.** I have more conflicts than most people around me.
_____ **7.** I like to get potential conflicts on the table as soon as I'm aware of them.
_____ **8.** I try not to make decisions under pressure.
_____ **9.** I have trouble communicating my *feelings* when I am in a conflict.
_____ **10.** I have trouble communicating my *thoughts* when I am in a conflict.
_____ **11.** I am the person who tries to work out compromises between conflict factions.
_____ **12.** I like a good healthy verbal fight.
_____ **13.** I often create more internal stress for myself than exists externally.
_____ **14.** In my experience, men and women tend to approach conflicts differently.
_____ **15.** Negative feedback should not be given unless it is requested.
_____ **16.** I remain clear about my options when in a conflict.
_____ **17.** I can usually figure out what the other person is going to do in a conflict.
_____ **18.** People should be able to work out their conflicts without any outside help.
_____ **19.** I seldom feel powerless.
_____ **20.** I am afraid when people become overtly angry.
_____ **21.** Once I try to resolve a conflict, I just don't give up.
_____ **22.** Somebody always loses in conflict.
_____ **23.** I usually feel that I've lost in conflict.
_____ **24.** I act differently in conflicts depending on the context.
_____ **25.** Overt conflict characterizes my past family life.
_____ **26.** There's a lot of overt conflict in my current living situation.
_____ **27.** I enjoy winning.
_____ **28.** When I am in a low power position I handle conflict productively.
_____ **29.** When I am in a high power position, I handle conflict productively.
_____ **30.** I have experienced many productive conflicts.

After you have completed the Conflict Attitudes Questionnaire, pair off with a partner. Find one or two items where you have the largest point spread (where the two of you had the most dissimilar answers). One of you begins by asking the other the following questions:

1. Why did you answer as you did?
2. How does this response to conflict work for you?
3. Any other open-ended questions that will facilitate discussion.

When the others first two responses are understood, you ask other open-ended questions.

After you have explored general attitudes toward conflict, you can measure general predispositions toward conflict by using the Predispositions toward Conflict scale generated by Yelsma (1981) and Brown, Yelsma, and Keller (1981). Global assessments of family systems can be specified with the FACES scale (Olson, Sprenkle, and Russell 1979), which quantifies the degrees of cohesion and adaptability in a family. The Areas of Change questionnaire can be used to identify the changes one spouse desires in the other, which correspond to content areas where conflicts are likely to have occurred (Patterson 1976; Weiss and Perry 1979; Weiss, Hops, and Patterson 1972).

Conflict parties' communication behavior can be rated on either global or specific levels using the inventories developed by Bienvenu (1970) and Hobart and Klausner (1959), or the more lengthy 400–item Spouse Observation Checklist (Patterson 1976; Weiss, Hops, and Patterson 1972; Weiss and Margolin 1977). The latter has been shortened to 179 items and retitled the Marital Observation Checklist (Christiansen and Nies 1980). Gurman (1981), Gurman and Knudson (1978), and Margolin (1981) provide extensive reviews of these two instruments. One instrument specifically designed for use with spouse disagreements is the Problem Inventory (Gottman et al. 1976). All of these instruments are self-reports by spouses on a variety of behaviors, including conflict.

Coding schemes that external observers can use for conflict behavior are the MICS (Marital Interaction Coding Scheme; Hops et al. 1972) and the shortened MICS (Resick et al. 1977, 1980; Welsh-Osga, Resick, and Zitomer 1979). In addition, the widely cited Coding Scheme for Interpersonal Conflict (Raush et al. 1974) is particularly comprehensive for coding conflict behaviors. A shortened version is available for observation of small-group conflict (Baxter 1982).

Conflict style scales have received considerable attention in both workshops and research. Many of the scales essentially duplicate one another, especially those based on Blake and Mouton's (1964) Managerial Grid. For training use, the instruments by Lawrence and Lorsch (1969) and Kilmann and Thomas (1975) are useful. Research on their dimensions, however, has been limited or insufficient. Putnam and Wilson (1982) have provided another scale that can be used, especially in classroom and training contexts, and although it was designed for assessing personal styles in organizations, it has utility in other conflict settings. Also, it can be adapted to assess both self and other conflict styles (as can most instruments).

The best researched instrument on self-reports of conflict styles is now the Rahim ROCI-II (Rahim Organizational Conflict Inventory II). This measure of self-reports on conflict styles now has forms A, B, and C to measure conflict with one's superiors, subordinates, and peers. This is a copyrighted instrument and can be secured from Consulting

Psychologists Press at 3803 East Bayshore Road, Palo Alto, California, 94303 (phone: 415-969-8901). The measure can be found in Rahim (1983) and data on the reliability and validity of the measure can be found in Rahim and Magner (1995). One final instrument measures perceptions of the spouse's style, but there is some doubt as to the generalizability of its a priori dimensions (Rands, Levinger, and Mellinger 1981).

All of these style instruments measure *self-reports* of one's conflict style. The instruments can be revised to assess (1) party A's perceptions of self and other and (2) party B's perceptions of self and other. The comparison of how each conflict party sees the self and the other yields some useful information on the discrepancy in perceptions. Typical findings were noted in chapter 5, "Styles and Tactics." One word of caution: Before using any of the style instruments, take a thorough look at some of the options, including critiques of each of the instruments. Reread the critique of measuring styles presented in chapter 5 of this book and consult Knapp, Putnam, and Davis (1988) and the other articles in the same issue.

Power in conflict can also be measured. The work by Cavanaugh et al. (1981a, 1981b) attempts to specify individual values about power, and it provides information similar to "attitudes toward conflict" approaches. Power per se is a difficult concept to measure, and before selecting an approach, the reviews by Berger (1980), Cromwell and Olson (1975), Turk and Bell (1972), Galvin and Brommel (1986), McCall (1979), McDonald (1980), and Gray-Little and Burks (1983) should be consulted. Further, assessments have tended to specialize in either process (interaction) or outcome (decision-making) approaches. Process approaches are represented by the work of Rogers and Farace (1975), Rogers-Millar and Millar (1977), Ellis (1979), Aldous (1974), and Mishler and Waxler (1968). Outcome stances are represented by the work of Blood and Wolfe (1960), Safilios-Rothschild (1970), Heer (1963), Kenkel (1957), Olson and Straus (1972), Olson and Rabunsky (1972), and McDonald (1980). Tactical options can be measured quantitatively through self-reports or observational methods. Some self-report methods are provided by Brown and Levinson (1978), who organize tactics according to whether they support or attack the other's presentation of "face" or self. For a typology of "compliance-gaining" tactics (which are limited by their one-way view of social interaction), consult Marwell and Schmidt (1967) and additional sources cited in chapter 5. Kipnis (1976) discusses "means of influence" from a similar one-way perspective. Finally, Straus, et al., (1996) Conflict Tactics Scale is noteworthy for its inclusion of physical violence in the scale.

There are a variety of observational coding systems for classifying conflict tactics. In negotiation settings, one can use Donohue's work (1981a, 1981b). For coding tactics in everyday conflicts, the approaches of Raush et al. (1974) and Chafetz (1980) might be useful. Particularly well-documented is the work of Sillars, whose tactical categories were overviewed earlier in this book. You can secure the newest revision of his coding manual by writing to him at the Communication Studies Department, University of Montana, Missoula, Montana, 59812. Conflict assessment always involves some choice making. If you want a clear sense of the overall pattern of a conflict, a broad view of the rules and repetitive patterns in the system are needed. Such a "macro" view provides richness of description and creativity at the expense of quantitative specificity. The quantitative approaches, although providing reliable specificity in a given area, do not place those specifics within a comprehensive framework. This chapter concludes with two overall assessment guides that can be used as organizing schemes for probing conflicts. These guides supply perspectives, not answers, and they need to be adapted for your particular purposes.

Comprehensive Assessment Guides

These two comprehensive assessment guides stress open-ended, participant-based data as the path to understanding conflict processes. Such approaches are particularly useful for third parties such as intervention agents and students wishing to study a particular conflict. As a party to the conflict you can use the guides to collect information about your own and the other party's views about the conflict. In either case, one needs to use primary information from the parties—for they are the ones who created and maintain the conflict.

Two assessment guides are (1) the Wehr Conflict Mapping Guide and (2) the Wilmot-Hocker Conflict Assessment Guide. Depending on the purpose of the assessment, the guides can be combined or altered to specifically address one's assessment goals. All conflicts change over time, and an assessment is limited to the time period in which it was collected—one might obtain different information by assessing earlier or later in the conflict process.

Wehr's Conflict Map

In his book *Conflict Regulation,* Wehr (1979) provided a Conflict Mapping Guide to give "both the intervener and the conflict parties a clearer understanding of the origins, nature, dynamics, and possibilities for resolution of conflict" (19). The map includes the following information:

I. *Summary Description* (one-page maximum)

II. *Conflict History.* The origins and major events in the evolution of both the conflict and its context. It is important to distinguish between the interactive conflict relationship among the parties and the context within which it occurs.

III. *Conflict Context.* It is important to establish the scope and character of the context or setting within which the conflict takes place. Such dimensions are geographical boundaries; political structures, relations, and jurisdictions; communication networks and patterns; and decision-making methods. Most of these apply to the full range of conflict types, from interpersonal to international levels.

IV. *Conflict Parties.* Decisional units directly or indirectly involved in the conflict and having some significant stake in its outcome.

- **A.** *Primary.* Parties whose goals are, or are perceived by them to be, incompatible and who interact directly in pursuit of those respective goals. When the conflict parties are organizations or groups, each may be composed of smaller units differing in their involvement and investment in the conflict.
- **B.** *Secondary.* Parties who have an indirect stake in the outcome of the dispute but who do not feel themselves to be directly involved. As the conflict progresses, secondary parties may become primary, however, and vice versa.
- **C.** *Interested third parties.* Those who have an interest in the successful resolution of the conflict.

Pertinent information about the parties, in addition to who they are, would include the nature of the power relations between/among them (e.g., symmetrical or asymmetrical); their leadership; each party's main goal(s) in the conflict; and the potential for coalitions among parties.

V. *Issues.* Normally, a conflict will develop around one or more issues emerging from or leading to a decision. Each issue can be viewed as a point of disagreement that must be resolved. Issues can be identified and grouped according to the primary generating factor:
   - **A.** *Fact-based.* Disagreement over *what is* based on the parties' perceptions. Judgment and perception are the primary conflict generators here.
   - **B.** *Value-based.* Disagreement over *what should be* as a determinant of a policy decision, a relationship, or some other source of conflict.
   - **C.** *Interest-based.* Disagreement over *who will get what* in the distribution of scarce resources (e.g., power, privilege, economic benefits, respect).
   - **D.** *Nonrealistic.* Originating elsewhere than in disparate perceptions, interests, or values. Style of interaction the parties use, the quality of communication between them, or aspects of the immediate physical setting, such as physical discomfort, are examples.

With few exceptions, any one conflict will be influenced by some disagreement emerging from each of these sources, but normally one source is predominant. It is useful not only to identify each issue in this way but to identify as well the significant disparities in perception, values, and interests motivating each party. (*Values* are here defined as beliefs that determine a party's position on any one issue [e.g., economic growth is always desirable]. *Interests* are defined as any party's desired or expected share of scarce resources [e.g., power, money, prestige, survival, respect, love].)

VI. *Dynamics.* Social conflicts have common though not always predictable dynamics that if recognized can help an intervener find a way around the conflict. The intervener must seek to transform these into dynamics of regulation and resolution. Common dynamics include the following:
   - **A.** *Precipitating events* signaling the surfacing of a dispute.
   - **B.** *Issue emergence, transformation, and proliferation.* Issues change as a conflict progresses—specific issues become generalized, single issues multiply, and impersonal disagreements become personal feuds.
   - **C.** *Polarization.* As parties seek internal consistency and coalitions with allies, and leaders consolidate positions, parties in conflict tend toward bipolarization that can lead both to greater intensity and to simplification and resolution of the conflict.
   - **D.** *Spiraling.* Through a process of reciprocal causation, each party may try to increase the hostility or damage to opponents in each round, with a corresponding increase from the other parties. Also possible are de-escalatory spirals, in which opponents reciprocally and incrementally reduce the hostility and rigidity of their interaction.
   - **E.** *Stereotyping and mirror-imaging.* Opponents often come to perceive one another as impersonal representations of the mirror-opposite of their own exemplary and benign characteristics. This process encourages rigid positioning, miscommunication, and misinterpretation between conflict parties.

VII. *Alternative Routes to Solution(s) of the Problem(s).* Each of the parties and often uninvolved observers will have suggestions for resolving the conflict. In conflicts within a formal policy-making framework, the options can be formal plans. In interpersonal conflicts, alternatives can be behavioral changes suggested to (or by) the parties. It is essential to identify as many "policies" as possible that have already surfaced in the conflict. They should be made visible for both the conflict parties and the intervener. The intervener may then suggest new alternatives or combinations of those already identified.

VIII. *Conflict Regulation Potential.* In each conflict situation, resources are available for limiting and perhaps resolving the conflict. The mapping process notes these resources, albeit in a preliminary way. They may include the following:

- **A.** *Internal limiting factors* like values and interests the conflicting parties have in common, the intrinsic value of a relationship between them that neither wishes to destroy, or cross pressures of multiple commitments of parties that constrain the conflict.
- **B.** *External limiting factors* like a higher authority who could intervene and force a settlement or an intermediary from outside the conflict.
- **C.** *Interested or neutral third parties* trusted by the parties in conflict who could facilitate communication, mediate the dispute, or locate financial resources to alleviate a scarcity problem.
- **D.** *Techniques of conflict management,* both those familiar to the different conflict parties and third parties and those known to have been useful elsewhere. Such methods range from the well-known mediation, conciliation, and rumor control to fractionating issues and extending the time range to encourage settlement.

IX. *Using the Map.* The conflict map is most useful (and quite essential) as the initial step in conflict intervention. Mapping permits an informed judgment about whether the intervention should continue. The map is also helpful in assisting conflict parties to step back from and make sense out of a process to which they are too close. If the mapper decides to further intervene, sharing the map can loosen up the conflict, making it easier to resolve. Finally, the map helps demystify the process of conflict that, for so many people, seems a confusing, unfathomable, inexplicable, and thoroughly frustrating phenomenon.

Wilmot-Hocker Conflict Assessment Guide

This guide is composed of a series of questions focusing on the components of conflict discussed in part 1 of this book. It can be used to bring specific aspects of a conflict into focus and as a check on gaps in information about a conflict. The guide is best used in its complete form so that the interplay of conflict elements can be clearly highlighted. For important, recurring, long-term conflicts, you might want to use each question for your assessment. Another way of using the guide is to pick several questions from each section that appear to apply to your conflict. Even seemingly small interpersonal conflicts benefit from a careful, objective assessment. You might do this in writing, in guided discussion with others, or for your own reflection.

I. Orientation to the Conflict

- **A.** What attitudes toward conflict do participants seem to hold?
- **B.** Do they perceive conflict as positive, negative, or neutral? How can you tell?

C. What metaphoric images do conflict participants use? What metaphors might you use to describe the conflict?
D. What is the cultural background of the participants? What is the cultural context in which the conflict takes place?
E. How might gender roles, limitations, and expectations be operating in this conflict?

II. Nature of the Conflict
A. What are the "triggering events" that brought this conflict into mutual awareness?
B. What is the historical context of this conflict in terms of (1) the ongoing relationship between the parties and (2) other, external events within which this conflict is embedded?
C. Do the parties have assumptions about conflict that are discernable by their choices of conflict metaphors, patterns of behavior, or clear expressions of their attitudes about conflict?
D. Conflict elements:
1. How is the struggle being expressed by each party?
2. What are the perceived incompatible goals?
3. What are the perceived scarce resources?
4. In what ways are the parties interdependent? How are they interfering with one another? How are they cooperating to keep the conflict in motion?
E. Has the conflict vacillated between productive and destructive phases? If so, which elements were transformed during the productive cycles? Which elements might be transformed by creative solutions to the conflict?

III. Goals
A. How do the parties clarify their goals? Do they phrase them in individualistic or systemic terms?
B. What does each party think the other's goals are? Are they similar or dissimilar to the perceptions of self-goals?
C. How have the goals been altered from the beginning of the conflict to the present? In what ways are the prospective, transactive, and retrospective goals similar or dissimilar?
D. What are the content, relational, identity, and process goals?
E. How do the CRIP goals overlap with one another?
F. Which goals seem to be primary at different stages of the dispute?
G. Are the conflict parties "specializing" in one type or the other?
H. Are the identity and relational issues the "drivers" of this dispute?
I. Are any of the goals emerging in different forms?
J. Is there "shape shifting" of the goals over time in the dispute? How do they change during the prospective, transactive, and retrospective phases?

IV. Power
A. What attitudes about their own and the other's power does each party have? Do they talk openly about power, or is it not discussed?
B. What do the parties see as their own and the other's dependencies on one another? As an external observer, can you classify some dependencies that they do not list?

C. What power currencies do the parties see themselves and the other possessing?
D. From an external perspective, what power currencies of which the participants are not aware seem to be operating?
E. In what ways do the parties disagree on the balance of power between them? Do they underestimate their own or the other's influence?
F. What impact does each party's assessment of power have on subsequent choices in the conflict?
G. What evidence of destructive "power balancing" occurs?
H. In what ways do observers of the conflict agree and disagree with the parties' assessments of their power?
I. What are some unused sources of power that are present?

V. Styles and Tactics
A. What individual styles did each party use?
B. How did the individual styles change during the course of the conflict?
C. How did the parties perceive the other's style?
D. In what way did a party's style reinforce the choices the other party made as the conflict progressed?
E. Were the style choices primarily symmetrical or complementary?
F. From an external perspective, what were the advantages and disadvantages of each style within this particular conflict?
G. Can the overall system be characterized as having a predominant style? What do the participants say about the relationship as a whole?
H. Do the participants appear to strategize about their conflict choices or remain spontaneous?
I. How does each party view the other's strategizing?
J. What are the tactical options used by both parties?
K. Do the tactical options classify primarily into avoidance, competition, or collaboration?
L. How are the participants' tactics mutually impacting on the other's choices? How are the tactics interlocking to push the conflict through phases of escalation, maintenance, and reduction?

VI. Assessment
A. What rules of repetitive patterns characterize this conflict?
B. What triangles and microevents best characterize the conflict?
C. How destructive is the tone of this conflict?

VII. Personal Intervention
A. What options for change do the parties perceive?
B. What philosophy of conflict characterizes the system?
C. What techniques for self-regulation or system regulation have been used thus far? Which might be used productively by the system?
D. How might anger be managed more productively?

VIII. Attempted Solutions
A. What options have been explored for managing the conflict?
B. Have attempted solutions become part of the problem?

C. Have third parties been brought into the conflict? If so, what roles did they play and what was the impact of their involvement?

D. Is this conflict a repetitive one, with attempted solutions providing temporary change but with the overall pattern remaining unchanged? If so, what is that overall pattern?

E. Can you identify categories of attempted solutions that have *not* been tried?

The Conflict Assessment Guide can be used in a variety of contexts. Students who are writing an analysis of a conflict can use the questions to check the components of conflict. Constructing interviews or a questionnaire based on the guide enables one to discover the dynamics of a conflict. The guide can also be used for analyzing larger social or international conflicts, but without interviewing or assessing the conflict parties, one is restricted to highly selective information.

A consultant to organizations can also use the guide by modifying it for direct use. Similarly, an intervener in private conflicts, such as those of a family, can solicit information about the components of a conflict in an informal, conversational way using the guide as an outline of relevant topics. In either case, care should be taken to modify the guide for the particular task, conflict parties, and intervention goals.

The guide can also be used as a form of self-intervention for conflict participants. You can use it to highlight what you and the other party perceive about your conflict. The questionnaire should be constructed for both parties to answer, and once the data are collected, the parties can discuss the similarities and differences in their perceptions of the conflict.

Whatever your preferred assessment technique, or combination of techniques, the assessment devices in this chapter enable you to see some order and regularity in conflicts that at first appear confusing and overwhelming. With careful assessment, the dynamics of conflict come into focus so you can fashion creative, productive options for management.

Summary

Conflicts are often perplexing to both participants and outsiders. Usually, however, an interpersonal conflict is operating as a system of relations, complete with repetitive behavior, rules, and other identifiable dynamics. There are many possible ways to assess conflict patterns. Metaphoric/dramatic approaches search for the images of the process held by the participants and use those as stepping stones for creative management options. Diagramming triangular relations also provides useful information about system dynamics. Sculpting is a nonverbal, spatially based technique for identifying patterns of communication within a larger system. One can also focus on system rules, the prescriptions for what one ought to do in a given situation. Microevents are observable, recurring patterns of behavior that can be analyzed for underlying conflict structure. Finally, interviews and simple observation are essential tools of conflict analysis.

If one wishes to quantitatively assess the components of either conflicts produced by simulation or games or natural conflicts accessed through self-reports of the parties, many options are available. For example, one can measure general orientations toward conflict, code behaviors enacted in an episode, identify conflict styles, assess power balances, or isolate the tactics used in a conflict. The Wehr and Wilmot-Hocker guides are two overall assessment guides used to generate information about the dynamics of specific conflicts; they can be used either by conflict participants or outside observers.

Chapter 7

Negotiation

The Importance of Negotiation

The word "negotiation" usually brings to mind labor and management representatives negotiating a work contract. In fact, most of the literature on negotiation restricts itself to that context. Yet negotiation occurs every day in both private and public contexts. The following situations call for negotiation:

- Your friend wants to have you over for dinner at 9:00 P.M., and you want to come earlier.
- You have a defective computer disk and want more time for completion of a paper.
- Your elderly mother, who has lived alone for decades, has fallen and broken her hip, and you and the other siblings need to talk about possible nursing home care.

- Your father agrees to pay for four years of college for you, but you now need one extra semester beyond four years to complete school.
- You and your roommate, who were best friends, bought many household items together. Recently, because you both want to date the same person, you have had a serious falling out with each other. You agree to stop rooming together but now have to decide who gets what items in the apartment.
- You are manager of a work team, and there is disagreement over who gets assigned what tasks.
- You are an hourly employee, and your boss says, "I don't care what hours you guys work just so the store is covered, so the four of you decide what hours you want to work."
- You buy carpet from a store and clearly tell the salesperson that you want the old carpet saved so that you can give it to your best friend. You come home at the end of the day, and the new carpet looks nice, but the old carpet is gone. A quick phone call reveals that it was taken to the landfill and cannot be retrieved.

Opportunities for negotiation are everywhere. In both our personal and work lives, we are faced with making decisions that are acceptable to both us and others. One survey found that human service administrators spend 26 percent of their time negotiating (Files 1981). Further, with the advent of "self-directed work teams" the ability to negotiate both within the team and from the team to the wider organization takes on added importance (Barker, Melville, and Pacanowsky 1993; Turner 1990; Sinclair 1992). Negotiation occurs whenever labor and management bargain for wages and fringe benefits.

A subset of conflict, negotiation presumes interdependence, motivation to engage with each other, and both similar and dissimilar interests (Bartos 1974). When people bargain or negotiate they "attempt to settle what each shall give and take, or perform and receive" (Rubin and Brown 1975, 2). Negotiation allows conflict parties to state their preferences, discuss their relationship, restrain themselves from certain actions, and increase predictability about each other (Wall 1985). It covers a wide range and falls midway between avoidance and domination, as shown in figure 7.1.

Although some writers distinguish between bargaining and negotiation (Keltner 1994), most people treat them as virtually synonymous terms. The definitions in most dictionaries send you into a loop between *bargaining* ("to negotiate") and *negotiation* ("to bargain"). For the remainder of this chapter, the two terms will be used equally to represent the same activity. Negotiation presumes the following:

- Participants engage in the conflict rather than avoid.
- Parties resist using domination or power-over tactics.
- All of the elements of a conflict situation are present.
- Parties have reached an active, problem-solving phase in which proposals are traded.

In the active negotiation process, all the parties depend on their assessment of the power and the structure of the situation, *regulate their own behavior to maximize their own gains,* and *search for acceptable proposals so resolution can be achieved.* Parties must be able to provide resources and to influence goal achievement, and they must be willing to do so through cooperation (Donohue and Kolt 1992). No purpose is served by negotiating with

Figure 7.1 The location of negotiation in a conflict spectrum

someone who has nothing to offer you. You need to be induced to struggle together to achieve common and individual goals. Parties in conflict agree tacitly to a framework of ground rules to manage conflict (Putnam and Poole 1987). The case of the "Cheap Statue" illustrates one type of negotiation.

The Cheap Statue

Wallace, a U.S. citizen, was new to Kathmandu. He had been told by his friend Liz to "be a hard bargainer" when in this culture, where sellers thrive on negotiation. His first day on the streets, many vendors approached him and Liz as they strolled about. One young man, in particular, would not go away. He was selling "good, high quality statues" for, as he said, a "rock price" (rock-bottom price). When the statue vendor first approached, Wallace stopped and looked intently at the statue. The vendor then stayed close to him for almost an hour, with Wallace saying, "I don't want to buy," but knowing that his looking at the statue made this protest sound rather hollow.

The vendor started at 500 rupees (about ten dollars). Throughout this first hour, Wallace gave in and started bargaining. His final offer was 300 rupees, which the vendor would not accept. Wallace and Liz left and returned to the market square some six hours later. The vendor spied them and started tagging along. Wallace bargained for a few minutes then said, "OK, I now will give you only 250 rupees for the statue." The vendor, after giving a speech about his family starving, and wringing his hands in agony, completed the sale and handed over the statue. Just as Wallace was beginning to feel smug about his fine bargaining ability, the vendor turned to Liz and said, "I'll sell you one for 175 rupees."

In contemporary Western cultures, we receive contradictory messages about negotiation. On the one hand, you are supposed to "get a good deal," but on the other, you are expected to walk into commercial establishments and pay their listed prices. No wonder some of us are confused about negotiation and its role in management potential disputes. Examine the following situations and decide in which ones you would go along with others and in which ones you would negotiate:

Negotiable?

- The price of a new house
- The part(s) of the apartment/house/dorm room you and your roommates will use
- The price of a used car
- The price of an item on sale at a chain store (CD, book, portable radio, etc.)
- The price of pens and paper at the college bookstore
- The salary offered at McDonalds or Burger King for you to "flip burgers"

- The time you work at your job
- The final paper assignment in your class
- The final grade you receive in your conflict class
- The price of a used toaster at a garage sale
- The person(s) who will care for your aging parents

As you can see, some items are negotiable and others are not. Each culture designates areas that are off-limit to negotiation and areas in which negotiation is acceptable. In Kathmandu, for example, Wallace found that everything was *not* negotiable, such as the price of booking a trek in Nepal. Decide where *you are comfortable* negotiating and where you are not. We differ considerably from one another in our comfort with and willingness to negotiate in different situations. For some of us negotiation in private relationships is fine, whereas for others of us it is off-limits. Similarly, many people take along a friend to negotiate for them when they buy a large item like a car because they are not comfortable "haggling over price."

Developmental Ability in Negotiation

When your partner in a conflict says, "Don't be such a child," he or she is suggesting that you should choose more "grown-up" conflict tactics. Although such comments are demeaning, they do suggest that children handle conflict and negotiation at a more basic level than do adults. Provocative research on the interpersonal negotiation abilities of children demonstrates that as children mature, their abilities for more complex negotiation strategies increase. As Selman et al. (1986) found, "The capacity for expressing reciprocal or collaborative strategies in interpersonal negotiations may still be developing beyond the juvenile and early adolescent period of chumship" (456).

Which specific communicative behaviors reflect "maturity" in negotiation? Selman et al. (1986, 453) have set forth an illuminating coding scheme for levels of "interpersonal negotiation strategies." Table 7.1 shows the scoring system used by observers to code the negotiation behaviors of children ages eleven to nineteen. One's level of interpersonal negotiation begins at level 0 in each category and proceeds to level 3. For example, in "Definition of problem," the basic level is "No reference to the problem" and shows little comprehension of the interpersonal problem between the two people. However, as one matures, progress is made toward level 3, "Reference to a shared problem." Varying levels of maturity exist for (1) definition of the problem, (2) action taken, (3) justification of strategy, and (4) complexity of feelings. As one matures and becomes more communicatively complex, the level of negotiation moves from 0 to 3 across the four levels.

As a child progresses toward a synthesis of self and other interests (Dien 1982), he or she is moving toward a collaborative approach in negotiations. On the other hand, when someone says, "I don't care—just shut up and do what I say," they are at one of the lower levels—level 1 of "Action taken." As children mature, they demonstrate a greater ability to use compromising techniques (Clark, O'Dell, and Willihnganz 1986; Selman et al. 1986). Stated another way, they develop "socially oriented behavior" (Selman and Demorest 1984), which incorporates (1) their wishes, (2) the other's wishes, and (3) some notion of the relationship between the two people. Young children, then, cannot be expected to

Table 7.1 Levels of Interpersonal Negotiation

Numeric value	Scoring category
	Definition of problem
0	No reference to the problem except to restate the protagonist's actions
1	Reference to the problem between self and other in terms of the wants or desires of the person viewed as having the most power
2	Reference to the reciprocal context of the relationship between self and other with a focus on one of the two persons having a priority of needs but the other's needs also having validity
3	Reference to a shared problem with consideration of both persons' needs or wants
	Action taken
0	Physical, noncommunicative methods
1	One-way directives or requests
2	Reciprocal communication with a balance of perspectives
3	Verbal collaboration with other
	Justification of strategy
0	No justification or anticipation of consequences expressed
1	Self-protective justification
2	Relationship or empathic concerns without attention to long-term consequences
3	Concern for long-term effects on the relationship
	Complexity of feelings
0	Consequences of strategy do not include reference to feelings
1	Simple, unidimensional feelings expressed in a self-protective, undifferentiated way
2	Simple, unidimensional feelings expressed in an empathic way
3	Complex, multiple, or changing feelings of self or other expressed

Source: Reprinted, by permission of the publisher, from R. L. Selman, W. Beardslee, L. H. Schultz, M. Krupa, and D. Podorefsky, "Assessing Adolescent Interpersonal Negotiation Strategies: Toward the Integration of Structural and Functional Models," *Developmental Psychology* 22 (1986): 453.

use high-level strategies; their one-way orientation is entirely appropriate for their age group.

One intriguing study demonstrated that unpopular children use inappropriate, negative strategies when in conflict with other children (Renshaw and Asher 1992). Another study found, not too surprisingly, that adolescent girls negotiate at a higher level on average than adolescent boys (Selman and Demorest 1984). However, children as young as those in the fourth grade can be taught how to compromise (Clark, O'Dell, and Willihnganz 1986).

Given that different levels of negotiation require different levels of thought and communication, it is no wonder that many amateur negotiators use lower-level strategies—they are easier to use and more readily learned. In many organizations, for example, managers often threaten their subordinates—a handy, quick way to "negotiate." However, although lower-level strategies are easier to learn, less taxing, and less time-consuming, they are more likely to boomerang and damage an ongoing relationship. When a relationship itself is as important or more important than the specific items being negotiated, high-level strategies must be learned to maintain the relationship. Yet, there are many circumstances in which negotiations do not require such a high level of functioning.

Argumentation

What comes to mind when someone says, "Oh, he is just arguing again"? For many people it implies that he is disagreeing on content and using a disagreeable tone. The following quotation from a student paper exemplifies this common stance:

> When I get into an argument with a person over something I really stand for, then I really like to get involved and have a good battle. If my competitor has a good stand on his issues, then I like to "rip" at him until he breaks or if things go wrong, I break. The excitement of confrontation when I'm battling it out with another person has a tremendous thrill for me if I come out as the victor. I love it when we are at each other's throats.

Content and relationship issues, as demonstrated earlier, can be separated. For example, you can disagree on content and be pleasant (maintaining the relationship component) at the same time. Or, you can offer forcible opinions about an issue yet protect the face/identity of the other and follow the procedural rules (one talking at a time, for example). In negotiation situations the following phrases allow participants to disagree on content without being "disagreeable":

I'm sorry, but I don't agree with your position about the election.
I'm pretty firm about not agreeing with you, but tell me more.
We still disagree about the role of government in our private lives.
John, that sure isn't my memory about what I agreed to about the deposit.

As you can see from these examples, one doesn't have to destroy the relational dimension in order to carry a strong content argument. In fact, the whole tradition of debate (such as college debate and the presidential debates during campaign years) rests on *agreeing on process rules to protect identity, procedural, and relationship dimensions* so that the arguments can focus on content. In professional debate circles, it is considered a logical fallacy to attack the other debater personally. It is called *argumentum ad hominen,* which means "argument against the man." If you are a professional advocate in a courtroom, there are strict rules about not attacking the other side personally, and the rules are interpreted and enforced by the judge—ensuring that argument will occur on the content level. The judge won't let you, for example, make the following statement: "The other attorney is just a jerk, and I can't believe the defendant is wasting his money employing him."

Argument, then, is "reason giving" (Benoit 1992; Rowland and Barge 1991), trying to convince others of your side of the issue. One makes claims and backs them up (Keough 1992). The arguer tries to get others to "recognize the rightness" of his or her beliefs or actions (Benoit 1983, 550). Interpersonal argumentation, then, has a place in our everyday conflicts and negotiations (Trapp 1981, 1989). One of the positive features of interpersonal arguments (in the sense defined here) is that they are comprised of exchanges between two people who feel powerful enough to set forth reasons for their beliefs. If two people are arguing, it is because they are balanced enough in power (or in their desire to reestablish a power balance) to proceed. Lack of argument, in fact, may show that one of the parties feels so powerless that he or she avoids engaging directly with the other (Cloven and Roloff 1993b).

Interpersonal argument, done properly, may in fact be the heart and soul of modern-day interpersonal problem solving and conflict management. We trade positions, set forth evidence, and let the free exchange of ideas reign. But we do not destroy our relationships with others, personally attack or destroy their face, or violate standards of procedure. When arguments get out of control and become destructive, some principle of argumentation is being violated. One may distort content by withholding or lying about facts. One may cite more support for an idea than is warranted. Often, people try to intimidate, demean, condescend to, or threaten the other—all examples of manipulating the relationship level of the conflict to get what they want. When one person says something sarcastic (an indirect attack), such as, "I wouldn't expect you to understand. You're sitting on a trust fund and couldn't be expected to know the value of money to ordinary people," the relationship and identity levels become the field of argument, with destructive effects. In many organizations, people argue about the appropriateness of consensus decision making, executive power, the role of the board, or how much input stuff members should have, thus dodging policy issues, relationship issues, and face-saving issues. In constructive conflicts, arguments focus on levels of discourse that will move the conflict toward resolution. When argument focuses on relationship or identity issues, the conflict may generate much heat but little light. As in classical debate, the honorable approach is to engage on those issues that are real and will help the dialogue. Anything else blocks progress. In ancient Rome, Quintilian, one of the earliest rhetoricians, wrote of the characteristics of an effective orator: intelligence, character, and goodwill. These attributes describe the effective negotiator as well.

The renewed call to "civility" in public discourse comes from experiences of personal attacks and unproductive negotiation tactics. In civil argumentation and negotiation, cordial, firm, and passionate communication takes place, but attacks on on the personhood of the other do not.

Perspectives on Negotiation

Negotiation depends on the communicative behavior of the participants. You will notice a similarity between specific negotiation tactics and some of the conflict tactics discussed earlier. In negotiation, however, the tactics are employed with one clear purpose—*to reach settlement* with the other. This chapter will demonstrate advanced techniques that are useful for successful negotiation with conflict participants.

Most views of negotiation present a limited perspective. Since negotiation is such a common and pervasive conflict management process, it is little wonder that scores of books have been written about it. Unfortunately, some of the popular advice reinforces a win-lose perspective. For instance, one book offers "examples to guide you in *getting the upper hand every time!*" or "33 ways to use the power in you to get *your* way in any situation" (Ilich 1981). Likewise, much of the research on bargaining and negotiation focuses exclusively on aggressive maneuvers of negotiators and views negotiation as a debate (Putnam and Jones 1982). Further, many popular authors see bargaining as a "game of managing impressions and manipulating information. Bargaining is a struggle for advantage, for with the advantage comes beneficial outcomes" (Walker 1988, 219). It is not surprising, then, that amateur negotiators often adopt a win-lose view of negotiation (Bazerman and Neale 1983).

Another limited view of negotiation is seeing it as a "series of compromises" (Haynes 1983, 79). From this perspective, negotiation is simply a trade-off in which each gives up something to reach a middle ground, ignoring the development of creative options. One final limitation of most literature on negotiation is that it centers on (1) formal negotiations, between (2) negotiating representatives, where (3) the beginning and endings of the negotiations are clearly delineated. International negotiators, labor management representatives, and lawyers negotiating for their clients all engage in *explicit negotiations.* We will discuss many aspects of such negotiations; however, most of us will never be professional negotiators. Therefore, this chapter will emphasize the process and outcomes of negotiations that can be used in everyday situations, ranging from explicit interpersonal negotiations, such as advocating for your chuld at school, to tacitly bargaining with your spouse or roommate.

In *implicit* negotiations, the communication is often indirect, in the form of hints, signs, and obscure intimations (Wall 1985). Still, the conflict parties are choosing to settle their differences without resorting to force or avoidance. They use commonly understood ground rules and advance offers and suggestions without losing face (Holloway and Brager 1985).

Everything you have learned about conflict so far will be useful in the negotiation situations you face. The key items to consider are the CRIP—content, relationship, identity, and process—goals of you and the other party, as these are what you will negotiate about. There are two main approaches to negotiation, competitive and collaborative, and they differ in the way they deal with CRIP goals. Each type of negotiation will be discussed in detail, but figure 7.2 illustrates some of the key conceptual differences between competitive and collaborative stances to negotiation.

As shown in figure 7.2, the two main approaches to negotiation differ widely from each other. Each of these two types will be discussed in turn, and the communication patterns underlying each type of negotiation will be specified. When most of us hear the word "negotiation," it triggers a competitive mind frame—winner and loser, power against, staking out a position in a gamelike stance. Most media coverage of conflict in general, and negotiation in particular, tends to cast relationships in a competitive light. As Brinson (1992) says, "Television seems to require a 'winner' and a 'loser' to enhance the dramatic tension" (101). In the following section, both competitive and collaborative negotiation will be presented, along with communication patterns characterizing each and general principles of effective negotiation.

Figure 7.2 Comparison of negotiating approaches

Competitive negotiating		**Collaborative negotiating**
	Content	
Zero-sum gain	⟷	**Joint gain**
(Win-lose)		(Win-win)
	Relationship	
Hard	⟷	**Soft**
(Unfriendly)		(Friendly)
	Identity/face-saving	
Rigid	⟷	**Flexible**
(Confrontational)		(Supportive)
	Process	
Solution-rationalizing	⟷	**Solution-building**
(Positional bargaining)		(Interest-based bargaining)

Source: Adapted from Roy H. Andes, "Message Dimensions of Negotiation," in *Negotiation Journal* 8, no. 2 (April 1992):137. Copyright Plenum Publishing Corporation, New York. Reprinted by permission.

Competitive Approaches

Assumptions

Competitive or "distributive" negotiations are what most people think of when discussing negotiation. For example, you and your sister both want to use your dad's fly rod. Competitive negotiators assume that the conflict is win-lose (or "zero-sum" in game theory terms). What you win, she loses, and vice versa. The rewards in such a conflict are seen as a "fixed pie" to be distributed between the parties, thus the name "distributive" bargaining (Walton and McKersie 1965). In competitive or distributive negotiations, each party usually has a "resistance point" or a "bargaining range" beyond which he or she will not go (Popple 1984). For example, from a competitive approach the relevant information for buying a house is this:

Buyer's range: $85,000–$90,000
Seller's range: $88,000–$93,500

Each person's range determines his or her offers and counteroffers. The seller lists the house for $95,500. The buyer makes a first offer of $85,000. After negotiations, the buyer offers $88,000. The seller says that she will not part with the house for less than $92,000. Buyer and seller slowly move toward their "settlement range" (between $88,000 and $90,000) and, after the seller agrees to pay the loan costs, settle on $89,300.

Typically, the distributive bargainer is not concerned about the future relationship with the other party and is trying to maximize gain and minimize loss. The basic assumptions of distributive or competitive negotiation are as follows:

- The negotiating world is controlled by egocentric self-interest.
- The underlying motivation is competitive/antagonistic.
- Limited resources prevail.
- One can make independent choices: tomorrow's decision remains unaffected materially by today's.
- The resource distribution system is distributive in nature (either-or).
- The goal is to win as much as you can—and especially more than the other side. (Murray 1986)

Communication Patterns

Since competitive bargaining assumes that the goals of the parties are in direct conflict and that what you gain the other loses (Walker 1988), you gain a competitive advantage by starting with a high or extreme offer (Fisher 1985). For instance, if you sue someone else, you will ask for large amounts of money—for what the other loses you gain. Similarly, if you are a competitive negotiator negotiating for a new job and employers ask you, "What salary do you want?" you will say "$35,000," knowing you would be happy with $32,000. Competitive bargainers withhold data from each other and try to throw off each other's ability to predict responses, meanwhile learning as much as possible about each other's position (Putnam and Poole 1987). The competitive bargainer:

- Makes high opening demands and concedes slowly
- Tries to maximize tangible resource gains, within the limits of the current dispute
- Exaggerates the value of concessions that are offered
- Uses threats, confrontations, argumentation, and forceful speaking
- Conceals information
- Manipulates people and the process by distorting intentions, resources, and goals
- Tries to resist persuasion on issues
- Is oriented to quantitative and competitive goals rather than relational goals (adapted from Murray 1986; Lax and Sebenius 1986)

The competitive bargainer times concessions (giving in and moving toward the other's position) carefully and moves in a stepwise fashion—giving a little bit at a time until a settlement range can be reached with the other (Popple 1984). Since both people are probably in a competitive mode, each is trying to get the other to make concessions. However, one is more likely to receive concessions from someone else when one can convince the other that one *cannot* make a concession (Schelling 1960). Thus, each negotiator is trying to convince the other that he or she cannot "give" anymore and that the only way the negotiations can reach settlement is if the *other* gives in (Edwards and White

1977). Former President Jimmy Carter spoke about his role as mediator in the Camp David accords, in which Anwar Sadat of Egypt and Menachem Begin of Israel spent thirteen days in isolation negotiating peace in their region. To convince Sadat of his seriousness, Begin had taken a religious oath that he would strike off his right hand if he gave up land in the Gaza Strip. Carter came up with the idea that the Israeli parliament, not Begin personally, could enact the moves that would give land back to Egypt. Begin saved face and was able to go ahead with a plan he personally endorsed, after days of negotiating.

There is an infinite array of well-known competitive strategies that can be used to advance one's own goals. You only behave cooperatively if it helps you attain a larger share of the pie. You see the "game" of negotiation as one of picking the right maneuvers, much like a military strategy, and you must present a strong defense and try to stay on the offensive. If you show elements of "weakness"—showing your hand or offering concessions too large or too early (Wall 1985)—these weaknesses will work against you. If you are a competitive negotiator you will go to great lengths to convince the opponent that you will not be swayed. When you say, "This is my bottom line!" you are trying to convince the other that you *will not* make concessions, so the other party had better make some. The shopper in a country in which bargaining is used walks away from the merchant saying, "All I can offer is $110—that's final," hoping the merchant will respond by saying, "OK, you can have the coat for $110."

Disadvantages

Disadvantages to a competitive approach to negotiations abound. As Follett (1940) observed many years ago, working out a position without first consulting others "blocks conflict management." The following list summarizes the most prominent negative features of a competitive approach to negotiations:

- *Has a strong bias toward confrontation,* encouraging the use of coercion and emotional pressure as persuasive means; is hard on relationships, breeding mistrust, feelings of separateness, frustration, and anger, resulting in more frequent breakdowns in negotiations; and distorts communication, producing misinformation and misjudgment
- *Guards against responsiveness and openness* to opponent, thereby restricting access to joint gains
- *Encourages brinkmanship* by creating many opportunities for impasse
- *Increases difficulty in predicting responses of opponent* because reliance is on manipulation and confrontation to control process
- *Contributes to an overestimation of the payoffs of competitive actions* such as litigation because the focus is not on a relatively objective analysis of substantive merits (Murray 1986, 184)

The situations most appropriate for a competitive approach to negotiations are those that are truly win-lose where one party stands to lose and the other stands to gain. For example, most lawsuits for malpractice can be seen as win-lose. When no ongoing relationship with the person is predicted, a competitive approach can make sense—take what you can get and leave. Such an approach, obviously, is only acceptable in a culture in which individual gain is valued and relationships are given secondary consideration. If someone is truly Machiavellian, planning each move in life strategically to obtain a payoff, competitiveness is at the center of his or her worldview. Someone with an extreme "dog-eat-dog" worldview may say such things as "I have to treat him well because someday I'll need him." A truly competitive person keeps his or her eyes on the prize at all times!

Collaborative Approaches

> Negotiation requires ongoing back-and-forth use of reflective listening and assertion skills by one or both parties. Management of conflict through effective negotiation requires listening to the other party; indicating that you understand his or her concerns; expressing your feelings; stating your points in a firm but friendly manner; linking your points to points expressed by the other party; and working toward a joint resolution that builds on the ideas of both parties and addresses all concerns.
>
> —Umbreit, *Mediating Interpersonal Conflicts*

Competitive or distributive negotiations assume that what one person wins the other loses. Integrative or collaborative bargaining, on the other hand, assumes that the parties have both (1) *diverse interests* and (2) *common interests* and that the negotiation process can result in both parties gaining something. There are *mixed motives*—separate needs and interdependent needs. Whereas the competitive model assumes that someone loses and someone wins, collaborative negotiation assumes that creativity can transcend the win-lose aspect of competitive negotiations.

The classic example, often repeated in a variety of forms, comes from Mary Parker Follett (1940), who coined the term *integrative.* She illustrates an integrative solution to a conflict that at first appears to be competitive.

> In the Harvard Library one day, in one of the smaller rooms, someone wanted the window open, I wanted it shut. We opened the window in the next room, where no one was sitting. This was not a compromise because there was no curtailing of desire; we both got what we really wanted. For I did not want a closed room, I simply did not want the north wind to blow directly on me; likewise the other occupant did not want that particular window open, he merely wanted more air in the room. (32)

Although she doesn't detail her bargaining process, the result was clearly integrative—it integrated the needs of both parties. Integrative or collaborative negotiations emphasize maximizing joint benefits for both parties, often in creative ways (Bazerman, Magliozzi, and Neale 1985). Such bargaining places value on the relationship between the conflict parties, requires trust, and relies on full disclosure of relevant information (Walker 1988).

One of the assumptions of collaborative or integrative negotiation is that *polar opposites are not necessarily in conflict.* For example, if two people are negotiating, sometimes they can reach a satisfactory solution precisely *because* they want different things. Fisher, Ury, and Patton (1991, 74) list some of the polar opposites that can be reconciled in integrative negotiation.

One party cares more about	Other party cares more about
form, appearance	substance
economic considerations	political considerations
internal considerations	external considerations
symbolic considerations	practical considerations
immediate future	more distant future
ad hoc results	the relationship
hardware	ideology
progress	respect for tradition
precedent	this case
prestige, reputation	results
political points	group welfare

Recall chapter 3, "Goals," which suggested that conflict parties often specialize in certain goals? If you are most concerned about "getting things done" (results) and your work associate is more concerned about "looking good" (prestige, reputation), your needs are not necessarily incompatible. For instance, you may want to make sure the work is done for your campus committee and the other may want to make sure there is newspaper coverage of the event you are sponsoring. He can help you get the job done, and you can put him in touch with a reporter you know. Collaborative approaches treat assumed opposites as connected and not incompatible.

Follett (1940) relates yet another story that provides insight into collaborative, integrative negotiations. Two sisters were fighting over an orange and, after much acrimony, agreed to split the orange in half—a compromise. One sister used her half of the orange for juice and the other sister used the peel of her half of the orange for a cake. They overlooked the integrative or collaborative elements of negotiation. They each could have had a full orange since they wanted different parts! As Walton and McKersie (1965) note, integrative or collaborative negotiators engage in joint problem-solving, jointly devising solutions that maximize benefits for both parties. This process of joint improvement is sometimes called "problem-solving" bargaining (Karrass 1970).

Assumptions

Just as the competitive model of negotiation has basic assumptions, so does the integrative, collaborative, problem-solving model of negotiation. The process presumes the following:

- The negotiating world is controlled by enlightened self-interest.
- Common interests are valued and sought.
- Interdependence is recognized and enhanced.
- Limited resources do exist, but they can usually be expanded through cooperation.
- The resource distribution system is integrative (joint) in nature.
- The goal is a mutually agreeable solution that is fair to all parties and efficient for the community. (Murray 1986)

As you can see, the collaborative approach has very different assumptions about the world. Rather than a "dog-eat-dog" view, it presumes that we can, even in the midst of a conflict, work from "enlightened self-interest." We get what we need from others but do it in a way that also helps them achieve some of their goals. The collaborative bargainer is interested in preserving the relationship with the other. Therefore, driving a hard bargain at the expense of the other is not seen as a victory. Collaborative bargainers must maintain some interest in the other while holding out for their own goals. Unlike a win-lose situation, both of you can come away from the negotiation with an intact relationship, willing to trust and work with each other in the next bargaining situation.

Communication Patterns

The obvious next question is, "How does one *do* collaborative negotiations?" Unless we can specify communicative behaviors that can activate a collaborative negotiation set, the basic principles won't take us very far. All of the collaborative tactics we discussed in chapter 5, "Styles and Tactics," can be put to use by the collaborative negotiator. You might want to review that section as a basis for collaborative negotiation. Also worthy of note are some specific techniques that lead to collaborative outcomes. If you want more lengthy treatment of these techniques consult Rubin, Pruitt, and Kim (1994) and Lewicki and Litterer (1985).

Expanding the pie encourages collaborative outcomes because most conflicts are based on the perception of scarce resources; expanding the resources alters the structure of the conflict. For example, if Jane wants to go to the mountains and Sandy wants to go to the seashore, they might collaborate to find a mountainous seashore. Although it won't be the perfect mountain and the shore may have some limitations, they will get to spend their vacation together—they have expanded the pie. Often, children squabble with one another because of the perception that there is not enough parental care and consideration to go around. They fight, say mean things to one another, and struggle over the available love. As the parent, if you refuse to "parcel out" the love and attention, giving each child attention and focus without leaving out the other, you have expanded the pie. Whether the "pie" is actual or metaphorical, its expansion alters the conflict.

"You've Got to Do It!"

Caitlin, an entry-level employee who had just received her B.A., worked for a veteran's program. The program was underfunded, with many demands being placed on the staff members. The program director of the family services division asked Caitlin to design and teach a family communication program to families with preschool children. Caitlin felt unprepared, pushed too far and too fast, and unsupported for this high-visibility program (it would be filmed and put on public-access TV). Although Caitlin was newly hired, she had been given a lot of responsibility and did have legitimate power in the organization. She also wanted to work for the organization so didn't want to resign under the pressure of three times too much work. Two possible scenarios follow:

Competitive Mode

Boss: Caitlin, you've got to do this program, and it has got to be good. Our grant funding for next year depends on delivering this service, which we said we'd provide.

Caitlin: I'd need a master's degree, at least, to be able to design and teach this course. I can't do it and keep track of the after-school program, too. I have too little secretarial support and too many projects that are needing my attention right now. I'm so stressed out I don't know whether I can keep on.

Boss: I hired you to run this entire program. If you didn't think you could do it, you shouldn't have applied. Drop something less important and do this. Then I'll give you some extra time off.

Collaborative Mode

Boss: Caitlin, I really need to get this program on family communication done. Our grant funding for next year depends on delivering this service, which we said we'd provide. Could you take it on?

Caitlin: I don't see how. I have to keep track of the after-school program, and there are a lot of other things that are half-done, too. And I'm stressed out and have almost no secretarial support. Besides, I don't have the training to put this course together. I'd need a master's degree, at least.

Boss: What if I get you some staff help from social work? There's a graduate student over there who said he'd like to do an internship with us. Maybe he could do the program development with you.

Caitlin: That sounds great, but I still need some secretarial help. Could you loan my program someone from your office?

Boss: I can't do that permanently, but you can bring work over and I'll delegate it.

Caitlin: OK. I'll see what I can do. (She continues planning with the boss.)

In the example of the overworked employee, *nonspecific compensation,* a process in which one of the parties is "paid off" with some creative form of compensation, can also help break a competitive spiral and begin a collaborative set. For instance, the boss could have offered extra time off after the project was finished or offered to move up Caitlin's evaluation, which would result in the possibility of an early promotion. If two roommates are bargaining over use of a car, one may say, "OK, you can have my car, but I get to have the apartment for an all-night party after graduation." Another example is purchasing a house and discovering that the owner is more interested in moving rapidly than in getting the stated purchase price. Your cousin owns a moving company, so you arrange to have the house owner moved at no cost. Your cousin charges you less than the going rate, and you get the house for less money than was originally asked. If the deal is sealed, you have created a form of nonspecific compensation. You have found some dimension that is valued by the other and have made an offer to offset your gains in the negotiation.

Logrolling is similar to nonspecific compensation, only one offers to "trade off" issues that are the top priority for the other. The parties have to find multiple issues in the conflict (for example, time is of the essence to you, money to him). Then, you arrange agreements so that each of you gets the top priority item while giving on the lower priority item. You "roll the logs" and shuffle the issues until the top priority issues come to the top of the pile. In one organization the supervisor wanted more work from a particular employee. The employee wanted a fairer evaluation at the end of the year. With the help of an outsider, they negotiated so that (1) the evaluation process would involve discussion before memos were sent, and (2) the employee would take on some extra work. Each received acknowledgment of his main concern and gave on the item that was vitally important to the other.

Cost cutting minimizes the other's costs for going along with you. For example, you want to go skiing with your friend. She is overloaded with work, so you offer to ski only half a day and not let her incur the "cost" of missing all her work time. Alternatively, you are negotiating with your romantic partner about going on vacation. He is tied up and feels he can't take off so many days, yet you both want to vacation together. So you offer to drive your car to the resort you wish to visit, giving you the "decompression time" that you value, and he flies to join you two days later. You shorten his total vacation time yet make it possible for the two of you to vacation together at the resort you want to visit.

Bridging invents new options to meet the other side's needs. You want to rent an apartment, but it is too expensive. You discover that your landlord is concerned about the appearance of the property. So you offer her a rent somewhat below what she wants but agree to do fifteen hours of "fix-it work" each month. She receives property improvements, and you receive reduced rent.

Everyone gains!

In collaborative negotiations, parties brainstorm to invent new and creative options to meet everyone's needs. For example, Sally is negotiating with her work partner. She is frustrated about the job not being done, and Chuck is feeling that the work intrudes too much on his personal time. So, she offers to do more of the work on the spreadsheet if he will bring her coffee and sandwiches. Chuck gains more free time, Sally sees the project moving ahead, and both of them contribute to the task while maintaining their working relationship.

Bargainers who employ collaborative approaches view negotiation as complex; thus, they find creative ways to "package" agreements and invent new options (Raiffa 1982). The collaborator moves from "fighting" to "conferring" (Follett 1940), assuming that *working with* the other will bring joint benefit. Information serves as fact-finding material for the bargainers rather than as a wedge that drives between the two parties. With information, one problem solves, explores causes, and generates alternative solutions (Lewicki and Litterer 1985).

Principled Negotiation

Fisher and Ury (1981) present a practical approach to collaborative negotiation based on four principles: *people, interests, options,* and *criteria.* Fisher and Ury term this process "negotiation on merits" or "principled negotiation."

1. *People: Separate the people from the problem.* The participants should come to see themselves as working side by side on a problem, attacking the problem instead of each other. The overarching process goal is "We, working together, can solve this problem that is confronting us." It is in the self-interest of both conflict parties to preserve a workable relationship; focusing on the problem instead of the other person assists in relational maintenance. The problem is faced as one would face an enemy, working cooperatively with one's conflict partner to solve the problem. For example, a divorcing couple, rather than asking, "Why are you causing me difficulties?" might ask, "What can we, working together, create that will be in the best interests of the children?"

   In collaborative negotiations, relational preservation becomes a *superordinate goal* (Sherif and Sherif 1956). In the classic description of superordinate goals, groups of boys at camp were placed in situations that created conflicts of interest between the two groups. The researchers then introduced a common enemy, thus stimulating the two groups to work together, which reduced their intergroup hostility. For partners in interpersonal conflicts, long-term relational or content goals can become superordinate goals that reduce conflict over short-term goals, but only if partners can separate "the people" from "the problem."
2. *Interests: Focus on interests, not positions.* In the Harvard Negotiation Project, researchers found that when people stated their goals in terms of positions that had to be defended, they were less able to produce wise agreements. The more you clarify your position and defend yourself, the more committed you become to the position. Arguing over positions endangers ongoing relationships, since the conflict often becomes a contest of wills. Researchers found that "whether a negotiation concerns a contract, a family quarrel, or a peace settlement among nations, people routinely engage in positional bargaining. Each side takes a position, argues for it, and makes concessions to reach a compromise" (Fisher and Ury 1981, 3).

   Focusing on interests, not positions, was exemplified by the parties in the library earlier in this chapter. Rather than starting with "Do you want the window closed or open?" (a position), each party searched for their own underlying interest. Interests always underlie positions, and many possible positions can be derived from one's interests. But a position is a specific solution to an interest; if you start with the position, you will overlook many creative options for meeting the interests. Interests are more diffuse than positions and sometimes are difficult to identify, but they keep the process of collaboration in motion when you focus on them.

The Language of Common Interests

The following phrases are useful in the search for common interests:

What if we tried . . . ?
What will it take?
Why not?
What would be the perfect situation?
How do you like to be treated?
What problems are we trying to solve?
What is your goal?
What concerns you the most?
When are you most irritated? Most satisfied?
What do you want? What would it mean if you got it?
Would you listen to what I want? (Adapted from Yarbrough and Wilmot 1994)
What process might we use?
What are two other ways to get what you want?
Why do you feel so strongly?
Before this conflict started, what did you want?
What would help you feel better?

3. *Options: Generate a variety of possibilities before deciding what to do.* Trying to resolve a conflict in the face of an adversary narrows one's vision. Pressure reduces creative thinking at the very time when creativity is most needed. Searching for the one right solution may be futile. You can get around this problem by setting up time to focus on new solutions instead of defending your prospective goals endlessly. Goal setting continues throughout the period of active conflict management, and afterward as well. A good decision is one that springs from many options generated by concerned conflict parties.
4. *Criteria: Insist that the result be based on some objective standard.* One person's will is not enough to justify a conflict solution. Some principle of fairness or objective judgment should be used. One can develop objective criteria by using fair procedures (equalizing power in the process) and by seeking fair standards. Menzel (1991) suggests six external standards for fairness: simple success at reaching an agreement, compliance with the agreement, cost of the agreement, efficiency through which the agreement is reached, access to justice presented to disputants, and stability of the agreement over time. These standards might be important to a court, to a branch of the government such as the department of family services, to family members, or to managers overseeing an agreement in their department. Other fair standards can be based on the following:

   market value
   costs
   precedent
   what a court would decide
   scientific judgment
   moral standards
   professional standards
   equal treatment
   efficiency
   reciprocity
   (Fisher and Ury 1981, 89)

An individual may effectively use the four principles of collaboration by informally adopting and using them in one-on-one conflicts that arise. The following are some statements that you might use when you are in conflict over perceptions of incompatible goals.

Collaborative Principle	Sample Statement
People	"This is a problem you and I haven't had to face before. I'm sure we can work it out."
Interests	"What is it that you are most hoping for?" or "Let's figure out where we agree, and that will give us a base to work from."
Options	"I'd like to postpone making a decision about filing a grievance until our next meeting. Today I want to explore all the options that are available to us in addition to filing a grievance. Is that all right with you?"
Criteria	"I can't be satisfied with getting my way if you're disgruntled. Let's get an example of market value from an objective source."

From the standpoint of a competitive approach, one can be assumed to be "weak" if one "gives in" to the superior strength and force of one's opponent. Interestingly, the collaborative bargainer can be just as "tough" as the competitive bargainer. However, you get tough about *different aspects*. You remain firm about your goals but flexible regarding how to accomplish them—what Pruitt (1983a) calls *firm flexibility*. You work with the other party, but you don't capitulate; your goals are always firm in your mind, but the means you use are flexible and adapted to the other person's needs as well. As Follett (1940, 48) noted, "Mushy people are no more good at this than stubborn people."

Disadvantages

As with competitive tactics, collaborative approaches have some disadvantages. Probably the biggest overall difficulty is that they require "a high order of intelligence, keen perception and discrimination, and, more than all, a brilliant inventiveness" (Follett 1940, 45). If it hasn't been modeled in the home or on the job, collaboration may require specific training. Unless the beginning bargainer (whether an attorney, spouse, friend, or coworker) has some level of training, the usual approach is to equate "good" bargaining with competitive tactics.

Murray (1986) has provided a comprehensive list of the disadvantages of collaborative, problem-solving, integrative bargaining approaches. According to Murray, collaborative negotiation

- is strongly biased toward cooperation, creating internal pressures to compromise and accommodate that may not be in one's best interests
- avoids strategies that are confrontational because they risk impasse, which is viewed as failure
- focuses on being sensitive to other's perceived interests; increases vulnerability to deception and manipulation by a competitive opponent; and increases the possibility that the settlement may be more favorable to the other side than fairness would warrant
- increases the difficulty of establishing definite aspiration levels and bottom lines because of the reliance on qualitative (value-laden) goals

- requires substantial skill and knowledge of the process to do well
- requires strong confidence in one's own assessment powers (perception) regarding the interests/needs of the other side and the other's payoff schedule (184).

Collaborative negotiations, then, are not easily used in every conflict. They require considerable skill on the part of the negotiator, who strives to keep the negotiations from disintegrating into a win-lose approach.

Developing a Collaborative Framework

As has been true throughout this book, no specific set of techniques will assure collaboration. Collaboration is an approach, a mind-set, or even a philosophy as much as a set of techniques. If one does not believe that energetic mutual cooperation will provide better solutions than competitive techniques, all the language of collaboration that could be memorized will not ultimately produce collaboration. Sometimes, however, you may get stuck looking for the right phrase to help a negotiation move toward collaboration. If so, consider some of the phrases presented in the following box.

The Language of Collaboration

I know this is difficult, but we can work it out.

I can understand why you want to "split the difference," but let's try for some creative alternatives.

I certainly appreciate your stance. Let's also talk about what I need to be satisfied.

Your threat tells me how important this issue is to you, but it will work better with me not to threaten. Can we back this up and come at it another way?

I don't see any conflict in both of us getting more of what we want, but we have been acting as if what we each gets the other loses.

I really do want a fair and durable settlement for both of us. That requires, of course, more direct information about what we each want. Let's explore that awhile.

I will discuss with you as long as it takes to reach a settlement that will work for both of us.

Yes, I see that you think that is the best solution. Remember, however, that there are two of us here. Let's see if both of us can be satisfied with an outcome.

Most people approach negotiations from a competitive frame of mind—assuming both sides have to lose part of the pie. The competitive or collaborative approaches are more a function of the bargainers than of any other factors. In fact, you can be in a cooperative negotiation in which one person takes a cooperative and the other a competitive stance (Walker 1988). If you take a competitive approach, whether you are negotiating about how to spend the evening with a friend or how much to offer on a house, the negotiation process will probably be a competitive, win-lose experience. On the other hand, if you stick firmly to a collaborative approach, you will find creative options that someone with a competitive approach simply would not find. Creative options are often available (Fogg 1985), but unless the negotiators believe it possible and work to jointly produce those options, the negotiations will begin and end on a win-lose footing. Having had experience negotiating and serving as third-party interveners, we are always gratified by how many creative, jointly satisfying options are available and how difficult they are for the parties to initially see.

The Gender Lens

The Impact of Gender

More than fifty years of turmoil and change in gender roles have resulted in research that is often confusing and inconclusive regarding the negotiating behaviors of men and women. The actual behavior of men and women is most likely changing as rapidly as research is completed, further obscuring the description of gender differences. A number of studies report significant difference in styles, whereas others find no clear-cut differences (Papa and Natalle 1989; Fitzpatrick and Winke 1979; Berryman-Fine and Brunner 1987). Indicative of the confusing nature of the research, one study demonstrated that (1) males are more likely than females to report that they compete in conflicts; (2) females are more likely than males to report that they compromise in conflicts; and (3) regardless of gender, all subjects are more likely to report using an accommodating style if the other person is female (Berryman-Fine and Brunner 1987). The subjects in this study may be reporting on gender expectations rather than actual behavior; nevertheless, these expectations influence negotiation behavior.

Intimate communication provides a special setting for negotiation. Some studies indicate that couples' satisfaction with marriage is related to the degree of coercive versus collaborative communication between partners (Koren, Carlton, and Shaw 1980). White (1989) found that in dissatisfied marriages, men are more likely to assume a coercive position in relation to their partners, whereas women are more likely to assume a "joining with" position. It is difficult to know whether these results are based primarily on social and economic power or on other gender differences, or a combination of both. Overall, the persons who perceived themselves as having more power than their partners were more likely to use direct, coercive strategies.

Negotiation styles of managers seem less related to gender than to position in the organization (Renwick 1977). In general, both genders use a more competitive strategy at work than at home and use the accommodation style more frequently at home than at work. People who are reasonably satisfied with their long-term, intimate relationships consistently use more accommodating and collaborating strategies within those relationships than coercive or competitive strategies. It is reasonable to assume, then, that consistently choosing active, collaborating strategies of negotiation at work would improve the trust level, satisfaction, and sense of fairness among work associates. The easy way out, using power over others when one has the power, may well result in short-term gain and long-term pain.

Children show sex-linked differences early in their development. Girls are more likely than boys (ages five to seven) to use communication that diffuses or de-escalates conflict, whereas boys are more likely than girls to engage in heavy-handed conflict before trying less confrontive means of resolution (Miller, Danaher, and Forbes 1986). Boys tend to behave the same way with both boys and girls, whereas girls tend to only use heavy-handed tactics with boys. Since girls' patterns with boys resemble boys' patterns when they are interacting with boys, it may be that even though boys are centered more toward direct persuasion and girls toward harmony, a dual path, at least for girls, is learned throughout childhood (Sanders-Garrett 1993). In adolescence, however, a striking change occurs (Brown and Gilligan 1992). Girls in early adolescence become aware that they have to take their "voice," in the form of argument, confrontation, plain speaking, and spontaneous expression, out of conversation with boys in order to maintain relationships—a culturally reinforced norm. Open conflict and free speaking that were part of girls' daily lives were found, in a long-term study of girls' development, to give way to more covert ways of responding to hurt feelings or disagreements. For girls at adolescence "to say what they are feeling and thinking often means to risk, in words of many girls, losing their relationships and finding themselves powerless and all alone" (217). This cultural development confuses boys, as well, who begin to think during adolescence that they cannot understand girls because girls use a special language to say what they mean. They may begin to assume that girls are by nature more manipulative or devious. Girls, fearing that conflict will ruin relationships, learn to avoid asking directly for what they want. This learned behavior directly influences women's ability to negotiate, especially in intimate relationships. The "covering up" of direct wishes prohibits women from expressing proposals in a negotiating situation.

As noted in chapter 1, "Perspectives on Conflict," in many ongoing marriages, the woman argues whereas the man withdraws. In observed conflicts, women and men seem to behave more similarly than differently (Canary, Cupach, and Messman 1995). The real issue here isn't whether women and men behave differently, but *what behaviors are enacted by the two parties* regardless of their gender.

A Transformative Approach

Recent work by Kolb and Putnam (in press) and Putnam (1996) suggests that conflict cannot simply be broken down into competitive and collaborative approaches. They examined the deep structural assumptions of both competitive and collaborative negotiations and found some common assumptions underlying them both. They argue that neither of these two approaches allow for adequate "transformation," or reconceptualization of the conflict. For example, collaborative "negotiators are advised to build trust with their counterparts in order to facilitate settlement. Face saving of self and others are defined as impression management strategies necessary to attain instrumental goals. Concern for relationships is transformed from an expressive interest to an instrumental one" (Kolb and Putnam in press). Collaborative "moves," therefore, should not be analyzed as genuinely collaborative if the intent is still, as in a competitive system, to promote self-interest at the expense of the other. Kolb and Putnam rightly point out the difference between a relational approach used for personal gain, which is manipulative, and true collaboration. As long as predetermined goals benefiting the self are pursued, the underlying assumptions of *both* competitive and collaborative modes are

- self-interest
- competitiveness
- rationality
- an individualistic focus
- the exchange model

These underlying assumptions limit the transformative potential of negotiation. Transformation creates something new from what existed before. New ways to cooperate emerge, new feelings arise, and new solutions become possible. The transformative approach to negotiation rests on

- community concerns
- cooperativeness
- subjectivity
- intuition
- emotion (Putnam 1996)

A negotiator following such a set of assumptions would focus on relationships, using connectedness, transformation, dialogue, and storytelling (Kolb and Putnam in press). Such approaches reflect a relational unit of analysis (Wilmot 1995), which transcends the individualistic "I have to have mine," or seeing the self as separate from the other. The unit of analysis would not be the individual but rather the ongoing exchange produced from the joint actions of the participants. The Kolb and Putnam approach highlights many aspects of negotiation taken for granted even in collaborative approaches and is worthy of serious consideration, argumentation, and examination. For an extensive treatment of some common assumptions, ranging from individualistic to spiritual levels of communication, see chapter 2, "Self and Other in Relation," in Wilmot (1995).

You may be thinking, "Why negotiate from a shared perspective?" When relationships are ongoing and the current dispute is just one of a series to be solved over time, no one gains from a narrowly focused, self-interested perspective. A common phrase from the ecology movement is "we are all downstream from each other," referring to the fact that there is no safe place for toxic wastes or pollutants to be dumped—someone will be adversely affected. Many conflicts are like this: downstream of the current conflict, another will surface, and if the relationship becomes polluted, the entire future will be poisoned.

Read the "Rainbow Development Water Problem" and answer these questions:

- What different assumptions would (1) competitive, (2) collaborative, and (3) transformative approaches bring to defining this problem?
- How can the issues be addressed, relationships be preserved, and solutions be found?
- What communicative moves from each of the three groups would enhance rather than destroy the ongoing relationships?
- If you were a negotiator for one of the groups, how might you approach the problem?

The Rainbow Development Water Problem

A group of summer home owners in the high mountains of Colorado faces an ongoing problem with their water well, which keeps testing as polluted, thus making it necessary for the residents to boil or buy their water. Recently some of the elected officials of the volunteer board authorized a road to be built so heavy equipment could reach the wellhead and the well could be dug out and rebuilt. The road was built through wetlands, raising some federal legal problems, and through a pristine meadow cherished by some of the residents as a quiet, beautiful spot at the end of the property. The road goes through commonly owned property, skirting the edge of privately owned lots. Three factions have erupted, and full-scale conflict is engaged with letters, private conversations, procedural challenges, content arguments, relationship destruction, and face-saving struggles going on at a high level of intensity. Thirty-five or so families are involved. It is a long-standing group of friends and acquaintances who have considerable monetary and emotional investment in the property and dramatically different ecological, political, financial, and community values.

1. **The "water first" group:** This group consists primarily of engineers, scientists, builders, and practical people who are sick and tired of dealing with a half-solution to the water problem year after year. They want to get a new well, install purification systems if needed, and assess the membership for what is required. They rely on scientific studies of the water quality as a database. In their view, the road was simply a means to an important end. They are convinced that their mandate was clear: to provide potable water for the group. They can't understand the outrage of the other group. Many of this group have volunteered countless hours through the years for the practical maintenance of the roads, water system, fences, and governing system. This group is concerned with content goals and face-saving. They argue that the content goals are the most important and that they did what they had to do (face-saving).
2. **The "road has to go" group:** This group consists of a few older home owners and their adult children. The views of this group are that environmental concerns are primary. They will not tolerate compromise about the sensitive wetlands along the stream and feel outraged at the destruction of the most beautiful area of common property. They think the board acted without proper authorization of the membership and feel strongly that not only should the road never have been built but that it must be taken out and the area reclaimed. They prefer any solution, including boiling water for drinking, to the degradation of the environment. Many of this group will be second-generation home owners when they inherit the property from their parents. However, these group members have no vote in the association, since only property owners can vote. This group as a whole is concerned about appropriate process and have strongly held content goals.
3. **The "we simply have to live with it" group:** This group sees itself as the middle group between two extremes. Many of these people feel disappointed or angry about the gravel road and the fact that the water problem still is not solved. They want to support the elected board but don't like all the conflict and alienation in what used to be a very close and friendly group, which had potlucks, birthday celebrations, and outings together. Now that the road is in, they think it should be accepted and used to solve the water problem. This group is concerned with relationships and face-saving for the board. They keep their private opinions, whatever they might be, to themselves. They look to the future.

Phases: From Competitive to Collaborative

Negotiations are characteristically complex. Early in negotiations, it is common for the participants to begin with a fixed-sum assumption (Bazerman, Magliozzi, and Neale 1995). Bargainers can, regardless of their initial positions and approaches, move to integrative or collaborative outcomes (Tutzauer and Roloff 1988; Gulliver 1979; Lewicki and

Litterer 1985). Many negotiations travel between cooperative and competitive phases, often returning to collaborative phases when someone stresses the gains to be had by both sides (Popple 1984; Holmes 1992).

The central finding from phase research is that *successful* negotiations eventually move toward collaborative or integrative processes (Holmes 1992; Gulliver 1979). Further, collaborative and competitive processes can be seen as intertwined—as the participants utilize more competitive approaches, a natural tension builds to move toward collaboration (Putnam 1986, 1988b). Usually the bargainers begin with a competitive orientation and, through the process of bargaining, move toward a collaborative stance (Jones 1988). The bargainers can be seen as moving from *differentiation*—stressing their differences with each other, attacking each other's positions, and venting emotions—to *integration* or *collaboration*—the negotiators adopt a problem-solving orientation. These processes would look, sequentially, like this:

1. Extreme statements of positions.
2. Clash and arguments about positions.
3. De-emphasis of differences and decreased use of antagonistic tactics (Jones 1988, 472).

An almost identical set of stages has also been specified:

1. Lengthy public orations characterized by a high degree of "spirited" conflict.
2. Tactical maneuvers and arguments for and against proposals.
3. Reducing alternatives to formal agreements (Putnam and Jones 1982a).

Note that these phases have been used in negotiations that resulted in agreements. Also, they are more characteristic of explicit bargaining situations, such as negotiations, than contracts or formal mediation sessions. There simply has not been enough research on implicit, informal bargaining processes to specify the phases and stages they involve. Clearly, however, successful negotiations typically accomplish workable agreements by arriving at collaborative phases.

As noted previously, most inexperienced bargainers automatically assume a competitive stance to negotiations since they believe that "toughness" can only be achieved through competitive tactics. Since collaborative tactics generally have to be learned, people often have difficulty understanding them. Yet, for negotiations to come to fruition, collaborative tactics have to be called on, or there is a strong possibility of negotiations breaking down and the relationship between the parties being damaged. One's choice of negotiation strategies sets forces into motion that may be difficult to alter. For example, using pressure tactics increases competitiveness (Tutzauer and Roloff 1988); spirals of competitiveness tend to bring impasse (Putnam 1988b); competitive strategies lessen satisfaction with the process (Putnam and Folger 1988); and a competitive orientation coupled with time pressure secures poorer agreements (Carnevale and Lawler 1986). Basically, cooperative and competitive climates are self-reinforcing—competition encourages more competition and collaboration brings collaboration in return (Folger and Poole 1984; Carnevale and Lawler 1986; Pace 1988).

How, then, can one move toward collaboration during the negotiation process? Surely, the mental set you have about negotiations is important and determines whether you see bargaining as essentially competitive or collaborative (Gulliver 1979). On most cases it is your orientation toward negotiating rather than facts about a particular conflict that determine your style of negotiating during that conflict. Practiced collaborative negotiators are able to work with the other even when a conflict "objectively" seems to be zero-sum or win-lose.

The mental set you have toward collaboration, however, only works in a conflict situation if you can *communicate collaboratively.* Although there are limits to learning about collaboration by reading about it, some collaborative communicative moves can be learned in this manner. These specific communicative moves can lead one toward a collaborative stance in negotiations.

The following list of collaborative actions has proven useful to facilitators and conflict parties alike. These principles may be helpful in leading you toward a collaborative approach to negotiations.

1. *Join "with" the other:*
   Use "we" language.
   Seek common interests.
   Consult before acting.
   Move closer nonverbally.
2. *Control the process, not the person:*
   Use setting, timing, and other factors creatively.
   Limit or increase the number of people involved.
   Encourage the other to expound fully—listen actively even when you disagree.
3. *Use principles of productive communication:*
   Be unconditionally constructive.
   Refuse to sabotage the process.
   Separate the people from the problem.
   Persuade rather than coerce.
   Refuse to hate the other.
4. *Be firm in your goals and flexible in your means:*
   Be provisional—seek alternate means to your goals.
   Separate content and relationship issues.
   Focus on interests, not positions.
5. *Assume there is a solution:*
   Invent options for mutual gain.
   Approach issues one at a time.
   First tackle issues that you can easily agree upon.
   Refuse to be pessimistic.

These principles may be helpful in adopting a collaborative approach to negotiations, in particular, and conflict, in general. These guidelines serve as a reminder that in all conflict situations, parties using a collaborative approach *can* find solutions that will benefit both parties.

Summary

Negotiation is one mechanism for solving ongoing struggles with others. Negotiation allows us to resolve conflicts peacefully by recognizing the stake that all parties have in the successful resolution of conflict. Although most of the literature on bargaining and negotiation focuses on formal negotiations where representatives are bargaining, results of that research may be extended to everyday negotiation situations. Argumentation, in both public and private contexts, is one key still in effective negotiation. The ability to negotiate develops as one matures; young children do not typically have the maturity to take into account the other party's needs.

The two major types of negotiations are (1) *competitive* and (2) *collaborative*. There are assumptions, communication patterns, and downsides associated with each type of negotiation. Negotiations also pass between phases, often beginning with a competitive tone and concluding with a collaborative tone. Successful negotiators are eventually able to collaborate with the other party, even if the initial stance involved extreme positions, lack of concession, and hostility. In addition to the two major types of negotiation, a third perspective has recently emerged that presumes a relational orientation.

The following are specific communicative moves that induce a collaborative atmosphere: (1) join with the other; (2) control the process, not the people; (3) use productive communication; (4) be firm in your goals and flexible in your means; and (5) remain optimistic about finding solutions to your conflict.

Chapter 8

Transforming Your Conflicts: Engagement in the Midrange

A father in his early twenties was busy at the children's slide in the city park. He was keeping track of two young children plus his own two-year-old daughter. She kept heading for the ladder on the slide to go up by herself, and each time he said, "Cristy, if you don't wait for me, I'll spank you." Then, he would join her, and they would slide together. After one particular trip down the slide, she went to their small black puppy who was off to the side. When she picked him up by the neck, the father came running, spanked her four hard swats, and said in a loud voice, "Damn it, you shouldn't hurt animals smaller than you."

The father was inadvertently teaching his child to handle conflict by using force. In the half hour they were sliding, he hit the youngster on the rear end three times, each time saying something like, "Now, listen to your dad." This father clearly could profit from mastering techniques other than threat and physical force for dealing with his daughter.

What Can Be Changed?

Parties to conflicts, like the father in the previous example, have three basic options for altering the conflict:

1. *Try to change the other party*. This is a natural response, usually highly unsuccessful. Just as you choose your stance for what you believe are good reasons, the other party does the same. You will appear as unreasonable to the other as the other does to

you—and your efforts to change the other will be met with his or her efforts to change you.

2. *Try to alter the conflict conditions.* If you can increase scarce resources, alter the nature of a problematic interdependence, change perceptions of incompatible goals, or make some other alteration in the conflict elements, you will be able to change a conflict.
3. *Change your own communication and/or perceptions.* This is usually the most difficult and, paradoxically, the most successful way to alter a conflict. Changing what you do and what you think about the other will quickly and profoundly affect the conflictual elements in the relationship.

This chapter highlights the philosophy that regulation of conflict "from the inside out," through personal change, is an effective technique for productive conflicts. This kind of change is generated by the individual instead of by rules imposed by someone higher up—you can alter your own conflict behavior. Just as the Environmental Protection Agency regulates the amount of toxins in air and water, individuals may discipline themselves to monitor the intensity of conflict, use of destructive tactics, displays of unequal power, unfair goals, or demeaning and unproductive styles. *The conflict parties themselves are responsible for the direction of their relationship.* If you are in an unproductive or destructive conflict with another, you are responsible for making choices that will not feed into the destructive spiral. People create the systems of interaction that later encircle and entrap them into repetitive rounds of destructive conflict.

Change in one individual's communication or thoughts changes the entire system. Boulding (1989) calls this the *watershed principle* based on where water flows along the Continental Divide. On one side, it flows toward the Atlantic, yet just a few feet over, it flows toward the Pacific. Very small changes can produce enormous effects. Similarly, in conflict interactions, *small changes reverberate throughout the entire system* and bring results that are much larger than you would ever imagine.

Take the case of two friends who have been avoiding a budding conflict over doing the dishes. Instead of letting it build and then blasting the other, one of them decides to ask the other to lunch and discuss the conflict calmly in public. As a result, the spiral of avoidance and resentment is broken—sending their relationship to a new level of problem solving and collaboration. Or maybe you and your romantic partner find that you continually escalate and complain to your friends about each other. If you agree, instead, that during a conflict neither of you will talk to others until you have resolved it with each other, you will develop a new type of interaction and save face for both of you.

Research on teacher-student interaction graphically illustrates the watershed principle. Marginal elementary students who often did not do their work, disrupted class, acted arrogantly, and engaged in other behavior considered unacceptable by teachers were given special training to modify the behavior of the teachers who were most hostile to these students. The students were taught to verbally reinforce the teachers for any positive attention and to point out to them in socially acceptable ways which teacher behaviors were harmful and which were helpful to the students. For instance, the children were taught to say things like, "I'd appreciate it if you would warn me about talking before sending me out of the room." The results, of course, were astonishing: many of the students experienced large increases in their self-esteem and were socialized back into their classrooms, and teachers felt much more positively about the students (Gray, Graubard, and Rosenberg 1974).

Because self-change in a conflict is difficult, it usually requires prerequisites. If you are going to alter your own behavior rather than assert that your actions are "natural" or "only in response to what she did," you have to care about the relationship. If the relationship is of no consequence to you, then you feel little impetus to change. In addition, you have to be willing to accept that your own choices are influencing the conflict process—even if you cannot identify the effects. Finally, you have to be willing to give up whatever you are gaining from the conflict. Some possible "gains" in the midst of trauma are that (1) the relationship keeps going, though destructively; (2) you receive pleasure from proving to family or friends how wrong the other is (and how innocent and purely motivated you are); and (3) you are able to exert overt power. Each party to an ongoing conflict receives some gain from the conflict, even in the midst of the negative consequences.

Striving for the Midrange

It is no accident that Aristotle wrote about the "Golden Mean" and Buddha preached about the "Middle Way." In our struggles with others, moderated conflicts have the greatest potential for productive management, whereas suppressed, avoided conflict and unrestrained, runaway conflict spirals are *equally* unproductive. Figure 8.1 illustrates the potential for productive conflict depending on the degree of conflict.

Low productivity occurs when interpersonal conflicts are not identified or openly expressed to the other party. The unexpressed frustration prevents you from working through the conflict, gives you the entire burden of negative feelings, and precludes the other from joining you in creating solutions to the difficulty. You neither share the pain nor experience the productive release of pent-up feelings.

Figure 8.1 Continuum of conflict intensity

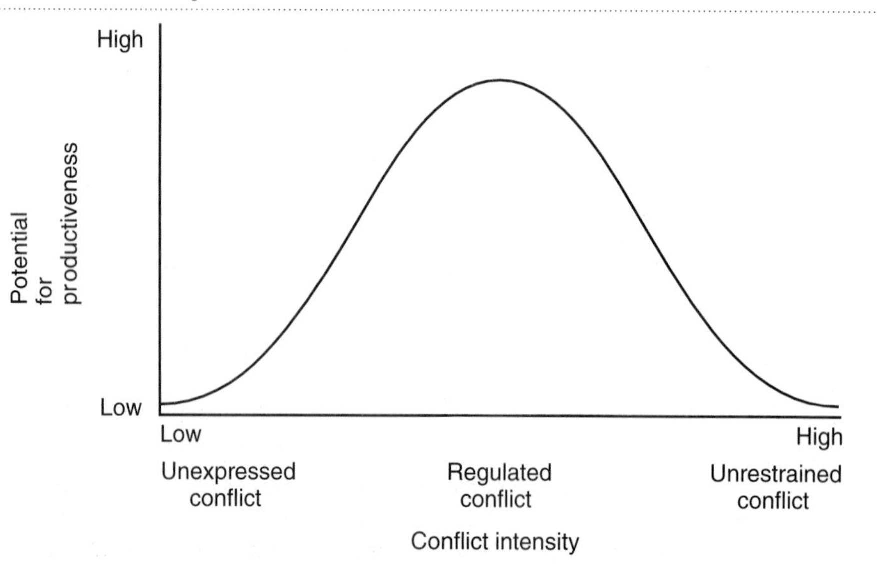

At the other extreme, with few restraints on conflict expression, a runaway destructive conflict spiral damages all. Two businessmen who have no restraints on their competition would logically end the conflict by burning down each other's businesses! Similarly, the lack of regulation in personal relationships is damaging. For instance, a divorcing couple attempting to share the custody of their two children were close to agreement when the ex-wife exploded in the mediation session, saying, "He's selfish! He always was and he always will be!" Her unregulated outburst ruined the chance for collaboration on their problem. Regardless of the specific conflict, after an episode has passed, the other person will recall what you did during the conflict. This, in turn, sets the stage for the next enactment of conflict in your relationship. People have long memories for poor treatment. Keeping a conflict in the midrange through self-regulation will mitigate these negative long-term effects.

If people are successful at keeping their conflicts in the midrange or bringing them into midrange from avoidance, they can expect some distinct advantages. Conflict regulation

1. alters the escalatory conflict spiral and halts destructive behavior
2. allows for self-discovery; when you use restraint, you have the time to explore sources of power you can use and to consider your own needs and goals for this particular conflict
3. allows for more creative conflict management options than either party could generate singly; each individual is induced into innovation
4. prevents you from taking actions that you will later regret or have to justify
5. makes productive use of energy that was previously being diverted into frustration

Overcoming Avoidance

People choose avoidance for a lot of reasons. Patterns of avoidance (summarized in chapter 5) range from denial to shifting the topic to making irrelevant remarks. You do almost anything to keep from engaging the other in dispute. It is difficult to alter avoidance because (1) we are supported by others for not engaging (e.g., "I wouldn't tell him either, he is such a jerk"); and (2) it is self-reinforcing—avoidance begets more avoidance. In destructive conflict, avoidance basically comes in two forms:

- Avoidance that leads to a downward spiral of avoidance
- Avoidance that leads to escalation, then more avoidance, then more escalation, and so on

In either form, avoidance sets the stage for unproductive conflict. Failure to take action keeps you stuck. Regardless of which form of avoidance you use, you refrain from engaging the other conflict party because

- you feel that the other "wouldn't like it" or is so fragile he or she would fall apart if you brought up the issue
- you feel that you don't have the "right" to bring up the issue or engage the other
- you feel that you lack the skills to deal with the conflict

A vice president and program director illustrated the first reason for avoidance. The vice president said to a third-party mediator, "I can't tell her that she is boring me to death. When she begins talking it goes on for an hour. But it would destroy her if I told her that."

Meanwhile, the program director said, "I can't tell the vice president what I want—she is going through a divorce and is too fragile right now." When the two of them were convened by the mediator, they very cautiously began to tell each other their concerns. When the vice president told the program director that "I need you to not take so much of my time—when we begin talking I feel like it will never end," the program director said, "Yeah, I kind of knew that; I hear that all the time. How about if we make an agenda for our meetings?" Then it was her turn. When she said, "I can't talk to you about the finances for my unit because I feel like you are too fragile, going through a divorce and all," the vice president gave a hearty laugh and said, "Well, gal, given what I've been going through personally, this sure isn't going to push me over the edge. What kind of financial support does your unit need?" They were both amazed that they had imagined totally different responses from each other.

Feelings of "They couldn't take it" or "It will blow things sky high" are almost always inaccurate. Actually, avoidance allows one to protect one's own identity without being corrected by the other. When you engage the other in productive conversation you will find that (1) your behavior is being misinterpreted by the other and (2) your preception of the other is skewed. These misperceptions cannot be corrected if you continue to practice avoidance.

The second major reason for avoidance is that people feel they don't have the "right" to engage the other. This hesitation often comes from low power in an organization or family rules that prohibit straight talk about difficulties. As a result, people try not to feel and think as they do, but due to avoidance, they never receive correction from the other party. Students often think, "Professor X wouldn't have time for me" and convince themselves they are not important enough to have some of his or her time. Yet, if the issue is important, it will usually jump out at some inopportune time. If you have a relationship with someone, you have a right (perhaps even an obligation) to initiate dialogue to clear up misperceptions.

The third reason for avoidance is that you may feel you don't have the skills to engage the conflict. Consultants, mediators, and therapists often "coach" others on what to say. Conflict parties may know that they want to engage but not know how to start. Take the case of Tara, a hard-driving director of an innovative program. She has two separate offices in different cities but is usually at the home office. She is an attorney by training and can fight on paper with the best of them. Yet when an employee needs correction, Tara can't figure out what to say. A new employee in the home office, Merrie, began parking in Tara's parking space. Rather than taking her aside and saying, "Merrie, I'm sorry, but the reserved parking space is for my use only. I come and go so much that I can't spend time finding parking spaces," Tara just steamed. She called her other office and ranted and raved for two days about how Merrie "is trying to get the upper hand" in the office. After she got some coaching on how to engage the issue yet still be supportive so Merrie could save face, Tara easily handled the situation.

When you move out of avoidance you

1. assert yourself as a legitimate party
2. verbalize the content issues of which the other may be unaware
3. recognize the mutual dependence and importance of the relationship
4. allow solutions to emerge from both parties

What can you do to break the spiral of avoidance? To assert yourself as a legitimate party, you can (1) remind yourself that the other needs your help in order to correct whatever misperceptions have formed and (2) recognize that not sharing important information does no good for either you or the other. If you find yourself criticizing someone when he or she is not there, *recognize it as indirect anger and a clue that you need to engage that person.* When you begin to criticize, stop and ask yourself, "What is it that I need to tell him or her?"

The avoid/criticize pattern can keep one from ever engaging at all. Some people perfect the art of criticizing others, but never to their face. As the other does things to displease you, you talk to all your friends and family members but *never to the other party.* As a result, no corrective action takes place. You stay mad, the other doesn't get a direct request for change, and things stay stuck. The following skill-building technique, "Moving from Complaints to Requests," can be very helpful in breaking this logjam.

Moving from Complaints to Requests

One effective management technique to help us break free from avoidance is to write down our complaints, *transpose* them into requests, and voice the requests to the other person. The object is to clarify for both you and the other what you need from the other, rather than staying stuck in the complaint cycle. Here are some examples:

Complaint	*Request*
You are too cold.	I need more warmth. I need you to look at me when you talk. I would like it if you would answer my questions.
You are unprofessional.	I want you to answer all my E-mail messages. It would work best for me if you would keep your appointments. When you don't give me information I request, I can't do my job well.

List your complaints	*Transpose them into requests*
______________________	______________________
______________________	______________________
______________________	______________________
______________________	______________________
______________________	______________________
______________________	______________________

This technique works well for work relationships as well as for personal relationships. The person who has been avoiding bringing up an issue is able to lay it on the table *in a form the other party can hear.* If you say, "You are manipulative," chances are the other person will not respond positively. On the other hand, if you say, "I need you to discuss important items with me before you go public with them," the other will hear the request. The request format also helps the avoider clarify what he or she wants rather than globally blasting the other person. Thinking through specific requests keeps you responsible and increases the chances that the other will be responsive.

When you are altering avoidance spirals, it is helpful to *practice on small conflicts* before taking on big ones. Start small and gradually build up the confidence to talk to your boss, parent, teacher, overseer, or employee. Obtaining assertiveness training can be quite helpful—you gain a sense that you have the right to speak assertively, and you learn some specific phrases to use.

Reframing can also be used to deal with avoidance. In reframing, you alter the way you think and speak. You change the categories you use for the other person, yourself, or the conflict issues that are keeping you stuck in avoidance. Here are some examples of reframing, based on the three main reasons people use avoidance.*

Original Thought	Reframed Thought
He is fragile.	He will be more fragile if friends don't help him. He has made it this far without falling apart.
It isn't my place to tell him.	If his best friends don't let him know when he blows it, who will? It is probably better if an employee who shows concern for him fills him in. This relationship is important to him, right? Wouldn't he want to know I am unhappy?
I don't know how to tell him.	Wouldn't it be better to make an honest, less-than-perfect attempt than to wait until I have it perfectly analyzed? He will probably appreciate my attempt anyway. He will be appreciative of my effort, knowing how hard it is for me to speak up.

A final note about avoidance: Even though the negative impacts of engaging in a conflict are almost always overestimated by parties, sometimes your only choice really is to avoid. If you are totally under the control of someone else, you may have to avoid or else pay serious consequences. People living in occupied countries, abused spouses, and others in dangerous circumstances usually find that avoidance is their only option. The rest of us, however, usually continue avoidance because we convince ourselves that we have no power and that engaging the other "won't do any good anyway."

Ending Escalation

Destructive conflict, as you know by now, has two faces—avoidance and escalation. When we think of destructive conflict, we almost all think of unending escalation, downward spirals, and negative behaviors breeding negative behaviors. As discussed in chapter 2, "The Nature of Conflict," this pattern describes a *destructive conflict spiral.*

* For specific treatment of different types of reframing used in mediation settings, see Yarbrough and Wilmot (1995, 135–139).

Recall that destructive spirals are when the thoughts and actions of parties degenerate into worse and more damaging forms of communication. The interactions and perceptions feed one another and cycle out of control. It happens at work, in families of origin, and in friendships and romantic relationships. Beck (1988) aptly characterizes this process in the case of romantic couples:

> When a relationship goes downhill, the partners begin to see each other through a negative frame . . . ("He's mean and manipulative"; "She's irresponsible") that each attributes to the other. . . . Even positive acts may be given a negative coloring. . . . When you and your spouse clash, the less desirable aspects of your personality become accentuated, leading to a vicious cycle in which hitherto pleasing qualities come to be seen as unpleasant. (207–209)

A brief excursion into a philosophy of nonviolence will set the stage for techniques used to end the naturally entrapping effects of escalation.

Nonviolent Philosophy in Interpersonal Conflict

Principles of nonviolence in relationships lay the groundwork for the kind of constructive, collaborative conflict interaction taught in this book. Many people who do not come from a historic peace church or a particular religious background that espouses nonviolence nevertheless do attempt to ground their interactions in principles of mutual empowerment and restraint from coercion. Some of the principles of nonviolence, with introductory material on its recent history as a way of thinking, will be applied to interpersonal conflict in this section. Think about principles that guide your behavior. Self-regulation requires one to have a set of values and principles that guide actions. You may want to write down or discuss your guiding principles and determine which ones you find most difficult to uphold.

Nonviolent principles warn against the buildup of arms in the service of peace. The Romans are well known for the credo *Si vis pacem, para bellum,* "If you want peace, prepare for war." Because of the precarious nature of threats, the difficulty of balancing power when harm is suspected, and the anxiety that accompanies another's higher power, deterrence does not work well to reduce conflict. In interpersonal relationships, the equivalent of an arms buildup might be such things as fostering private coalitions, keeping secrets to use against an opponent if needed, keeping a "paper trail" of warnings and complaints, telling only part of the truth in the hopes of not having to play all your cards, using the threat of blackmail, such as "If you don't make a C average or better, you can pay your own way to school next year," gathering harmful gossip and spreading it against people who irritate you, and writing unsigned letters that disclose devastating information about someone you are in conflict with. Too many people focus on developing "first-strike capability" even in close relationships. Energy and personal resources are used up in the stockpiling of personal power rather than in the building of new problem-solving strategies.

Nonviolent confrontation is not a move toward compromise. It is a respectfully stubborn insistence that principles of right and fairness cannot be compromised, along with the insistence that former enemies or potential opponents working together can produce a better solution than presently exists through coercion. Gandhi's satyagraha movement in India resulted in the freeing of millions of Indians from British control without resorting to violence. Gandhi's approach and principles are not as well-known as they were in the 1960s when Martin Luther King used many of the same principles in the civil rights movement in the United States. Gandhian principles were based on strong leadership and a continuous application of the brakes of nonviolence (Wehr 1979, 5). In interpersonal conflict situations, the same principles apply. They depend on a firmly grounded refusal to violate the boundaries of someone else and a belief that, working together, people can find an ethically just solution to even the most difficult conflict. Some of Gandhi's principles are summarized in the following box.

Gandhian Nonviolent Responses to Destructive Conflict

Destructive conflict forces	Gandhi's strategy
1. Movement from specific to more general issues and from original to new issues	Tie each campaign to a single issue in a sharply limited arena.
2. Movement from disagreement to antagonism as the conflict develops	Reduce threat by stressing the maintenance of good personal relations with opponents while pressing the issue, simultaneously providing for confrontation and maximizing the potential for conciliation.
3. Distortion of information	Openly discuss tactics; eliminate secrecy and misinformation to reduce the perceived threat to opponents.
4. Mutual reinforcement of response (escalatory spiral)	Use positive reciprocal causation; nonviolent action promotes a nonhostile response.

(Adapted from Wehr 1979, 60–62)

Nonviolent, noncoercive conflict management can be as effective as power-over approaches. Research on interpersonal negotiation demonstrates that collaborative, integrative solutions come from "vigorous discussions or mild arguments" (Pruitt 1981, 192) rather than from competitive tactics. Of course, when no restraints, inner or outer, exist on the other party, mutual power approaches may fail. When the power balance is seriously disparate, the low-power person may not be able to bring about change through traditional nonviolent techniques. However, as discussed in chapter 4, "Power," people usually have more potential sources of power than they recognize. Often the leap into violence is made in ignorance of nonviolent possibilities. No list of techniques can substitute for the development of your own philosophy of personal action to guide your conflict interactions. As you think through your own values and approaches to conflict, consider adding some of the following self-regulation techniques to your repertoire.

Self-Regulation Techniques

In this section, you are asked to take responsibility for internal change as part of your mastery of interpersonal conflict techniques. Self-awareness provides a base for choosing flexible, effective techniques. One of the primary goals in constructive conflict interaction is to analyze and act instead of to react without thinking. The more you understand about anger, other feelings associated with low power, dialogue possibilities, the effectiveness of restraint, and the skill of fractionation, the more confident you will feel in the middle of explosive, threatening conflicts. You will also feel more confident in conflicts characterized by avoidance spirals. You can teach yourself to act thoughtfully instead of acting out of fear or anger.

Dynamics of Anger

Angry emotion threatens most people; few healthy people enjoy feeling angry or having others direct anger at them. Anger differs from aggression in that aggression is an attack, whereas "anger is the feeling connected to a perceived unfairness or injustice" (Young-Eisendrath 1993). Anger is also the emotion connected to *fear.* Consider the following diagram of the dynamics of anger:

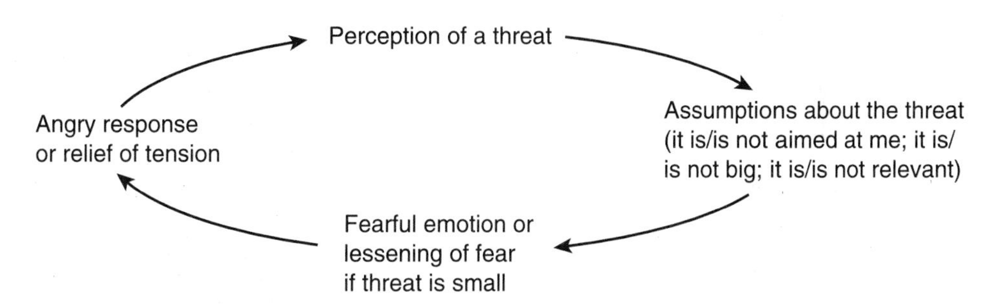

Even though anger, when felt in the body, seems instinctive and unavoidable, it is actually a *secondary emotion* rather than a primary emotion. Anger has no direct bodily expression, only indirect avenues for expression such as heightened blood pressure, flushed face, sweating, muscle tightness, fast breathing, and a loud or high voice tone. Underneath every angry emotion, outburst, or withdrawal, one can find a fearful emotion. Fear makes human beings experience vulnerability that we transform into anger, which is more socially acceptable, especially for adults, than fear. Anger is also based on *frustration of unmet needs* or *thwarted desires.* In the definition of conflict offered earlier, the opposition is seen as *interfering with desired goals.* If another way to achieve the desired goal cannot be easily found, anger may well be the final result. Again, anger is the secondary emotion to frustration, which is a form of fear that one's needs will not be met. Anger is our response to a situation in which our sense of security is threatened, our self-esteem damaged, and our feelings hurt. In such a situation, the last thing we really want is to get into a fight. Our real need is to be understood, loved, and supported. As someone once said of teenagers, the time they need love most is the time they seem most unlovable (Mace 1987, 96–97).

Anger was termed "the moral emotion" by the ancients because it is based on a reflective judgment that we or our values have been wronged, threatened, or treated unjustly. Anger "is rooted in reason; it is equally of the heart and the head" (Young-Eisendrath 1993, 154). Tavris's exhaustive reviews (1982, 1989) of research on anger concluded that expressing anger in an unrestrained way simply makes people angrier and does not discharge the emotion in a way that helps reduce the feeling. In conflict situations, if one acts directly on the anger, feeling justified and self-righteous, the more primary issues will likely not be discussed. List some of your angry moments and see if you can "back up" through the anger/fear cycle to assess the threat. Once you have identified the underlying threat, clarify the original communication. The following are examples of fear, threats to self-esteem or well-being, or unjust treatment that might lead to feelings of anger:

1. A woman is angry at her friend for calling her a name in public. (She is fearful of not being accepted by others.)
2. A newly promoted employee is angry because his secretary didn't get the final report to him on time. (He is afraid that his own supervisor will think he is not working hard enough, and he really needs this job.)
3. A husband is furious that his wife has disclosed their private life to others in a hurtful way. (He is frightened that their bond is no longer strong and that their relationship is ending.)
4. A single parent overreacts to a child misbehaving at a family reunion by raising his voice and ordering the child into a time-out. (He is afraid that other family members will criticize his parenting.)
5. An intimate partner casually indicates that she might change her plans and not visit when she had planned. Her partner says, "Well, if you have better things to do than honor your commitments, go ahead." (He has asked an old friend to visit to meet his significant other and fears looking foolish after speaking in glowing terms about the wonderful woman he wants his friend to meet. He is afraid he is unimportant to her.)

Anger Regulation and Expression

A Poison Tree*

I was angry with my friend;
I told my wrath, my wrath did end.
I was angry with my foe;
I told it not, my wrath did grow.

William Blake

Anger is of paramount importance in conflict situations. How we deal with both our own and other's anger often determines whether a conflict is productive or destructive. Therefore, specific suggestions for the productive use of anger will now be outlined.

Anger is a healthy emotion. It arises across cultures and in both personal and public relationships. It is basic to the human experience. Anger informs us about the importance of an issue. When one gets angry at a roommate or work associate, the emotion provides

* From *Poetry and Prose of William Blake* edited by Geoffrey Keynes (1967, 76).

information that someone has interfered with one's preferences and goals. As such, it crops up in all types of relationships. *Anger can be expressed in healthy ways.* However, most people view anger from one of two perspectives:

1. At one extreme is the "never let it out" school that believes in *suppressing* rather than *expressing* anger. Someone with this viewpoint might use the following phrases:
   It isn't nice to get angry.
   If you can't say something nice, don't say anything at all.
   Chill out.
   It's no big deal.
   Don't make a mountain out of a molehill.
   It'll all blow over.
   Don't sweat the small stuff.
2. At the other extreme is the *ventilation* or *catharsis* view suggesting one should release anger by venting or expressing it fully. This viewpoint is reflected in the following phrases:
   Hot tempers run in my family.
   It's good to let off steam.
   The pressure will build until you explode.
   Let them have it.
   Go ahead, get it out of your system.

Each of these polar positions on anger presents some difficulties. The problem with suppressing anger and never expressing it is that such bottling up leads to resentment and physical ailments because the conflict "simmers" and cannot be engaged or resolved (Tavris 1989; Rubin 1980).

One can learn to *responsibly* express anger in a way that does not hurt the relationship. Responsible anger expression, a specific form of regulated conflict, bridges the two non-productive poles—unrestrained anger and unexpressed anger. Responsible expression allows one the "expression" supported by the catharsis school while maintaining the respect and responsibility supported by the suppression view of anger. On both the international and interpersonal levels, limited and regulated expressions will keep large-scale, uncontrollable explosions from occurring (Levy and Morgan 1984).

Mace (1987) suggests the following guidelines for responsible expression of anger:

1. *Verbally state the anger.* Just as one says, "I am hungry," say, "I am angry."
2. *Distinguish between venting and acknowledging anger.*
3. Agree that you will *never attack each other* in a state of anger.
4. Work to *find the stimulus for the anger.* It won't go away just by expressing it.

Mace summarizes his approach (for use with intimate partners) as follows: "I find myself getting angry with you. But you know I am pledged not to attack you, which would only make you angry, too, and alienate us. What I need is your help to get behind my anger to what is really causing it, so that we can do something about it together." The response to this is: "I don't like you being angry with me, but I don't blame you for it. And since I know you won't attack me, I needn't put up my defenses and get angry with you in turn. I appreciate your invitation to help you get through to the underlying cause of your anger, because I care about our relationship, and it should help both of us to find out what is really happening to us." (97)

Often, finding the right words to communicate anger is difficult. The *X-Y-Z formula* will help one express anger (Gottman et al. 1976). Using the X-Y-Z formula to responsibly express anger can have profound impact on relationships. Here are its components:

- When you do X
- In situation Y
- I feel Z

A secretary might say, "When you interrupt me (X) when I am on the phone (Y), I feel hassled and belittled (Z)." Her response, taking responsibility for feeling angry yet giving the other person the information to know what produced the anger, is more likely to result in a constructive solution than if she had said, "I don't get any respect around here!" The X-Y-Z skill has the advantage of clarifying the issue of concern for the recipient of the anger and urging the sender to take responsibility for his or her emotional reaction. While X-Y-Z does not prescribe the desired change, the complaint is lodged in a specific, descriptive form so that the recipient might reduce defensiveness and respond appropriately.

Reception of Anger

As a recipient of anger, the natural tendency is to experience your own fear and respond defensively, such as, "I only interrupt you when it is important to me—get off my case." Remember, however, that when someone is angry at you, he or she needs to responsibly express that anger or the anger will build. You can't "argue" or "reason" someone out of his or her anger. When you say, "You shouldn't be angry," this injunction doesn't reduce the anger but adds frustration because you are devaluing the other's experience. Put another way, *feelings are facts.* When people feel intensely, their emotion provides important information about the conflict. The following are some useful steps to take when someone is angry with you:

1. Acknowledge the person's feelings.
2. Clarify the specific behaviors involved.
3. Gauge the intensity and importance of the issue.
4. Invite the other to join you in working toward solutions.
5. Make an optimistic relational statement.

The following dialogue illustrates both (1) responsible expression and (2) helpful reception of anger.

Roommate to Roommate

Angry person: When you leave your clothes on the floor (X) and I have people in after my night class (Y), I feel disgusted (Z).

Recipient: So my clothes on the floor really get you mad? (#1). Does it make you mad at the time or just if people are coming over? (#2). Is this a big deal that bothers you a lot, or is it a minor irritation, or somewhere in between? (#3). Let's both come up with some ideas. I bet we'll figure something out (#4). It's important to me that we give and take because I like having you as a roommate (#5).

When another's expression of anger is out of control, *you have a responsibility to protect yourself from verbal abuse.* Listening to belittling, hostile blame, ridicule, demeaning, untrue accusations, sarcastic name-calling, or actual physical threats is not good conflict management. The other person should be told, firmly and consistently, "I won't listen to this kind of talk. I can't hear anything important you're trying to say when you're this out of control." Then you can leave or hang up the phone, giving the other person a chance to cool off. You can say, "Wait!" or "Stop!" in a firm voice. Never try to argue with a person who is engaged in verbal abuse (it's like arguing with an alcoholic—nothing healing can happen until the person is not drinking). But just as you would move to stop the abuse of a child, you have the responsibility to stop verbal abuse in a conflict. It leads to escalation or withdrawal, hinders conflict resolution, and lowers the dignity and self-esteem of all parties. Productive reception of someone's anger may not be possible until boundaries are reset and conversation takes a more constructive tone. Conflict is not always polite, but constructive conflict is never abusive or violent.

One other helpful approach to managing our conflicts is, first and foremost, to *reduce fear*. As noted earlier, threat and counterthreat lead to damaged relationships. Similarly, ignoring the fear behind others' anger only intensifies their anger. They want to be heard, just as we do when we are angry. If you can reduce another's fear, that person can more successfully collaborate with you to work through the difficulties that naturally arise in all important relationships. When both parties can move past either suppressing or venting anger, they can *process anger* and utilize it for a more viable relationship, whether it be a marriage, work association, roommate situation, or any other type of relationship. Mace (1982) capsulizes the need for *both* parties in a marriage to learn to deal with anger productively:

> In observing marriages over the years, I have been interested in recognizing various combination of types: venters married to venters are inveterate fighters; venters married to suppressors end up with a tyrant-slave relationship; suppressors married to suppressors achieve a peace-at-any-price relationship, which is drearily respectable but without warmth and tenderness. Processors, unfortunately, must exist in pairs, because this is an approach to anger that has to be cooperative. So a processor, unless married to another processor, must convert a venting or suppressing partner to become a processor too! (98–99)

If you want to, then, you can manage and control anger. The following box presents a list of techniques that have been useful for many people in managing anger and that are worth your perusal and discussion. Read the list one strategy at a time, reflect on how you might use the strategy, and give one or more strategies a try.

Strategies for Managing and Transforming Anger

1. Reason with yourself
2. Stop hostile thoughts, feelings, and urges
3. Distract yourself
4. Meditate
5. Avoid overstimulation
6. Assert yourself
7. Care for a pet
8. Listen
9. Practice trusting others
10. Take on community service
11. Increase your empathy
12. Be tolerant
13. Forgive
14. Have a confidant
15. Laugh at yourself
16. Become more spiritual or religious
17. Pretend today is your last
18. Do what comes unnaturally to you—talk to conflict partners, move toward them
19. Ask for third-party help—mediate the dispute
20. Focus on your fear, not your anger

(The first seventeen come from *Anger Kills* by Williams and Williams, 1994)

The View from the Downside

Other emotions in addition to anger characterize the conflict cycle. Almost no one experiences exhilaration or creative energy surges when stuck in a low-power situation over time. People who are in positions of low power, such as entry-level workers in corporations, practical nurses in hospitals, children in abusive or neglectful families, night shift workers, medical and psychological interns, and support staff in organizations find themselves spending time and energy "psyching out" the people with the power. This safety skill requires vigilance and often creates anxiety and a lack of spontaneity. Remember how you felt when you were visiting someone else's family or in a new job, sports team, or living group. You undoubtedly watched and listened to others more closely than usual. Now imagine having that degree of watchfulness virtually all the time. When the low-power person realizes that his or her needs will not be met regardless of their reasonableness, frustration, irritation, or anger are initially felt and expressed. If nothing changes, a depressing numbness takes over. When people feel helpless to change their situation, they slowly give up, withdraw, and "numb out." This state may not lead to actual clinical depression, but people begin performing at a lowered capacity, expecting little and feeling alienated, sad, or cynical. If attempts to gain support from peers or to leave the situation do not work, the person may settle into resentment and repression. Resentment is unexpressed anger that has nowhere to go. Repression means the low-power person tries to block out the depressing situation by focusing on upcoming vacations, break times, or social activities. With constructive conflict skills people in low-power situations might be able to employ constructive confrontation to break the downside cycle. The following box portrays what one woman experienced when she was stuck "on the downside."

> **"The Number Six Man"**
>
> Shannon was a forty-year-old woman who had worked for years in a manufacturing plant, operating heavy machinery and working in an almost all male environment. When a job opened up on the night shift at a larger manufacturing plant, she applied and was given a job operating a huge log splitter, a mechanical and technical operation that involved lifting. It also required coordinating timing with a work crew of five others and taking direction from a foreman. Shannon was "number six man" on the crew. Since the pay and benefits were so good, she wanted to make this job work because she was recently divorced and was supporting two children at home. Problems began almost immediately. When Shannon asked the foreman and the first and second men on the crew to tell her how she was doing, they made jokes, changed the subject, or taunted her with statements like "if you can't stand the heat go back to your own kitchen." Quickly, Shannon experienced frustration and anger and the growing realization that she was not going to receive cooperation from the crew. She talked with the few women on other shifts, who suggested she go to the foreman privately. She asked the foreman for a transfer, but no positions were open, and things became worse when the crew learned she had gone to the foreman. Her attempts to tease back, stay silent, or not show her feelings did not work. Finally, she left the job with physical disabilities exacerbated by stress and filed a lawsuit.

What could Shannon have done? Since none of her original attempts were helpful, she would have needed to continue up the hierarchy until she found help—in the human resources department, for example, which monitors sexual harassment. But Shannon did not know this and saw no choice but to resign. She was depressed, ill, physically injured, and deeply discouraged. Now the conflict remains stalemated until the trial.

Not all cases are so bleak. Remember, however, when you begin to feel cynical, depressed, numb, resentful, or that you need to hide your feelings, you will need to invoke low-power strategies reviewed in chapter 4, "Power," to break the cycle.

The Dialogue Process

One's communication both indicates and creates the level of conflict intensity (Waln 1981). Dialogue differs from usual conversation because although you may dislike what the other person advocates, you still listen and work to value the person. Although "you can't value all human behavior positively, . . . you can value each human positively" (Stewart 1978). Dialogue is possible only between two persons or two groups whose power relationship is more or less in balance (Tournier 1978). One constructively confronts the other so that "the answer to a conflict emerges 'between' the conflicting parties" (Arnett 1980a, 113). In this dialogic view of conflict, neither party alone possesses truth; truth emerges during the struggle with each other (Buber 1972; Stewart 1978). As you can well imagine, dialogue is not easy. As Keller says, "The true test of dialogue is in conflict, not in casual conversation" (Arnett 1980a, 124). Engaging in dialogue requires an "immense toughness of self," demanding that we confirm the opposing party while in conflict (Brown and Keller 1973). Engaging a person in dialogue is an act of commitment to the relationship and to one's own principles at the same time. If a person can find the courage to meet aggression with calm friendliness, this may have a powerful inhibiting effect (Frank 1978). Dialogue leads to collaboration.

One of the ways dialogue differs from normal conversation is that in dialogue, both people speak and listen to help each other clarify what is being said. One actively asks questions and probes what the other means to say, not for purposes of refutation but to help even an opposing viewpoint become crystallized and understood. This radical, active listening requires belief in the transformative power of hearing and being heard. Quality dialogue is slow, careful, full of feeling, respectful, and attentive. One "moves toward bad news" so that an opposing opinion can be fully heard. This movement toward an apparently opposing viewpoint must be learned; few develop this approach to others without a deep sense of the importance of each human being and a belief in collaboratively searching for new solutions that honor each person.

In summary, the following steps can lead highly interdependent parties such as close friends, work partners, couples, or family members toward conversational dialogue to deepen the level of collaboration:

1. *Explore different assumptions.* Listen with respect, without attacking the other's point of view.
2. *Develop an objective view and description of the conflict, as if you were outside the conflict.* Practice describing your opponent/partner's position.
3. *Give up persuasion in favor of exploration of different perspectives.* Treat each person as intelligent and worthy of attention.
4. *Look critically at all sides to the controversy.* All sides have strengths and weaknesses that can add to the analysis (adapted from Freeman, Littlejohn, and Pearce 1992).
5. *Express hope, belief in the good will of the other person, and your intention to work out your differences.*

Self-Restraint

Another principle of nonviolence is that of self-control, or maintaining belief in an internal locus of control (Elliott 1980). Since "conflict resolution is largely the discovery of a means to break into escalatory reciprocal causation and reverse its direction" (Wehr 1979, 63), self-restraint and self-control do create change in the conflict system. Proponents of nonviolence maintain that one always has a choice about how to respond to provocation. Even if the choice (at an extreme) is to submit with grace to coercion and to feel pity for the person perpetrating the violence, a choice remains. One may experience a flash of anger but choose to take actions that reflect a different feeling. For instance, parents are often furious with their children. They report to counselors that they have fantasies about hurting their children, abandoning them, or wishing them dead. Yet most parents are able to restrain their occasional outbursts of destructive feeling. They exercise self-control in the interest of the larger, loving relationship. *We do not have to act the way we feel.*

Restraint includes the difficult task of holding back one's desire to act on vengeful feelings. Revenge is the attempt to inflict harm in return for harm and leads to an escalatory spiral. Revenge is considered for many reasons. One seeking revenge may wish to deter future unfair treatment, may have an exaggerated view of the other's power to harm, may long to revenge an injustice, or may have become locked into a spiral of feuding and vengeance in which the original conflict has been overshadowed by the vengeful acts (Kim and Smith 1993).

In classroom discussions in which students were asked to disclose an outrageous act they contemplated but did not perform, the most common reasons for restraint were the following:

- Fear of reprisal
- Wanting to save face and not look foolish
- Believing that what goes around comes around
- Moral principles
- Fear of loss
- Fear of breaking the law
- Regaining common sense after a cooling-off period
- Choosing to write out anger instead (some mailed these letters, some did not)
- Believing that getting even never solves anything
- Not wanting to act the same way as the other ("sink to his/her level")

Even people who have not studied philosophies of nonviolence commonly realize that better ways have to exist. By itself, self-restraint doesn't solve the problem, but it doesn't exacerbate the problem either.

Fractionation

The basic conflict reduction tactic known as *fractionating* was an idea developed by Follett (1940) and later called "fractionation" by Fisher (1971). They suggest that conflict can be reduced by focusing attention on the *sizing* of disputes. Conflicts can be broken down from one big mass to several smaller, more manageable conflicts. Fractionating conflict does not make it disappear, of course; it simply makes the components of large conflicts more approachable by parties who are trying to manage their disputes. Conflicts "do not have objective edges established by external events" (158). Rather, conflicts are like a seamless web, with indistinguishable beginnings and endings. Choices are almost always available as to how to size, and therefore manage, conflicts.

A group of ten townspeople recently met at the instigation of one of the members to determine what should be done about the deteriorating quality of the town's air. Due to the poor quality of the air, residents suffered from respiratory problems, allergies, and asthma attacks, and several people had recently been hospitalized. In the group's opinion, the major culprit was the town's large paper mill, which had, they suspected, been violating air quality standards. One way to size the conflict would be to mount an all-out attack to try to close down the plant. One step down from that mode of attack would be to conceptualize the conflict as being between the citizens of the town and the management of the company. Defining the parties in this way suggests certain negotiation devices that might be used to resolve the conflict. An even smaller sizing might be to conceptualize the conflict as being between some concerned citizens and the county commissioners who enforced the air quality standards. If the conflict were conceptualized in this way, yet another plan of management would be appropriate. The smallest sizing of the conflict would be one between the committee of ten and the engineers who monitor the air quality machinery at the plant. The group succeeded in reducing the conflict by defining the conflict carefully, assessing their resources, talking to the "other side," and carefully planning an incremental campaign to get more citizens involved in the issue. By fractionating the conflict for purposes of analysis, they were later able to successfully manage the conflict. After all, closing the plant would have had negative consequences for the town, too.

Fractionation not only involves defining conflict parties but also involves making small conflicts out of larger ones. This simple idea is one of the most useful conflict management tactics. Almost all conflicts can be made smaller without trivializing or devaluing them. In a student-teacher conflict, for instance, the students might come into the classroom one day and ask for the abolition of all the grading in the course. The teacher could escalate the issue by becoming defensive or polarize the issue by resorting to rules or external authority. But the issue could be reduced in size if the teacher asked the students what they most objected to in the tests and then talked with the students about those features. By looking for subissues in the "Let's not have tests" statement, the teacher might find that the tests are misscheduled, unexpected, unclear, or too long. Then the parties could handle these small issues instead of expending their relational power over an issue that is too extreme and that probably cannot be resolved satisfactorily.

Some phrases that aid in the process of fractionation follow:

What part of that problem is most important to your group right now?

Who are the people most immediately involved?

Whom could we go talk to about this? (This approach personalizes instead of stereotypes the other side.)

Maybe we'll have to resort to that, but let's see what we might try first. (This statement acknowledges the possibility of escalation but expresses a preference for sizing the conflict.)

I want to hear more about your objections. Please tell me what is not working for you. (This statement joins with the other party, inviting dialogue rather than setting up a competitive stance.)

You probably know I cannot accept what you are saying. That approach would violate what I hold most dear. I want to know what makes that decision your first choice. Then I can work with you to meet both our needs. (This statement reiterates that certain principles cannot be breached but that you are continuing the dialogue.)

Choosing a Format for Interaction

Personal intervention in one's own conflicts involves self-regulation and the wisdom to be able to *choose a format* for conversation during conflict. Often, the security of a structure helps people move through stages of conflict, strong feelings, and seemingly impossible impasses. In the next chapter, forms of facilitated intervention will be presented. The rest of this chapter will present sample formats you might find useful when you, yourself, are part of the conflict. They can be adapted to meet your needs. Many come from couple and family interaction, since these long-term relationships make such intense focus on process worthwhile. Structured but informal formats also make sense in organizations. Too often organizations use the formal staff meeting or business meeting, in which reports are given, votes are taken, and announcements are made, but the constructive flow of conflicting opinions is not allowed. Then the conflict goes underground, only to surface in an inconvenient place. One of the reasons businesses use consultants to help resolve disputes is because consultants have the outside legitimacy to help the organization structure conversations. As a member of an organization, you can suggest that some form of the following structures be adapted to your organization's needs. Often, leadership can be shared, with one person taking charge of the content discussion and another facilitating the process. Creative use of conversations can help organizations as well as families and couples deal with their own conflicts earlier in the process, ideally in the preventive phase. You can make a positive contribution to conflict management by thinking about what format would help everyone be heard and further problem solving.

Conflict Containment Model

Stuart's (1980) model provides an overall outline for conflict containment based on his work with married couples. He notes that issue expansion (Raush et al. 1974) and personal attacks accompany destructive conflicts, thus his model offers guidelines for containing and regulating the exchange. Stuart's model involves three primary foci:

1. *Emphasizing a present orientation.* The focus is on the present, not the past. Rather than searching for the roots of conflict in the past, participants should search for solutions in the present. *Why* questions are replaced by *how* questions.
2. *Adopting a "conciliatory set."* This requires (1) labeling the behavior of the other in the most positive light and (2) planning moves to "resolve the issue equitably" rather than by winning. For instance, Margaret arrives home for dinner an hour late. Burt decides that she has no regard for his feelings, so he gets mad and labels her "selfish." He could have labeled Margaret's behavior differently, such as, "She has trouble managing time," or "She gets really involved in her work." Either of these attributions would have allowed him to respond differently to the trigger event (292–293). Labeling one person as the villain merely sets off counterattacks.
3. *Seeking solutions in small steps.* Address issues one at a time and sequentially. Sometimes writing is helpful in slowing the process down. One complaint is dealt with at a time, and each person takes a turn.

These basic techniques are adapted to the various stages of conflict outlined in the following box.

Stuart's Conflict Containment Stages

1. *Trigger stage* (you first recognize the conflict, often with an emotional reaction). Pause before responding and use that time to ask yourself these questions:
   a. Exactly what is the issue?
   b. Exactly what would satisfy me?
   c. Is the goal important?
   d. Have I tried to get what I want through problem solving?
   e. How much conflict am I willing to risk to get what I want?
2. *Reflex stage* (you respond to the other, often with the expression of anger). You can put your threatening messages into focus by asking yourself these four questions;
   a. Have I qualified my statement by accepting my anger?
   b. Have I expressed respect for the other person while communicating my displeasure with his or her actions?
   c. Have I made a threat that is modest and therefore credible?
   d. Have I asked for a specific and reasonable change?
3. *Reflex fatigue stage* (the reaction from having expressed one's anger). A useful two-step approach can move the interaction from conflict to problem solving:
   a. Express recognition of the other's anger.
   b. Refocus it by asking what he or she would like to do in the future.
4. *Commitment stage* (you and the other maneuver for relationship gain in the form of more power in future exchanges. You both harden into positions temporarily.) You can assist the other by announcing your intentions before the fact, such as, "I am going to tell you how frustrating this has been for me so that you can understand my position." If you are the recipient, listening quietly and respecting the other's anger as legitimate will assist in its reduction.
5. *Reconsolidation stage* (you engage the problem mode). You can learn to signal the other when you are ready to problem solve, such as, "OK, I'm ready to begin working on how to stop this from happening again." People develop private signals that indicate their readiness to communicate, such as, "Let's work on it."
6. *Reapproachment stage* (you summarize what you have learned, acknowledge the lesson, and make agreements to change). Obviously, without this "learning" stage, the conflict will be left to simmer and erupt again. You need to take action to demonstrate to the other your willingness to alter elements of the conflict.

(From Stuart, *Helping Couples Change,* 1980, 295–300)

These stages may be useful to you in several ways. Use them as a guide to help understand conflicts or to pinpoint the stage at which a conflict gets bogged down. Observers can help with Stuart's three recommended approaches (emphasizing the present, adopting a conciliatory set, and seeking solutions in small steps). Application of these three approaches, as well as others made throughout the book, will help parties move quickly through the stages of conflict containment. Finally, one person can employ self-limitation with an eye toward productive conflict even if the other person does not. The following box presents an example of such a situation.

Brenda and Gerry

(The following is a shortened version of a conflict in which Brenda tries to self-limit and Gerry does not.)

Gerry: You never have understood how important my work is to me. Now you're trying to get me to stop working on my computer program for the new game. Somebody has to take work seriously.

Conciliatory Set

Brenda: I want to work this out. It's not working for me to constantly ask for more time from you and for you to feel guilty and lock yourself in your study.

Gerry: You didn't want me to go into programming from the beginning.

Present Set

Brenda: I don't want to change your profession at all. I want more time from you this year—I don't want to wait until vacation to spend time alone with you.

Gerry: I guess I should quit doing creative work and just punch the old time clock. Would that make you happy?

Small Steps Conciliatory Set

Brenda: No, it wouldn't. I can't be happy if you're doing something you hate. We ought to be able to work out time together and some time for your new game. I miss you.

Gerry: What is it you want so badly to do?

Small Steps

Brenda: I want to spend good time with you. We can work out how and what together.

Family Meetings

"Family meetings" can be used by families, work groups, roommates, or any intact system that is small enough for all the parties to convene. The meeting can be facilitated at first by a third party as an external check on the process as it unfolds; groups can also conduct such meetings without third-party assistance. The purpose of the meeting is to increase the number of positive behaviors and break out of dead-end destructive spirals through the use of (1) gripe time, (2) agenda building, and (3) problem solving (Gottman et al. 1976).

The family meeting outlined above is useful for making specific plans for change, especially if the family or group has tried to change before but has failed because the members tried to "have a better attitude" or "show more love" or other kinds of nonspecific change attempts. Some feel the format of the negotiation meeting is too rigid, that it does not allow for expression of feeling. Yet for the group that needs help in learning that they can indeed change and that small steps need to be taken, the method works very well. This step-by-step procedure can be used with small children, who can follow pictured symbols on a chart to help them keep up with the steps. Some families use the meeting on a weekly basis, thus assuring that problems do not build up over a long period of time. Care needs to be taken to help more reticent members participate and to encourage more assertive members to take their turn fairly.

The Family Meeting

Stage	Your Job
Gripe time	**1.** State clearly the gripes you have about your spouse, parent, or child. **2.** Follow the rules for constructive leveling. **3.** Listen and accept others' gripes as legitimate feelings. **4.** Work to understand gripes by summarizing and paraphrasing them. **5.** Help to turn "negative nebulous" (fuzzy and nonspecific) gripes into specific negative gripes.
Agenda building	Decide on one or, at most, two gripes you feel are the most important to work on in the problem-solving stage. Other members do the same. Reach consensus about which gripes to solve.
Problem solving	**1.** Together with spouse or family member, turn the specific negative gripes (chosen during agenda building) into suggestions for increasing the frequency of a positive behavior that will answer the gripe. **2.** Form a contract in which you agree to increase a positive behavior. Determine the reward you will get for increasing your behaviors.

In one family meeting, Mom stated a negative nebulous gripe to son Dan, a fourteen-year-old boy, by saying, "I wish you would show respect to your father and me." The family agreed to work on this gripe, which was in Dan's interest to negotiate, since he had just been grounded by Mom for "not showing respect." The younger siblings were helpful in specifying exactly when Dan and Mom got into a negative spiral over respect. All made suggestions for how Mom and Dan could change their behavior. Not surprisingly, Dad and the younger brother and sisters had suggestions that involved them, too. They were able to agree on several suggestions made by the family, on a form like the one shown in the following box.

Negotiation Agreement

Dan	Mom
1. I will call home if I'm going to be more than thirty minutes late.	**1.** I will call around to see if our curfew is similar to that of Dan's friends.
2. I will tell Mom and Dad where I am going.	**2.** Dan may go see friends in the neighborhood before dinner without telling us where he is.
3. I will not use sarcasm when I'm asked about my plans.	**3.** I will ask Dan privately what his plans are instead of in front of his friends.

The reward I will receive for this behavior at the end of a week is ______________ (Dan)

____ (Mom)

Signed ______________________ Date ______________________

Note that the agreements negotiated are *noncontingent,* that Dan and Mom do not wait to see whether the other will comply before they are obligated to follow their part of the agreement. Noncontingent contracts work well if there is a basic level of trust; if the group or family is seriously distrustful, a contingent agreement may have to be negotiated at first. When a negotiated agreement is contingent, it is usually a quid pro quo (Lederer and Jackson 1968). *Quid pro quo* means "getting something for something." Each party offers to alter some behavior if the other will also. For example, if two roommates are continually arguing over their apartment chores and each is angry at the other for "not doing her share," they can negotiate on a contingent basis. Susan might say, "OK, if you will take out the garbage during the week, I'll shovel the snow off the walk." This principle could be extended into other areas as well, with each person specifying what she will do in exchange for the other's efforts. The key to a successful quid pro quo is treating each other as equals in order to consummate the trade. Regardless of the specific agreements, if both parties are full participants, the agreement will be of like value to both of them.

Practical Crisis Management

In a family (and other groups as well) the participants will often find themselves continually in crises, with tempers flaring and negative communicative behaviors rebounding with increased frequency. Gottman et al. (1976) suggests that in such a crisis, you should

1. *Stop action.* Halt the destructive exchanges.
2. *Be active.* Take action toward some solution. Imperfect solutions are better than none.
3. *Be agreeable.* Even if you fee hurt and wronged, both of you have to be agreeable to some solutions to reach accommodation.

In addition, the following seven suggestions can be used to tip the balance of interaction in a positive direction. Usually, these are utilized after conflict participants are out of crisis.

1. *Set up ground rules.* For example, agree on "no more behavior X" (screaming, stomping out of the room, etc.).
2. *Define structure.* "Set rules for behaviors and interaction both inside and outside of the home" (129). Avoid actions that typically produce high conflict.
3. *Engage in shaping.* Once you and the other begin to act more positively, give concrete praise, rewards, and attention to each other.
4. *Stop acting out.* As Gottman et al. say, "No acting out, just talking out" (10). Acting out is any desperate behavior—threatening to run away or leave, threatening to kill oneself or harm others, and so forth.
5. *Use ABCD analysis.* Describe the conflict process in sequence, making suggestions for change, as follows:
    Antecedents: What led up to the crisis? What were the precipitating events?
    Behaviors: How did each person act in response to the crisis?
    Consequences: What were the consequences of these behaviors?
    Do differently: What can be done differently now?
6. *Negotiate a temporary agreement.* After the problematic behaviors are identified, specify the changes each person can make. List these in a written contract.

The analysis, recording, and alteration of specific behaviors on the part of the participants leads to more productive patterns of communicating. Parents, especially, can teach these self-limiting steps to themselves and to their children.

A Postscript on Further Education

The techniques in the preceding section are oriented toward individual use in conflicts, although many require some level of cooperation from conflict partners. Further education about effective communication can allow for lifelong training in effective conflict management. Destructive conflict sometimes results from ignorance or lack of practice in growth-producing communication. When we know only destructive tactics, those are the tactics we use. If you are interested in further study in conflict management techniques specifically adapted for individuals, families, and groups, many such opportunities exist. Human relations and management workshops and short courses are offered around the country every month.

If certain kinds of conflict continually create tension and result in destructive outcomes in your life, you might want to seek further training in conflict skills, such as taking college-level courses in communication. Many people who initially felt that their only option was to continue a destructive pattern have transformed their conflicts. Productive conflict management requires examining your choices and determining what alterations will bring better results for both you and the other party.

Summary

It is advisable to keep conflict in the middle range between avoidance and escalation. You can overcome avoidance by transforming complaints to requests. You can stop escalation by following nonviolent principles of conflict and techniques of self-regulation. Anger is a secondary emotion, and one effective technique for managing anger is the XYZ format, which helps one responsibly engage an issue. Dialogue with the other can also be used to lessen escalation. Furthermore, one can fractionate—"downsize" a conflict. You can be an intervention agent in conflicts within your own family or organization by suggesting structured formats for conflict conversation. Three helpful approaches are Stuart's containment model, family meetings, and practical crisis management.

Chapter 9

Third-Party Intervention

Conflicts often exceed the abilities of the involved parties to constructively deal with them. Attempts at negotiation and self-regulation are not sufficient—the conflict continues and the participants stay stuck, angry, or withdrawn and engage in destructive tactics. At such times, third parties can help. One or more of the parties asks for help, turning to a pastor, friend, parent, coworker, unit manager, personnel officer, outside arbitrator, or mediator or to the courts. Third parties serve crucial roles by guiding the conflict participants to agreement on issues and, if possible, transforming ongoing relationships so the parties can continue to function effectively. Third-party intervention is appropriate in situations such as these:

- A woman is getting ready to file for divorce but doesn't want it to be as destructive as other divorces she has seen, so she asks her sister for a recommendation for a mediator.
- Two ranchers dispute constantly about their property line; their bitterness affects the entire community.
- An employee is injured on the job and goes to a hearing to argue for benefits.
- A customer tries to return a defective product, but the retailer refuses to accept it.
- A labor union and the management call off contract talks because negotiations are stalled.

- Only one worker, a relative of the supervisor, gets a raise. The rest of the employees decide to protest the action by calling in someone from personnel to mediate.

Parties in all the preceding incidents can benefit from the services of a third party. You may become involved in conflict intervention by (1) serving as a third party yourself; (2) assisting your work associates, family members, or friends to find qualified third parties; or (3) asking for third-party assistance for your own conflicts. Third-party intervention into ongoing disputes is part of many professional jobs, such as dormitory head resident, counselor, social worker, juvenile and adult probation officer, teacher, mediator, minister, and hearings officer or judge. A head resident, for example, may intervene when two roommates are unplugging each other's alarm clocks, hiding stereos, and refusing to take phone messages for each other.

Many conflicts require the use of a competent third party who does not have a vested interest in a specific outcome. Intervention, whether informal or formal, occurs more than most of us realize. Aunt Sarah talks to John to keep him from escalating a dispute over the repair of his car. A teacher talks to two grade-schoolers to keep them from fighting on the playground. A mutual friend asks the executive director and program director to sit down and work through the concerns each has about the other. A pastor counsels a husband and wife at the same time, trying to work through their issues about spending money. Third-party intervention is so common that the real question is not whether people will be involved in others' conflicts, but *what form the intervention will take* and *how competent the third party will be.* As you shall see, there are particular skill sets that are important to employ when intervening in others' disputes.

Whether formal or informal, *the goal of all intervention is to assist in a transformation of the conflict elements.* The transformation may take many forms. It may

- change the expression of conflict
- alter the degree of interdependence between the parties
- change their perceptions or their goals so they are not seen as incompatible
- modify the actual or perceived scarcity of resources
- adjust the actual or perceived interference by the opposing parties

After third-party intervention, coworkers may be able to speak to the boss directly instead of forming coalitions, and the boss may agree to give negative feedback in person instead of in writing. Parents may agree to help their eighteen-year-old daughter go to college in a different state, or a conflict over scarce parking space may be redefined so that coworkers can talk about their relational conflicts instead of the content conflict. A judgment may be rendered that alters a company's hiring practices. Competent intervention *transforms the conflict* so that issues can be put to rest and people can move on.

The Intervention Continuum

Intervention modes differ according to the *degree to which conflict parties determine the final outcome.* In some forms of third-party intervention, the intervener serves as a facilitator to parties who make their own decisions, whereas other forms impose a resolution to the conflict upon the parties (see the following).

Degree to which the conflicting parties determine the solutions to their conflicts		*Representative modes of intervention*
	High ↑	• Facilitation • Mediation • Counseling and therapy • Organizational development • Conciliation • Quasi-judicial bodies • Informal tribunals • Arbitration of all types
	Low ↓	• Criminal and civil justice system

In many interventions, combinations of these approaches are used. For instance, some forms of conciliation use both mediation and arbitration, usually decided by the third party who is assisting the parties in reaching agreement (Buzzard and Eck 1982). Similarly, contracts between labor and management often specify a sequence of steps such as (1) negotiation, (2) mediation, and, if necessary, (3) arbitration. Divorce mediators often specify that if the mediation breaks down on a specific issue, that particular issue is taken to an arbitrator, then the parties return to mediation to finish their work (Coogler 1978; Moore 1986).

When an Outsider Decides

Adjudication

Adjudication is a process in which parties go before a judge or jury. Adjudication assumes that parties are unable to solve their own conflicts, and a decision must be imported from outside. It is similar to arbitration in that a third party decides, but adjudication can be put into motion without mutual consent. In adjudication, you can sue the other party, forcing a decision whether the other wants to participate or not. Additionally, the officials of the criminal justice system can initiate charges, for instance in cases of bodily assault, robbery, and related offenses. Adjudication further assumes that the full exposition of each side to a conflict will allow a judge or jury to make a just decision. Figure 9.1 illustrates the *communication structure* that is common to both adjudication and arbitration.

As figure 9.1 illustrates, once a suit or petition has been filed with the court (or filed for arbitration), lawyers or other advocates negotiate with each other, often instructing the litigants to not talk to each other. In this structure, it is easy for the litigants (the conflict parties) to set into motion a struggle that the lawyers act out. The original conflict metamorphoses into a conflict between the two lawyers (Irving and Bohm 1978). The prime players become the attorneys, who negotiate with each other, trying to estimate what the judge (or jury) will do with the case. Each lawyer's estimate of the judge's, jury's or arbitrator's probable response becomes the basis of his or her negotiation strategy. The lawyers then try to persuade each other about their views.

Court processes are fairly well-known. One party files charges, suit, or a petition in court and the other must appear to respond to the charges. Between the time of the filing and the court date, the lawyers usually negotiate with each other regarding the case. For example, a landlord charges a tenant with violation of a lease agreement because the tenant signed a one-year lease and moved after four months. The landlord files suit to recover

Figure 9.1 Lines of communication with professional advocates. (Solid lines indicate heavy communication; broken lines signify that the judge or jury is used as a reference point for the attorneys, often without direct communication; absence of lines signifies no direct communication.)

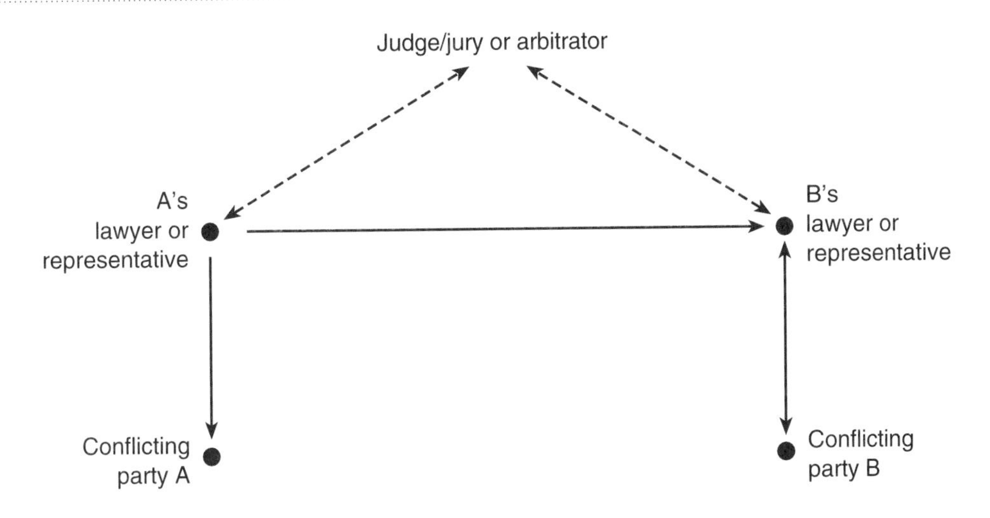

the rent for the eight months the renter was not living there. The two lawyers typically begin negotiations, calling and writing back and forth. If they are not able to reach settlement, the case goes to court; a judge or jury, after hearing testimony and evidence from both sides, may decide that the tenant must pay the eight months' rent, plus attorney fees. If no appeal is filed, the resolution process will end with the enforcement of the action.

Litigating a dispute is both an alternative to negotiating and at the same time a way to force negotiation. Since most lawsuits settle before trial, it is useful to view litigation not only as a way to "go to court" but also as a highly structured negotiation game, a "refined and constrained version of competitive bargaining" (Goodpaster 1992, 221). Filing a lawsuit forces a nonresponding party to attend to the complaint—avoidance is not possible once a suit is filed. The law enables lawyers to translate the dispute into a form that can be adjudicated. Many parties negotiate a settlement because of high costs, time delays, and practical advice from their attorneys. Because of the form of litigation, these negotiations will be competitive in nature (Goodpaster 1992, 234).

Adjudication as a form of conflict management has a number of positive features. "Equal protection of the law" allows everyone access to a resolution process and does not require the agreement of the other party. As such, adjudication serves as a power-balancing mechanism. For example, individuals can sue large corporations. And in the case of abused or neglected children, a state agency can bring the parents before a court to determine their suitability for continued parenting. The children's representative acts as their agent. As Wehr (1979) notes, "Asymmetrical conflict is best resolved through intervention that empowers the weaker party" (37).

A second positive feature of adjudication is that it provides rules for fairness, such as the admission of evidence. In some interpersonal conflicts, one party monopolizes the process, with few restraints. Process restraints are, however, built into the legal system. Each party has equal right to speak. The process rules allow both parties to fully explicate their positions.

Third, the use of professionals to speak for the conflict parties is an advantage for parties who need assistance in preparation or presentation of their case. The trained legal expert can develop the best case for the client, ensure fair procedures, and set forth the case with vigor.

Finally, adjudication serves as a backup for other conflict management procedures. When arbitration, mediation, conciliation, and negotiation fail to produce agreement, the disputants can go to court. The appeal process allows people to present their case in a higher court if they dislike an earlier judgment. The moral as well as physical power present in our judicial and criminal justice system provides a last-resort option when necessary.

However, the judicial system also has some limitations in dealing with conflict. First, it has been overutilized and, as a consequence, is overburdened and misused. Former Chief Justice Warren Burger, referring to the legal profession, said, "The obligation of our profession is to serve as healers of human conflicts" (Ray 1982), but "suing has become an American parlor game" (Marks 1981). As a result, there is an "unprecedented demand upon the judicial system, leading to considerable frustration and delay. . . ." (Sander 1977, 2).

Guarantees of speedy justice are difficult to receive; delays of as much as two years between filing and first court appearances are common. As Judge Evans of the Court of Civil Appeals says, "There are certain elements . . . that are inappropriate. They are not efficient, they are not effective" (Ray 1982, 52). Because the judicial system has been used and talked about so much, many individuals automatically think of it as the way to "get even" for some wrong. They often do not realize they have chosen a mode of conflict resolution until "they find themselves caught up in it with apparently no way out" (Coogler 1978, 6). One legal scholar concludes, "It seems clear that it is simply too cumbersome and expensive for most (minor) disputes" (Sander 1977, 24). A continuing round of court battles in order to "win" can deplete almost anyone's finances.

A second disadvantage of using the legal system for conflict resolution is that conflict parties no longer make their own decisions. For example, in a dispute involving a community (such as an environmental issue), "Litigation takes the decision out of the hands of the communities who must live with its consequences" (Wehr 1979, 123). Similarly, if two people are involved in a protracted domestic dispute such as a contested divorce, the parties stop dealing directly with each other and the attorneys take over the negotiation process.

Sometimes the conflict parties, after seeing the communication structure inherent in adjudication, decide to go a different route. For example, Sharon and her ex-husband, Ted, had been divorced for three years and were having difficulties agreeing on child visitation arrangements. They lived in different towns, and each had consulted an attorney about visitation options. One day in April, Sharon flew to Ted's city and called him, only to discover that his attorney had told him, "Don't talk to her, and hold out for all you can get." Sharon told Ted that she had received the same advice from her attorney. They realized that if they both followed their lawyers' advice, they would be in for a protracted court battle. The two of them wisely decided to empower themselves. They met the next day and worked out an agreement—though the process was difficult for them. They were the original parties to the dispute and are the ones who have to live with the long-term results of a decision. Therefore, turning over the decision to their representatives did not seem desirable.

A final disadvantage of adjudication is that the adversarial system operates on a win-lose set of conflict assumptions that encourages escalation tactics (Menkel-Meadow 1986; Hartje 1984). Often the lawyer is seen as each client's only champion in a hostile world. This belief promotes escalation when, in fact, it might not be necessary. In order to file an action, one has to blow up the magnitude of the conflict to a "You owe us" or "We'll get you" frame of mind; one tries to win at the other's expense. Filing an action is a signal of serious conflict, but unfortunately, filing sets an escalatory process in motion. Because attorneys are charged with solely representing the interests of their client, "The client's interest is always perceived as being in opposition to the interests of the other party. The lawyer cannot and does not regard the parties as having a common problem which he or she will help resolve" (Coogler 1978, 7). The gathering of evidence for one side of the conflict disregards the relational and face-saving interests of both parties. Parties cooperate in following procedure, but this level of commonality does not open up many potentially creative outcomes. The escalatory, win-lose atmosphere is often difficult to disengage from once it has been set into motion. Suits and countersuits reflect continual escalation, with each "loser" trying again on some other basis until resources or options are exhausted.

Arbitration

In arbitration, as in adjudication, a third party is empowered to decide the outcome of a conflict. Parties who cannot resolve their conflict unassisted mutually empower an arbitrator to solve their conflict, are ordered to do so by a judge or manager, or are compelled by contract to seek arbitration.

The arbitration process varies according to the type of dispute and the needs of the parties. For example, a grievance procedure initiated by a worker who feels unfairly treated may be long and require numerous others to testify. Contract disputes are a common form of "rights" arbitration; many managers and line workers routinely sign contracts with a clause calling for arbitration in the case of disagreement. For instance, if you buy a car, have to make numerous repairs, and cannot get compensation from the dealer, you can ask for arbitration. The arbitrator listens to both sides of the dispute, questions you and the car dealer (or your representatives), and renders a judgment. When the parties contractually agree to arbitration, the arbitrated judgment is enforceable in court. This process is called *binding arbitration;* the judgment is final. Voluntary or *nonbinding arbitration* is sometimes used when the parties will not agree to binding arbitration. It allows for further arbitration or the initiation of a court case if parties do not accept the judgment.

Arbitration has some distinct features that make it useful as a form of third-party intervention. First, unlike adjudication, both parties enter into arbitration voluntarily. Neither party can force the other into the process, and as a result, neither party will feel coerced into a settlement situation. Second, it keeps one party from using passive aggressive or impasse tactics on the other—sooner or later the issue will be resolved (Coogler 1978). Third, in many cases the arbitrator has special training in the content area of the dispute, such as in contract arbitration. When the arbitrator has special expertise in the content of the arbitration, he or she can often offer creative solutions. Fourth, arbitration is readily available for use in situations in which the participants experience a communication breakdown and are no longer able to solve their own problems (McGillicuddy, Welton, and Pruitt 1987). Finally, arbitration is a process that can be used for a wide variety of content areas, ranging from contract disputes, medical malpractice, or landlord-tenant conflicts to domestic relations (Alper and Nichols 1981; Tyler 1987; Keltner 1994).

Arbitration does have some limitations. First, it tends to resolve conflicts solely on a content basis. Arbitration typically does not address the relational or face-saving aspects of the dispute, which is unfortunate in that if parties can reach some accord in their relationship, the content issues can often be worked out. Second, arbitration reinforces the assumption that the parties cannot learn to manage their own difficulties—that only a third party can find a solution. Third, arbitration reinforces escalation as a legitimate tactic because intransigence will automatically bring the help of an outsider. Despite these disadvantages, arbitration is still a widely used alternative in conflict management because it places boundaries on parties' choices, thus binding them procedurally to seek resolution. The prerequisite that parties agree to arbitrate (either contractually before the dispute begins or voluntarily once they are in conflict) enhances the chances for productive conflict management.

Forms of ADR

When most people think of third parties, they automatically focus on legal and quasi-legal remedies like adjudication and arbitration. The newspapers are full of stories about lawsuits, where one party seeks redress from the other—whether over some defective product that caused difficulties, libelous speech, or contract violation. So, when someone feels aggrieved or damaged by someone, they shout, "I'm going to sue him."

In the past few years, in response to the overuse of the courts, the ADR (Alternative Dispute Resolution) movement has made considerable headway. ADR procedures are *alternatives to litigation* where a third party *other than a judge or jury* is asked to help resolve a dispute. Given the breadth of the procedures, it might be better if "ADR" stood for "Appropriate Dispute Resolution." The term lumps together very different processes—arbitration and mediation. When someone says "use ADR" they may be calling for arbitration, which follows the structure outlined in figure 9.1, or mediation, which is an entirely different process. "ADR," then, is sometimes not the best term to use because, conceptually, it may refer to very different dispute resolution structures. In this chapter, the more precise terms "arbitration" and "mediation" are used rather than "ADR."

Mediation: The Parties Decide

> The mediator has no power to render a decision or impose a solution. Instead, the mediator helps the parties themselves to work out their differences and to construct a mutually acceptable solution.
>
> —Gray, *Collaborating: Finding Common Ground for Multiparty Problems*

Mediation is a vastly different process from adjudication and arbitration.* In mediation, rather than having an "authority" decide the issues, mediators help the parties negotiate so they can reach agreement. Mediation is the "art of changing people's positions with the explicit aim of acceptance of a package put together by both sides, with the mediator as

* For an excellent, in-depth treatment of both arbitration and mediation and the essential differences between the two, see Keltner (1994).

Figure 9.2 Mediation (the solid lines indicate flow of communication)

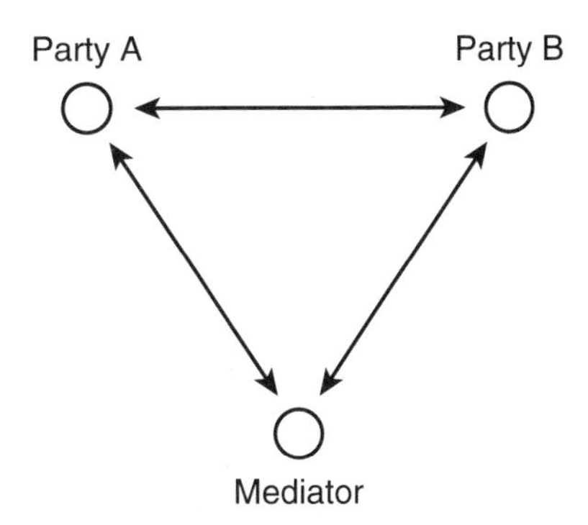

listener, the suggestor, the formulator of final agreement to which both sides have contributed" (Alper and Nichols 1981, 31). As Keltner (1983) says, "Your job is to *facilitate* the parties to the dispute to reach an agreement *themselves"* (2). As shown in figure 9.2, the structure of communication differs profoundly between the mediation model and the adjudication/arbitration model. Note that the mediator is there to facilitate communication between the parties. The mediator is the convener, the facilitator, but *not* the one who makes the decision. The communication in the initial stages might consist of the parties talking mostly to the mediator, but as mediation progresses, the parties talk more and more to each other with the mediator guiding the process. The mediator is there to *control the process*—not letting the participants interrupt, call names, or engage in other destructive moves. But, the mediator *does not control the outcome*—the solutions to the dispute come from the parties themselves. Sometimes mediators engage in "shuttle diplomacy," in which they keep the parties separate and bring messages back and forth. Separation of the parties is common in intense disputes such as war, court-ordered divorce mediation, or other situations in which the parties are unable to be in the same room with each other. However, the bulk of mediation is performed with the parties in the same room, with the mediator controlling the communication process for their mutual benefit.

The process of mediation *assumes that conflict is inevitable and resolvable.* It further assumes that a conflicted relationship has enough common interest to bring about an agreement and that the parties are ultimately responsible for settling their own conflict. It assumes that agreements between parties will be more responsive to their needs than a settlement imposed by a third party (Moore 1996).

Mediation brings three distinct advantages to the management of conflict. First, because it relies on the parties' active negotiation and involvement, it promotes a mutual stake in the resolution; solutions derived through the process are more likely to be carried out by the parties. The agreement is theirs, not imposed, and as a result there is no "loser" who feels compelled to strike back. The parties created the conflict, and they work for its management. Their active involvement is a source of mutual empowerment; they take ownership of the conflict and, with the mediator's assistance, impose some limits on the process. Mediation recognizes that the parties "have had some sort of prior relationship that will continue long after the dispute has been resolved" (Alper and Nichols 1981, 13).

Second, since mediated agreements represent the work of all concerned, the solutions are more likely to be integrative and creative. Rather than choosing between two interlocked, nonnegotiable positions, new solutions can be generated (Pruitt 1981). As Fisher and Ury (1981) suggest, behind each specific position are more general issues. A mediated agreement can focus on interests rather than on particular positions. Often, someone who is holding out for a monetary reward is more satisfied with an apology than with a sum of money!

Third, mediation is usually cheaper than *either* adjudication or arbitration. For instance, in one study of 449 cases, mediation settled 78 percent of them with an average cost of $2,750 compared to $11,800 for arbitration (Brett, Barsness, and Goldberg 1996).

Limitations to the use of mediation as a settlement option do exist. First, not all conflict parties will agree to work through their conflict with the "enemy." They may either not want to talk openly about their difficulties with the other or not want to be in the presence of the other person. Many conflicts escalate to the point where conjoint constructive work is not possible. The conflict may be so protracted and the trust level so low that the only solution is a win-lose structure in which an outside party decides. In addition, if someone thinks he or she can win by going to court, that person is less likely to want mediation. For example, in one study of couples who either did or did not choose mediation during their divorce, the man's perceived chances of winning in the adversarial system affected his willingness to try mediation (Pearson, Thonnes, and Vanderkooi 1982). Furthermore, attorneys who do not favor mediation will not refer clients to mediation. Older attorneys who have not been exposed to nonadversarial methods of conflict resolution are less likely to refer clients to mediation.

A second limitation of mediation is that it may not be appropriate for certain types of relationships. Mediation involves considerable commitment to work on the conflict. However, many parties are not prepared to reinvest in a relationship that has been problematic for them; they would rather try other routes to settlement or just continue the conflict. For example, Kressel et al. (1980) discovered that enmeshed couples were so intertwined in their dynamics that mediation was not successful for them. Similarly, couples with weak relationship bonds were not good candidates for mediation. Both too much involvement and too little involvement with the other work against mediation.

A final limitation of mediation is that for some disputes, involvement in mediation is not worth the effort. Many small disputes may be more efficiently handled by third-party adjudication than by the disputants trying to work with each other. The conflict may not be serious enough to warrant "working through" by the conflict parties.

Mediation Settings

Mediation may be applied to a wide variety of settings and disputes. It has been used successfully in such diverse arenas as

- home disputes
    - separation and divorce
    - estate distribution after a death
    - parental conflicts

  - parent-child concerns
  - disputes between romantic partners who are splitting up
  - grandparental visitation of children
  - financial concerns
- business disputes
  - partnership concerns
  - contract disagreements
  - management team disputes
  - entire work groups split into coalitions
  - employee grievances
  - sexual harassment
  - employee disputes
- educational settings
  - disputes over grades or treatment in class
  - relationships between students and campus groups
  - student-faculty relationships
- community/neighborhood disputes
  - barking dogs
  - property line disputes
  - small claims
  - landlord-tenant disputes
- the criminal justice system
  - juvenile court situations
  - VOR (victim-offender restitution)
  - treatment in detention facilities
- labor-management conflicts
- international conflicts

The entire field of mediation cannot be tackled here, but a few examples will indicate the usefulness of mediation across settings ranging from community disputes to business disputes.

Community mediation programs continue to expand across much of the United States with high rates of success in settling a variety of disputes. In Massachusetts, New York, North Carolina, and other states the success rates for mediating community disputes range from 75 to 95 percent (Umbreit 1995, 59). Community centers typically rely on volunteers who are trained by the local Dispute Resolution Center. Community mediation programs offer excellent training, supervision, and guidance, as well as opportunities to help others resolve disputes. Complaints range from noisy neighbors to "He took my parking space"—almost any issue one can image that arises in a neighborhood. The National Association for Community Mediation (address listed in the appendix) can be contacted to see if your community has an ongoing center where you might volunteer and receive training.

In the "community" of schools and universities, considerable mediation is occurring. For instance, many grade schools, middle schools, and high schools have instituted programs of peer mediation. These programs train students, teachers, and administrators in constructive conflict resolution, teach mediation skills to peer mediators, and provide mediators for disputes ranging from playground difficulties to teacher-student problems. One of the originators of peer mediators in schools was the Community Board Program in

San Francisco (address listed in the appendix). As an example of peer mediation, here are the tasks for fourth- and fifth-grade mediators when they see a conflict beginning:

1. When you see a conflict brewing during recess or lunch, introduce yourself and ask both parties if they want to solve their problem.
2. If they do, go to the area designated for solving problems. Explain and get agreement to the four basic rules: (a) agree to solve the problem, (b) don't call each other names, (c) do not interrupt, and (d) tell the truth.
3. Decide who will talk first. Ask that person what happened and how he or she feels, using active listening skills to repeat back what is said. Do the same with the other person.
4. Ask the first party and then the second party for alternative solutions.
5. Work with the students toward a solution that they both think is good.
6. After the agreement is reached, congratulate the parties and fill out the Conflict Manager Report Form (Umbreit 1995, 78).

School mediation programs have had considerable success. Of 137 disputes between students in Honolulu, 92 percent resulted in complete agreement, and after the institution of peer mediation in New York schools, suspensions decreased by more than half in many schools. Clearly, school mediation is a viable form of third-party intervention for a variety of disputes (Umbreit 1995; Burrell and Cahn 1994). In the university and college setting, campus mediation centers deal with disputes over grades and classroom behavior, and in dorms and married-student housing. Some of the centers provide family mediation services to students as well. A current list of campus mediation programs is now available on the Web via Nova Southeastern University, with links to other valuable mediation and conflict management sites. By visiting this site you can find out which programs are up and running as well as find materials for your use (http://www.nova.edu/ssss/DR/univ.html). Among other items, this site will give you a list of conflict resolution programs in higher education so that you can study mediation in more depth.

Family mediation takes many forms, the most common application being separation and divorce. With almost half of all marriages ending in divorce and the pain of going through the court system all too evident, mediation of separation and divorce is becoming increasingly common. It is not a replacement for the legal process but an adjunct to it. The judge retains all the authority to decide the details of a divorce, but a cooperative couple that comes to a judge with a fair agreement will find the process much easier than trying to "prove the other one wrong." The couple, with the mediator's help, fashions (within the constraints of the law) an agreement that will work best for their unique situation. The acrimony, lingering conflict, and repeated trips to court by couples who take the legal adversarial approach has fueled the mediation movement. One study concluded the following after examining mediation in divorces:

> Despite the high levels of stress, anxiety, and fear associated with the breakup of a marriage, the vast majority of the parties in mediation believed that their needs and interests had been considered by the mediator and that the agreements reached in mediation were substantively fair to both parties, and they recommended the mediation process to others. Long-term satisfaction with the agreements was demonstrated by the continued compliance with the original agreements and changes by mutual consent, modifications that were reached through constructive private discussion or by a return to mediation. (Meierding 1993, 169)

In the family context, family business and estate mediation is becoming more popular. When a family owns a small business, for example, and the time comes for Mom or Dad to retire, mediation involves all family members in the decision making so options can be charted that work best for all. Whether it is the family pharmacy, ranch, or Subway franchise, (1) content, (2) relationship, (3) identity, and (4) process issues need to be carefully addressed. Mediation provides a framework for discussing important family issues, in addition to the usual issues of taxes, estate planning, finances, control of decisions, and inheritance. With mediation, all the issues can be brought to the surface and dealt with, thus bringing the participants to a mediated agreement that serves the entire family. The following article demonstrates the advantages of using mediation in estate planning.

The Family Estate*

Reader: My mother, in her late 70s, is worried about her fairly sizable estate. It includes real estate, stock and our long-time family cabin in the mountains. She wants to do the "right" thing for her three grown children and their grown families so we won't fight or bicker after she's gone. She vividly remembers a nephew who, after her father's death, broke into the family house and took one of his guns. After 25 years, the family still talks about it! Should Mom think about using mediation?

Mediators: Absolutely. The two biggest mistakes people make about their estates, as well as in other types of mediation are (1) not preplanning and (2) not dealing with relationship issues.

One cannot, should not, and must not try to pass on a sizeable estate without specialized legal help. Estate and tax laws are complex and impose severe consequences for the unprepared (read "$$$"). Issues abound, such as whether to create a trust, if so, what kind, and how to handle the $10,000 annual gift exemption. These "content" issues need careful thought and expert advice.

Equally however, your mother dares not neglect the relational issues in her family—how she and the three children react to the content issues. Before, during and after consulting with attorneys, she should listen to and address the concerns of each person affected. Current research starkly paints the picture: If one tries to plan an estate using only legal and financial advisors, the children left out of the discussion will react negatively *regardless* of the elegance of the plan. Just ask families who've tried to craft even the most thorough estate plan without involving all the impacted players—smouldering resentments and "what ifs" remain.

In the safe environment of mediation, both the content and relational issues can be put on the table and examined. Assumptions about people's needs and feelings can be checked out, before they're locked into the text of a will. Creative problem solving can be used to derive solutions that work for the whole family. We have seen cases of people (1) retaining the family business intact in the face of children reluctant to participate and (2) passing on financial assets in ways that work for everyone.

Find a competent, experienced mediator to work with the family and with your estate lawyer, and your chances of somebody stealing the guns will diminish.

* Reprinted from *The Missoulian,* September 23, 1996, by Bill Wilmot and Roy Andes, 210 North Higgins, Missoula, MT 59812.

Mediation can be used in conjunction with counseling to resolve adolescent-parent conflicts—those natural calamities that arise in most families. Whereas for some, adolescence is a minor inconvenience, for others it is "a painful exhausting journey that cuts into the bond between parent and child" (Umbreit 1995, 116). A trained mediator can help both the adolescent and the parent(s) develop workable agreements to get them through this often contentious stage of family life. Whatever the need for family mediation, mediators who are members of the Academy of Family Mediators follow specific standards for practice (see appendix for address).

VOR (Victim Offender Restitution) is a specialized form of mediation designed for cases in which someone is guilty of a crime. Rather than resolving the issue between the defendant and the court system, VOR brings the victim into the process. Both the victim and the perpetrator tell their story and review options for compensation of the victim. Such an approach allows the victim participation, brings the reality of the crime home to the offender, and sets the conditions under which the offender can compensate the victim for what was done. It recognizes the victim's rights, allows the offender to take responsibility for what he or she has done, and provides avenues for restoration. Good reviews of VOR can be found in Umbreit (1995) and in a special issue of *Mediation Quarterly* (vol. 12, no. 3, 1995). A poignant example of a creative use of mediation for a minor crime is presented in the following box.

"I Stole Your TV"

An example taken from the files illustrates the constructive use of mediation to achieve both symbolic and actual restitution. An elderly woman returned to her home one afternoon to find her television set gone. The youth who had stolen it was apprehended and admitted that he had sold the set to a fence. Rather than face a fine or continuance under probation, the defendant, in the presence of the mediation board and of the victim, sat down to work out a non-punitive resolution to submit to the judge for his approval. The woman broke down in the course of telling the boy, "I watch television all day. This is all I do. I watch sixteen hours a day. You have taken the heart of my life away." Confronted with personal implications of his act, the youth agreed to accept a job in order to buy the widow a new set. In addition, he agreed that he would accompany her to the bank to cash her weekly check and escort her to the market to do her shopping. A postscript to the case reports that after inviting the boy to have coffee with her, the woman learned from him that his mother had died and that he lived in an uncongenial relationship with his father and brother. Thereafter these Saturday morning coffee hours became a weekly feature. The closing entry reports that the boy had volunteered to paint the woman's kitchen (Alper and Nichols 1981, 146–147).

Mediation is beginning to be used in the business setting as well. When a dispute arises between two coworkers, between a supervisor and an employee, or within a self-directed work team, mediation allows the parties to address the issue in a confidential way. Advantages to using mediation in the workplace include the following:

- Mediation reduces the cost of protracted disputes.
- Mediation increases everyone's satisfaction with the outcomes of the dispute.
- Mediation enhances relationships among people.
- Mediation reduces the recurrence of conflict (Yarbrough and Wilmot 1995, 3).

Some examples of the use of mediation in business settings are as follows: A man and wife were co-owners of a business, and he took out loans against the business without consulting her. With the ongoing help of the mediator, they restored their working relationship, got their employees out of the middle of their struggles, and began cooperating fully with each other. A male supervisor in a large institution was investigated by the personnel office for sexual harassment. After he was found not guilty of harassment, something had to be done to reestablish the working relationship between him and his female administrative aide. The mediator worked with the two of them to (1) set clear boundaries on appropriate behavior on both their parts, (2) stop "end runs" to higher authorities, and (3) establish clear protocols for how to run the office. These are samples of the kinds of disputes that can be successfully handled via mediation. Yarbrough and Wilmot (1995) provide numerous examples of the mediation of diverse organizational disputes ranging from employee-employee disputes to disputes within management teams.

Mediation: Agreement or Transformation?

Mediators' *views* of the mediation process differ in two primary ways: (1) what issues are tackled in sessions and (2) what the goals are for the mediation. Some mediators (usually those with technical and/or legal training) will only mediate the *content* issues. For example, many legal jurisdictions have a "settlement week" when they convene groups of attorneys to mediate cases that are backlogged on the court calendars. This type of mediation is usually quite different from, for example, family mediation that deals with *content, relationship, identity,* and *process* issues. Both types of mediation have their place, but as a user of the services you should be aware that the mediators' views of mediation can result in vastly different processes. A local attorney who was going to mediate between two different factions (an insurance company with an attorney and a tribal elder with a representative) called for advice. In the phone call, it became apparent that his only considerations were content issues. The case did settle the content issues exclusively, primarily because of the natural empathy of the attorney whom everyone sees as a warm and friendly person. Disputants who have an ongoing relationship are more satisfied and more willing to adhere to agreements when mediators expand the issues being considered. The results of research on family mediation are quite clear—when mediators bypass the relational issues and focus only on "facts," they have trouble obtaining agreement from the parties (Donohue 1991; Donohue, Allen, and Burrell 1988; Donohue, Drake, and Roberto 1994).

Mediators also have different goals for mediation. Bush and Folger (1994) have detailed goals that range from getting agreement (problem solving) to transformation. Many mediators just want agreement—to settle the conflict. Others want to see clients undergo transformation—a change in how they see themselves and the other. *Transformation* occurs when clients experience empowerment and give recognition. Clients are empowered when they more clearly realize their goals (empowerment of goals), become aware of a wider range of options (empowerment of options), increase their skills (empowerment of skills), gain new awareness of resources (empowerment of resources), and make conscious decisions about what they want to do (empowerment of decision making). As Bush and Folger note, "When these kinds of things occur within relationships, the party experiences a greater sense of self-worth, security, self-determination, and autonomy" (87). In a similar vein, one gives recognition by (a) having the desire to recognize the other, (b) thinking about giving recognition, (c) giving recognition in words, and (d) giving recognition in actions. When these things occur, "The party realizes and enacts his capacity to acknowledge, consider and be concerned about others" (91).

The problem-solving approach to mediation, Bush and Folger argue, is more aligned with an individualistic world view, in which we see ourselves as separate, concrete entities. On the other hand, the transformative view has as its underpinnings a relational view—that we are all interconnected and part of an organic whole. For an overview of these two world views and how they might affect one's mediation, see Bush and Folger (1994) and Wilmot (1995).

Mediation Process and Skills

Depending on the *type of mediation,* different skill sets are needed. Two of the more comprehensive lists of mediational skills can be found in Keltner (1994) and Yarbrough and Wilmot (1995). Keltner quotes the late William Simkin, former director of the Federal Mediation and Conciliation service, in listing these mediational qualities:

- The patience of Job
- The sincerity and bulldog characteristics of the English
- The wit of the Irish
- The physical endurance of a marathon runner
- The broken-field dodging abilities of a halfback
- The guile of Machiavelli
- The personality-probing skills of a good psychiatrist
- The confidence-retaining characteristics of a mute
- The hide of a rhinoceros
- The wisdom of Solomon (107).

The mediator needs to have an expansive set of skills to control communication, affirm both parties, and move them toward creative content and relational solutions, all the while within legal and cultural parameters. Yarbrough and Wilmot (1995) go a step further and specify the primary skills that are necessary at each stage of the mediation process. Figure 9.3 shows that the mediator needs to have both "reflective" skills (shown on the right side of the S curving through the diagram) and "directive" skills (shown on the left side). The stages of mediation illustrated in the diagram are as follows:

- Entry
- Diagnosis
- Negotiation
- Agreements
- Follow-up

Figure 9.3 Mediation skills

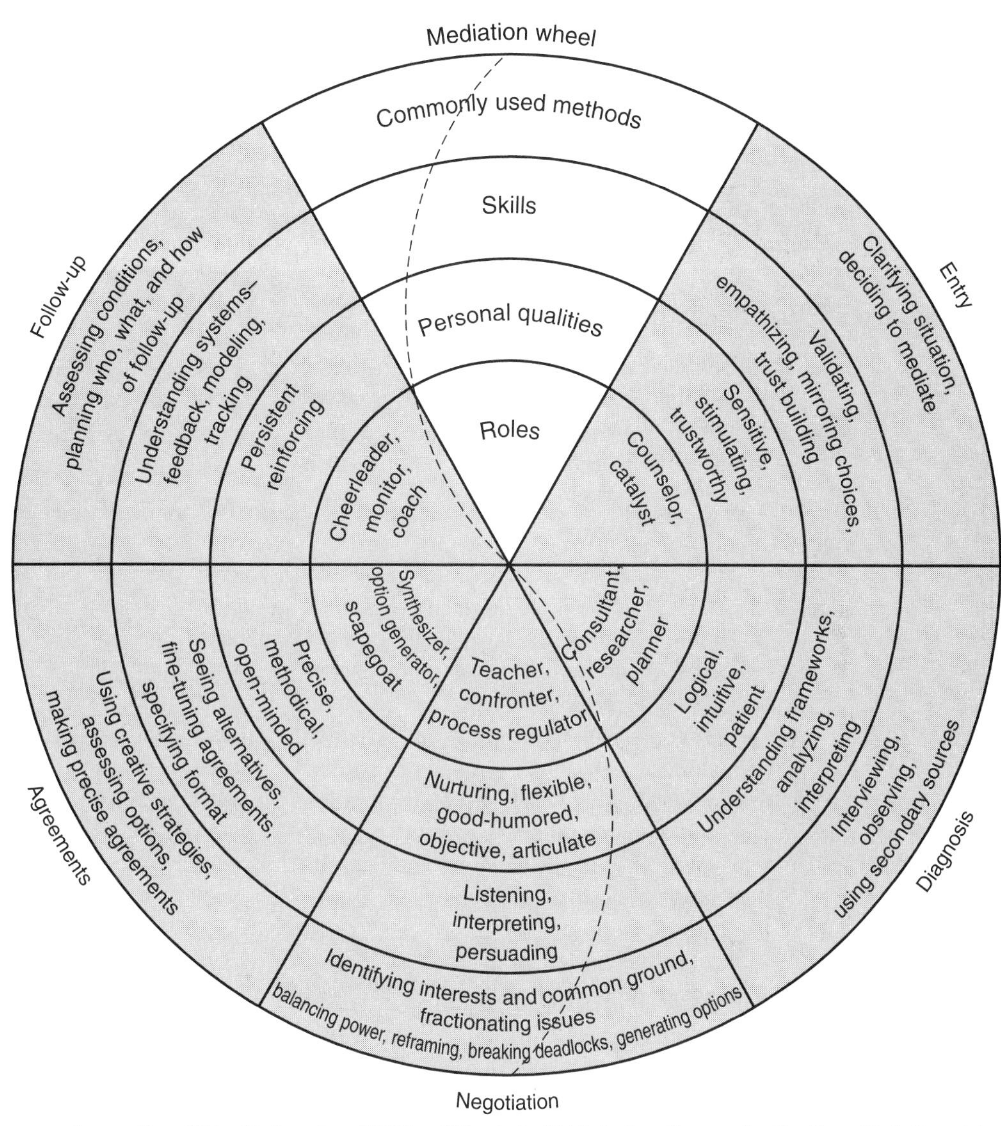

Source: From Elaine Yarbrough and William Wilmot, *Artful Mediation: Constructive Conflict at Work.* Copyright © 1995 Cairns Publishing, Boulder, Colorado. Reprinted by permission.

As you progress through the mediation, the skill set required at each stage differs. You will move from "counselor/catalyst" at the entry stage to "cheerleader, monitor, and coach" in the follow-up stage.

The key to effective mediation is the level of competence of the mediator. It is imperative, if you are to be a mediator or other type of third-party intervenor, that you (1) receive extensive training in the necessary skills, (2) have the opportunity to try those skills with co-mediators or mentors, (3) are supervised by experienced mediators, and (4) continue your skill training and exposure to the literature on mediation. One cannot learn mediational skills from a book—they have to be practiced, critiqued, and evaluated. Similarly, it is important to juxtapose the skills against conceptual knowledge. For example, if you are a skilled mediator with lots of cases under your belt, it is worthwhile to read the Bush and Folger (1994) book and reflect on the variety of mediation you practice. Finally, it is important to continually question *all* of your assumptions about what mediation is and what it can accomplish. The following section on cultural assumptions about mediation illustrates some of the ideas being gathered from other cultures.

Culture and Third Parties

A study of how other cultures use third parties to manage disputes highlights the automatic assumptions derived from one's own culture. Much can be learned from forms used in other cultures. For instance, look at the steps for resolving conflict in a Hawaiian context, based on ancient Polynesian culture. *Ho'oponopono* consists of

1. gathering of the disputants by a high-status family or community member who knows the parties
2. opening prayer to the gods (or God)
3. a statement of the problem to be solved or prevented from growing worse
4. questioning of involved participants by the leader
5. replies to the leader and a discussion channeled through the leader
6. periods of silence
7. honest confession to the gods (or God) and to each of the disputants
8. immediate restitution or arrangements to make restitution as soon as possible
9. "setting to right" of each successive problem that becomes apparent as Ho'oponopono proceeds (repeating the preceding steps if necessary)
10. mutual forgiveness of the other and releasing him or her from guilt, grudges, and tensions for the wrongdoing
11. closing prayer
12. a meal or snack (Wall and Callister 1995)

In different cultures, the forms of intervention, selection of intervenor, and methods used by the third party to move the parties to resolution vary dramatically. In most Asian approaches to third-party involvement, for example, face-saving and relationship building play a more predominant role than in Western approaches. Social harmony is paramount, rather than the disputants "getting what they want" (Wall 1993). The disputants might not initiate the intervention; rather, a family or community member might ask the third party to intervene (Ma 1992).

Ury (1995) studied the Kalahari Bushmen, who follow a sequence of solving conflicts that taps the "third force"—the power of the community. The disputants actually meet in front of others and work the conflict through with the participation of others.

> In every serious dispute between two individuals or groups, then, there is a third party at work. The third party is usually not a single individual but a collectivity of third parties: a third force of concerned relatives, friends, and elders. These third parties are typically "insider third

> parties" with strong ties to either one or both sides. There can be no private disputes of any seriousness because a dispute affects everyone. (396).

The role of spirit or religion in resolving disputes is also recognized in other societies. In Malay society, for example, the spiritual elements play a prominent role, and the mediator meets the disputants in all kinds of contexts—attending family gatherings and weddings, for example. Native American cultures that keep their spiritual traditions alive continue to use spiritual force to resolve conflicts. Umbreit (1995) provides a comprehensive overview of some of these approaches and says this about Native American traditions of dispute resolution:

> A model of mediation that is culturally sensitive to Native Americans and aboriginal people in Canada would be quite different from the dominant Western models. Such a model is likely to include consensus decision making; preference for co-mediation; separate premediation sessions with each person; involvement of elders in the mediation; presence of chosen family members; circular seating; silence as comfortable; interruptions as inappropriate; nonlinear agenda; and the use of cultural metaphors and symbols. From this culture perspective, mediation occurs within a large cultural context. (37)

Although we cannot import other cultural forms into mainstream Western culture without modification, neither can we export Western modes directly into other cultural situations. Similarly, when there are subcultures within Western society, one needs to adapt dispute resolution mechanisms to address their special situations. As Buitrago (1996) says, "with Hispanics the issue of trust is as essential for a positive outcome as for any conflictive party, but can be harder to obtain due to variables like discrimination and powerlessness" (16). Many community mediation centers solicit volunteers who are from unique groups as a way to bridge the gap between traditional mediation techniques and the special needs of subcultures.

Umbreit (1995) provides a step-by-step look at some of the central differences between mediation in modern cultures and mediation in traditional cultures. As you peruse table 9.1, notice just how different each stage is. For example, in a modern culture, mediation might end with a written and signed agreement, whereas in a traditional culture, mediation often ends with participants giving their personal word.

Dispute Systems Design

The pioneering work of Ury, Brett, and Goldberg (1988) revealed the need to analyze the entire system to decide how best to match dispute resolution to the specific needs of the involved parties. For example, third-party involvement is best used after the parties have had a chance to work out their problem themselves. For example, a typical sequence of a dispute between two employees would be

- direct discussion with each other
- involvement of their immediate supervisor
- involvement of a neutral third party, such as human resource personnel
- filing a grievance
- going to court

Table 9.1 Continuum of Cultural Expectations in Mediation

Stages of Mediation	(Components) Elements	(Modern) "Pure formal"	(Traditional) "Pure informal'
1. Entry (context setting and ground rules)	1.1 Setting	Public bureaucratic style	Private interpersonal style
	1.2 Mediator chosen	Professional, impersonal, anonymous	Known and trusted person, friend, or social leader; known and in network
	1.3 Expectations shared by third party and disputants	Restricted access to mediator's time	Unrestricted access to time and involvement
		Facilitate direct address	Provide surrogate, or go-between, for indirect communication
		Focus on issues and goals	All aspects of relationship may be involved
		Autonomous decisions made by each party	Appropriate groups will be involved in decisions
2. Introduction to session (monologue by mediator)	2.1 Process	Directive monologue	Nondirective introduction
	2.2 Structure	Formalized	Assumed in social customs
	2.3 Rules of talk	Directed by mediator	Familiar social process
	2.4 Priorities	Tasks confronted first	Relationships come first
	2.5 Roles	Formalized	Natural social roles of participants in community
3. Story-telling	3.1 Interaction made	Face-to-face	Through third party(ies)
	3.2 Focus (topic)	Disputants' demands (I-topics) stated early	Disputants' demands (I-topics) stated later
	3.3 Sequence	Issues one-at-a-time	Multiple related issues
	3.4 Style	Analytical, linear causation	Relational, entwined stories
4. Problem solving	4.1 Time function	Linear (monochronic)	Cyclical-personal (polychronic)
	4.2 Purpose	Focus on issues	Reconcile relationships
	4.3 Person/context understanding	Issues must be resolved in isolation from the social network	Issues are embedded in the social network so both are interrelated

Table 9.1 Continuum of Cultural Expectations in Mediation—*Continued*

Stages of Mediation	(Components) Elements	(Modern) "Pure formal"	(Traditional) "Pure informal'
5. Agreement	5.1 Form	Written and signed	Personal word given
	5.2 Continuing relationship to third party	No continuing relationship	Symbols of reconciliation exchanged; ongoing responsibility to parties and for implementation of agreement

Such a sequence allows the participants to solve their conflict themselves, and if they are unsuccessful at an early step, to move the dispute slowly to where they have less control over the outcome—grievance and then court. Furthermore, these steps can be expanded (for an excellent example in health care, see Slaikeu 1989, 399).

Ury and others suggest these principles for designing dispute systems:

1. *Focus on interests.* Examine the driving interests behind disputes rather than letting the parties rush into positional statements. As was noted in the goals and negotiation chapters, once the driving interests are uncovered, the management of the dispute proceeds rapidly.
2. *Build in "loop-back" procedures that encourage disputants to return to negotiation.* Provide cooling-off periods when participants get locked into power or rights struggles. Or, make sure the parties meet with each other before strong tactics, such as strikes, are used.
3. *Provide low-cost rights and power back-up procedures.* Provide arbitration or other mechanisms to settle issues rather than having parties go to adjudication. Use combinations of mediation and arbitration (med-arb), or use "final offer arbitration" in which you "threaten" to choose between the parties' positions, usually resulting in the parties moving closer together so that they won't "lose" the decision.
4. *Build in consultation before, feedback after.* Work to notify parties, keep them in communication with each other, and provide postdispute analysis and feedback. For example, companies and unions might establish common interest forums after a dispute to refocus on what they have in common with each other.
5. *Arrange procedures in a low-to-high cost sequence.* Work to establish settlement at the lowest possible cost. For example, try to catch the dispute early by resolving it through negotiation, bring in upper-level executives in labor-management disputes, if necessary, and move on to more extensive mechanisms later.
6. *Provide the motivation, skills, and resources necessary to make the procedures work.* Provide training for participants so that the mechanisms of intervention can be

successful. The entire system must support proactive conflict so that when disputes arise, parties are supportive of settlement efforts.*

One can adapt these same principles to all types of interpersonal conflicts in dormitories, families, and the workplace. The key is to think ahead about what type of dispute design will best serve the participants and manage the conflict with a minimum of time, expense, and public posturing.

Informal Intervention

Many everyday conflicts are settled out of court or without the aid of a professional helper through the assistance of informal mediators, such as friends, neighbors, and others (McGillis 1981). These interveners serve the same objective as more defined agents, that is, "to interrupt a self-maintaining or escalating-malevolent cycle in one way or another and to initiate a de-escalating-benevolent cycle" (Walton 1969). In some circumstances, third parties pass messages back and forth (Rubin and Brown 1975). You may have informed a friend when her angry boyfriend was ready to talk over a conflict or told your brother that your younger sister was upset and needed to talk.

Informal third parties enter conflicts through diverse routes. Parties may ask for help indirectly. Children, for instance, seem to sense that parents will step into the role as a third party when they get beaten up on the playground, when "Jill won't give me back my teddy bear," or when big brother picks on them behind their parents' backs. The complaint, accompanied by anger or tears, serves as a request for help. A friend may call to discuss a potential romantic breakup. You may guess that he wants you to carry a message or come over to talk with the unhappy couple. A staff person may say, "What would you think about coming to the meeting Tuesday with Julie and Chris? I think we could use your level head."

The following are indirect cues indicating that your help may be needed:

1. A person spends more time with you than usual, asking for advice and sharing feelings.
2. A person shares private information with you.
3. A person indicates that a crucial decision is impending.
4. A person makes you understand that his or her life is not smooth, that distress is present, or that things seem out of control.
5. A person makes dramatic, noticeable changes.

A teacher may notice that a student, usually happy and in love with life, talks more and more of negative feelings and events. Accounts of events may shift from balanced to blaming. A student who says, "They won't hire me. They don't think I have any useful experience" may be indirectly asking for the teacher's intervention in the form of a phone call or letter of recommendation.

If you have decided to offer to help people resolve their conflict, you must now choose when to intervene, what your role will be, what your intervention style will be, and what

* Note that these suggestions are most appropriate for labor-management disputes. For more detail consult Ury, Brett, and Goldberg (1988).

skills you will bring to the conflict. Before you make a commitment to help, answer the following questions:

1. Are they ready for a third party? What evidence do you have to indicate such readiness?
2. How certain are you that your help has been requested? If the request was indirect, clarify your understanding of the request.
3. How do you know that they want *you* to help?
4. What skills prepare you to help them? Can you best help by referring them to someone else?
5. Is your role free and flexible enough so you can help, or are you biased, committed to one of the parties, grinding your own ax, or unable to help because of time, position, or other matters?
6. Can you say no? If not, then you are probably too involved in the conflict to be an effective helper.

If you are satisfied with the answers to these questions, take the time to think about the consequences of your intervention. Remember, someone else's problem is not necessarily your problem—you have a choice. If you think you have no choice, you cannot be useful as an informal intervener. Many adults get involved in conflicts between their parents only to discover the futility of trying to solve marital problems not of their making. If you do not want to get involved in a conflict but think that you should, your lack of enthusiasm for the role will result in lessened energy and creativity, a lack of sensitivity, and ineffective intervention. If you don't want to help, don't.

If you do choose to take a role in the conflict, however informal or nonspecific that role may be, take special care to retain your neutrality. Informal third parties often take sides (Van de Vliert 1981, 1985). If one of the parties succeeds in allying with the helper, the resulting alliance lessens the other side's power in the conflict and creates a new issue in the conflict—that of unfair bonding. Consultants to organizations are trained to avoid such biased behavior, but friends and relatives may slip into taking sides only to find that their "help" has made the conflict worse. The following result from siding with one party:

- Siding implies that the outsider adopts the win-lose thinking of the principal parties, reinforcing the destructive effects of such thinking.
- Siding creates a winner (the chosen party) and a loser (the rejected party) precipitating escalation by the rejected party.
- Siding increases the number of conflict participants.
- By adding views, siding complicates the conflict issues.
- The siding outsider invests energy, increasing the stake of the parties in the conflict outcome.

(Adapted from Van de Vliert 1981, 497–498)

Siding with one conflict party, although not wise for an intervener, does have its place. If, for example, your close friend is breaking off a relationship with her fiancé, you may choose to side with her to give her support. Anything else would be unrealistic. However, you should be aware that siding with one of the conflict parties precludes you from being an effective neutral helper; you will become an additional party to the conflict.

Refusing to take sides can result in (1) your not being involved in the conflict or (2) your readiness to be an effective change agent. A new employee of a hospital was approached by persons on opposite sides of a conflict over whether the assignment of nursing shifts should be based on seniority only or on seniority and experience. The new nurse found himself being pushed toward the middle—both sides wanted him to persuade the other side of the rightness of their position. He wisely told all parties, "I am too new to have an informed opinion. Besides, I value my relationships with all of you. I choose not to help with this problem."

On a university campus, a faculty member's neutrality set the stage for an effective intervention. The faculty member heard from a student who wanted to graduate early that another faculty member refused to consider a petition to waive or substitute a required course. The neutral faculty member offered to intervene by privately asking the resistant faculty member to discuss the issue in a meeting. The resulting meeting transformed the two-party conflict into a discussion of the principles of fairness and the desirability of requests to waive or substitute courses. The intervening professor did not take sides; she provided a forum for handling the matter creatively.

If you are going to intervene, clarify any change in your role from your habitual role with the conflict parties. If you have been a buddy, boss, romantic partner, coworker, or casual acquaintance, any change in that role needs to be negotiated. For example, a fourteen-year-old girl, Toni, lived with a couple in their midfifties who cared for her as foster parents. The state children's service worker, Anne, had functioned in the past as a person who found placements for Toni, certified potential foster homes for her, and provided her with ongoing counseling. Mr. and Mrs. Black began to quarrel about whether to continue providing care for Toni, since their own children were out of the home and they were beginning to want time without children. Mrs. Black wanted to wait until Toni graduated from high school to request another placement, whereas Mr. Black wanted Toni to be moved during the summer. Anne was able to act as a third party to their conflict, after making clear that her first loyalty was to Toni's best interests. Since all three people agreed on the interests, they were able, with Anne's help, to find a solution to the conflict. Unless Anne had clarified her role, which involved not taking sides with either parent and keeping Toni's interests prominent, both parents would have tried to elicit Anne's support for their side.

Several cautions are in order for the intervener who is a friend or coworker. Be certain the parties want help in managing their conflict. Any time a third party enters into an existing relationship, the relationship is changed. Be careful that the successful conflict management of the original parties is not built at the expense of the third party—they may cast you as the enemy, thus temporarily bonding with each other and excluding you. Remember, you are entering an already existing system, whether it is two friends, two employees, or any greater number of interdependent persons. *Your focus, even if you are taking an informal rule, is the relationship.* If you become a common enemy by pushing the parties too hard, they will not solve their problem and you will lose two relationships. In addition, you must constantly remain aware of attempts to convince you of the rightness of a particular side. Once you coalesce with one person, you lose your helpful role and weaken the relationship between the two parties. Although you cannot predict ahead of time exactly what will happen when you involve yourself, you do need to monitor the interactions to watch for shifts in coalitions or destruction of the original bond. If you begin thinking, "No wonder he is struggling with her; she is completely unreasonable," you have formed a coalition and lost your effectiveness. Honest and helpful assistance can heal conflicts and further an ongoing relationship. Just remember to intervene for the people who want your help and not for your own purposes.

You may at some point need to request the help of an outside consultant for your organization, family, or personal relationship. You can be helpful to the consultant by asking for what you want and clarifying what you do not want. Asking someone to train your staff in conflict management results in a different process than asking for mediation. Once the work is completed, the third party exits from the system. In both formal and informal intervention, the goal is to train the parties to manage their own relations. An intervener who does not work himself or herself out of a job is not doing the job properly; the parties must become independent of the third party. In one mediated conflict, the leaders of two departments agreed to set up weekly meetings to discuss ongoing or potential conflicts. A three-month follow-up meeting with the original conflict parties was scheduled to assess how the weekly meetings were working—and to make sure the meetings were occurring. An effective third party trains people in the process of conflict management so that the clients will not need ongoing services. In either formal or informal roles, an intervener who provides the impetus for altering the parties' relations over time has contributed a valuable and reusable resource to the system.

Summary

The purpose of intervening in conflict is to transform the conflict elements, thereby allowing for effective management. Intervention modes differ according to how much the original conflict parties determine the outcome. In both adjudication and arbitration, an outsider (judge, jury, or arbitrator) decides the outcome of the dispute. Mediation, on the other hand, involves the participants in the management of their own struggle. The mediator facilitates communication and helps the parties reach an agreement that will work for both of them. Various settings for mediation exist, ranging from family disputes to business concerns all the way to international conflicts. For instance, school mediation programs are useful throughout all levels of schools.

Although some mediators want agreement, others strive for transformation of the conflict parties. Regardless of the desired outcome, however, mediation processes and skills vary depending on the particular stage of mediation, beginning with softer skills such as listening and ending with setting rules so the parties can keep their agreements. There are profound differences in terms of third-party intervention across cultures; Eastern cultures, for example, often use extended networks of people to help parties keep agreements, whereas Western cultures generally do not. Interveners can focus attention on the proactive design of dispute systems to handle conflicts as they arise. Informal intervention occurs frequently, such as within groups of friends.

Appendix

Organizations, Resources, Training Opportunities, and Materials on Conflict and Mediation

The following resources are a very select list. Rather than try to encompass a vast and rapidly growing set of resources, those most pertinent to the topics of this book are included. The easiest and fastest way to search for topics on conflict and mediation is to visit some of the following sites on the Internet or to use an Internet search engine to find new sites.

Topic/Web Site/Phone Number	Name/Address
Peace and conflict resources http://www.contact.org/uspeace.htm	U.S. Peace and Conflict Resolution Resources
Family mediation training, standards, and resources (617) 674-2663 http://www.igc.apc.org/afm	Academy of Family Mediators 4 Militia Drive, Lexington, MA 02173
Listing of graduate programs in conflict, campus mediation centers, and more http://www.nova.edu/ssss/DR/univ.html	Nova Southeast University
An organization for arbitration and mediation, with many publications and resources http://www.adr.org/overview.html	American Arbitration Association
A consortium of multifaceted organizations and resources on conflict http://www.igc.apc.org/igc/issues/cr/	ConflictNet

Professional society for mediators and arbitrators
(202) 783-7277
http://www.igc.apc.org/spidr

Society of Professionals in Dispute Resolution (SPIDR)
815 Fifteenth Street NW, Suite 530, Washington, DC 20005

Professional association
(714) 836-8100
http://www.igc.org/voma

Victim Offender Mediation Association
c/o St. Vincent de Paul Center, 777 South Main Street, Suite 200, Orange, CA 92668

Violence prevention resources
http://www.cyfe.umn.edu/other/PREVRESOURCE.HTM

Biannual international conference
(703) 993-2440
http://web.gmu.edu/departments/NCPCR

National Conference on Peacemaking and Conflict Resolution
George Mason University, University Drive, Fairfax, VA 22030-4444

Conflict Resolution
Education Network & Other Resources
(202) 466-4767

N.I.D.R. (National Institute for Dispute Resolution)
1726 M. St. NW, Suite 500
Washington, D.C. 20036

References

Acitelli, L. K., E. Douvan, and J. Veroff. 1993. Perceptions of conflict in the first year of marriage: How important are similarity and understanding? *Journal of Social and Personal Relationships* 10: 5–20.

Alberts, J., and G. Driscoll. 1992. Containment versus escalation: The trajectory of couples' conversational complaints. *Western Journal of Communication* 56: 394–412.

Albrecht, T. L., and B. W. Bach. 1997. *Communication in complex organizations: A relational approach.* New York: Harcourt Brace College Publishers.

Aldous, J. 1974. Family interaction patterns. *Annual Review of Sociology* 3: 105–135.

Alexander, J. F. 1973. Defensive and supportive communication in normal and deviant families. *Journal of Consulting and Clinical Psychology* 40: 223–231.

Alper, B. S., and L. W. Nichols. 1981. *Beyond the courtroom.* Lexington, Mass.: Lexington Books.

Andes, R. H. 1992. Message dimensions of negotiation. *Negotiation Journal* 8: 125–130.

Apfelbaum, E. 1974. On conflicts and bargaining. *Advances in Experimental Social Psychology* 7: 103–156.

Applegate, J. L. 1982. The impact of construct system development on communication and impression formation in persuasive contexts. *Communication Monographs* 49 (December): 277–286.

Argyle, M., and A. Furnham. 1983. Sources of satisfaction and conflict in long-term relationships. *Journal of Marriage and the Family* 45: 481–493.

Argyris, C. 1970. *Intervention theory and method: A behavioral science view.* Reading, Mass.: Addison-Wesley Publishing.

Arnett, R. C. 1980a. *Dialogical foundations of conflict resolution.* Paper presented to the Speech Communication Association Convention, New York, November 16.

———. 1980b. *Dwell in peace: Applying nonviolence to everyday relationships.* Elgin, Ill.: Brethren Press.

Arnold, W. E. 1977. Crisis communication. In *Communicating through behavior,* edited by W. E. Arnold and R. O. Hirsch. St. Paul, Minn.: West Publishing.

Augsburger, D. W. 1992. *Conflict mediation across cultures: Pathways and Patterns.* Louisville, Ky.: Westminster/John Knox Press.

Bach, G. R., and H. Goldberg. 1974. *Creative aggression: The art of assertive living.* New York: Avon Books.

Bach, G. R., and P. Wyden. 1968. *The intimate enemy: How to fight fair in love and marriage.* New York: Avon Books.

Barker, J. R., C. W. Melville, and M. E. Pacanowsky. 1993. Self-directed teams at Xel: Changes in communication practices during a program of cultural transformation. *Journal of Applied Communication Research* 21: 297–312.

Barnlund, D. C. 1989. *Communicative styles of Japanese and Americans: Images and realities.* Belmont, Calif.: Wadsworth.

Baron, R. A. 1984. Reducing organizational conflict: An incompatible response approach. *Journal of Applied Psychology* 69: 272–279.

Barry, W. A. 1970. Marriage research and conflict: An integrative review. *Psychological Bulletin* 73: 41–54.

Bartos, O. J. 1974. *Process and outcome of negotiations.* New York: Columbia University Press.

Bartunek, J. M., A. A. Benton, and C. B. Keys. 1975. Third party intervention and the bargaining behavior of group representatives. *Journal of Conflict Resolution* 76, no. 3: 535–555.

Bateson, G. 1972. *Steps to an ecology of mind.* New York: Ballantine Books.

———. 1980. *Mind and nature: A necessary unity.* New York: Bantam Books.

Baumeister, R. R., A. Stillwell, and S. R. Wotman. 1990. Victim and perpetrator accounts of interpersonal conflict: Autobiographical narratives about anger. *Journal of Personality and Social Psychology,* 59: 994–1005.

Baxter, L. A. 1982. Conflict management: An episodic approach. *Small Group Behavior* 13, no. 1: 23–42.

Baxter, L. A., W. W. Wilmot, C. A. Simmons, and A. Swartz. 1993. Ways of doing conflict: A folk taxonomy of conflict events in personal relationships. In *Interpersonal communication: Evolving interpersonal relationships,* edited by P. J. Kalbfleischs. Hillsdale, N.J.: Erlbaum Associates.

Bazerman, M. H., and M. A. Neale. 1983. Heuristics in negotiation: Limitations to effective dispute resolution procedures. In *Negotiating in organizations,* edited by M. Bazerman and R. Lewicki. Beverly Hills, Calif.: Sage Publications.

Bazerman, M. H., T. Magliozzi, and M. A. Neale. 1985. Integrative bargaining in a competitive market. *Organizational Behavior and Human Decision Processes,* 35: 294–313.

Beck, A. T. 1988. *Love is never enough.* New York: Harper & Row.

Belenky, M., B. Clinchy, N. Goldberger, and J. Tarule. 1986. *Women's ways of knowing: The development of self, voice, and mind.* New York: Basic Books.

Bell, D. C., J. S. Chafetz, and L. H. Horn. 1982. Marital conflict resolution: A study of strategies and outcomes. *Journal of Family Issues* 3: 111–131.

Bell, J., and A. Hadas. 1977. *On friendship.* Paper presented at Wyotana Conference, University of Montana, Missoula, June.

Bell, R. A., and J. A. Daly. 1984. The affinity-seeking function of communication. *Communication Monographs* 51: 91–115.

Bell, R. Q. 1968. A reinterpretation of the direction of effects in studies of socialization. *Psychological Review* 75: 81–95.

———. 1971. Stimulus control of parent or caretaker behavior by offspring. *Developmental Psychology* 4: 63–72.

Benoit, P. J. 1983. Characteristics of arguing from a naive social actor's perspective. In *Argument in transition: Proceedings of the third summer conference on argumentation,* edited by D. Zarefsky, M. O. Sillars, and J. Rhodes, 544–559. Annandale, Va.: Speech Communication Association.

———. 1992. Introduction, special issue: Interpersonal argumentation. *Argumentation and Advocacy* 29: 39–40.

Berger, C. R. 1980. Power and the family. In *Persuasion: New directions in theory and research,* edited by M. E. Roloff and G. R. Miller, Beverly Hills, Calif.: Sage Publications.

Bergmann, T. J., and R. J. Volkema. 1994. Issues, behavioral responses and consequences in interpersonal conflicts. *Journal of Organizational Behavior* 15: 467–471.

Bernard, M., and J. Bernard. 1983. Violent intimacy: The family as a model for love relationships. *Family Relations* 32: 283–286.

Berne, E. 1964. *Games people play.* New York: Grove Press.

Bernstein, L. 1981. *Disarmament.* Address to Johns Hopkins University.

Berryman-Fine, C., and C. C. Brunner. 1987. The effects of sex of source and target on interpersonal conflict management styles. *Southern Speech Communication Journal* 53: 38–48.

Betz, B., W. R. Fry. 1995. The role of group schema in the selection of influence attempts. *Basic and Applied Social Psychology* 16: 351–365.

Bienvenu, M. J. 1970. Measurement of marital communication. *Family Coordinator* 19: 26–31.

Bjorkqvist, K., K. Osterman, and K. M. J. Lagerspetz. 1994. Sex differences in covert aggression among adults. *Aggressive Behavior* 20: 27–33.

Bjorkqvist, K., K. Osterman, and M. Hjelt-Back. 1994. Aggression among university employees. *Aggressive Behavior* 20: 173–184.

Blake, R. R., and J. S. Mouton. 1964. *Managerial grid.* Houston, Tex.: Gulf Publishing.

Blake, R. R., A. Shepard, and J. S. Mouton. 1964. *Managing intergroup conflict in industry.* Houston, Tex.: Gulf Publishing.

Blau, P. M. 1964. *Exchange and power in social life.* New York: John Wiley & Sons.

Blood, R. O., Jr., and D. M. Wolfe. 1960. *Husbands and wives: The dynamics of married living.* Glencoe, Ill.: Free Press.

Bochner, A. P. 1976. Conceptual frontiers in the study of communication in families: An introduction to the literature. *Human Communication Research* 2, no. 4: 381–397.

Bochner, A. P., D. L. Krueger, and T. L. Chmielewski. 1982. Interpersonal perceptions and marital adjustments. *Journal of Communication* 32: 135–147.

Bolger, N., A. DeLongis, R. C. Kessler, and E. A. Schilling. 1989. Effects of daily stress on negative mood. *Journal of Personality and Social Psychology* 57: 808–818.

Borisoff, D., and D. A. Victor. 1989. *Conflict management: A communication skills approach.* Englewood Cliffs, N.J.: Prentice Hall.

Boulding, K. 1962. *Conflict and defense: A general theory.* New York: Harper Torchbooks.

———. 1987. Learning peace. In *The quest for peace,* edited by R. Vayrynen. London: Sage Publications.

———. 1989. *Three faces of power.* Newbury Park, Calif.: Sage Publications.

Bowers, J. W. 1974. Beyond threats and promises. *Speech Monographs* 41: ix–xi.

Bowers, J. W., and D. J. Ochs. 1971. *The rhetoric of agitation and control.* Reading, Mass.: Addison-Wesley Publishing.

Braiker, H. B., and H. H. Kelley. 1979. Conflict in the development of close relationships. In *Social exchange in developing relationships,* edited by R. L. Burgess and T. L. Huston. New York: Academic Press.

Brammer, L. M. 1973. *The helping relationship.* Englewood Cliffs, N.J.: Prentice Hall.

Breggin, P. B. 1992. *Beyond conflict: From self-help and psychotherapy to peacemaking.* New York: St. Martin's Press.

Brett, J. M., Z. I. Barsness, and S. B. Goldberg. 1996. The effectiveness of mediation: An independent analysis of cases handled by four major service providers. *Negotiation Journal* 12: 259–269.

Brinson, S. L. 1992. TV fights: Women and men in interpersonal arguments on prime-time television dramas. *Argumentation and Advocacy* 29: 89–104.

Brockner, J., and J. Z. Rubin. 1985. *Entrapment in escalating conflicts: A social psychological analysis.* New York: Springer-Verlag.

Brockriede, W. 1972. Arguers as lovers. *Philosophy and Rhetoric* 5 (Winter): 1–11.

Brown, B. R. 1977. Face-saving and face-restoration in negotiation. In *Negotiations,* edited by D. Druckman, 275–299. Beverly Hills, Calif.: Sage Publications.

Brown, C. T., and P. W. Keller. 1973. *Monologue to dialogue.* Englewood Cliffs, N.J.: Prentice Hall.

Brown, C. T., P. Yelsma, and P. W. Keller. 1981. Communication-conflict predispositions: Development of a theory and an instrument. *Human Relations* 34, no. 12: 1103–1117.

Brown, L. D. 1983. *Managing conflict at organizational interfaces.* Reading, Mass.: Addison-Wesley Publishing.

———. 1992. Normative conflict management theories: Past, present and future. *Journal of Organizational Behavior* 13: 303–309.

Brown, L. M., and C. Gilligan. 1992. *Meeting at the crossroads: Women's psychology and girls' development.* Cambridge, Mass.: Harvard University Press.

Brown, P., and S. Levinson. 1978. Universals in language use: Politeness phenomena. In *Questions and politeness: Strategies in social interaction,* edited by E. Goody. New York: Cambridge University Press.

Browning, J., and O. Dotton. 1986. Assessment of wife assault with the conflict tactics scale: Using couple data to quantify the differential reporting effect. *Journal of Marriage and the Family* 48: 375–379.

Brutz, J., and C. M. Allen. 1986. Religious commitment, peace activism, and marital violence in Quaker families. *Journal of Marriage and the Family* 48: 491–502.

Brygger, M. P., and Edleson. 1984. Gender differences in reporting of battering incidents. Paper presented at the Second National Conference for Family Violence Researchers, University of New Hampshire, Durham.

Buber, M. 1972. *Between man and man.* New York: Macmillan.

Buehler, C., A. Krishnakumar, C. Anthony, S. Tittsworth, and G. Stone. 1994. Hostile interparental conflict and youth maladjustment. *Family Relations* 43: 409–417.

Buitrago, Y. 1997. Mediation through a Hispanic lens. Paper presented to the Intercultural Communication Division of Western State Communication Association, San Diego, California.

Bullis, C. 1983. *Conflict behavior: An inductive examination of deductive measures.* Paper presented at the Western Speech Communication Association Convention, Albuquerque, New Mexico, February.

Burggraf, D., and A. Sillars. 1987. A critical examination of sex differences in marital communication. *Communication Monographs* 54: 276–294.

Burleson, B. R., A. W. Kunkel, W. Samter, and K. J. Werking. 1996. Men's and women's evaluations of communication skills in personal relationships: When sex differences make a difference—and when they don't. *Journal of Social and Personal Relationships* 13: 201–224.

Burrell, N. A., and D. D. Cahn. 1994. Mediating peer conflicts in education contexts: The maintenance of school relationships. In *Conflict in personal relationships,* edited by D. D. Cahn, 79–94. Hillsdale, N.J.: Lawrence Erlbaum Associates.

Burrell, N. A., W. A. Donohue, and M. Allen. 1988. Gender-based perceptual biases in mediation. *Communication Research* 15: 447–469.

Bush, R. A. B. and J. P. Folger. 1994. *The promise of mediation: Responding to conflict through empowerment and recognition.* San Francisco: Jossey-Bass.

Buunk, B. P., C. Schaap, and N. Prevoo. 1990. Conflict resolution styles attributed to self and partner in premarital relationships. *Journal of Social Psychology* 130: 821–823.

Buzzard, L. R., and L. Eck. 1982. *Tell it to the church: Reconciling out of court.* Elgin, Ill.: David C. Cook Publishing.

Cahill, M. 1982. *Couples' perceptions of power.* Paper for Interpersonal Communication 595: Advanced Conflict Management, University of Montana.

Cahn, D. D. 1994. *Conflict in personal relationships.* Hillsdale, N.J.: Lawrence Erlbaum Associates.

Camara, K. A., and G. Resnick. 1989. Styles of conflict resolution and cooperation between divorced parents: Effects on child behavior and adjustment. *American Journal of Orthopsychiatry* 59, no. 4: 560–575.

Campbell, J. 1988. *The power of myth.* New York: Doubleday.

Canary, D. J., and B. H. Spitzberg. 1987. Appropriateness and effectiveness perceptions of conflict strategies. *Human Communication Research* 14: 93–118.

Canary, D. J., and W. R. Cupach. 1988. Relational and episodic characteristics associated with conflict tactics. *Journal of Social and Personal Relationships* 5: 305–322

Canary, D. J., E. M. Cunningham, and M. J. Cody. 1988. Goal types, gender, and locus of control in managing interpersonal conflict. *Communication Research* 15: 426–447.

Canary, D. J., W. R. Cupach, and S. J. Messman. 1995. *Relationship conflict.* Thousand Oaks, Calif.: Sage Publications.

Carey, C. M., and P. A. Mongeau. 1996. Communication and violence in courtship relationships. In *Family violence from a communication perspective,* edited by D. D. Cahn and S. A. Lloyd, 127–150. Hillsdale, N.J.: Lawrence Erlbaum Associates.

Carkhuff, R. 1969. *Helping and human relations,* 2 vols. New York: Holt, Rinehart & Winston.

Carnes, P. J. 1981. *Family development. Vol. 1, Understanding us.* Minneapolis: Interpersonal Communication Programs.

Carnevale, P. J. D., and E. J. Lawler. 1986. Time pressure and the development of integrative agreements in bilateral negotiations. *Journal of Conflict Resolution* 30:636–659.

Cate, R., J. Henton, J. Koval, R. Christopher, and S. Lloyd. 1982. Premarital abuse: A social psychological perspective. *Journal of Family Issues* 3: 70–90.

Cavanaugh, M., C. Larson, A. Goldberg, and J. Bellow. 1981a. Power. *Communication* 10, no. 2: 81–107.

———. 1981b. *Power and communication behavior: A formulative investigation.* Unpublished manuscript. Department of Speech Communication, University of Denver.

Chafetz, J. S. 1980. Conflict resolution in marriage: Toward a theory of spousal strategies and marital dissolution rates. *Journal of Family Issues* 1: 397–421.

Chanin, M. N., and J. A. Schneer. 1984. A study of the relationship between Jungian personality dimensions and conflict-handling behavior. *Human Relations* 37, no. 10: 863–879.

Christiansen, A., and D. C. Nies. 1980. The spouse observation checklist: Empirical analysis and critique. *American Journal of Family Therapy* 8: 69–79.

Clark, R. A., L. L. O'Dell, and S. C. Willihnganz. 1985. Training fourth graders in compromising and persuasive strategies. *Communication Education* 34: 331–342.

———. 1986. The development of compromising as an alternative to persuasion. *Central States Speech Journal* 37, no. 4: 220–224.

Cloven, D. H., and Roloff, M. E. 1991. Sense-making activities and interpersonal conflict: Communicative cures for the mulling blues. *Western Journal of Speech Communication* 55: 134–158.

———. 1993a. The chilling effect of aggressive potential on the expression of complaints in intimate relationships. *Communication Monographs* 60: 199–219.

———. 1993b. Sense-making activities and interpersonal conflict. Part 2, The effects of communicative intentions on internal dialogue. *Western Journal of Speech Communication* 57: 309–329.

———. 1995. Cognitive tuning effects on anticipating communication on thought about an interpersonal conflict. *Communication Reports* 8: 1–9.

Cody, M. J., and M. McLaughlin. 1980. Perceptions of compliance-gaining situations: A dimensional analysis. *Communication Monographs* 47 (June): 132–148.

Cody, M. J., M. L. McLaughlin, and M. J. Schneider. 1981. The impact of intimacy and relational consequences on the selection of interpersonal persuasive strategies: A reanalysis. *Communication Quarterly* 29: 91–106.

Coleman, D. H., and M. A. Straus. 1986. Marital power, conflict, and violence in a nationally representative sample of American couples. *Violence and Victims* 1: 141–157.

Comstock, J. 1994. Parent–adolescent conflict: A developmental approach. *Western Journal of Communication* 58: 263–282.

Comstock, J., and Strzyzewski. 1990. Interpersonal interaction on television: Family conflict and jealousy on prime time. *Journal of Broadcasting and Electronic Media* 34: 263–282.

Conrad, C. 1991. Communication in conflict: Style-strategy relationships. *Communication Monographs* 58: 135–155.

Coogler, O. J. 1978. *Structured mediation in divorce settlement.* Lexington, Mass.: D. C. Heath & Company.

Coser, L. A. 1967. *Continuities in the study of social conflict.* New York: Free Press.

Courtright, J. A., F. E. Millar, L. E. Rogers, and D. Bagarozzi. 1990. Interaction dynamics of relational negotiation: Reconciliation versus termination of distressed relationships. *Western Journal of Speech Communication* 54: 429–453.

Crohan, S. E. 1992. Marital happiness and spousal consensus on beliefs about marital conflict: A longitudinal investigation. *Journal of Social and Personal Relationships* 9: 89–102.

Cromwell, R. E., and D. H. Olson. 1975. *Power in families.* Beverly Hills, Calif.: Sage Publications.

Cuber, J. F., and P. B. Haroff. 1955. *The significant Americans: A study of sexual behavior among the affluent.* New York: Appleton-Century.

Cupach, W. R. 1980. *Interpersonal conflict: Relational strategies and intimacy.* Paper presented to the Speech Communication Association Convention, New York.

———. 1982. Communication satisfaction and interpersonal solidarity as outcomes of conflict message strategy use. Paper presented at the International Communication Association Convention, May.

Dahl, R. A. 1957. The concept of power. *Behavioral Science* 2: 201–215.

———. 1963. *Modern political analysis.* Englewood Cliffs, N.J.: Prentice Hall.

Davis, A. M., and R. A. Salem. 1984. Dealing with power imbalances in mediation of interpersonal disputes. In *Procedures for guiding the divorce mediation process,* edited by J. A. Lemmon, 17–26. *Mediation Quarterly*, no. 6. San Francisco: Jossey-Bass.

Deal, J. E., and K. S. Wampler. 1986. Dating violence: The primacy of previous experience. *Journal of Social and Personal Relationships* 3: 457–471.

Delia, J. G., and R. A. Clark. 1977. Cognitive complexity, social perception and the development of listener-adapted communication in six-, eight-, ten-, and twelve-year-old boys. *Communication Monographs* 44, no. 4: 326–345.

Deturck, M. A. 1987. When communication fails: Physical aggression as a compliance-gaining strategy. *Communication Monographs* 54: 106–112.

Deutsch, M. 1949. A theory of competition and cooperation. *Human Relations* 2: 129–151.

———. 1958. Trust and suspicion. *Journal of Conflict Resolution* 2: 265–279.

———. 1973. Conflicts: Productive and destructive. In *Conflict resolution through communication,* edited by F. E. Jandt. New York: Harper & Row.

Deutsch, M., and R. M. Krauss. 1960. The effect of threat upon interpersonal bargaining. *Journal of Abnormal and Social Psychology* 61: 181–189.

Dien, D. S. F. 1982. A Chinese perspective on Kohlberg's theory of moral development. *Developmental Review* 2: 331–341.

Dobash, R., and R. Dobash. 1979. *Violence against wives.* New York: Free Press.

Dollard, J., L. W. Dobb, N. Miller, O. H. Mower, and R. R. Sears. 1939. *Frustration and aggression.* New Haven, Conn.: Yale University Press.

Donnellon, A., and D. M. Kilb. 1994. Constructive for whom? The fate of diversity disputes in organizations. *Journal of Social Issues* 50: 139–155.

Donohue, W. A. 1981a. Development of a model of rule use in negotiation interaction. *Communication Monographs* 48: 106–120.

———. 1981b. Analyzing negotiation tactics: Development of a negotiation interact system. *Human Communication Research* 7, no. 3: 273–287.

———. 1991. *Communication, marital dispute, and divorce mediation.* Hillsdale, N.J.: Lawrence Erlbaum Associates.

Donohue, W. A., and R. Kolt. 1992. *Managing interpersonal conflict.* Newbury Park, Calif.: Sage Publications.

Donohue, W. A., L. Drake, and A. J. Roberto. 1994. Mediator issue intervention strategies: A replication and some conclusions. *Mediation Quarterly* 11: 261–274.

Donohue, W. A., M. Allen, and N. Burrell. 1988. Mediator communicative competence. *Communication Monographs* 55: 104–119.

Duhl, F. A., D. Kantor, and B. S. Duhl. 1973. Learning, space and action in family therapy: A primer of sculpture. In *Techniques of family psychotherapy,* edited by D. Bloch. New York: Grune & Stratton.

Dunn, C. W., and C. M. Tucker. 1993. Black children's adaptive functioning and maladaptive behavior associated with quality of family support. *Journal of Multicultural Counseling and Development* 21: 79–87.

Edwards, H. T., and J. J. White. 1977. *Problems, readings and materials on the lawyer as a negotiator.* St. Paul, Minn.: West Publishing.

Elkouri, F., and E. Elkouri. 1985. *How arbitration works.* 3d ed. Washington, D.C.: Bureau of National Affairs.

Elliott, G. C. 1980. Components of pacifism: Conceptualization and measurement. *Journal of Conflict Resolution* 24, no. 1: 27–54.

Ellis, D. G. 1979. Relational control in two group systems. *Communication Monographs* 46, no. 3: 153–166.

El-Sheikh, M. 1994. Children's emotional and physiological responses to interadult angry behavior: The role of history of interparental hostility. *Journal of Abnormal Child Psychology* 22: 661–679.

El-Sheikh, M., and J. Cheskes. 1995. Background verbal and physical anger: A comparison of children's responses to adult-adult and adult-child arguments. *Child Development* 66: 446–458.

Emerson, R. M. 1962. Power-dependence relations. *American Sociological Review* 27: 31–41.

Evans, P. 1992. *The verbally abusive relationship.* Holbrook, Mass.: Bob Adams.

Falbo, T. 1977. Multidimensional scaling of power strategies. *Journal of Personality and Social Psychology* 35: 537–547.

Falbo, T., and L. A. Peplau. 1980. Power strategies in intimate relationships. *Journal of Personality and Social Psychology* 38: 618–628.

Files, L. A. 1981. The human services management task: A time allocation study. *Public Administration Review* 41: 686–692.

Fisher, L. 1982. Transactional theories but individual assessment: A frequent discrepancy in family research. *Family Process* 21 (September): 313–320.

Fisher, R. 1971. Fractioning conflict. On *Conflict resolution: Contributions of the behavioral sciences,* edited by C. Smith, 157–169. Notre Dame: University of Notre Dame Press.

———. 1972. Third party consultation: A method for the study and resolution of conflict. *Journal of Conflict Resolution* 16 (March): 67–94.

———. 1985. Beyond yes. *Negotiation Journal* 1: 67–70.

———. 1986. Dealing with conflict among individuals and nations: Are there common principles? *Psychoanalytic Inquiry* 6: 143–153.

Fisher, R., and S. Brown. 1988. *Getting together: Building a relationship that gets to yes.* Boston, Mass.: Houghton Mifflin.

Fisher, R., and W. H. Davis. 1987. Six basic interpersonal skills for a negotiator's repertoire. *Negotiation Journal* 3: 117–125.

Fisher, R., and W. Ury. 1981. *Getting to yes: Negotiating agreement without giving in.* Boston, Mass.: Houghton Mifflin.

Fisher, R., W. Ury, and B. Patton. 1991. *Getting to yes.* 2d ed. New York: Penguin Books.

Fiske, S. T. 1993. Controlling other people: The impact of power on stereotyping. *American Psychologist* 48 (June): 621–628.

Fitzpatrick, M. A., and J. Winke. 1979. You always hurt the one you love: Strategies and tactics in interpersonal conflict. *Communication Quarterly* 27: 3–11.

Flannery, D. J., R. Montemayor, M. Eberly, and J. Torquati. 1993. Unraveling the ties that bind: Affective expression and perceived conflict in parent-adolescent interactions. *Journal of Social and Personal Relationships* 10: 495–509.

Foa, U. G., and E. B. Foa. 1974. *Societal structures of the mind.* Springfield, Ill.: Charles C. Thomas.

Fogg, R. W. 1985. Dealing with conflict: A repertoire of creative, peaceful approaches. *Journal of Conflict Resolution* 29: 330–358.

Folger, J. P., and M. S. Poole. 1984. *Working through conflict: A communication perspective.* Glenview, Ill.: Scott, Foresman & Company.

Folger, J. P., M. S. Poole, and R. Stutman. 1993. *Working through conflict: A communication perspective.* Glenview, Ill.: Scott, Foresman & Company.

Follett, M. P. 1940. *Dynamic administration: The collected papers of M. P. Follett.* Edited by H. C. Metcalf and L. Urwick. New York: Harper & Brothers.

Foss, S., and C. L. Griffin. 1995. Beyond persuasion: A proposal for an invitational rhetoric. *Communication Monographs* 62 (March): 2–18.

Frank, J. D. 1978. *Psychotherapy and the human predicament: A psychosocial approach.* New York: Schocken Books.

Franz, C. R., and K. G. Jin. 1995. The structure of group conflict in a collaborative work group during information systems development. *Journal of Applied Communication Research* 23: 108–127.

Freeman, S. A., S. W. Littlejohn, and W. B. Pearce. 1992. Communication and moral conflict. *Western Journal of Communication* 56: 311–329.

Frentz, T., and J. H. Rushing. 1980. *A communicative perspective on closeness/distance and stability/change in intimate ongoing dyads.* Unpublished manuscript, University of Colorado, Boulder.

Friedman, P. H. A., and E. Yarbrough. 1984. *Training strategies from start to finish: Designing and conducting training and retraining programs and workshops.* Englewood Cliffs, N.J.: Prentice Hall.

Gallessich, J. 1982. *The profession and practice of consultation.* San Francisco, Calif.: Jossey-Bass.

Galvin, K. M., and B. J. Brommel. 1982. *Family communication: Cohesion and change.* Glenview, Ill.: Scott, Foresman & Company.

———. 1986. *Family communication: Cohesion and change.* 2d ed. Glenview, Ill.: Scott, Foresman & Company.

Garber, R. J. 1991. Long-term effects of divorce on the self-esteem of young adults. *Journal of Divorce and Remarriage* 17: 131–137.

Gayle, B. M. 1991. Sex equity in workplace conflict management. *Journal of Applied Communication Research* 19: 152–169.

Gayle-Hackett, B. 1989a. Do females and males differ in the selection of conflict management strategies: A meta-analytic review. Paper presented to the Western Speech Communication Association Convention, Spokane, Washington, February 17.

———. 1989b. Gender differences in conflict management strategy selection: A preliminary organizational investigation. Paper presented to the Western Speech Communication Association Convention, Spokane, Washington, February 17.

Gelles, R. 1981. The myth of the battered husband. In *Marriage and family* 81/82, edited by R. Walsh and O. Poes. New York: Guilford Press.

———. 1987. *The violent home.* Beverly Hills, Calif.: Sage Publications.

Gelles, R. J., and C. P. Cornell. 1990. *Intimate violence in families.* 2d ed. Newbury Park, Calif.: Sage Publications.

Gerzon, M. 1994. *A choice of heroes.* Boston, Mass.: Houghton Mifflin.

Gilmore, S. K., and P. W. Fraleigh. 1992. *Style profile for communication at work.* Eugene, Oreg.: Friendly Press.

Glick, B. R., and S. J. Gross. 1975. Marital interaction and marital conflict: A critical evaluation of current research strategies. *Journal of Marriage and the Family* 37, no. 3: 505–512.

Goffman, E. 1967. *Interaction ritual: Essays on face to face behavior.* Garden City, N.Y.: Doubleday.

Goldberg, A. A., M. S. Cavanaugh, and C. E. Larson. 1983. The meaning of "power." *Journal of Applied Communication Research* 11, no. 2: 89–108.

Goodpaster, G. 1992. Lawsuits as negotiations. *Negotiation Journal* 8, no. 3: 221–239.

Goodrich, D. W., and D. S. Boomer. 1963. Experimental assessment of modes of conflict resolution. *Family Process* 2: 15–24.

Goodrich, T. J. 1991. Women, power, and family therapy: What's wrong with this picture? In *Women and power: Perspectives for family therapy,* edited by T. J. Goodrich, 3–35. New York: W. W. Norton & Company.

Goodwin, R. 1991. A re-examination of Rusbult's "responses to dissatisfaction" typology. *Journal of Social and Personal Relationships* 8: 569–574.

Gottman, J. M. 1982. Emotional responsiveness in marital conversations. *Journal of Communication* 32, no. 8: 108–120.

———. 1994. *What predicts divorce? The relationship between marital processes and marital outcomes.* Hillsdale, N.J.: Lawrence Erlbaum Associates.

Gottman, J. M., and L. J. Krokoff. 1989. Marital interaction and satisfaction: A longitudinal view. *Journal of Consulting and Clinical Psychology* 57: 47–52.

Gottman, J., C., Notarius, J. Gonso, and H. Markman. 1976. *A couple's guide to communication.* Champaign, Ill.: Research Press.

Gray, B. 1989. *Collaborating: Finding common ground for multiparty problems.* San Francisco, Calif.: Jossey-Bass.

Gray, F., P. S. Graubard, and H. Rosenberg. 1974. Little brother is changing you. *Psychology Today* (March).

Gray-Little, B. 1982. Marital quality and power processes among black couples. *Journal of Marriage and the Family* 44, no. 3: 633–646.

Gray-Little, B., and N. Burks. 1983. Power and satisfaction in marriage: A review and critique. *Psychological Bulletin* 93, no. 3: 513–538.

Grenyer, G. F. S., and L. Luborsky. 1996. Dynamic change in psychotherapy: Mastery of interpersonal conflicts. *Journal of Consulting and Clinical Psychology* 64: 411–416.

Grych, J. H., and F. D. Fincham. 1990. Marital conflict and children's adjustment: A cognitive conceptual framework. *Psychological Bulletin* 108: 267–290.

Gudykunst, W., and S. Ting-Toomey. 1988. *Culture and interpersonal communication.* Beverly Hills, Calif.: Sage Publications.

Guerin, P. J., Jr., L. F. Fay, S. L. Burden, and J. G. Kautto. 1987. *The evaluation and treatment of marital conflict: A four-stage approach.* New York: Basic Books.

Guggenbuhl-Craig, A. 1971. *Power and the helping professions.* Translated by M. Gubitz. Dallas, Tex.: Spring Publications.

Guisinger, S., and S. Blatt. In press. Dialectics of individuality and interpersonal relatedness: An evolutionary perspective. *American Psychologist,* 42, no. 2.

Gulliver, P. H. 1979. *Disputes and negotiations: A cross-cultural perspective.* New York: Academic Press.

Gurman, A. S. 1981. *Questions and answers in the practice of family therapy.* New York: Brunner/Mazel.

Gurman, A. S., and R. W. Knudson. 1978. Behavioral marriage therapy: A psychodynamic systems analysis and critique. *Family Process* 17: 121–138.

Gwartney-Gibbs, P. A., and D. H. Lach. 1994. Gender differences in clerical workers' disputes over tasks, interpersonal treatment, and emotion. *Human Relations* 47: 611–639.

Gyrl, F. E., S. M. Stith, and G. W. Bird. 1991. Close dating relationships among college students: Differences by use of violence and by gender. *Journal of Social and Personal Relationships* 8: 243–264.

Haferkamp, C. J. 1991–92. Orientations to conflict: Gender, attributions, resolution strategies, and self-monitoring. *Current Psychology: Research and Reviews* 10: 227–240.

Haley, J. 1959. An interactional description of schizophrenia. *Psychiatry* 22: 321–332.

———. 1976. Development of a theory: A history of a research project. In *Double bind: The foundation of the communicational approach to the family,* edited by C. E. Sluzki and D. C. Ransom. New York: Grune & Stratton.

Hall, J. 1969. *Conflict management survey.* Conroe, Tex.: Teleometrics.

Hample, D., and M. Dalinger. 1995. A Lewinian perspective on taking conflict personally: Revision, refinement, and validation of the instrument. *Communication Quarterly* 43: 297–319.

Han, G., and B. Park. 1995. Children's choice in conflict: Application of the theory of individualism-collectivism. *Journal of Cross-Cultural Psychology* 26: 298–313.

Hanson, T. L., S. S. McLanahan, and E. Thomson. 1996. Double jeopardy: Parental conflict and stepfamily outcomes for children. *Journal of Marriage and the Family* 58: 141–154.

Harre, R. 1974. Some remarks on "rule" as a scientific concept. In *Understanding other persons,* edited by T. Mischel. Oxford: Basil Blackwell.

Harrell, W. A. 1990. Husband's masculinity, wife's power, and marital conflict. *Social Behavior and Personality* 18: 207–216.

Harris, L. M., K. J. Gergen, and J. W. Lannamann. 1986. Aggression rituals. *Communication Monographs* 53: 252–265.

Harsanyi, J. C. 1962a. Measurement of social power in n-person reciprocal power situations. *Behavioral Science* 7: 81–91.

———. 1962b. Measurement of social power, opportunity costs, and the theory of two-person bargaining games. *Behavioral Science* 7: 67–80.

Hart, R. P., and D. M. Burks. 1972. Rhetorical sensitivity and social interaction. *Speech Monographs* 39, no. 2: 75–91.

Hartje, J. H. 1984. Lawyer's skills in negotiations: Justice in unseen hands. *Missouri Journal of Dispute Resolution:* 119–192.

Hatfield, E., M. K. Utne, and J. Traupmann. 1979. Equity theory and intimate relationships. In *Social exchange in developing relationships,* edited by R. L. Burgess and T. L. Huston. New York: Academic Press.

Hathaway, W. 1995. A new way of viewing dispute resolution training. *Mediation Quarterly* 13: 37–45.

Hawes, L. C., and D. Smith. 1973. A critique of assumptions underlying the study of communication in conflict. *Quarterly Journal of Speech* 59: 423–435.

Hayakawa, S. I. 1978. *Language in thought and action.* 4th ed. New York: Harcourt Brace Jovanovich.

Haynes, J. M. 1983. The process of negotiations. In *Dimensions and practice of divorce mediation,* edited by J. A. Lemmon. *Mediation Quarterly,* no. 1. San Francisco: Jossey-Bass.

Heer, D. M. 1963. The measurement and bases of family power: An overview. *Marriage and Family Living* 25: 133–139.

Heilbrun, C. 1988. *Writing a woman's life.* New York: Ballantine Books.

Heitler, S. 1990. *From conflict to resolution: Skills and strategies for individual, couple, and family therapy.* New York: W. W. Norton & Company.

Hermone, R. H. 1974. How to negotiate and come out the winner. *Management Review* 1: 19–25.

Hirschman, A. O. 1970. *Exit, voice, and loyalty: Responses to decline in firms, organizations, and states.* Cambridge, Mass.: Harvard University Press.

———. 1974. Exit, voice and loyalty: Further reflections and a survey of recent contributions. *Social Science Information* 13: 7–26.

Hobart, C. W., and W. J. Klausner. 1959. Some social interaction correlates of marital role disagreement and marital adjustment. *Marriage and Family Living* 21: 256–263.

Hocker, J. 1974. The implications of theories of bargaining on interpersonal conflict resolution. Unpublished dissertation, University of Texas.

———. 1984. Change in marital satisfaction and positive communication behavior in enrichment couples using a self-help manual: A multiple baseline study. Unpublished dissertation, University of Montana.

Hocker, J. L., and B. W. Bach. 1981. Functions of metaphor in couples' descriptions of conflicts. Unpublished paper, University of Montana.

Hoffman, L. 1981. *Foundations of family therapy: A conceptual framework for systems change.* New York: Basic Books.

Holloway, S., and G. Brager. 1985. Implicit negotiations and organizational practice. *Administration in Social Work* 9: 15–24.

Holmes, M. E. 1992. Phase structures in negotiation. In *Communication and negotiation,* edited by L. L. Putnam and M. E. Roloff, 83–105. Newbury Park, Calif.: Sage Publications.

Honeycutt, J. M., B. L. Woods and K. Fontenot. 1933. The endorsement of communication conflict rules as a function of engagement, marriage and marital ideology. *Journal of Social and Personal Relationships* 10: 285–304.

Hops, H., T. A. Wills, G. R. Patterson, and R. L. Weiss. 1972. *Marital interaction coding system.* Eugene, Oreg.: University of Oregon & Oregon Research Institute.

Howard, A. M., and J. L. Hocker. 1981. Youths' descriptions of their place in the family: A qualitative study using metaphorical data. Paper presented to the Language Behavior Interest Group, Western Speech Communication Association Convention, San Jose, California.

Huston, T. L. 1983. Power. In *Close relationships,* edited by H. H. Kelley, E. Berscheid, A. Christensen, J. H. Harvey, T. L. Huston, G. Levinger, E. McClintock, L. A. Peplau, and D. R. Peterson. New York: Freeman Press.

Ilich, J. 1981. *Power negotiating: Strategies for winning in life and business.* Boston, Mass.: Addison-Wesley Publishing.

Infante, D. A., and C. J. Wigley III. 1986. Verbal aggressiveness: An interpersonal model and measure. *Communication Monographs* 53: 61–69.

Infante, D. A., B. L. Riddle, C. L. Horvath, and S. A. Tumlin. 1992. Verbal aggressiveness: Messages and reasons. *Communication Quarterly* 40: 116–126.

Infante, D. A., K. C. Hartley, M. M. Martin, M. A. Higgins, S. D. Bruning, and G. Hur. 1992. Initiating and reciprocating verbal aggression: Effects on credibility and credited valid arguments. *Communication Studies* 43: 182–190.

Infante, D. A., S. A. Myers, and R. Buerkel. 1993. Argument and verbal aggression in constructive and destructive family and organizational disagreements. Paper presented at Speech Communication Association, Miami.

Irving, H. H., and P. E. Bohm. 1978. A social science approach to family dispute resolution. *Canadian Journal of Family Law* 1, no. 1: 39–56.

Jamieson, D. W., and K. W. Thomas. 1974. Power and conflict in the student-teacher relationship. *Journal of Applied Behavioral Science* 10: 321–333.

Jandt, F. E., ed. 1973. *Conflict resolution through communication.* New York: Harper & Row.

Jaycox, L. H, and R. L. Repetti. 1993. Conflict in families and the psychological adjustment of preadolescent children. *Journal of Family Psychology* 7: 344–355.

Jennings, A. M., C. J. Salts, and T. A. Smith Jr. 1991. Attitudes toward marriage: Effects of parental conflict, family structure, and gender. *Journal of Divorce and Remarriage* 17: 67–79.

Johnson, B. 1977. *Communication: The process of organizing.* Boston, Mass.: Allyn & Bacon.

Johnson, D. W., R. Johnson, B. Cotten, D. Harris, and S. Louison. 1995. Using conflict managers to mediate conflicts in an inner-city elementary school. *Mediation Quarterly* 12: 379–390.

Johnson, P. 1976. Women and power: Toward a theory of effectiveness. *Journal of Social Issues* 32: 99–110.

Jones, D. C. 1992. Parental divorce, family conflict and friendship networks. *Journal of Social and Personal Relationships* 9: 219–235.

Jones, T. S. 1988. Phase structures in agreement and no-agreement mediation. *Communication Research* 15: 470–495.

Jordan, 1984. Empathy and self-boundaries. In *Work in Progress.* Stone Center Working Paper Series. Wellesley, Mass.: Stone Center, Wellesley College.

———. 1990. Courage in connection: Conflict, compassion, creativity. In *Work in progress.* Stone Center Working Paper Series. Wellesley, Mass.: Stone Center, Wellesley College.

———. 1992. Relational resilience. In *Work in progress.* Stone Center Working Paper Series. Wellesley, Mass.: Stone Center, Wellesley College.

Jordan, J., S. Kaplan, J. Miller, I. Stiver, and J. Surrey. 1991. *Women's growth in connection.* New York: Guilford Press.

Jouriles, E. N., and A. Farris. 1992. Effects of marital conflict on subsequent parent-son interactions. *Behavior Therapy* 23: 355–374.

Jouriles, E. N., W. J. Bourg, and A. M. Farris. 1991. Marital adjustment and child conduct problems: A comparison of the correlation across subsamples. *Journal of Consulting and Clinical Psychology* 59: 354–357.

Kalmuss, D. S., and M. A. Straus. 1982. Wife's marital dependency and wife abuse. *Journal of Marriage and the Family* 44: 277–286.

Kaplan, R. E. 1975. Maintaining interpersonal relationships. *Interpersonal Development* 6: 106.

Karambayya, R., and J. Brett. 1989. Managers handling disputes: Third-party roles and perception of fairness. *Academy of Management Journal* 4: 687–704.

Karrass, C. 1970. *The negotiating game.* New York: Thomas Y. Crowell.

———. 1974. *Give and take: A complete guide to negotiating strategies and tactics.* New York: Thomas Y. Crowell.

Kaschak, E. 1992. *Engendered lives: A new psychology of women's experience.* New York: Basic Books.

Katz, L. F., and J. M. Gottman. 1993. Patterns of marital conflict predict children's internalizing and externalizing behaviors. *Developmental Psychology* 29: 940–950.

Kaufman, S., and G. T. Duncan. 1988. The role of mandates in third party intervention. *Negotiation Journal* 4, no. 4: 403–412.

Keashly, L., and J. Newberry. 1995. Preference for and fairness of intervention: Influence of third-party control, third-party status and conflict setting. *Journal of Social and Personal Relationships* 12: 277–293.

Kellermann, K., and B. C. Shea. 1996. Threats, suggestions, hints and promises: Gaining compliance efficiently and politely. *Communication Quarterly* 44: 145–165.

Keltner, J. (Sam). 1983. You are the mediator. Unpublished guide, Department of Speech Communication, Oregon State University.

Keltner, J. W. 1987. *Mediation: Toward a civilized system of dispute resolution.* Annandale, Va.: Speech Communication Association.

———. 1994. *The management of struggle: Elements of dispute resolution through negotiation, mediation and arbitration.* Cresskill, N.J.: Hampton Press.

Kenkel, W. W. 1957. Influence differentiation in family decision making. *Sociology and Social Research* 43: 18–25.

Keough, C. M. 1992. Bargaining arguments and argumentative bargainers. In *Communication and negotiation,* edited by L. L. Putnam and M. E. Roloff, 109–127. Newbury Park, Calif.: Sage Publications.

Kilmann, R., and K. W. Thomas. 1975. Interpersonal conflict-handling behavior as reflections of Jungian personality dimensions. *Psychological Reports* 37: 971–980.

Kim, S. H., and R. H. Smith. 1993. Revenge and conflict escalation. *Negotiation Journal* 9, no. 1: 37–43.

Kimmel, M. J., D. G. Pruitt, J. M. Magenau, E. Konar-Goldband, and P. J. D. Carnevale. 1980. Effects of trust, aspiration, and gender on negotiation tactics. *Journal of Personality and Social Psychology* 38: 9–22.

King, A. 1987. *Power and communication.* Prospect Heights, Ill.: Waveland Press.

Kipnis, D. 1976. *The powerholders.* Chicago: University of Chicago Press.

Kipnis, D., S. Schmidt, and I. Wilkerson. 1980. Intraorganizational influence tactics: Explorations in getting one's way. *Journal of Applied Psychology* 65: 440–452.

Knapp, M. L., L. L. Putnam, and L. J. Davis. 1988. Measuring interpersonal conflict in organizations: Where do we go from here? *Management Communication Quarterly* 1: 414–429.

Knox, D., C. Schacht, J. Turner, and P. Norris. 1995. College students' preference for win-win relationships. *College Student Journal* 29: 44–46.

Knudson, R. M., A. A. Sommers, and S. L. Golding. 1980. Interpersonal perception and mode of resolution in marital conflict. *Journal of Personality and Social Psychology* 38, no. 5: 751–763.

Kochan, T. A., and T. Jick. 1978. The public sector mediation process: A theory and empirical examination. *Journal of Conflict Resolution* 22, no. 2: 209–240.

Kolb, D. M. 1983. Strategy and the tactics of mediation. *Human Relations* 36, no. 3: 247–268.

———. 1987. Dealing with organizational conflict: Implications from theory. *Negotiation Journal* 3: 123–125.

Kolb, D., and B. Sheppard. 1985. Do managers mediate, or even arbitrate? *Negotiation Journal* 1: 379–388.

Kolb, D., and L. Putnam. 1992. The multiple faces of conflict in organizations. *Journal of Organizational Behavior* 13: 311–324.

———. In press. Through the looking glass: Negotiation theory refracted through the lens of gender. In *Frontiers in dispute resolution in industrial relations and human resources,* edited by Sandra Gleason. East Lansing, Mich.: Michigan State University Press.

Korabik, K., G. L. Baril, and C. Watson. 1993. Managers' conflict management style and leadership effectiveness: The moderating effects of gender. *Sex Roles* 29, no. 5/6: 405–418.

Koren, P., K. Carlton, and O. Shaw. 1980. Marital conflicts: Relations among behaviors, outcomes and distress. *Journal of Consulting and Clinical Psychology* 48, no. 4: 460–468.

Kressel, K., N. Jaffee, B. Tuchman, C. Watson, and M. Deutsch. 1980. A typology of divorcing couples: Implications for mediation and the divorce process. *Family Process* 19, no. 2: 101–116.

Krokoff, L. J., J. M. Gottman, and A. K. Roy. 1988. Blue-collar and white-collar marital interaction and communication orientation. *Journal of Social and Personal Relationships* 5: 201–221.

Kurdek, L. A. 1994. Areas of conflict for gay, lesbian, and heterosexual couples: What couples argue about influences relationship satisfaction. *Journal of Marriage and the Family* 56: 923–935.

———. 1995. Predicting change in marital satisfaction from husbands' and wives' conflict resolution styles. *Journal of Marriage and the Family* 57: 153–164.

Laing, R. D., H. Phillipson, and A. R. Lee. 1966. *Interpersonal perception.* Baltimore, Md.: Perennial Library.

Lakoff, G., and M. Johnson. 1980. *Metaphors we live by.* Chicago: University of Chicago Press.

Lange, J. I. 1993. The logic of competing information campaigns: Conflict over old growth and the spotted owl. *Communication Monographs* 60: 239–257.

Langhinrichsen-Robling, J., P. Neidig, and G. Thorn. 1995. Violent marriages: Gender differences in levels of current violence and past abuse. *Journal of Family Violence* 10: 159–176.

Larson, C., and F. LaFasto. 1989. *Teamwork.* Newbury Park, Calif.: Sage Publications.

Lawrence, P. R., and J. W. Lorsch. 1969. *Organization and environment.* Homewood, Ill.: Irwin.

Lax, D., and J. Sebenius. 1986. *The manager as negotiator.* New York: Free Press.

Leas, S., and P. Kittlaus. 1973. *Church fights: Managing conflict in the local church.* Philadelphia: Westminster Press.

Lederer, W. J., and D. D. Jackson. 1968. *Mirages of marriage.* New York: W. W. Norton & Company.

Legge, N. J., and W. K. Rawlins. 1992. Managing disputes in young adult friendships: Modes of convenience, cooperation and commitment. *Western Journal of Communication* 56: 226–247.

Lenton, R. L. 1995. Power versus feminist theories of wife abuse. *Canadian Journal of Criminology* 20: 305–330.

Lerner, H. G. 1989. *The dance of intimacy.* New York: Harper & Row.

Levy, J. S., and T. C. Morgan. 1984. The frequency and seriousness of war. *Journal of Conflict Resolution* 28: 731–749.

Lewicki, R. J., and J. A. Litterer. 1985. *Negotiation.* Homewood, Ill.: Irwin.

Lewicki, R. J., S. E. Weiss, and D. Lewin. 1992. Models of conflict, negotiation and third party intervention: A review and synthesis. *Journal of Organizational Behavior* 13: 209–254.

Lilly, E. R. 1989. The determinants of organizational power styles. *Educational Review* 41: 281–293.

Lim, T., and J. Bowers. 1991. Face-work: Solidarity, approbation, and tact. *Human Communication Research* 17: 415–450.

Lindbergh, A. 1955. *Gift from the sea.* New York: Pantheon.

Lloyd, S. A. 1987. Conflict in premarital relationships: Differential perceptions of males and females. *Family Relations* 36: 290–294.

———. 1990. A behavioral self-report technique for assessing conflict in close relationships. *Journal of Social and Personal Relationships* 8: 265–272.

———. 1996. Physical aggression, distress and everyday marital interaction. In *Family violence from a communication perspective,* edited by D. D. Cahn and S. A. Lloyd, 177–198. Hillsdale, N.J.: Lawrence Erlbaum Associates.

Lloyd, S. A., and B. C. Emery. 1994. Physically aggressive conflict in romantic relationships. In *Conflict in personal relationships,* edited by D. D. Cahn, 27–46. Hillsdale, N.J.: Lawrence Erlbaum Associates.

Lloyd, S. A., and R. M. Cate. 1995. The developmental course of conflict in dissolution of premarital relationships. *Journal of Social and Personal Relationships* 2: 179–194.

Lorenz, V. C. 1989. Some treatment approaches for family members who jeopardize the compulsive gambler's recovery. *Journal of Gambling Behavior* 5: 303–312.

Lulofs, R. S. 1994. *Conflict: From theory to action.* Scottsdale, Ariz.: Gorsuch Scarisbuck Publishers.

Lustig, M. W., and S. W. King. 1980. The effect of communication apprehension and situation on communication strategy choices. *Human Communication Research* 7, no. 1: 74–82.

Ma, R. 1992. The role of unofficial intermediaries in interpersonal conflicts in the Chinese culture. *Communication Quarterly* 40: 269–278.

Mace, D. R. 1987. *Close companions: The marriage enrichment handbook.* 1982. Reprint, New York: Continuum.

Mace, D., and V. Mace. 1976. Marriage enrichment: A preventive group approach for couples. In *Treating relationships,* edited by D. H. L. Olson. Lake Mills, Iowa: Graphic Publishing.

Mack, R. M., and R. C. Snyder. 1973. The analysis of social conflict—toward an overview and synthesis. In *Conflict resolution through communication,* edited by F. E. Jandt. New York: Harper & Row.

Madanes, C. 1981. *Strategic family therapy.* San Francisco: Jossey-Bass.

Mager, R., and P. Pipe. 1970. *Analyzing performance problems: Or you really oughta wanna.* Belmont, Calif.: Fearon Publishers.

Marano, H. E. 1996. A saga of spouse abuse. *Psychology Today,* May/June, 56–77.

Margolin, G. 1981. Behavior exchange in distressed and nondistressed marriages: A family cycle perspective. *Behavior Therapy* 12: 329–343.

Marin, M. J., J. C. Sherblom, and T. Shipps. 1994. Contextual influences on nurses' conflict management strategies. *Western Journal of Communication* 58: 201–228.

Marks, M. A. 1981. *The suing of America.* New York: Seaview Books.

Marshall, L. L. 1994. Physical and psychological abuse. In *The dark side of interpersonal communication,* edited by W. R. Cupach and B. H. Spitzberg, 281–311. Hillsdale, N.J.: Lawrence Erlbaum Associates.

Martin, B. 1990. The transmission of relationship difficulties from one generation to the next. *Journal of Youth and Adolescence* 19: 181–199.

Martin, M. M., C. M. Anderson, and G. L. Horvath. 1996. Feelings about verbal aggression: Justifications for sending and hurt from receiving verbally aggressive messages. *Communication Research Reports* 13: 19–26.

Marwell, G., and D. Schmidt. 1967. Dimensions of compliance-gaining behavior: An empirical analysis. *Sociometry* 39: 350–364.

May, R. 1972. *Power and innocence: A search for the sources of violence.* New York: Dell Publishing.

McCall, M. W., Jr. 1979. Power, authority, and influence. In *Organizational behavior,* edited by S. Kerr. Columbus, Ohio: Grid Publishing.

McClelland, D. C. 1969. The two faces of power. *Journal of International Affairs* 24: 141–154.

McCorkle, S., and J. Mills. 1992. Rowboat in a hurricane; Metaphors of interpersonal conflict management. *Communication Reports* 5, no. 2: 57–66.

McDonald, G. W. 1980. Family power: The assessment of a decade of theory and research. *Journal of Marriage and the Family* 42, no 4: 841–854.

McGillicuddy, N. B., G. L. Welton, and D. G. Pruitt. 1987. Third-party intervention: A field experiment comparing three different models. *Journal of Personality and Social Psychology* 53: 104–112.

McGillis, D. 1981. Conflict resolution outside the courts. *Applied Social Psychology Annual* 2: 243–262.

McGinnis, K., and J. McGinnis. 1981. *Parenting for peace and justice.* MaryKnoll, N.Y.: Orbis Books.

McGonagle, K. A., R. C. Kessler, and E. A. Schilling. 1992. The frequency and determinants of marital disagreements in a community sample. *Journal of Social and Personal Relationships* 9: 507–524.

McGonagle, K. A., R. C. Kessler, and I. H. Gotlib. 1993. The effects of marital disagreement style, frequency, and outcome on marital disruption. *Journal of Social and Personal Relationships* 10: 385–404.

Meierding, N. R. 1993. Does mediation work? A survey of long-term satisfaction and durability rates for privately mediated agreements. *Mediation Quarterly* 11: 157–170.

Menkel-Meadow, C. 1986. The transformation of disputes by lawyers: What the dispute paradigm does and does not tell us. *Missouri Journal of Dispute Resolution,* 25–44.

Menzel, K. E. 1991. Judging the fairness of mediation: A critical framework. *Mediation Quarterly* 9, no. 1: 3–20.

Merrill, D. M. 1996. Conflict and cooperation among adult siblings during the transition to the role of filial caregiver. *Journal of Social and Personal Relationships* 13: 399–413.

Metcoff, J., and C. A. Whitaker. 1982. Family microevents: Communication patterns for problem solving. In *Normal family processes,* edited by F. Walsh. New York: Guilford Press.

Mettetal, G., and J. M. Gottman. 1980. Affective responsiveness in spouses: Investigating the relationship between communication behavior and marital satisfaction. Paper presented to the Speech Communication Association, New York, November.

Metz, M. E., B. R. S. Rosser, and N. Strapko. 1994. Differences in conflict-resolution styles among heterosexual, gay, and lesbian couples. *Journal of Sex Research* 31: 293–308.

Meyer, J. 1992. The collaborative development of power in children's arguments. *Argumentation and Advocacy* 29: 77–88.

Millar, F. E., and L. E. Rogers. 1987. Relational dimensions of interpersonal dynamics. In *Interpersonal processes: New directions in communication research,* edited by M. E. Roloff and G. R. Miller, 117–139. Vol. 14 of *Sage Annual Reviews of Communication Research.* Newbury Park: Sage Publications.

———. 1988. Power dynamics in marital relationships. In *Perspectives on marital interaction,* edited by O. Noller and M. A. Fitzpatrick, 78–97. Clevedon, England: Multilingual Matters.

Miller, G. R., and M. Steinberg. 1975. *Between people: A new analysis of interpersonal communication.* Chicago: Science Research Association.

Miller, G., F. Boster, M. Roloff, and D. Siebold. 1977. Compliance-gaining message strategies: A typology and some findings concerning effects of situational differences. *Communication Monographs* 44: 37–54.

Miller, J. B. 1986. What do we mean by relationships? In *Work in progress.* Stone Center Working Paper Series, no. 22. Wellesley, Mass.: Stone Center, Wellesley College.

Miller, J. B. 1991. Women's and men's scripts for interpersonal conflict. *Psychology of Women Quarterly* 15: 15–29.

Miller, P., D. Danaher, and D. Forbes. 1986. Sex-related strategies for coping with interpersonal conflict in children aged five and seven. *Developmental Psychology* 22, no. 4: 543–548.

Miller, S., D. Wackman, E. Nunnally, and C. Saline. 1981. *Straight talk.* New York: New American Library.

Minuchin, S. 1974. *Families and family therapy.* Cambridge: Harvard University Press.

Mishler, E. G., and N. E. Waxler. 1968. *Interaction in families: An experimental study of family processes and schizophrenia.* New York: John Wiley & Sons.

Moore, C. 1986. *The mediation process.* San Francisco, Calif.: Jossey-Bass.

Moore, C. 1996. *The mediation process.* 2d ed. San Francisco, Calif.: Jossey-Bass.

Moos, R. H., and B. S. Moos. 1976. A typology of family social environment. *Family Process* 15: 357–371.

Morrill, C. 1991. Conflict management, honor, and organizational change. *American Journal of Sociology* 97: 585–621.

Murray, J. A. 1986. Understanding competing theories of negotiation. *Negotiation Journal* 2 (April): 179–186.

Napier, A., and C. Whitaker. 1978. *The family crucible.* New York: Harper & Row.

Neale, M., and M. Bazerman. 1985. When will externally set aspiration levels improve negotiator performance? A look at integrative behavior in a competitive market. *Journal of Occupational Behavior* 6:19–32.

Neill, J. R., and D. P. Kniskern. 1982. *From psyche to system: The evolving therapy of Carl Whitaker.* New York: Guilford Press.

Neimeyer, G. J., and R. A. Neimeyer. 1985. Relational trajectories: A personal construct contribution. *Journal of Social and Personal Relationships* 2: 325–349.

Nelson, M. C., and W. R. Sharp. 1995. Mediating conflicts of persons at risk of homelessness: The helping hand project. *Mediation Quarterly* 12: 317–325.

Newmark, L., A. Harrell, and P. Salem. 1995. Domestic violence and empowerment in custody and visitation cases. *Family and Conciliation Courts Review* 33: 30–62.

Noller, P., J. A. Feeney, D. Bonnell, and V. Callan. 1994. A longitudinal study of conflict in early marriage. *Journal of Social and Personal Relationships* 11: 233–252.

Oggins, J., J. Veroff, and D. Leber. 1993. Perceptions of marital interaction among black and white newlyweds. *Journal of Personality and Social Psychology* 65: 494–511.

O'Leary, K. D., J. Barling, I. Arias, A. Rosenbaum, J. Malone, and A. Tyree. 1989. Prevalence and stability of physical aggression between spouses: A longitudinal analysis. *Journal of Consulting and Clinical Psychology* 57: 263–268.

Oliver, P. 1984. Rewards and punishments as selective incentives. *Journal of Conflict Resolution* 28: 123–148.

Olson, D. H., and C. Rabunsky. 1972. Validity of four measures of family power. *Journal of Marriage and Family* 34, no. 2: 224–233.

Olson, D. H., and M. A. Strauss. 1972. A diagnostic tool for marital and family therapy: The SIMFAM technique. *Family Coordinator* 21: 251–258.

Olson, D. H., and R. G. Ryder. 1970. Inventory of marital conflict (IMC): An experimental interaction procedure. *Journal of Marriage and the Family* 32: 443–448.

Olson, D. H., D. H. Sprenkle, and C. Russell. 1979. Circumplex model of marital and family systems. Part 2, Cohesion and adaptability dimensions, family types and clinical applications. *Family Process* 18: 3–28.

Ortony, A. 1975. Why metaphors are necessary and not just nice. *Educational Theory* 25, no. 1: 45–53.

Ottaway, R. N. 1983. The change agent: A taxonomy in relation to the change process. *Human Relations* 36, no. 4: 361–392.

Pace, R. C. 1988. Communication patterns in high and low consensus discussions: A descriptive analysis. *Southern Speech Communication Journal* 53: 184–202.

Papa, M. J., and E. A. Pood. 1988a. Coorientational accuracy and differentiation in the management of conflict. *Communication Research* 15: 400–425.

———. 1988b. Coorientational accuracy and organizational conflict: An examination of tactic selection and discussion satisfaction. *Communication Research* 15: 1, 3–28.

Papa, M. J., and E. J. Natalle. 1989. Gender, stratgy selection and discussion satisfaction in interpersonal conflict. *Western Journal of Speech Communication* 53: 260–272.

Papp, P., O. Silberstein, and E. Carter. 1973. Family sculpting in preventive work with "well" families. *Family Process* 12, no. 1: 197–212.

Parker, A. O. 1981. A comparison of divorce mediation versus lawyer adversary processes and the relationship to marital separation factors. In *Compilation of unpublished research about divorce.* Corte Madera, Calif.: Center for the Family in Transition.

Patterson, G. R. 1976. Some procedures for assessing changes in marital interaction patterns. *Oregon Research Institute Bulletin,* no. 16.

Paul, J., and M. Paul. 1983. *Do I have to give up me to be loved by you?* Minneapolis: CompCare Publications.

Pearson, J. 1981. The Denver custody mediation project. In *Compilation of unpublished research about divorce.* Corte Madera, Calif.: Center for the Family in Transition.

Pearson, J. C., L. H. Turner, and W. Todd-Mancillas. 1991. *Gender and communication.* 2d ed. Dubuque, Iowa: William C. Brown Communications.

Pearson, J., N. Thonnes, and L. Vanderkooi. 1982. The decision to mediate profiles—individuals who accept and reject the opportunity to mediate contested child custody and visitation issues. *Journal of Divorce* 6 (Winter): 17–35.

Percival, T. Q., V. Smitheram, and M. Kelly. 1992. Myers-Briggs type indicator and conflict-handling intention: An interactive approach. *Journal of Psychological Type* 23: 10–16.

Pervin, L. A. 1982. The stasis and flow of behavior: Toward a theory of goals. In *Nebraska symposium on motivation,* edited by M. E. Page, 1–51. Lincoln, Nebr.: University of Nebraska Press.

Peterson, C. C., and J. L. Peterson. 1990. Fight or flight: Factors influencing children's and adults' decisions to avoid or confront conflict. *Journal of Genetic Psychology* 151: 461–471.

Peterson, D. R. 1983. Conflict. In *Close relationships,* edited by H. H. Kelley et al. New York. W. H. Freeman and Company.

Phillips, G. M., and N. Metzger. 1976. *Intimate communication.* Boston, Mass.: Allyn & Bacon.

Pike, G. R., and A. L. Sillars. 1985. Reciprocity of marital communication. *Journal of Social and Personal Relationships* 2: 303–324.

Pondy, L. R. 1992. Reflections on organizational conflict. *Journal of Organizational Behavior* 13: 257–262.

Popple, P. R. 1994. Negotiation: A critical skill for social work administrators. *Administration in Social Work* 8: 1–11.

Portello, J. Y., and C. Long. 1994. Gender role orientation, ethical and interpersonal conflicts, and conflict handling styles of female managers. *Sex Roles* 31: 683–701.

Prager, K. J. 1991. Intimacy status and couple conflict resolution. *Journal of Social and Personal Relationships* 8: 505–526.

Pruitt, D. G. 1981. *Negotiation behavior.* New York: Academic Press.

———. 1983a. Achieving integrative agreements. In *Negotiating in organizations,* edited by M. H. Bazerman and R. Lewicki. Beverly Hills, Calif.: Sage Publications.

———. 1983b. Strategic choice in negotiation. *American Behavioral Scientist* 27: 167–194.

———. 1986. Trends in the scientific study of negotiation and mediation. *Negotiation Journal* 2: 237–244.

Pruitt, D. G., and D. F. Johnson. 1970. Mediation as an aid to face saving in negotiation. *Journal of Personality and Social Psychology* 14, no. 3: 239–246.

Putnam, L. L. 1986. Negotiation of intergroup conflict in organizations. Lecture delivered at Baylor University, Waco, Texas, October 21.

———. 1988a. Communication and interpersonal conflict in organizations. *Management Communication Quarterly* 1: 293–301.

———. 1988b. Reframing integrative and distributive bargaining: A process perspective. Revised manuscript, Purdue University, Spring.

———. 1996. A gendered view of negotiation. Address to Communication Studies Department, University of Montana, September 26.

Putnam, L. L., and C. E. Wilson. 1982. Communicative strategies in organizational conflicts: Reliability and validity of a measurement scale. In *Communication yearbook.* Vol. 6. Edited by M. Burgoon. Beverly Hills, Calif.: Sage Publications, International Communication Association.

Putnam, L. L., and J. P. Folger. 1988. Communication, conflict, and dispute resolution: The study of interaction and the development of conflict theory. *Communication Research* 15: 349–359.

Putnam, L. L., and M. S. Poole. 1987. Conflict and negotiation. In *Handbook of organizational communication: An interdisciplinary perspective,* edited by F. M. Jablin, L. L. Putnam, K. H. Roberts, and L. W. Porter. Newbury Park, Calif.: Sage Publications.

Putnam, L. L., and T. S. Jones. 1982a. Reciprocity in negotiations: An analysis of bargaining interaction. *Communication Monographs* 49: 181–191.

———. 1982b. The role of communication in bargaining. *Human Communication Research* 8: 162–280.

Putnam, L. L., S. A. Van Hoeven, and C. A. Bullis. 1991. The role of rituals and fantasy themes in teachers' bargaining. *Western Journal of Speech Communication* 55: 85–103.

Rahim, M. A. 1983. A measure of styles of handling interpersonal conflict. *Academy of Management Journal* 26: 368–376.

———. 1986. *Managing conflict in organizations.* New York: Praeger.

Rahim, M., and G. Buntzman. 1989. Supervisory power bases, styles of handling conflict with subordinates, and subordinate compliance and satisfaction. *Journal of Psychology* 123: 195–210.

Rahim, M. A., and N. R. Magner. 1995. Confirmatory factor analysis of the styles of handling interpersonal conflict: First-order factor model and its invariance across groups. *Journal of Applied Psychology* 80: 122–132.

Raiffa, H. 1982. *The art and science of negotiation.* Cambridge, Mass.: Harvard University Press, Belknap Press.

Rancer, A. S., R. L. Kosberg, and R. A. Baukus. 1992. Beliefs about arguing as predictors of trait argumentativeness: Implications for training in argument and conflict management. *Communication Education* 41: 375–387.

Rands, M., G. Levinger, and G. D. Mellinger. 1981. Patterns of conflict resolution and marital satisfaction. *Journal of Family Issues* 2, no. 3: 297–321.

Raush, H. C., W. A. Barry, R. Hertel, and M. A. Swain. 1974. *Communication, conflict and marriage.* San Francisco: Jossey-Bass.

Raven, B. H., and A. W. Kruglanski. 1970. Conflict and power. In *The structure of conflict,* edited by P. Swingel, 69–109. New York: Academic Press.

Raven, B. H., and J. R. P. French Jr. 1956. A formal theory of social power. *Psychological Review* 63: 181–194.

Ray, L., ed. 1982. *Alternative dispute resolution: Bane or boon to attorneys?* Washington, D.C.: Special Committee on Alternative Means of Dispute Resolution of the Public Services Division, American Bar association.

Renshaw, P. D., and S. R. Asher. 1982. Social competence and peer status: The distinction between goals and strategies. In *Peer relationships and social skills in childhood,* edited by K. A. Rubin and H. S. Ross. New York: Springer-Verlag.

Renwick, P. 1977. The effects of sex differences on the perception and management of superior-subordinate conflict: An exploratory study. *Organizational Behavior and Human Performance* 19: 403–415.

Resick, P. A., B. Welsh-Osga, E. A. Zitomer, D. K. Spiegel, J. C. Meidlinger, and B. R. Long. 1980. Predictors of marital satisfaction, conflict and accord: Study I, a preliminary revision of the marital interaction coding system. Unpublished manuscript, University of South Dakota.

Resick, P. A., J. J. Sweet, D. M. Kieffer, P. K. Barr, and N. L. Ruby. 1977. Perceived and actual discriminations of conflict and accord in marital communication. Paper presented at the Eleventh Annual Convention of the Association for Advancement of Behavior Therapy, Atlanta, December.

Richardson, D. R., G. S. Hammock, T. Lubben, and S. Mickler. 1989. The relationship between love attitudes and conflict responses. *Journal of Social and Clinical Psychology* 8: 430–441.

Richmond, V. P., L. M. Davis, K. Saylor, and J. C. McCroskey. 1984. Power strategies in organizations: Communication techniques and messages. *Human Communication Research* 11: 85–108.

Robert, M. 1982. *Managing conflict from the inside out.* Austin, Tex.: Learning Concepts.

Rodman, H. 1967. Marital power in France, Greece, Yugoslavia, and the United States: A cross-national discussion. *Journal of Marriage and the Family* 29: 320–325.

———. 1972. Marital power and the theory of resources in cultural context. *Journal of Comparative Family Studies* 3: 50–69.

Rogan, R. G., and R. Hammer. 1994. Crisis negotiations: A preliminary investigation of facework in naturalistic conflict discourse. *Journal of Applied Communication Research* 22: 216–231.

Rogers, L. E., and R. Farace. 1975. Analysis of relational communication in dyads. *Human Communication Research* 1, no. 3: 222–239.

Rogers, L. E., A. Castleton, and S. A. Lloyd. 1996. Relational control and physical aggression in satisfying marital relationships. In *Family violence from a communication perspective,* edited by D. D. Cahn and S. A. Lloyd, 218–239. Hillsdale, N.J.: Lawrence Erlbaum Associates.

Rogers, M. F. 1974. Instrumental and infra-resources: The bases of power. *American Journal of Sociology* 79: 1418–1433.

Rogers-Millar, L. E., and F. E. Millar. 1977. A transactional definition and measure of power. Paper presented to the Speech Communication Association, Washington, D.C.

Rollins, B. C., and S. Bahr. 1976. A theory of power relationship in marriage. *Journal of Marriage and the Family* 38 (November): 619–627.

Roloff, M. E. 1976. Communication strategies, relationships, and relational change. In *Explorations in interpersonal communication,* edited by G. R. Miller. Newbury Park, Calif.: Sage Publications.

———. 1996. The catalyst hypothesis: Conditions under which coercive communication leads to physical aggression. In *Family violence from a communication perspective,* edited by D. D. Cahn and S. A. Lloyd. Hillsdale, N.J.: Lawrence Erlbaum Associates.

Rommetveit, R. 1980. On "meanings" of acts and what is meant and made known by what I said in a pluralistic social world. *The structure of action,* M. Brenner, 108–149. Oxford: Basil Blackwell.

Rosen, K. H. 1996. The ties that bind women to violent premarital relationships: Processes of seduction and entrapment. In *Family violence from a communication perspective,* edited by D. D. Cahn and S. A. Loyd. Hillsdale, N.J.: Lawrence Erlbaum Associates.

Ross, M., and D. Holmberg. 1992. Are wives' memories for events in relationships more vivid than their husbands' memories? *Journal of Social and Personal Relationships* 9: 585–604.

Ross, R., and S. DeWine. 1982. Interpersonal conflict: Measurement and validation. Paper presented to the Interpersonal and Small Group Communication Division, Speech Communication Association Convention, Louisville, Kentucky, November.

Rossi, A. M., and W. R. Todd-Mancillas. 1987. Male and female differences in managing conflicts. In *Communication, gender, and sex roles in diverse interaction contexts,* edited by L. P. Stewart and S. Ting-Toomey. Norwood, N.J.: Ablex.

Roush, G., and E. Hall. 1993. Teaching peaceful conflict resolution. *Mediation Quarterly* 11: 185–191.

Rowe, M. P. 1990a. People who feel harassed need a complaint system with both formal and informal options. *Negotiation Journal* 6: 61–172.

———. 1990b. Helping people help themselves: An ADR option for interpersonal conflict. *Negotiation Journal* 6, no. 3: 239–248.

Rowland, R. C., and J. K. Barge. On interactional argument. *Argumentation and Advocacy* 28: 24–34.

Rubin, J. Z. 1980. Experimental research on third party intervention in conflict: Toward some generalizations. *Psychological Bulletin* 87: 379–391.

———. 1996. Proliferation process in conflict. Address to faculty and students. University of Montana, Missoula, May.

Rubin, J. Z., and B. R. Brown. 1975. *The social psychology of bargaining and negotiation.* New York: Academic Press.

Rubin, J. Z., D. G. Pruitt, and S. H. Kim. 1994. Social conflict: Escalation, stalemate and settlement. 2d ed. New York: McGraw-Hill.

Ruhly, S. 1976. *Orientations to intercultural communication.* Palo Alto, Calif: SRA.

Rummel, R. J. 1976. *Understanding conflict and war: The conflict helix.* Vol. 2. New York: Sage Publications.

Rusbult, C. E. 1987. Responses to dissatisfaction in close relationships. In *Intimate relationships: Development, dynamics and deterioration,* edited by D. Perlman and S. Duck, 209–237.

Rusbult, C. E., D. J. Johnson, and G. D. Morrow. 1984. Impact of couple patterns of problem solving on distress and nondistress in dating relationships. *Journal of Personality and Social Psychology* 50: 744–753.

Rusbult, C. E., I. Zembrodt, and L. K. Gunn. 1982. Exit, voice, loyalty and neglect: Responses to dissatisfaction in romantic involvements. *Journal of Personality and Social Psychology* 43: 1230–1242.

Rushing, J. H. 1983. Rhetorical criticism as analogic process. Paper presented at the Speech Communication Association/American Forensic Association Summer Conference on Argumentation, Alta, Utah, July.

Rushing, J., and T. Frentz. 1995. *Projecting the Shadow: The cyborg hero in American film.* Chicago: University of Chicago Press.

Rusk, T., and R. Gerner. 1972. A study of the process of emergency psychotherapy. *American Journal of Psychiatry* 128: 882–886.

Ryder, R. G., and D. W. Goodrich. 1966. Married couples' response to disagreement. *Family Process* 5: 30–42.

Sabourin, T. C. 1995. The role of negative reciprocity in spousal abuse: A relational control analysis. *Journal of Applied Communication Research* 23: 271–283.

Sabourin, T. C., and G. H. Stamp. 1995. Communication and the experience of dialectical tensions in family life: An examination of abusive and nonabusive families. *Communication Monographs* 62: 213–242.

Safilios-Rothschild, C. 1970. The study of family power structure: A review 1960–1969. *Journal of Marriage and the Family* 32, no. 4: 539–549.

Sander, F. E. A. 1977. *Report on the national conference on minor disputes resolution.* Washington, D.C.: American Bar Association Press.

Sanders-Garrett, T. 1993. The effects of gender on conflict behaviors. Unpublished paper, University of Montana.

Satir, V. *Conjoint family therapy.* 1967. Palo Alto, Calif.: Science and Behavior Books.

———. 1972. *Peoplemaking,* Palo Alto, Calif.: Science and Behavior Books.

Scanzoni, J. 1979. Social processes and power in families. In *Contemporary theories about the family,* edited by E. Burr. New York: Free Press.

Schechter, S. 1982. *Women and male violence: The visions and struggles of the battered women's movement.* Boston, Mass.: South End Press.

Schelling, T. C. 1960. *The strategy of conflict.* Cambridge, Mass.: Harvard University Press.

Schmidt, S. M., and T. A. Kochan. 1972. Conflict: Toward conceptual clarity. *Administrative Science Quarterly* 17: 359–370.

Schnake, M. E., and D. S. Cochran. 1985. Effect of two goal-setting dimensions on perceived intraorganizational conflict. *Group and Organization Studies* 10: 168–183.

Shockley-Zalabak, P. 1981. The effects of sex differences on preference for utilization of conflict styles of managers in a work setting: An exploratory study. *Public Personnel Management Journal* 10: 289–295.

Schuetz, J. 1978. Communicative competence and the bargaining of Watergate. *Western Journal of Speech Communication* 41: 105–115.

Schutz, W. C. 1966. *The interpersonal underworld,* Palo Alto, Calif.: Science and Behavior Books.

Schwartz, G. E. 1989. *How people change: A systems perspective on integrating psychotherapies.* Invited address, Society for Exploration of Psychotherapy Integration, Berkeley, California.

Scott, M. B., and S. Lyman. 1968. Accounts. *American Sociological Review* 33: 46–62.

Selman, R. L., and A. P. Demorest. 1984. Observing troubled children's interpersonal negotiation strategies: Implications of and for a developmental model. *Child Development* 55: 288–304.

Selman, R. L., W. Beardslee, L. H. Schultz, M. Krupa, and D. Podorefsky. 1986. Assessing adolescent interpersonal negotiation strategies: Toward the integration of structural and functional models. *Developmental Psychology* 22: 450–459.

Selye, H. 1974. *Stress without distress.* New York: Lippincott & Crowell.

Sheldon, A. 1992. Conflict talk: Sociolinguistic challenges to self-assertion and how young girls meet them. *Merrill-Palmer Quarterly* 38: 95–117.

Sherif, M., and C. W. Sherif. 1956. *An outline of social psychology.* rev. ed. New York: Harper & Brothers.

Shimanoff, S. B. 1980. *Communication rules: Theory and research.* Beverly Hills, Calif.: Sage Publications.

Siegel, S., and L. E. Fouraker. 1960. *Bargaining and group decision making: Experiments in bilateral monopoly.* New York: McGraw-Hill.

Siegert, J. R., and G. H. Stamp. 1994. "Our first big fight" as a milestone in the development of close relationships. *Communication Monographs* 61: 345–360.

Sillars, A. L. 1980. Attributions and communication in roommate conflicts. *Communication Monographs* 47: 180–200.

———. 1981. Attributions and interpersonal conflict resolution. In *New directions in attribution research.* Vol. 3. Edited by J. H. Harvey, W. Ickes, and R. F. Kidd. Hillsdale, N.J.: Lawrence Erlbaum Associates.

———. 1986. Procedures for coding interpersonal conflict (revised). Unpublished manuscript, Department of Interpersonal Communication, University of Montana.

Sillars, A. L., and D. Parry. 1982. Stress, cognition, and communication in interpersonal conflicts. *Communication Research* 9: 201–226.

Sillars, A. L., and J. Weisberg. 1987. Conflict as a social skill. In *Interpersonal processes: New directions in communication research,* edited by M. E. Roloff and G. R. Miller, 140–171. Newbury Park, Calif.: Sage Publications.

Sillars, A. L., and M. D. Scott. 1983. Interpersonal perception between intimates: An integrative review. *Human Communication Research* 10: 153–176.

Sillars, A. L., S. F. Coletti, D. Parry, and M. A. Rogers. 1982. Coding verbal conflict tactics: Nonverbal and perceptual correlates of the "avoidance-distributive-integrative" distinction. *Human Communication Research* 9, no. 1: 83–95.

Simmel, G. 1953. *Conflict and the web of the group affiliations.* Translated by K. H. Wolff. New York: Free Press.

Simons, H. 1972. Persuasion in social conflicts: A critique of prevailing conceptions and a framework for future research. *Speech Monographs* 39: 227–247.

Sinclair, A. 1992. The tyranny of a team ideology. *Organization Studies* 13: 611–626.

Slaikeu, K. A. 1989. Designing dispute resolution systems in the health care industry. *Negotiation Journal* 5: 395–405.

Smith, M. J. 1975. *When I say no, I feel guilty.* New York: Bantam Books.

Soloman, L. 1960. The influence of some types of power relationships and game strategies upon the development of interpersonal trust. *Journal of Abnormal and Social Psychology* 61: 223–230.

Sowell, T. 1987. *A conflict of visions.* New York: William Morrow.

Sprey, J. 1972. Family power structure: A critical comment. *Journal of Marriage and the Family* 33 (May): 722–733.

Stets, J. E., and D. A. Henderson. Contextual factors surrounding conflict resolution while dating: Results from a national study. *Family Relations* 40: 29–36.

Stevens, A. 1989. *The roots of war: A Jungian perspective.* New York: Paragon House.

Stewart, J. 1978. Foundations of dialogic communication. *Quarterly Journal of Speech* 64: 183–201.

Strachan, C. E., and D. G. Dutton. 1992. The role of power and gender in anger responses to sexual jealousy. *Journal of Applied Social Psychology* 22: 1721–1740.

Straus, M. A. 1978. Wife beating: Causes, treatment and research needs. In *Battered women: Issues of public policy.* U.S. Commission on Civil Rights, Washington, D.C., January 30–31.

———. 1979. Measuring intrafamily conflict and violence: The conflict tactics (CT) scales. *Journal of Marriage and the Family* 41: 75–88.

———. 1987. Forward. In *The violent home,* edited by R. Gelles. Beverly Hills, Calif.: Sage Publications.

Straus, M. A., and R. J. Gelles. 1986. Societal change and change in family violence from 1975 to 1985 as revealed by two national surveys. *Journal of Mariage and the Family* 48: 465–479.

Straus, M. A., and S. Sweet. 1992. Verbal/symbolic aggression in couples: Incidence rates and relationships to personal characteristics. *Journal of Marriage and the Family* 54: 346–357.

Straus, M. A., R. J. Gelles, and S. K. Steinmetz. 1980. *Behind closed coors: Violence in the American family.* Garden City, N.Y. Doubleday.

Straus, M. A., S. L. Hamby, S. Boney-McCoy, and D. B. Sugarman. 1996. The revised conflict tactics scale (CTS2): Development and preliminary psychometric data. *Journal of Family Issues* 17: 283–316.

Strodtbeck, F. L. 1951. Husband-wife interaction over revealed differences. *American Sociological Review* 16: 468–473.

Stuart, R. B. 1980. *Helping couples change: A social learning approach to marital therapy.* New York: Guilford Press.

Stulberg, J. 1987. *Taking charge/Managing conflict.* New York: D. C. Heath & Company.

Sugarman, A. B., and G. T. Hotaling. 1989. Rating violence: Prevalence, context, and risk markers. In *Violence in dating relationships,* edited by M. A. Pirog-Good and J. E. Stets, 3–32. New York: Praeger.

Sundberg, N. D., J. R. Taplin, and L. E. Tyler. 1983. *Introduction to clinical psychology: Perspectives, issues and contributions to human service.* Englewood Cliffs, N.J.: Prentice Hall.

Szinovacz, M. E. 1983. Using couple data as a methodological tool: The case of marital violence. *Journal of Marriage and the Family* 45: 633–644.

Tannen, D. 1990. *You just don't understand: Women and men in conversation.* New York: William Morrow.

Tavris, C. 1989. *Anger: The misunderstood emotion.* 1982. Reprint, New York: Simon & Schuster/Touchstone.

Taylor, W. R. 1979. Using systems theory to organize confusion. *Family Process* 18: 479–488.

Tedeschi, J. T. 1970. Threats and promises. In *The structure of conflict,* edited by P. Swingle. New York: Academic Press.

Thomas, K. 1976. Conflict and conflict management. In *Handbook of industrial and organizational psychology,* edited by M. D. Dunnette. Chicago: Rand McNally.

Thomas, K. W., and R. Kilmann. 1977. Developing a forced-choice measure of conflict-handling behavior: The MODE instrument. *Educational and Psychological Measurement* 37: 390–395.

Thomas, K. W., and L. R. Pondy. 1977. Toward an "intent" model of conflict management among principal parties. *Human Relations* 30: 1089–1102.

Ting-Toomey, S. 1981. Conflict communication styles in blacks and whites. In *Interethnic communication: Current research,* edited by Young Yunkim. Beverly Hills, Calif.: Sage Publications.

Tjosvold, D. 1990. The goal interdependence approach to communication in conflict: An organizational study. In *Theory and research in conflict management,* edited by M. A. Rahim, 15–27. New York: Praeger.

Toulmin, S. 1958. *The uses of argument.* Cambridge, Mass.: Cambridge University Press.

Tournier, P. 1978. *The violence within.* Translated by E. Hudson. New York: Harper & Row.

Tracy, K., and J. Naughton. 1994. The identity work of questioning in intellectual discussion. *Speech Monograph* 61: 281–302.

Trapp, R. 1981. Special report on argumentation: Introduction. *Western Journal of Speech Communication* 45: 111–117.

———. 1989. Interpersonal argumentation: Conflict and reason-giving. *Communication Reports* 2: 105–109.

Triandis, H. C. 1980. *Handbook of cross cultural psychology.* Boston, Mass.: Allyn & Bacon.

Trubisky, P., S. Ting-Toomey, and S-L. Lin. 1991. The influence of individualism-collectivism and self-monitoring on conflict styles. *International Journal of Intercultural Relations* 15: 65–83.

Turk, J. L., and N. W. Bell. 1972. Measuring power in families. *Journal of Marriage and Family* 34, no. 2: 215–222.

Turner, D. G. 1990. Intraorganizational bargaining: The effect of goal congruence and trust on negotiator strategy use. *Communication Studies* 41: 54–75.

Tutzauer, F., and M. E. Roloff. 1988. Communication processes leading to integrative agreements: Three paths to joint benefits. *Communication Research* 15: 360–380.

Tyler, T. R. 1987. The psychology of disputant concerns in mediation. *Negotiation Journal* 3: 367–374.

Umbreit, M. S. 1995. *Mediating interpersonal conflicts.* West Concord, Minn.: CPI Publishing.

Ury, W. L. 1990. Dispute resolution notes from the Kalahari. *Negotiation Journal* 6: 229–238.

———. 1995. Conflict resolution among the Bushmen: Lessons in dispute systems design. *Negotiation Journal* 11: 379–389.

Ury, W., J. Brett and S. Goldberg. 1988. *Getting disputes resolved.* San Francisco, Calif.: Jossey-Bass.

———. 1989. Dispute systems design: An introduction. *Negotiation Journal* 5: 357–358.

van den Broucke, S., W. Vandereycken, and H. Vertommen. 1995. Conflict management in married eating disorder patients: A controlled observational study. *Journal of Social and Personal Relationships* 12: 27–48.

Van de Vliert, E. 1981. Siding and other reactions to a conflict. *Journal of Conflict Resolution* 25, no. 3: 495–520.

———. 1985. Escalative intervention in small-group conflicts. *Journal of Applied Behavioral Science* 21: 19–36.

van Goozen, S. H. M., N. H. Frijda, M. Kindt, and N. E. van de Poll. 1994. Anger proneness in women: Development and validation of the anger situation questionnaire. *Aggressive Behavior* 20: 79–100.

VanLear, C. 1992. Marital communication across the generations: Learning and rebellion, continuity and change. *Journal of Social and Personal Relationships* 9: 103–123.

Varney, G. H. 1978. Strategies for designing an intervention. *The 1978 annual handbook for group facilitators.* San Diego, Calif.: University Associates.

Vinacke, W. E., and A. Arkoff. 1957. An experimental study of coalitions in a triad. *American Sociological Review* 22: 406–414.

Vincent, J. P. 1972. *Problem-solving behavior in distressed and nondistressed married and stranger dyads.* Unpublished doctoral dissertation, University of Oregon.

Vissing, Y, and W. Baily. 1996. Parent-to-child verbal aggression. In *Family violence from a communication perspective,* edited by D. D. Cahn and S. A. Lloyd, 85–107. Hillsdale, N.J.: Lawrence Erlbaum Associates.

Vivian, D., and J. Langhinrichsen-Rohling. 1994. Are bi-directionally violent couples mutually victimized? A gender-sensitive comparison. *Violence and Victims* 9: 107–124.

Volkema, R. J., and T. J. Bergmann. 1989. Interpersonal conflict at work: An analysis of behavioral responses. *Human Relations* 42: 757–770.

Vroom, P., D. Fassett, and R. A. Wakefield. 1981. Mediation: The wave of the future? *American Family* 4, no. 4: 8–15.

———. 1982. Winning through mediation: Divorce without losers. *Futurist* 16 (February): 28–34.

Vuchinich, S. 1986. On attenuation in verbal family conflict. *Social Psychology Quarterly* 49: 281–293.

Waldron, V. 1991. Achieving communication goals in superior-subordinate relationships: The multifunctionality of upward maintenance tactics. *Communication Monographs* 58: 289–306.

Walker, G. B. 1988. Bacharach and Lawler's theory of argument in bargaining: A critique. *Journal of the American Forensic Association* 24: 218–232.

Wall, J. A., Jr. 1981. Mediation: An analysis, review, and proposed research. *Journal of Conflict Resolution* 25, no. 1: 157–180.

———. 1985. *Negotiation: Theory and practice.* Glenview, Ill.: Scott, Foresman & Company.

———. 1993. Community mediation in China and Korea: Some similarities and differences. *Negotiation Journal* 9: 141–153.

Wall, J. A., and R. R. Callister. 1995. Ho'oponopono: Some lessons from Hawaiian mediation. *Negotiation Journal* 11: 45–53.

Wall, V. D., Jr., and G. Galanes. 1986. The SYMLOG dimensions and small group conflict. *Central States Speech Journal* 37: 61–78.

Waller, W. 1938. *The family: A dynamic interpretation.* New York: Gordon.

Waln, V. 1981. Interpersonal conflict interaction: An examination of verbal defense of self. Paper presented to Speech Communication Association Convention, Anaheim, California.

Walsh, F. 1984. *Normal family processes.* New York: Guilford Press.

Walton, R. E. 1969. *Interpersonal peacemaking: Confrontation and third party consultation.* Reading, Mass.: Addison-Wesley Publishing.

Walton, R. E., and R. B. McKersie. 1965. *A behavioral theory of labor negotiations: An analysis of a social system.* New York: McGraw-Hill.

Warner, C. T., and T. D. Olson. 1981. Another view of family conflict and family wholeness. *Family Relations* 30, no. 4: 493–504.

Warner, R. L., G. R. Lee, and J. Lee. 1986. Social organization, spousal resources, and marital power: A cross-cultural study. *Journal of Marriage and the Family* 48: 121–128.

Watson, C. 1994. Gender versus power as a predictor of negotiation behavior and outcomes. *Negotiation Journal* 10: 117–127.

Watzlawick, P. 1966. A structured family interview. *Family Process* 5: 256–271.

Watzlawick, P., J. H. Beavin, and D. D. Jackson. 1967. *Pragmatics of human communication: A study of interaction patterns, pathologies and paradoxes.* New York: W. W. Norton & Company.

Wehr, P. 1979. *Conflict regulation.* Boulder, Colo.: Westview Press.

Weick, K. E. 1969. The social psychology of organizing. Reading, Mass.: Addison-Wesley Publishing.

———. 1979. *The social psychology of organizing.* 2d ed. New York: Addison-Wesley Publishing.

Weider-Hatfield, D., and J. D. Weider-Hatfield. 1996. Superiors' conflict management strategies and subordinate outcomes. *Management Communication Quarterly* 10: 189–208.

Weiss, R. L., and B. A. Perry. 1979. *Assessment and treatment of marital dysfunction.* Eugene, Oreg.: Oregon Marital Studies Program.

Weiss, R., and G. Margolin. 1977. Marital conflict and accord. In *Handbook for behavioral assessment,* edited by A. R. Ciminero, K. S. Calhoun, and H. E. Adams. New York: John Wiley & Sons.

Weiss, R. L., H. Hops, and G. R. Patterson. 1972. A framework for conceptualizing marital conflict: A technology for altering it, some data for evaluating it. In *Behavior change: Methodology, concepts and practice* (The Fourth Banff International Conference on Behavior Modification), edited by L. A. Hammerlynck, L. C. Handy, and E. J. Mash. Champaign, Ill.: Research Press.

Welsh-Osga, B., P. A. Resick, and E. A. Zitomer. 1979. Revising the marital interaction coding system: Study 2, extension and cross-validation. Paper presented at the meeting of the American Psychological Association, New York, September.

Whitchurch, G. G., and J. L. Pace. 1993. Communication skills training and interspousal violence. *Journal of Applied Communication Research* 21: 96–102.

White, B. 1989. Gender differences in marital communication patterns. *Family Process* 28: 89–104.

White, J. W., and J. A. Humphrey. 1994. Women's aggression in heterosexual conflicts. *Aggressive Behavior* 20: 195–202.

Wilhelm, R., trans. 1977. *The I Ching.* New Jersey: Princeton University Press.

Williams, R., and V. Williams. 1994. *Anger kills: Seventeen strategies for controlling the hostility that can harm your health.* New York: Harper Perennial.

Wilmot, W. W. 1976. The influence of personal conflict styles of teachers on student attitudes toward conflict. Paper presented to Instructional Communication Division, International Communication Association Convention, Portland, Oregon, April 15.

———. 1987. *Dyadic communication.* 3d ed. New York: McGraw-Hill.

———. 1995. *Relational communication.* New York: McGraw-Hill.

Wilson, C., and P. Gross. 1994. Police-public interactions: The impact of conflict resolution tactics. *Journal of Applied Social Psychology* 24: 159–175.

Wilson, S. R. 1992. Face and facework in negotiation. In *Communication and negotiation,* edited by L. L. Putnam and M. E. Roloff, 176–205. Newbury Park, Calif.: Sage Publications.

Witteman, H. 1992. Analyzing interpersonal conflict: Nature of awareness, type of initiating event, situational perceptions, and management styles. *Western Journal of Communication* 56: 248–280.

Witteman, H., and M. A. Fitzpatrick. 1986. Compliance-gaining in marital interaction: Power bases, processes, and outcomes. *Communication Monographs* 53: 130–143.

Womack, D. F. 1988. Assessing the Thomas-Kilmann conflict MODE survey. *Management Communication Quarterly* 1: 321–349.

Wood, J. T. 1994. *Gendered lives: Communication, gender, and culture.* Belmont, Calif.: Wadsworth Publishing.

Yarbrough, E. 1977. Rules of observation. Unpublished monograph, Department of Communication, University of Colorado.

Yarbrough, E., and W. Wilmot. 1995. *Artful mediation: Constructive conflict at work.* Boulder, Colo.: Cairns Publishing.

Yelsma, P. 1981. Conflict predispositions: Differences between happy and clinical couples. *American Journal of Family Therapy* 9: 57–63.

———. 1984. Functional conflict management in effective marital adjustment. *Communication Quarterly* 32, no. 1: 56–61.

———. 1995. Couples' affective orientations and their verbal aggressiveness. *Communication Quarterly* 43: 100–114.

Young, O. R. 1972. Intermediaries: Additional thought on third parties. *Journal of Conflict Resolution* 16 (March): 51–65.

Young-Eisendrath, P. 1993. *You're not what I expected.* New York: William Morrow.

Zehr, H. 1985. *Retributive justice, restorative justice.* Akron, Pa.: Mennonite Central Committee.

Zeitlow, P. H., and A. L. Sillars. 1988. Life-stage differences in communication during marital conflicts. *Journal of Social and Personal Relationships* 5: 223–245.

Name Index

G

H

I

J

K

L

M

N

O

P

R

S

T

U

V

W

Y

Z

Subject Index

A

B

C

D

E

F

G

H

I

J

K

L

M

N

O

P

Q

R

S

T

U

V

W